Foucauld in 1916.

Laperrine at the start of his career.

The Sword and the Cross

THE SWORD
AND THE
CROSS

TWO MEN AND
AN EMPIRE OF SAND

Fergus Fleming

GROVE PRESS
New York

First published in 2003 in Great Britain by
Granta Books, London, England

Printed in the United States of America
Published simultaneously in Canada

FIRST GROVE PRESS PAPERBACK EDITION

Library of Congress Cataloging-in-Publication Data

Fleming, Fergus, 1959–
    The sword and the cross / Fergus Fleming.
        p. cm.
    Includes bibliographical references (p.) and index.
    ISBN 0-8021-4173-0
    1. Sahara—Description and travel. 2. Foucauld, Charles de, 1858–
1916. 3. Laperrine, Henri, 1860–1920. I. Title.
DT333.F58 2003
966'.023'092—dc21   2003049071

Grove Press
an imprint of Grove/Atlantic, Inc.
841 Broadway
New York, NY 10003

04 05 06 07 08   10 9 8 7 6 5 4 3 2 1

CONTENTS

PREFACE AND ACKNOWLEDGEMENTS

When France invaded Algeria in 1830 she didn't particularly want to create a colony; events just took their course. In similar fashion, this book was never meant to be a biography or a chronicle of French imperialism in North Africa; yet it seems to have become a bit of both. If it succeeds on either level then it does so by accident. Essentially, this is a tale of two extraordinary men who lived in an extraordinary place during an extraordinary time. It is their story, rather than their history, that I have tried to tell.

The main protagonist, Charles de Foucauld, aristocratic roué turned hermit, is a well-known figure in France, where many volumes have been published on his life. Here, in Britain, he has been virtually ignored save for a flurry of post-war hagiographies. (Before the Second World War our interest was so minimal that one biographer, Sonia Howe, could only find a publisher by writing in French.) Most authors have taken the angle that he was either a saint or the nearest thing to one. Certainly he has influenced many people. T. S. Eliot, for example, lectured on him during his prolonged conversion to Catholicism; and Foucauldesque images of the desert can be found in many of his poems. Tens of thousands of followers from the

Thirties to the present day have hailed his life as a standard for theirs. (At present there are some 11,000 Little Brothers and Sisters of Jesus worldwide.) Whether he really was a saint, or whether he was just a disturbed fanatic – or, indeed, whether the two are mutually exclusive – are questions that fall outside the scope of this book.

Henri Laperrine is a more elusive character. To my knowledge, nothing has been written about him in English. He survives only in a few French biographies, the most recent of which dates back to 1940. He was not a great man, nor even a very famous one: nobody really knew about him until his death; and although he has since been immortalised on stamps and in the names of streets and schools, nobody really remembers him today. There are few photographs of him in action – here an indistinct outline on a camel; there a kepied figure pausing by a doorway within a mud fort. He did not care for fame. Yet as the creator of the Camel Corps he played an important role in the conquest of the Sahara and seems, in his own way, to have been as complex as his monkish friend. His (universally gushing) biographers praise his reticence and his compassion; they remember the cheery twinkle in his eye. Reticent and compassionate he may have been, but according to one contemporary his smile also contained a glint of malice. His record shows him to have been a pragmatic man, violent and scheming – though by all accounts great campfire company – who went about his business without spiritual angst. He was a soldier's soldier, just as Foucauld was a Catholic's Catholic.

Laperrine wrote little and what he did seems mostly to have been destroyed, leaving only a few letters and press articles. So shadowy has he become that accounts differ even as to his appearance. One author describes him as small, scruffy and squeaky-voiced, another as tall, impeccably dressed and strident. From photographs and contemporary descriptions he seems to have been an amalgam of the two, and this is how I have portrayed him. Foucauld, on the other hand, is disorientatingly well-documented. He wrote with fearful energy and his every utterance has been preserved. Whenever possible he posted at least three letters per week – sometimes per day, and sometimes in code – to friends, relatives and anyone he could think of. In the fifteen years before his death he wrote more than 700 letters to his cousin Marie de Bondy, another 700 to her husband Oliver de Bondy and some 6,000 more to scores of others. His correspondence with Bishop Guérin of the White Fathers, alone fills a book over 1,000 pages long. In addition he left more than 12,000 pages of assorted writings. Thanks to various French publishers – predominantly Nouvelle Cité – most of the material is now available in printed form.

Of secondary sources, Douglas Porch's *The Conquest of the Sahara* (1985) stands out not only for its wit but for the quality of its research. It is the bible for anyone interested in the subject. I have drawn on it heavily, both for quotes and for episodes that have little to do with Foucauld or Laperrine – such as the horrors of the Central African Mission – but which help place their careers in context. I have also relied on a medley of Foucauld biographers. René Bazin was the first of them. He knew Foucauld and wrote a definitive study five years after his subject's death. Most subsequent authors have to a greater or lesser extent relied on Bazin's material, the main difference being the manner in which they have interpreted it. Anne Fremantle's *Desert Calling* and Jean-Jacques Antier's *Charles de Foucauld* are not only well-written but offer the liveliest translations so I have preferred them, in places, over Bazin's slightly dated version. On the subject of translations, quotes from secondary sources have been verified wherever possible against the original. The notes at the back should reveal whether a particular passage has been translated by me or by someone else. In general, if it reads well then it's someone else's; if it's a dog's dinner then it's mine.

I would like to thank my agent Gillon Aitken; Sajidah Ahmad; my editor Neil Belton who has, as always, shown impeccable attention to the manuscript; Michael Graham-Stewart; Patrick Herring; Edward Hulton; David Macey for scrutinising the text for errors; Douglas Porch for pointing me in the right directions; Eugene Rae; Jane Robertson; Barnaby Rogerson; Lynne Thornton; Janet Turner and Joanna Wright. I would like further to thank the Bibliothèque

Nationale; the British Library; the State Historical Society of North Dakota; the Kensington and Chelsea Library; the London Library; the Royal Geographical Society and the School of Oriental and African Studies. Also, Claudia Broadhead, Sam Lebus and Matilda Simpson. Finally, thanks to Liz, Romar and Patrick for absolutely everything. This book is dedicated to my mother and my brother George, both of whom died during its preparation. I would like also to commemorate my aunt and godmother, Tish, who did likewise.

Terminology

In general, Saharan place names have been spelled as they were at the time. Frequently there were a variety of spellings – Tuat, Touat and Twat, for example, were used interchangeably; Tamanrasset was also Tamanghasset; Ouargla was sometimes Wargla, and so on. In these cases I have aimed only for consistency. To distinguish the modern country of Sudan from its nineteenth-century alternative – the band of territory lying to the south of the Sahara – I have written it as the French did then: Soudan. In Salah is known nowadays as Ain Salah but I have kept the old spelling. The term Tuareg (or Touareg) is currently used in the West to describe a person, a group, their language and their script. The correct declension is: I am a Targui, we are Tuareg, we speak Tamacheq and we write Tinifar. By authorial fiat I have rejected Targui but have kept Tamacheq and Tinifar. I have also followed Foucauld's example in using Tamacheq as a catch-all for its regional variations. In the Adrar des Iforas it is Tamacheq but in the Hoggar it is Tamahaq, in Niger Tamajaq and in Morocco Tamazight.

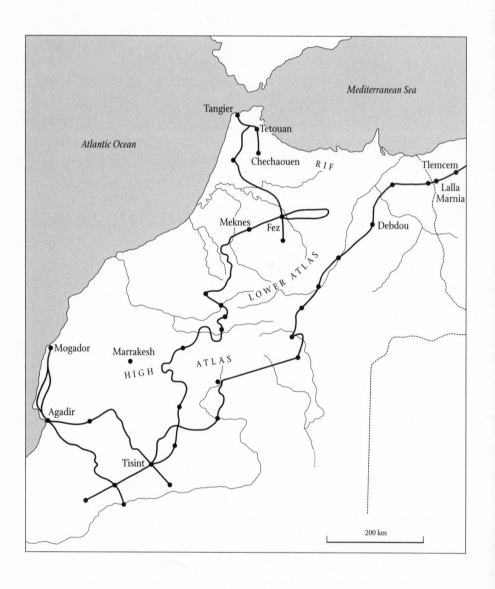

Mediterranean Sea

Atlantic Ocean

Tangier
Tetouan
Chechaouen
R I F
Tlemcem
Lalla
Marnia
Meknes
Fez
Debdou
L O W E R   A T L A S
Mogador
Marrakesh
H I G H   *A T L A S*
Agadir
Tisint

200 km

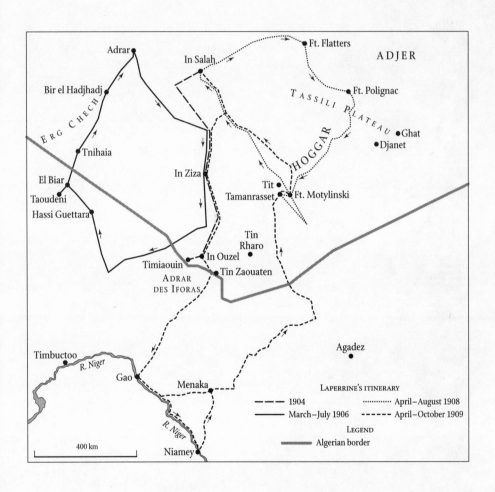

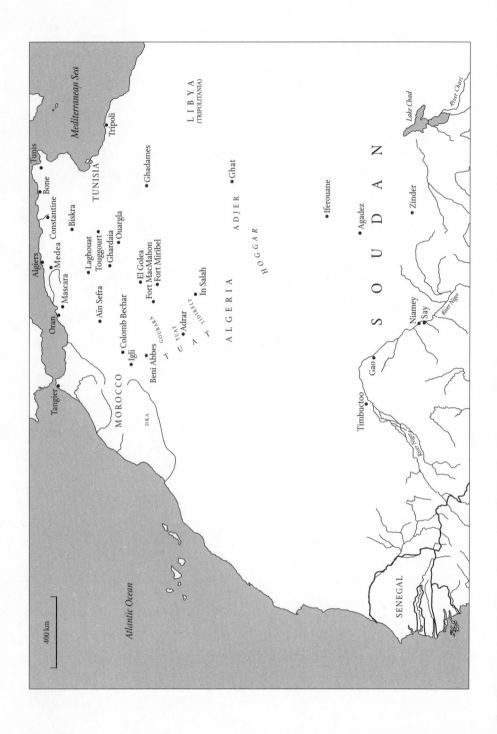

1

ABSINTHE AND
BARRACKS

In December 1880 the River Loire froze, giving Lieutenant Vicomte Charles de Foucauld the chance to hold an evening party for his fellow officers of the Fourth Hussars. By Parisian standards it was not particularly grand – a provincial *fête-champêtre*, at best – but there was no denying its host had a sense of style. When his guests descended from their carriages they were greeted by a remarkable sight. There, on the ice, Foucauld had created an al fresco ballroom: a section of the Loire had been roped off as a dance floor; a band was playing the latest tunes; on the bank, sideboards groaned under the weight of Parisian delicacies; meanwhile, vats of blazing rum punch cast a bluish glow over the scene. Everything had been taken care of, including the provision of skates for each officer, their shoe sizes having been obtained beforehand from the regimental quartermaster.

As Foucauld's guests cavorted over the ice, a sleigh carved in the shape of a swan drew up amidst a circle of flaming brands. It contained Foucauld's fur-swaddled mistress, Mimi. She was, he declared, their 'honorary colonel' for the evening. Breaking into song, the men whirled the sleigh across the dance floor while Foucauld skated casually alongside, murmuring to his mistress. He had news: orders had just come in, the Fourth Hussars were being posted to Algeria. Mimi, however, was not to worry. He was sure she could accompany him, and the move would do both of them good. As the jaded young aristocrat explained, 'I need a change of scene.'[1]

From Tunisia, the fertile zones of North Africa comprise a narrow strip of land that stretches west to Morocco, where the Atlas mountains, which form their southern boundary, dip southwards to create a triangular wedge of prosperity on the Atlantic coast. As one nineteenth-century writer put it, the effect is that of a verdant forage cap perched on the great, bald head of the continent. In the middle of this strip, sandwiched between Tunisia and Morocco, lies Algeria. Topographically, Algeria differs little from its neighbours: a Mediterranean littoral – the Sahel – followed by a stretch of good, crop-growing land – the Tell – and then a series of high valleys, suitable mainly for grazing – Les Hauts Plateaux – beyond which the snow-clad mountains plunge abruptly to the Sahara. Its cultivable area is small, extending approximately 250 kilometres inland from 900 kilometres of shoreline. Its history, however, is rich.

The Berbers, a pale-skinned race of semi-pastoralists, claim priority as the first inhabitants of North Africa. Their tutelage was disrupted by the Phoenicans, who set up coastal trading stations, the most impressive of which was Carthage. Later, the Ancient Romans assumed control of their possessions, moving inland to create substantial colonies whose main purpose was the harvesting of wheat and the processing of resources from the African interior – ivory, gold, feathers, furs, wild animals for the circuses and, above all, slaves. Between 800 and 1100 AD, as Arab invaders swept across North Africa and into Spain, Roman control gave way to a succession of Islamic dynasties. Then, in the seventeenth century, Algeria came under the sway of the Ottomans, forming the western limit of a vast empire that stretched eastward to Persia and all but encircled the Mediterranean. Ottoman rule, however, was weak. Theoretically under the fist of Constantinople, its outlying territories were run in practice by local rulers who paid mere lip service to the Sultan. One such ruler was the Dey of Algeria. It took the Deys very little time to realize that they could do more or less as they wished and that, while the trade in slaves continued very profitably, they could also, with the covert blessing of the Sultan, make a lot of money from piracy.

Algeria, or the Barbary Coast as Europeans knew and feared it, became the scourge of the Mediterranean – and of the Atlantic too. In 1644, Barbary pirates raided the British port of Penzance, seizing sixty people to be sold as slaves; forty-four years later they took 237 men, women and children from the Irish port of Baltimore. In the same century, so voluminous were the crowds of women, who came to London seeking restitution for breadwinners lost to Barbary corsairs, that Parliament allocated them the fines levied on Members who were late for morning prayers. It helped the women little and had no deterrent effect on the corsairs, whose reputation was by now so wide-spread that a group of Japanese pirates came to join in the fun. For two centuries the Barbary Coast disrupted European shipping with virtual impunity and in blithe disregard of world politics. In 1810, during the Napoleonic War, when Britain supposedly ruled the waves, Sir Arthur Paget, Commander of HMS *Thetis*, was forced to exchange a gold snuff-box valued at £500 for two British captives held by the pirates; in the same year London's Company of Ironmongers paid £465 for the return of another thirteen. This was too much. In 1816 a Royal Navy squadron anchored off Algiers and blew the pirates, their ships and their port to smithereens. Troops were sent to invest the rubble, which they did with notable success, using some of it to construct a new pier, before sailing home with the satisfaction that the Dey had been taught a lesson.

In 1830, France decided that the Dey needed another lesson – this time in manners. During the past fifteen years, the world had become increasingly interested in Ottoman North Africa. Nations as far afield as America and Sweden were intrigued by its commercial possibilities and despatched so-called 'Consuls' to pursue their interests. In every major port, therefore, could be found a group of foreigners – adventurers and spies for the most part – who manoeuvred for advantage in the eyes of the local ruler. The Deys of Algeria, however, kept a sharper eye on accounts than did most other rulers and in 1828 the current Dey invited the French Consul to discuss a debt that had been outstanding since the 1790s for a consignment of wheat. When the Consul refused to countenance payment, the Dey became so outraged that he struck the man with his fly whisk. For Charles X, the unpopular Bourbon monarch who had been placed on the French throne following the defeat of Napoleon, this was a perfect opportunity to detract attention from his failings at home. Declaring the incident 'an insult to the national honour',[2] he put Algiers under blockade. It was, alas, a seasonal blockade, and as soon as the French ships left for the winter, Algerian pirates snatched three ships from the Bay of Naples, sold them in Tangiers and returned home with the proceeds.

Therefore, in 1830, France inflicted a second bombardment on Algiers and sent marines to occupy the port. To the marines' surprise they met almost no resistance, so they moved inland. The process was repeated along the coast, at the ports of Oran and Bône. By the end of the year, France, which had intended at first only to rid the Mediterranean of a nuisance, and maybe at the same time flex its muscles on the international stage, found itself in possession of a small colony. Charles X would have been pleased, had he still been in power. He had, however, been deposed and his successor, Louis Philippe, the 'Citizen King', a ruler of more popularity and greater caution, needed no such venture to bolster his regime. In fact, colonization was the last thing he wanted. Afflicted, almost uniquely in Europe, by a diminishing population, and with its finances in disarray, France had neither the money nor the people to support new overseas possessions. To the government's dismay, its North African territory continued to expand. It was not a matter of policy but of practicality: once they had recovered from the initial shock, tribal leaders did their utmost to prevent the French advancing inland and the military responded by securing their outer limits or, as one commentator put it, 'the presence of enemies induced battle'.[3] Under the command of, among others, the grizzled veteran General Thomas-Richard Bugeaud, French troops marched ever deeper into Algeria.

For the invaders it was a glorious and exciting prospect, a chance to display their martial prowess and to prove that, despite the ignominy of Waterloo, they were still a formidable power. All they had to do to take Algeria was smite a few natives armed with swords, spears and the occasional musket. But, as they soon discovered, this was a land in which European notions of warfare did not apply. Massed battalions, long baggage trains and heavy artillery worked well enough in the urbanized coastal regions; but in the countryside matters were not so simple. The logistics alone were a nightmare. How was an offensive force and all its supplies to be hauled through a trackless, occasionally marshy and often mountainous hinterland? How were these cumbersome columns to defend themselves against a foe that refused to fight set-piece battles but pestered them with skirmishes and midnight raids, vanishing into the bush whenever artillery was brought into play? The French response was to advance by construction, consolidating each hard-won piece of territory by means of a fortified redoubt in which they could regroup before moving on. The result became one of the clichés of North African conquest: white soldiers huddled in mud-brick forts, awaiting the doubtful arrival of supplies, while disease and guerrilla action took their toll. Even the Foreign Legion failed to make an impression. Created in 1831 to siphon off undesirable elements of France's alien population, it fought its first battles in Algeria and later made its headquarters in the territory south of Oran. But, notorious as it was for its brutality, it, too, became just another part of the beleaguered garrison.

In the first year of their conquest the French had uttered vague promises about the rights of the natives: they could retain their property, their religion would be respected; they would be treated fairly. Some, predominantly those around the towns and in the agricultural zone of the Tell, had believed these promises, assuming that they had merely exchanged rule by the Ottomans for rule by the French. 'Far from being hostile to us, the Moors are friends of our civilization,' wrote one observer. 'By treating them well, by according them liberty and security, we will find the most useful support among them.'[4] It soon became obvious, however, that the promises were empty: one of

France's first acts was to transform Algiers' Ketchawa Mosque into a
church; Muslim feast days were no longer recognized as legal holi-
days; and large stretches of farmland were confiscated and handed
over to colonists. As the occupation continued, resentment increased.
There had always been divisions within the Algerian population, the
main one being that between the coastal regions, inhabited by Arab
communities, and the highlands, which were occupied by Berbers.
The two groups did not share a common language – Berbers spoke
their own tongue, with numerous dialects. They were also at odds in
their religion: while both practised Islam, the Berbers pursued their
own, unorthodox version that incorporated ancient, pre-Islamic customs. And their lifestyles differed – the Arabs were settled farmers,
the Berbers were pastoralists. The French had hoped to exploit these
differences but, to their dismay, both parties now came together in
opposition against them.

In the colony's outlying territories, settlers protected their villages
with ditches, walls and watchtowers. When they emerged to till their
fields they did so in armed groups and kept an eye out for the black
flag that was raised to warn them of danger. Raids were common-
place, torchings, kidnaps and murders a matter of weekly occurrence.
Initially, the attacking tribesmen ransomed their hostages; latterly,
they just decapitated them, finding that the colonists would pay as
much for a head as they would for the living person. The settlers
replied in kind, with or without military assistance. Outside the
narrow coastal strip, where some order reigned and whose native
inhabitants actually volunteered to serve in the French army, Algeria
was a bloody and very unpleasant place. Yet still Frenchmen wanted
to live there. Displaced aristocrats who had been supporters of
Charles X – they were nicknamed the 'gants jaunes' or 'yellow
gloves' – built large estates from which they enriched themselves
while remaining in the safety of the city. Property speculators were
attracted by the promise of quick, if dangerous, profits: on seeing that
a rebellious village was about to fall, one land agent rushed in with his
wallet; the conquering officer had to pay the man several thousand
francs for the land on which he wanted to construct his fort, plus a

premium for the parade ground. And even in the most dangerous areas settlers were united by a frontier spirit – the land might not have been theirs originally, but having shed blood for it, they were not going to give it up.

Paris fretted. In 1834 M. Dupin, Procureur-général, told the French Assembly that 'The thing to do was to reduce expenditure to the lowest possible limit, and hasten in every way the moment that would free France from a burden which she could not and would not support much longer.'[5] Three years later, M. Thiers, Foreign Minister, said: 'If we could secure a few leagues of land around Algiers, Oran and Bône, I should for my part be satisfied. I am no friend of a general occupation.'[6] Even at the front there were doubts. While dealing with his elusive enemy, a process that involved variously victory, submission, double-dealing and a corrupt but highly profitable bit of arms-dealing, General Bugeaud insisted that his task was a complete waste of time. 'Unfortunately,' wrote one of his officers, 'he professes these opinions all day, to every one, and at the top of his voice, which, although he may not be aware of it, is rather discouraging to the army.'[7] Nevertheless, it was thanks to Bugeaud that Algeria was finally vanquished. Discarding traditional European methods, he created a force of light infantry that moved swiftly, living off the land by means of *razzia*, or raids, in the same manner as its opponents. As one veteran described it, 'In Europe, once [you are] master of two or three large cities, the entire country is yours. But in Africa, how do you act against a population whose only link with the land is the pegs of their tents? . . . The only way is to take the grain which feeds them, the flocks which clothe them. For this reason, we make war on silos, war on cattle, [we make] the *razzia*.'[8]

Bugeaud's tactics were ideally suited to their context, and gave rise to a second cliché of colonial warfare, that of the infantry square blazing defiantly at circling hordes of savages. They would later be copied by other imperial powers – though it was the cliché rather than the practice that they imitated; Bugeaud preferred a line over a square on the grounds that it gave him greater manoeuvrability – but the immediate result was that European troops were for the first time able to beat indigenous forces at their own game. At the cost of tens of thousands of lives, which to read the official histories were largely French but were in fact almost entirely African, Bugeaud and his colleagues cut Algeria to pieces. In 1837 the French captured Constantine, a town of Roman origin, perched on an improbably precipitous outcrop that commanded the eastern wheatlands. The outposts of Kolea and Blida were garrisoned in 1838, Medea and Miliana in 1840, Biskra and Dellys in 1844. An attack from Morocco was repelled in 1844 and three years later the last and most potent chieftain, Abd-el-Kadir, surrendered.* Save for a small group of Berber tribesmen, who inhabited the Kabylia mountains east of Algiers and who presented no apparent threat to the new regime, Algeria was at last conquered.

It was a small conquest by contemporary standards. Set against Britain's rapid colonization of India, France's thirty-year struggle to command a 250-kilometre deep corridor of North African soil was embarrassingly inadequate. Worst of all, the French government did not even want the place. But, having been conquered, Algeria could not simply be thrown away; besides, the army supported Charles X and for political reasons could not be recalled. For a while, therefore, a curious policy prevailed whereby France promoted military expansion in Algeria while doing its utmost to prevent its citizens from settling there. There was no charge, for example, for a ticket from Marseilles to Algiers, but would-be colonists were required to invest punitive amounts of capital – 400 francs for a labourer, up to 3,000 francs for a landowner. Similarly, land was free to all who applied for it, but it was unimproved land, covered in dwarf palms, most of the best fields having already been taken. In the same vein, Paris decreed that French farmers must hire French workers instead of using cheap native labour, thus rigging the labour market in favour of immigrants,

---

*An honourable man, respected both by his troops and his enemies, Abd-el-Kadir has often been hailed as the father of Algerian nationalism. Exiled to Damascus, he later intervened to secure the release of thousands of Christians captured by Islamic rebels.

but the immigrants required high wages to offset the cost they had incurred simply by setting foot in Algeria, and the farmers, proportionally strapped for cash, could not afford to pay them. The result was an economy in which smallholders poked half-heartedly at the land while working part-time as café waiters or road-builders for the military. Foreigners were exempt from these regulations and could do as they pleased, which they did: hard-working Spaniards, Italians and Maltese formed large and reasonably prosperous communities, but for the average Frenchman, Algeria held little promise. By 1847 a mere 3,000 French settlers occupied less than 45,000 hectares of a potential thirty-six million on offer, while another 110,000 scrabbled a living in the towns. Algeria was a mess. Yet, as Marshal Bugeaud said, on quitting the territory in 1847, 'When France makes up her mind to occupy the country – when she makes up her mind seriously, I mean – she will, no doubt, achieve her object.'[9]

France made up its mind in 1848. In that year, Louis Philippe became one of the many rulers who fell before the wave of revolutions that swept Europe. His successor, Louis Napoleon, who brought down the short-lived Second Republic in 1851, was a populist dictator whose fondness for monarchical trappings was underlined in 1852 when he inaugurated the Second Empire with himself, as Napoleon III, at its head. He took a bullish attitude towards France's foreign possessions – there was, after all, not much point calling oneself an Emperor if one did not pursue imperial goals – and expansion became the theme of his twenty-year reign. He established a French presence in Indo-China, financed an eastward thrust towards Timbuctoo from France's West African colony of Senegal, affected a brief but unsuccessful colonization of Mexico in alliance with Austria and, above all, promoted the assimilation of Algeria as part of metropolitan France.

Millions upon millions of francs per annum were diverted towards the Algerian military. By 1860 the exact figure was 58,388,625 francs, or £2,500,000 (a sum that can be translated into modern sterling by a multiplication of approximately one hundred), which was spent not only on the maintenance of a 100,000-strong army of occupation but on the construction of roads, bridges and citadels. Millions more were sunk in the creation of a new capital, built by the British railway contractor, Sir Samuel Morton Peto, in perfect imitation of a French port, complete with quays, corniches, squares and boulevards, whose 1.5 kilometre-long, white façade rose from the Bay of Algiers like a set of false teeth. Further millions were spent on the construction of a residential suburb – Mustapha – where white villas, built in a *mélange* of styles that encompassed Islamic, Gothic and Classical, gleamed amidst the forests that sloped down to the bay. (Opinions were divided as to the scheme's aesthetic success: French apologists described Algiers as a diamond set amidst emeralds; British visitors were reminded of a hillside quarry; and to the American novelist Herman Melville it looked, from a distance, like a streak of guano on a rock.) Still more money turned the ports of Bône and Oran into lacklustre simulacra of Algiers. Inland, meanwhile, engineers went to work on Constantine, transforming it into a modern city that, with Algiers and Oran, became one of Algeria's three new regional capitals.

Everything was contrived to give the impression that Algeria was an integral but exotically flavoured offshoot of the motherland, in which the original inhabitants were left to their own devices while being cajoled paternally towards better things. The old Arab quarter of Algiers was left untouched, huddling incongruously behind the façades of the new city. Native land tenure and farming practices were allowed, with some exceptions and in certain areas, to continue as they always had. Provision was made for orphans and the unemployed: abandoned or parentless children were embraced by Roman Catholic institutes that taught them reading, writing, arithmetic and Christianity; and the landless younger sons of farmers found profitable futures in the army as spahis (cavalry) or *tirailleurs* (infantrymen). Vineyards were planted whose grapes ripened so heavily that those in France seemed mere berries in comparison; and tobacco plants flourished in such quantity that their leaves were occasionally used as fodder for donkeys. In Algiers and other centres the authorities created *jardins d'essai*, open-air forcing houses in which every conceivable variety of plant was tested for its suitability to African soil; those that proved adaptable were donated free of charge to farmers. As advertised under the regime of Napoleon III, Algeria was a wonderful place for visitors and colonists alike. Roman ruins abounded, the ground was fertile and the climate was healthy. Until the 1870s, when sanatoria were established in the Alps, tubercular patients flocked to Algiers for its clean, dry air. One writer went so far as to call it 'the New Playground'.

Yet, for all its attractiveness, the playground had a sullen atmosphere. It was divided into two distinct sections: the civilian ones, which encompassed the towns and their immediate surroundings in which white colonists were permitted to settle; and the military areas (everywhere else) in which the locals were allowed to carry on as before under the watchful eye of the Bureau Arabe, an educated elite of officers who administered the territory on behalf of the army. In both sectors, however, civilian government was non-existent, with everything from investment to taxes being controlled by the military. The roads were poor, communications were rudimentary and expensive; outside the main cities accommodation was basic. Despite the advantages of good soil and a conducive climate, farmers continued to struggle, the few who succeeded being those whose establishments received substantial injections of capital from a government keen to create showcases for the outside world. Mines and forests, two potential sources of wealth, were hampered by the high cost of transport and the low prices obtainable in a glutted European market. The *jardins d'essai*, magnificent in concept, operated poorly in practice, their plants resenting the move from well-irrigated, well-cultivated enclosures to dry, poorly tended fields. The much-touted sunshine was offset by frequent earthquakes, unreliable rainfall, plagues of locusts and the sirocco, a hot wind from the south that brought an enervating malaise called the *cafard*, whose symptoms were both physical (headaches and languor) and psychological (depression and irritability). Malaria was an omnipresent threat, outbreaks of cholera and smallpox came at regular intervals, and every few years there would be a visitation of bubonic plague. Even in the great white city of Algiers itself, there was a sense of impermanence and insecurity. By day its streets teemed with a multiracial throng,

French porters and merchants mingling with well-heeled tourists, Maltese fishermen, Arab hawkers, Berber villagers, tall, dark-skinned spahis, baggy-trousered Zouaves (French infantry who had been given a glamorous, Ottoman-style uniform) and a constant shuffling of blue-clad troops. Bougainvillea flowered in profusion and yellow roses poured over the walls of Mustapha's gardens. By night, however, the flowers lost their colour and the multitudes departed, leaving the city to a white, predominantly male master race who, having partaken of a hotel meal and a game of billiards, lounged in the empty streets, hungry for entertainment.

Simmering beneath it all was the anger of three million native Algerians – Arab and Berber – who resented France's disruption of their centuries-old, semi-autonomous existence. They adapted unwillingly but philosophically to the new regime, taking the French coin whenever a position was offered. Religious leaders looked forward to a time when a God-sent leader would drive the infidel into the sea – the precise date was fixed at one hundred years from the date of the French invasion – but for most people it was a matter of waiting and hating. Confident in their military capability, the French paid no attention to what their subjects thought. Other Europeans, however, were less certain. As one British tourist wrote: 'The natives, thoroughly crushed and beaten, will not stir by themselves; but if they found serious European backers, I should be sorry to deliver policies of insurance upon their lives to French residents in Algiers. One of the consequences of their conquest, and, far more, of their administration . . . has been that the French have concentrated upon themselves all the hatred of race and religion which this country can provide.'[10]

In reality, Napoleon III's Algerian dream was nothing more than a gimcrack marketing exercise, whose aim was to bolster his international prestige while drawing attention, like his predecessors, away from his failings at home. When France suffered from unemployment, for example, the burden of excess humanity was simply transferred to Algeria. In 1848, 13,000 potentially disruptive out-of-work Parisians were lured to Africa with the promise of ready-made villages and free implements with which to work the soil. The villages did not exist and the ploughs were unavailable. Those who did not die (3,000 did, within the first year) returned *en masse*, clamorous with discontent. Ten years later, by which time the entry fee for landowners had dropped from 3,000 francs to 300 for a twenty-four-hectare plot, the situation was little better. In 1857, of 80,000 people who sailed gratis for a place in the sun, 70,000 caught the first ship home and most of the remainder took the one after. In that year the French civilian population hovered around 130,000, not much larger than the number of troops required to safeguard their existence, and most of them were concentrated in the towns. Favourable tax concessions were introduced and Algerian produce was promoted at international exhibitions, but still, despite its vast annual subsidy, the colony failed to prosper. As for the promised assimilation, it was, like everything else, without foundation. Although laws were passed that theoretically offered a degree of equality between conquered and conqueror, they failed: colonists did not want to be on equal terms with the natives; and the natives had no desire at all to become like the colonists. Algiers, meanwhile, appeared ever more devoid of substance. One garden, for example, boasted a bust of Napoleon Bonaparte, Napoleon III's distant ancestor, whose plinth carried the inscription, '*Il avait rêvé cette conquête*' ('He had dreamed of this conquest'). Bonaparte, however, had never dreamed seriously of conquering Algeria, his single African foray having been to Egypt, with the purpose of seizing the valuable overland route between Europe and India. The bust was not only a piece of triumphal puffery but, worst of all, was seen as such. As one Scottish visitor wondered, 'Have Frenchmen any sense of the ludicrous?'[11]

In an age when imperialism was accepted as the route towards global progress and prosperity, foreigners were intrigued by Napoleon III's new version. In the late 1850s the *Times* journalist George Wingrove Cooke decided to investigate the colony. Impressed by the Algerian stand in the recent Paris Exhibition, he wrote that 'It is very important to know whether these are the healthy fruit of a hardy, thriving young tree, or only the precocious produce of a forced, sickly exotic. Will it last? and does it pay? What is its principal political object? and to what will it lead?'[12] His findings were unfavourable. The country was ill-managed and unprofitable; land distribution was afflicted by jobbery, favouritism and procrastination; there was little order outside the main urban centres and not, indeed, much order within them; the civilian and military populations seemed to work against each other, while the native population worked against both; above all, no overriding purpose was evident, everything being arranged *ad hoc* around the movements of the army. It was, he decided, a military dictatorship that had been allowed to run wild.

Cooke, admittedly, visited Algeria at the worst possible time as far as France was concerned. The Kabylia Berbers had risen in 1857, the year he arrived, and their slaughter of French farmers within a few score kilometres of Algiers had provoked a violent backlash. Within weeks, 15,000 troops were marching against the aggressor. Cooke was present when the first, retaliatory gunshots rang out. 'The sounds of a fearful vengeance echoed along the sides of those mountains. *"Ça sera l'affaire d'une quinzaine"* ["It'll be a fortnight's work"] philosophically remarked a French officer, while we were watching the troops form and march. What a hell of tragedies did that little word "Ça" import!'[13] Cooke did not personally witness the crushing of the Kabylia Berbers, but he described the chillingly calm manner in which it began.

> Let us go to dinner. The fare is good at the Hôtel de la Régence; – suppose we dine there today. There are two sentinels at the door. This signifies that Le Maréchal Randon, the Governor of Algiers and the leader of this new expedition, is dining upstairs. The Hôtel de la Régence has an excellent *salon*, well stored with little round tables with marble tops. There is one vacant, and I take it. In the opposite corner, as unpretending in appearance as any other guest, sits rather an elderly man of considerable corpulency, and of a firm but not unkindly countenance. Opposite to him is seated a lady, not perhaps in her *première jeunesse*, but with a face which

impresses you at once with the conviction that to know her
would be to esteem and love her. They are chatting
affectionately together as the dinner goes on, the husband
taking a minute or two from time to time to read some
document which lies by the side of his plate. The *café* and *petit
verre* are brought and despatched, and then the lady and
gentleman rise to go away. Several of the occupants of the
neighbouring tables – men and ladies – now leave their chairs.
A little levee takes place. Madame says something kind to
each lady – something polite to each gentleman. The ladies
wish the gentlemen *bon voyage*; the gentlemen bow low, for
they are going with him. Thus having eaten their dinner, and
said good-day to their friends, in this quiet, frugal fashion, they
walk out arm-in-arm.

   This was Marshal Randon, the Governor of Algeria, and his
lady, and the *bon voyage* upon which he is gone is that mission
of extermination by fire and sword, which will crush a
thousand domesticities ruder, but no less dear, than that we
have just looked upon.[14]

Cooke's reports were racist, jingoistic and, on occasion, exaggerat-
edly sentimental. Their political content, however, was perspicacious.
On his return to London, he concluded that 'the wealth and fertility of
this great portion of the earth, so close to our own shores, are altogether
unestimated and are almost unknown . . . There is a tremendous gulf
between what it has been and what it is, and perhaps, also, between
what it is and what it will be . . . Perhaps in the pressure upon these
North African shores the world is about to witness another siege of
Troy, another Punic War, another crusade.'[15]
   The crusade he foresaw was one in which France extended its
hegemony over Morocco and Tunisia, two countries which were as yet
uncolonized, but which were accepted as belonging respectively to
Spain and Italy should they want them. Spain was in decline and
Italy still fumbling its way to nationhood, so Cooke saw no reason why
France should not usurp their rights with the object of making 'the

Mediterranean Sea a French lake'.[16] The prospect was quite horrible to any Briton and for that very reason may have been part of Napoleon III's grand plan. (Eventually, France did conquer both territories, but it never wreaked the havoc on British trade that Cooke envisaged.) For the moment, however, Britain could sleep easily. Between 1861 and 1866 Algeria's population rose by a mere 890 (including births), making sideways expansion the last thing Napoleon III could afford. As the expense of his projects became apparent, he backed away from the idea of assimilating Algeria with France, stating instead his preference that it become an Arab kingdom with himself as titular ruler. When the settlers objected, he changed his mind: Algeria would be a colony like any other. Then, when the military warned him that the native population could only be controlled by force, he changed his mind again: Algeria, he said, was nothing but an enlarged parade ground.

Whatever Napoleon's haphazard ambitions might have produced will never be known. In 1871, following the unhappy outcome of the Franco-Prussian War, the Second Empire was replaced by the Third Republic and Napoleon went into exile. A civil administration seized power in Algeria – there were some among the colonists who wanted to make it a separate state – its integration with metropolitan France was complete, and the expansion of the settled areas proceeded apace. Its European population rose rapidly. Many of the newcomers were artisans attracted by Napoleon's public spending scheme, but a large proportion were also farmers. A certain amount of government intervention was still evident: French prostitutes were encouraged to move their business to Algeria in order to redress the balance of sexes in what was a predominantly male society; in addition, the inhabitants of Alsace-Lorraine, who had been displaced following Prussia's seizure of their homeland, were cajoled into rebuilding their lives in North Africa. Gradually, however, Algeria was assuming its own, independent identity. By 1880 its white population stood at 350,000 – the largest in Africa – of whom the majority were for once French.

Like its predecessors, the new government in Paris had doubts as to whether Algeria was worth the trouble – the natives continued to rebel, the costs continued to escalate, and white farmers continued to desert their holdings for a more secure and profitable life in the towns – but, ultimately, the prestige of possession outweighed all other concerns. There was also the public to consider. A small but vociferous number favoured colonization at all costs and pressed their case with every statistic to hand. For example, the birth rate for French families was far higher in Africa than it was at home – forty-one per thousand as opposed to twenty-six – which demonstrated, in their eyes, the invigorating effect of Algeria's climate.* It was, more-over, a climate suited ideally to the Latin races such as the French, and inimical to colonists from colder zones. A Swiss settlement, established at great cost, was an utter failure; as for German colonists, their death rate far exceeded their birth rate. And what could be more satisfactory than that? 'From the French point of view, it would be highly desirable to pass the whole of the Germanic race by drafts through the Algerian colander,' wrote one Briton, only partially in jest. 'Given time and patience, what might one not hope for?'[17]

To the aid of statistics came myth. The pro-colonial faction (few of whom had ever set foot in Algeria) propagated a frightful distortion of the past. They ignored the brutality of conquest – and it had, at times, been unspeakably brutal: once, when 800 villagers hid in caves to escape Bugeaud's flying columns, they were asphyxiated by the smoke from bonfires constructed at every entrance – casting the French troops instead as latter-day crusaders. The military was engaged in 'a magnificent and providential mission, a mission of order and peace, against enemies that formerly enriched themselves on the

---

*The invigorating effect was noticeably absent in Algiers, where a local news-paper, the *Akhbar*, published a 'Necrology . . . for the Fourth Quarter of 1879'. Of 716 deaths only thirty-eight were from old age. 'Wounds and Violent Death' accounted for twenty-four, 'Still-born' for fifty-nine and 'Teething', mysteriously, for nineteen. All the rest were attributable to disease of one kind or another. Bronchitis was the biggest killer (128), followed by consumption (114). At the bottom of the scale one person died of smallpox and two people succumbed (unfathomably) to thrush. The same report showed that most individuals died before they were twelve and that the survivors were lucky to live beyond fifty.

proceeds of pillage and rejoiced in cruelty; a mission to civilize people endowed with intelligence but in need of enlightenment and guidance; a divine mission on soil that our religion has watered with the blood of martyrs'.[18] The men with blue coats and guns were elevated, from a distance, to a height to which they had never aspired but which they were happy to command. It was a well-calculated piece of propaganda that gained credence with every year of Algeria's long colonial night.

For native Algerians the new regime meant only increased oppression and a steady theft of their land. During the last half-century their society had been virtually destroyed. Hundreds of thousands had died between 1840 and 1847 as the *razzias* of Bugeaud and his opponents flailed the country, and hundreds of thousands more had perished in subsequent campaigns. In 1868 alone, one failed uprising cost an estimated 300,000 lives, the majority succumbing to starvation and disease. Tens of thousands had fled to Morocco and Tunisia, initially to escape the killings but later because they were dispossessed by the influx of European settlers. For those who remained, the new Algeria was an alien world. Taxes were heavy and applied in a disastrous fashion. Unable or unwilling to recognize that Algeria was not a perpetual Eden and that a plentiful season might be followed by long periods of scarcity, the French extracted the maximum immediate tribute, leaving villagers with no surplus for lean years. (A policy which contributed directly to the horrific death toll of 1868.) Rural mosques had been smashed or deserted; urban mosques had been turned into tourist attractions, where their mosaics and tile-work had not been hacked off and sold at great profit by army officers in the 1830s. Officers of the Bureau Arabe now ran the legal system and local rulers were reduced to mere vassals. The traditional systems of charity-funded education and health-care had been abolished, and the old, urban-based Koranic values had given way to a peasant fundamentalism that was used by refugees to encourage further revolt. As the philosopher and political commentator Alexis de Tocqueville said, 'We have cut down the number of charities, let schools fall into ruins, closed the colleges. Around us the lights have gone out, the recruitment of men of religion and men of law has ceased. We have, in short, made Muslim society far more disorganized, ignorant and barbarous than ever it was before it knew us.'[19]

It was for this gratuitous, festering canker in North Africa, a society in which, according to Alphonse Daudet, 'the old Oriental perfumes are replaced by a strong blend of absinthe and the barracks',[20] that Charles de Foucauld sailed with the Fourth Hussars in 1880.

2

A PAINFUL VOID

Charles Eugène, Vicomte de Foucauld, was born at 5 a.m., 15 September 1858, in 3 Place de Broglie, Strasbourg, the main town of the province of Alsace. His family and his place of birth were both solidly French: generations of Foucaulds had served either in the military or the religious hierarchy, and 3 Place de Broglie was where, in 1792, Rouget de l'Isle had first sung his stirring composition, the 'Marseillaise'. By 1858, however, 3 Place de Broglie was just another house in an ordinary street, and its occupants were little different from any other members of the new bourgeoisie. Foucauld's mother, Élisabeth, was the daughter of an undistinguished soldiering family and his father, Édouard, was a civil servant employed by the Department of Woods and Waters.

The family Foucauld lived a peripatetic existence, movng from town to town as Édouard's job dictated. In 1861, when he was ordered to Wissembourg, Édouard became the father of a daughter – Marie. Two years later Élisabeth died in Strasbourg (perhaps from a miscarriage) at the age of thirty-five. The following year Édouard died in Paris – it was rumoured that he had killed himself – aged forty-four. The two children, Charles and Marie, were subsequently brought up in Strasbourg by their mother's father, Colonel Beaudet de Morlet, a precise, scholarly, impeccably groomed man, who was keen on archaeology and the classics.

Initially, Foucauld did not seem to be affected by the loss of his parents. With the deceptive adaptability of youth, the six-year-old simply carried on, went to school, achieved average grades (except on the history of Algeria, where he scored well), and walked with his grandfather, adopting the old man's likes and dislikes. When Prussia invaded Alsace in 1870, he moved with his grandfather and sister, with every appearance of placidity, first to Interlaken in Switzerland and then to Nancy from where Colonel de Morlet – who, unlike many Alsatians, had rejected the offer of relocation to Algeria – awaited a reoccupation of Alsace that did not occur. When Colonel de Morlet decided it was time for Foucauld to join the army, his pudgy, dark-eyed grandson acquiesced quite happily, stating only that he would rather not enrol in the École Polytechnique (Morlet's alma mater) but in St Cyr, the second of France's two great military academies. The reasons he gave were perfectly sensible: he was not particularly bright nor very fit but he did come from an aristocratic family. St Cyr had a reputation for preferring birth over brains or brawn and its entrance exams were supposedly easier than those of its rival. In 1875, Morlet sent him to a Jesuit boarding school in Paris for a spell of preparatory coaching. As always, Foucauld did what he was told was best for him.

The move proved to be a catalyst. Orphaned, rootless, spoiled and essentially friendless, Foucauld had only two constants in his ever-changing life: his family and his religion; among the few familiar objects he possessed from the past was a small bedroom altar given to him by his mother. In his teens, however, he lost his faith – or as one biographer puts it, 'what Charles really lost was his innocence'.[1] Now, boarding with the Jesuits, he felt he had lost his family too. Every two days he wrote letters, sometimes forty pages long, begging his grandfather to let him return home. When the answer was in the negative, he invented a new identity to cope with an unfamiliar world. He became the fat man of his class, a layabout who shirked his lessons

and adopted the self-indulgent attitude that was beginning to typify
fin de siècle Europe. 'I don't think I've ever been in such a bad state as
I was then,' he wrote thirteen years later. 'I've done worse things at
other times, but by then some good had grown alongside the evil: at
seventeen I was wholly an egoist, wholly vain, totally impious, wholly
given over to evil; I was as though crazy. As to my laziness, I hadn't
even in February cut the pages of the geometry book which I was
supposed to be studying since November!'[2] To the surprise of both
himself and his teachers he passed into St Cyr eighty-second out of a
list of 412 candidates though he very nearly failed the physical on
account of his obesity.

In 1928, Marshal Pétain, an old St Cyrien, described life at the acad-
emy: 'Here is a type of life entered upon without calculation or
interested ambition, a simple life, guided by a few straight rules: to
obey, to command.'[3] Foucauld was unimpressed. 'Nothing new at St.
Cyr,' he wrote in one letter. 'One always amuses oneself so much,
which is to say not much.'[4] In fact, he seems to have amused himself
a great deal. As he grew older he refined his man-of-the-world act,
making frequent excursions to escape the tedium of military academe,
drinking the finest champagne at lunch and developing such an
affected taste in cigars that he smoked only those that had been hand-
made according to his own recipe by a tobacconist in Paris. At night, in
his dormitory, he snacked on pâté de foie gras, specially ordered from
Strasbourg, which he ate straight from the tin with a little silver spoon.
He was, as one biographer says, 'ostentatious, vulgar, not particularly
good-looking or distinguished, but very amiable'.[5] Yet behind the
façade, there still lurked a child. 'You know how much I love pretzels,'
he wrote home. 'Very well, please arrange so that on Easter Monday at
lunch I can nibble half a dozen. Another thing no less important, I am
very fond of steaks roasted on the spit, of vegetable salad, and of water-
cress salad. I expect to eat these and lots more things during my stay.'[6]

He retained enough sense of duty to bother with his exams, and
was awarded 'stripes' for coming 143rd out of 391 at the end of his first
year. On 3 February 1878, however, his grandfather died. Once again
bereft, Foucauld abandoned all ideas of duty. He grew his hair,

dressed in slovenly fashion, appeared on parade with torn trousers and dirty uniform, and played truant. As he wrote to an old schoolfriend, 'You ask if on leaving St. Cyr I'll know whether to cry or laugh: *foutre*! yes, I know all right. I'm going to laugh – I'm going to laugh wildly and madly. It's dreadful. You cannot imagine what a hell St. Cyr is.'[7] His 'stripes' were removed on 11 April and when he graduated in August – 333rd out of a class of 386 – his record revealed that he had received forty-five official punishments and had spent forty-seven days under house arrest. He did not mind. On 15 September 1878, his nineteenth birthday, he received an inheritance of 840,000 francs, with a monthly interest worth 2,000 francs. It was a fortune – a labourer could keep an entire family very comfortably on less than a tenth of that sum. He immediately spent some of it on the rental of a Paris apartment from where he proceeded to dissipate the rest.

Foucauld's next stop was the cavalry school at Saumur. In the short break between St Cyr and Saumur, he was obliged to undergo yet another family upheaval. He and his sister Marie were now officially under the wing of their aunt, Inès, and her husband, M. Moitessier, who inhabited a big house at 52 Rue d'Anjou, Paris. No more bizarre a couple could be imagined. M. Moitessier was an elderly, dyspeptic boaster, who told stories of the time he had seen a man eaten alive by mosquitoes in Vera Cruz, of the occasion he had ripped the tongue from a mad dog's throat and of his fight with an assegai-wielding tribesman whom he had despatched with a thrust of his umbrella. Inès, on the other hand, was a society beauty whose face had been carved in stone on the Pont des Saints Pères as an emblem of French perfection, whose portrait had been painted twice by Ingres, and whose worldliness earned Foucauld's admiration – but not his love. Foucauld was lonelier than ever, failing even to connect with his sister who, although a fellow sufferer, remained, according to one biographer, 'self-effacing, colourless . . . a perpetual blancmange on the side board of Charles's heart'.[8]

At Saumur, Foucauld's depression manifested itself in further bouts of high living for which he found an admirable accomplice in the form of Antoine de Vallombrosa, Marquis de Morès, a companion from St Cyr with whom he now shared rooms. They were an odd couple: Vallombrosa was 'always on the go, a fine horseman, a sportsman, and Foucauld the stay-at-home, apathetic, and a dreamer'.[9] Foucauld had by now become so corpulent that he was nicknamed 'Piggy', but the two men complemented each other well enough. One of the younger cadets, Henri Laperrine, wrote that the menage 'became celebrated on account of the excellent dinners and long card parties which were held there, to keep company with the one under punishment, for it was very rare that one of the two occupants was not under arrest'.[10] Legends grew up around Foucauld's extravagance and disregard for authority. Once, he and Vallombrosa discovered a particularly fine wine at a restaurant and bought the entire cellar forthwith at a cost of 18,000 francs. There was the time when, confined to quarters for various dismeanours, Foucauld escaped in disguise to attend a party but on stopping at a restaurant for a snack was arrested as a spy when his false beard came unglued over the soup. He was placed under arrest for fifteen days. While serving his sentence he absconded yet again, this time wandering the countryside as a tramp, begging food from nearby farms. He was caught several days later when he jumped from a bridge onto a passing train. His gluttony was prodigious. 'He who discovers a new dish does more for humanity than he who discovers a new star,'[11] he liked to declaim. In pursuit of this philosophy he became fatter and fatter. He had his coaches lowered so that he did not have to climb their steps, and on visits home he impressed his relatives with his appetite. One cousin remembered that 'I was terrified if I saw Charles moving towards the children's table, for in a few seconds he invariably gobbled up all the cakes which had been set aside for us.'[12]

His exploits were extravagant to such a degree that M. Moitessier, fearing for his charge's financial health, resorted to the humiliating procedure of placing him under legal guardianship. It made little difference. The Inspector-General of Saumur noted with disapproval that 'M. Foucauld has a certain distinction and has been well brought up. But he is empty-headed and thinks of nothing but amusing himself.'[13] When he left Saumur in 1879 – eighty-seventh out of eighty-seven – and was commissioned as sub-lieutenant to the Fourth Hussars stationed at Pont-à-Mousson, he continued down his self-appointed path. At times he disgusted even himself. 'I felt a painful void, an anguish and a sorrow I never felt before or since;' he later wrote. 'This anguish returned each evening as soon as I found myself alone in my apartment; it was this that held me dumb, depressed, during what people call entertainments. I organized them, but when they were actually taking place, I spent them speechless in an infinite disgust.'[14] Those words, however, were written in retrospect and, if true, their sentiments seemed to have no effect on his behaviour. Barracks life provided as much opportunity for disgrace as had Saumur. For instance, having fallen foul of his Colonel, Foucauld took revenge on an evening when the Colonel was hosting a regimental occasion. It was a rainy night and, at the end of festivities, the Colonel went out in search of cabs for his guests. Carriage after empty carriage ignored him. Eventually the infuriated officer leaped into the street, wrestled a cab to a standstill and demanded to know why the driver had not stopped when requested. The man confessed that Vicomte de Foucauld had hired every cab in town and instructed them to drive in circles past the Colonel's home ignoring his signals. On another occasion the Colonel held a party but Foucauld acquired a list of his guests and invited them to a party of his own, leaving the Colonel to a full table and an empty room. In response the Colonel invited himself to the rival party and took great pleasure in telling Foucauld that he was being posted to Africa.

The stories were, perhaps, apocryphal – stock anecdotes of the type produced by every male institution – but they could equally have been true. To Foucauld, military life was a game. When the Fourth Hussars – renamed the Fourth Chasseurs D'Afrique – arrived at the garrison town of Sétif, inland and to the east of Algiers, Foucauld remained oblivious to the realities of his situation. He had no interest in his role as an officer in the army of occupation; he was untouched by the prospect of war. He investigated in a scholarly fashion the people he was meant to be subjugating; he studied Arabic and Berber dialects, and toured the Kabylia district to acquaint himself with local customs. (The knowledge gained was not exclusively academic: 'you must sleep with a black woman,'[15] he enthused to a friend.) But mostly he was struck by the tedium of his new position, the dreariness of which was exemplified by a dusty notice hanging in the mess of the adjoining infantry barracks: 'No discussion of any sort on any subject is permitted on sirocco days.'[16] Sétif, as he later wrote, was an 'ugly garrison and the job bored me'.[17]

Fortunately, Foucauld had come prepared. With him he had brought his mistress, Mimi, whom he settled in the town's best hotel under the pretence that she was his wife. For a while Vicomte and Vicomtesse de Foucauld were honoured guests at colonial dinners until his commanding officer discovered the truth. Foucauld was asked to explain. He replied that he had nothing to explain, that he was innocent of any crime, that the woman was not subject to military rules, that she could choose to stay in Sétif or not, as she wished, and that she was her own mistress. The Colonel replied that 'She may be her own mistress, but she is, unfortunately for her, also yours, and *you are* under my orders.'[18] Lieutenant Vicomte de Foucauld was imprisoned for thirty days. When, on his release, he continued to see Mimi, he was given a choice: he could dismiss her and stay, or he could take her and go. He settled for the latter. Removed temporarily from active service 'for lack of discipline and notorious misconduct',[19] according to the official record, or, as he put it casually in a letter, '*affaire d'une femme*',[20] he retreated with Mimi to a hotel near Evian from where he was able to admire the view, ponder his future and follow, in a desultory fashion, the news that came in from Africa.

His resignation lasted less than a year. In the spring of 1881 France invaded Tunisia. Simultaneously a tribal leader named Bou-Amama proclaimed a *jihad* or holy war against the invader. Leading an army across the Moroccan border, he overwhelmed the garrisons of southern Oran and sparked an insurrection that threatened to engulf the whole colony. Once again Algeria was aflame. Foucauld sought the immediate reinstatement of his commission. Either life with Mimi had become too dull, or he had at last decided to act rather than drift – or maybe he was impelled by patriotism; 'When the blood of France cries aloud, nothing can silence it,'[21] as one of his biographers wrote in 1923. Whatever the reason, he appealed directly to the Minister of War, stating his willingness to enrol as a spahi so long as he could help his comrades in their fight against the enemy. He had no need to change regiments. That year he rejoined the Fourth Chasseurs in Africa.

Although Foucauld did not know it, the war for which he sailed was not a localized conflict but one that had originated in France's wider imperial ambitions. Following the collapse of the Second Empire and the appointment of civilian governors, Algeria's military, which was always a law unto itself, had sought new avenues of self-determination. Morocco beckoned from the west, Tunisia and Tripolitania from the east, but these routes were, in the 1870s, charged with diplomatic perils. Much safer, for the moment, was the road that led south over the Atlas mountains. In the eyes of some strategists the uncharted, unclaimed desert represented great wealth, not necessarily for what it contained – nobody was very sure what it did contain: gold, diamonds, the lost kingdom of Prester John; anything was possible – but for what lay beyond it. If France's equatorial possessions were connected by conquest to Algeria it would effectively turn the whole of West Africa into a French colony. Moreover, if during the conquest it was possible to lay a railway line, the natural bounty of the tropics could be transmitted to France in a matter of days as opposed to the months it took by sea. It was the military's first probe in this direction that indirectly sparked Bou-Amama's uprising and the invasion of Tunisia and which changed Foucauld's life for ever. The Sahara, the great bald head of Africa, was about to become the next victim of French imperialism.

3

INTO THE DESERT

The Sahara is vast, a wasteland approximately the size of the United States, whose nine million square kilometres comprise the largest, most notoriously inhospitable desert known to humankind. Its name derives from the Arabic *Sah'ra*, meaning dun or mouse-coloured, being a literal description of the terrain the Arabs encountered on probing the southern limits of their North African conquests. The two Great Ergs, situated on Algeria's borders with Morocco and Tunisia, are the Sahara as portrayed in picture-books: razor-edged swells of sand stretching to the horizon. They are frighteningly huge – you could place some West European countries in them and still have dunes to spare – and they are also mysterious: occasionally, when the wind is in the right direction, the sand sings, a deep booming whose cause has yet to be explained by science. The Ergs, however, occupy only a small percentage of the Sahara. Between them lie rock-strewn plateaux whose surfaces have acquired a unique glaze, a black patina known as 'desert varnish', and which are riven by the dry river beds, or *oueds*, that lead from the mountains. And the Sahara does have mountains, not just hills but true mountains that catch the wind and rain like those in Europe. They are tectonic in origin, rather than volcanic or glacial, squeezed through the earth's mantle to form violent peaks and outcrops. But they serve the same purpose as any other mountain. When rain falls, as it does in the Sahara with greater frequency than most people realize, the water pours down the slopes and into the *oueds*, creating flash floods that produce a sudden flourish of greenery. The water, however, does not last long: a day or two every few years and then it is gone, leaving the desert as barren as before, save for a few springs that sustain life along the *oueds*.

The Sahara was not always thus. During the last ice age it was a Mediterranean savannah whose plants sustained a wide range of wildlife – lions, rhinoceros, elephants, giraffe, gazelle and buffalo – and an accompanying population of human hunter-gatherers. Then, over centuries, the climate changed: rivers that had once run overland retreated underground, emerging at brief intervals to form oases, and the land dried up, its rocks and soil drifting in clouds of silicate dust that blew across the landscape, gathering around rocks or other obstacles, where they attracted further accumulations of sand that grew into full-fledged dunes. The winds that formed the Great Ergs came, as they always had, from the equator. They still carried clouds and they still continued to deposit rain on the Sahara, but by now the earth was so dry and its temperature so high that more often than not the rain evaporated before it hit the ground. Wildlife and humans together moved south to the semi-arid territories bordering equatorial Africa, leaving the Sahara to its unpredictable weather and to the deep-rooted date palms that managed to survive in the oases. At some point, however, humans began to re-infiltrate the Sahara. They were the Tuareg, nomads related distantly to the Berbers of the north, who moved with small flocks of goats and camels from pasture to seasonal pasture. A loose-knit series of clans, centred on the mountainous areas of the Adjer to the south of Tunisia, the Hoggar above Lake Chad, and the Adrar des Iforas to its west, they lived not only off their animals but off the cultivation – by slaves and black tenants known as *harratin* – of dates and the occasional fields of wheat that flourished in the oases. Primarily, however, they thrived on the caravans that plied the trade routes linking North Africa to the equator. Indeed, banditry and extortion provided most of their livelihood, making them an evolutionary rarity: in almost no other quarter of the globe was there such a large and distinct populace whose lifestyle depended so heavily on robbing other humans. The Tuareg were masters of their environment, moving unpredictably through the desert, launching surprise attacks on any who had not paid for their protection and sometimes on those who had – the excuse, if offered, being that one leader's influence did not necessarily extend over the invisible and arbitrary frontier separating his clan's territory from that of its neighbours.

It was impossible to dispute the Tuareg's control of the Sahara. The army did not exist that could defeat such an elusive foe in such inhospitable terrain. Many had tried. All had failed. The annals of Ancient Greece contained stories of entire armies that had been swallowed without trace. A whole Roman legion had vanished in the sands. The Ottomans didn't even try, satisfying themselves with an accord that suited both sides: slaves from tropical Africa were delivered to the Mediterranean coast, no questions were asked, and money was made by all. Even had the Sahara not been desert it would still have been hard to overcome the Tuareg. The Hoggar, for example, was a massive natural fortress whose mountains rose more than 3,000 metres above sea level on a horseshoe-shaped plateau that was accessible only from the south. To take such a place by conventional means would have been difficult for any European force under any circumstance. To do so across the desert was impossible. Therefore, one can only admire France for its determination to do that very thing.

By the middle of the nineteenth century the Sahara was virtually unknown to white men. During the past fifty years some half dozen Europeans had departed from North Africa, using the old caravan routes as a means to explore the regions to the south. They had returned (sometimes) with uniformly discouraging tales of horrible terrain and aggressive inhabitants. In the 1850s, French troops poked their guns over the southern rim of the Atlas but occupied only the oases that lay in the mountains' shadow. They had no immediate need to go further as their reputation had preceded them. In 1854 a delegation of Tuareg offered promises of eternal friendship and guaranteed safe conduct as far as Timbuctoo, the fabled *non plus ultra* on the upper reaches of the River Niger, towards which most previous expeditions had been directed. Little, however, was really known about either the desert or the people that lived in it. In 1858 (the year in which Foucauld was born) a teenager named Henri Duveyrier decided to remedy the defect.

Duveyrier was an inexperienced but intelligent eighteen-year-old, who seemed to possess all the attributes required of a Saharan explorer. He was 'a botanist, geologist, versed in Oriental languages, thoroughly civilized, marvellously endowed for meeting and winning barbarians'.[1] Most importantly, he was willing to go, writing: 'Since my mind was first capable of reasoned judgement, I have been drawn invincibly to the African continent.'[2] He departed for the Adjer, preceded by messages of goodwill and accompanied by no more than a few servants. 'I am well aware,' he wrote in his diary, 'that the journey I am about to undertake is not without its dangers; but I am confident in my health and I hope that with prudence, patience and energy I will avoid them and will guide my expedition to a happy conclusion. Events will prove if I am mistaken.'[3] He was not mistaken. For three years he criss-crossed the northern Sahara, investigating its oases and spending many unmolested months among the Tuareg, before coming home in 1861, his mind and notebooks brimming with extraordinary images.

It was unfortunate that, on his return, he fell ill with a 'fever of the brain' – perhaps meningitis – and lost all recollection of his unique voyage. But from his journal he managed to recreate the first and fullest picture of Tuareg life to reach the Western world. The society he described in *Les Touaregs du Nord* (published eventually in 1864) could have been plucked from a manual of Romantic stereotypes. The men, he wrote, were almost Caucasian – white-skinned, thin-nosed, hard-working and hard-fighting. They were Muslims in theory but not in practice, the men wearing a veil that was dyed a traditional blue, while the women (who were extremely beautiful and with whom Duveyrier seems to have had several liaisons) kept their faces uncovered. Their diet obeyed no recognizable Islamic code: pork was acceptable, but it was forbidden to eat either fish, chicken or eggs. They had scant knowledge of the Koran, and although a few marabouts, or holy men, understood Arabic, they preferred in general to use their own language and their own script, which consisted of a blocky set of squiggles, possibly descended from Carthaginian, in which they daubed messages on the rocks that surrounded wells and oases. They were a matriarchal society, chieftainship of each clan passing to the son of the chief's wife, regardless of whether the chief was the father. Travelling mostly by night, they were expert astronomers, steering their way by constellations of a brilliancy that staggered Duveyrier and to which they gave evocative names. They were hospitable, generous, long-lived and poetic. They were fond of music, and played a one-stringed violin. They lived in low, black tents yet walked tall and bore themselves with impressive dignity. Above all, they were a kind, peaceful folk who would not obstruct France's ambitions. As one chief told Duveyrier, 'All Frenchmen who wish to explore the Hoggar will be very welcome, provided that they follow local customs.'[4] In short, they were the best and noblest of savages.

Duveyrier was awarded the Légion d'Honneur for his work – a magnificent accolade for one so young. But while his observations may have been accurate, his conclusions were flawed by youthful innocence and an understandable excitement at having done what no other had before him. His greatest error was in portraying the Tuareg as peaceful. Although willing to harbour a harmless stranger and to make polite advances to a powerful new neighbour, they had no intention of allowing themselves to be overrun. For both sides, Duveyrier had been an experiment: to France his findings suggested a trouble-free conquest; to the Tuareg, however, his stay was an insight into a culture they had no wish to be part of. These opposing interpretations resulted in frightful bloodshed.

In 1869 Mlle Tinne of Holland went into the desert. A practised shot, she came armed with pistols, maids and a caravan of luxurious goods.

She was murdered by the Tuareg. In 1870, two Frenchmen – Joubert and Dorneaux-Duprée – also went into the desert. They were murdered. In 1875 the newly created Cardinal of Algiers sent three fathers, Paulmier, Menorel and Bouchand, to convert the Tuareg. They, too, were murdered. So, in the same year, outside the Hoggar, were Lieutenant Louis Say and a journalist named Lemay. In 1876 the seasoned desert traveller Erwin du Barry was poisoned in Ghat. The reports of these deaths, as transmitted to Algiers by local rulers, made unpleasant reading. The Ottoman governor of Murzouk, for example, while apologizing fulsomely for the death of Mlle Tinne and condemning it wholeheartedly, dwelled with macabre glee on details which he could only have obtained from an intimate acquaintance with the perpetrators – when she reached for a pistol, he told the French, her right hand was severed by one stroke of a sword. A warning was clearly being sent to France. But France ignored it, just as it ignored the reports of those travellers whom the Tuareg did not kill but sent away with orders never to return. Rather than accept the evidence before them, the authorities preferred to rely on Duveyrier's misguided, outdated, yet comforting reassurances as to the pacific state of the interior.

Among those who reacted most positively to the idea of a safe Sahara was an engineer from Montpellier named Alphonse Duponchel. In 1879 Duponchel published a book called *Le Chemin de fer Trans Saharien* or *The Transsaharian Railway*. It was a gripping title, encompassing as it did the thrill of steam travel, the mystery of the desert and (never far from any European mind) the prospect of colonial conquest. The notion was glamorous, uplifting and, above all, patrotic in a very high-profile way. To a nation still recovering from its ignominious defeat in the Franco-Prussian War, Duponchel's plan was the perfect tonic.

What Duponchel proposed was simple. A railway would be driven from Algiers to the Soudan, the semi-arid region that separated the Sahara from the tropics. On reaching Timbuctoo it would split, one branch leading to Lake Chad, the other to Senegal. He breezed over the difficulties involved in its construction. Shifting dunes? Plant them over. No water? Sink a series of artesian wells, connected by pumps and pipes. Lack of workers? A perfect opportunity to put France's population of unemployed and criminal wastrels to profitable use. Hostile tribes? To be discounted absolutely: 'The prestige of our troops, the superiority of our weapons, and the well-known pusillanimity of the Sahara's inhabitants, whose warlike reputation has been greatly exaggerated, allow complete confidence in the successful outcome of the enterprise.'[5]

Duponchel ignored all practicalities. With what magical plant did he intend to stabilize the dunes? How would the convicts and idlers be pressed into service, and how would they be supplied once they were in the desert? Once the track had been laid, where would the locomotives recoal? And, on a minor political note, what business did France have laying a railway through lands it did not own: in the case of Chad ('discovered' by Britons) this might prove contentious. To Duponchel these were mere details. If his railway were built it would unite French colonies in West Africa with those in the North, creating an enclosure that, with Chad as its easternmost point, stretched north to the Mediterranean and west to the Atlantic. 'The great humanitarian crusade upon which Europe seems resolved to bring the African continent into the current of general civilization,' he wrote, 'can never succeed until we arrive in the heart of the country.'[6] Previously, Europeans had reached the 'heart' – i.e. Timbuctoo and Chad – either by travelling in native clothes, 'as beggars disguising their nationality',[7] or with the aid of detachments supplied by the Bey of Tripoli. Duponchel was uncertain which was the most disgraceful. If his Saharan railway was constructed, French merchants, explorers and colonists could dominate the territory in proper style, with all the puff, whistle and presence of the fastest means of locomotion then known to humankind. They would arrive with 'all of the material resources at our disposal, with all the prestige of irresistible power, which alone can impress the spirit of these barbarous peoples, used only to respect force and submit to its yoke'.[8]

Additionally the Transsaharian, as it became known, would open the interior to French trade, thus turning an estimated one hundred

million 'barbarians' into valuable customers. Reports showed that the
British monopolized regional trade with goods whose cheapness was
guaranteed by access to an Empire of raw materials and an advanced
factory system. In African marketplaces, British produce undercut
French by almost a third. These goods, however, had first to be transported to the coast by ship and then hauled overland, all of which cost
time and money. When the Transsaharian was in place, French products could reach central Africa in a trice, and the trains that took them
there could return with the limitless wealth of the Soudan. Duponchel
glided over the exact nature of this wealth: apart from palm oil (which
was produced, anyway, on the coast and was far better transported in
ships), the Soudan offered only feathers, pelts and small quantities of
ivory and gold. Nor did he explain precisely what products the Africans
were to purchase in exchange: French manufacturing was still relatively undeveloped and the nation's main exports were luxury goods
such as lace, perfume, gloves and wine. Instead, he emphasized the
joys of tourism. Within only *six days* people who sailed from
Marseilles could be on the coast of West Africa. Whether they would
like the notoriously unhealthy tropics was another matter. (As one
Briton said, 'Who the deuce wants to take a return ticket to
Timbuctoo?')[9] Duponchel thought it a very good idea nonetheless. It
was the concept rather than the reality that mattered.

Duponchel was not the man best qualified to pronounce on the
construction of a trans-Saharan railway. Less an engineer than a tech-
nological fantasist, he overflowed with grandiose projects. One was
the construction of a pipeline to carry wine from Beziers to Paris.
Another was the use of compressed water to blast a canal through the
Panama Isthmus. On a grander scale, he proposed the use of high-
pressure water jets to artificially erode the Pyrenees so that the
marshes of south-western France would be covered by fertile soil.
None of these madcap ideas received much attention. The
Transsaharian, however, struck a chord with the public. Colonization
was very much on the national mind. There was an increasing despair
that France was being left behind while other nations – particularly
Britain – gobbled up the world's unexploited spaces. Paul Gaffarel, a

professor from Dijon, expressed the mood in one of his many books on the subject. 'How many times,' he asked, 'have we heard someone say, or indeed, said ourselves, "France does not know how to colonize."'[10] He rejected the current theory that colonies were dangerous to establish and that their maintenance was a drain both on the population and on the public purse. No, he said, 'we must colonize, colonize at all costs; not only is colonization safe but it is patriotic and of absolute necessity'.[11] To convince his readers he drew up a league table showing which countries owned how much land, governed how many people, and what the ratio was between their colonial and home populations. Britain, naturally, was at the top with 200 million foreign subjects (a ratio of seven to one) and there at the bottom was France with six million (a humiliating ratio of one to six). Even Portugal, a country that belonged to the fifth rank in the accepted rating of European power, came ahead of France in Gaffarel's calculations. 'Our inferority is flagrant,'[12] he wrote.

Gaffarel, whose books were widely read, told people what he thought should be done. 'In extending our political influence immeasurably, in opening to our etiolated industry, dormant capital and bored youth, such untold wealth and prosperity, what do we have to do? Nothing but reach the unexploited region! Nothing but build a railway!'[13]

The pressure of people like Gaffarel and Duponchel was irresistible and, eventually, the French government bowed to it. In January 1880 Colonel Paul Flatters, a middle-aged, under-employed officer in the Bureau Arabe, was sent to the desert. His orders were to survey the route over which the Transsaharian might run and, while doing so, to reassure the calm, peaceful, complaisant Tuareg that a railway through their territory was just what they needed. Flatters departed with a large armed escort, which was probably the only reason he returned alive a few months later with depressing news. The Tuareg, he said, did not want a railway built on their land. The government was uncertain what to do. After some deliberation, it decided that Flatters had manifested himself in too threatening a guise and that he should return the following year with less firepower.

Flatters was uncertain about the value of a railway. Privately, he opined that if he had to go, then the more men and guns he had the better. But, despite his reservations, he agreed to the new conditions. He wanted a job, some excitement, something whereby (like every nineteenth-century explorer) he could make his name. So, in late 1880, leading a reduced force of forty-seven Algerian *tirailleurs*, or riflemen, and eleven Frenchmen, including one officer and two sergeants, plus thirty-one cameleers and seven guides drawn from the Chaamba, a semi-nomadic Berber tribe from the northern desert, Flatters rode once again into the Sahara. He did, indeed, make his name, but not as he would have wished and in a manner that shook France to its core.

Travelling south for the Hoggar, Flatters fell prey to standard Tuareg tactics. At first he received messages that all was well, that he was welcome wherever he might wish to go. His fears assuaged and his resolution stiffened, Flatters moved deeper into Tuareg territory. In the letters he sent home he wrote that the expedition was proceeding smoothly. But things were not going satisfactorily at all. He suffered from sciatica and, despite injections of morphine and 'cauterizations with a hot iron',[14] could not walk for more than thirty minutes at a stretch and was only comfortable when lying down. Moreover, his camels were dying. He had grown to distrust his Chaamba guides: once, he threatened to shoot them if they did not lead him directly to his destination. Luckily, a Tuareg guide came to his assistance and by 26 January 1882 Flatters could see the distant foothills of the Hoggar. Three days later he wrote to his wife, 'When you receive this we shall be in the Soudan.'[15] But on 2 February, his Tuareg guide said he could not remember the way. On 10 February a second guide arrived, who had a better memory – which came at a price of 1,000 francs. On 11 February thirty armed Tuareg visited Flatters's camp, slapped his back, accepted gifts, inspected his goods, congratulated him on his pluck, stole two camels, and thereafter lurked threateningly on the horizon. By 16 February the expedition was running out of water. That same day the new guide announced that he was lost. He was certain, however, that a well was somewhere nearby. Infuriated, Flatters mounted his horse and with four other Frenchmen led his guides in search of water. Twelve *tirailleurs* were instructed to unload their supplies and follow as swiftly as possible with the camels. Forty soldiers and two civil engineers under a Lieutenant Dianous and Sergeant Pobeguin stayed behind to guard the camp.

Flatters did, eventually, reach the well. It was situated in a valley approachable only by a narrow, rocky ravine. He and his fellows dismounted to inspect it. At that moment the Tuareg rose from behind the hills. Flatters's band was hacked to pieces. His accompanying *tirailleurs* put up a brief defence before their ammunition ran out and they, too, were slaughtered. A few men escaped, staggering back to camp with the information that 200 armed Tuareg were on the rampage. Lieutenant Dianous, who was later criticized for not leading an immediate offensive action, ordered his men to make a stockade using their supply chests. From this impromptu redoubt he hoped to repel the attack he was sure was imminent. But no attack came: the Tuareg were too busy squabbling over the spoils. That night, Dianous ordered a quiet retreat to the oasis of Ouargla.

Ouargla was almost 1,600 kilometres to the north. The road was reasonably well furnished with wells and they had rifles as well as ample ammunition. But it was food that Dianous's column now needed. They had only what could be carried either by themselves or on three camels (all the others having been lost to the Tuareg) and their supplies soon ran out. They grubbed in the sand for roots and chewed on pieces of shoe leather. One man tried to shoot himself. Meanwhile, the Tuareg shadowed them, now making protestations of friendship, then making half-hearted defences of the wells, then selling them some of the stores they had been forced to leave behind (loaded, humiliatingly, on two of their own camels). Occasionally small bands of *tirailleurs* were invited to collect provisions from the enemy camp. They never returned. On 9 March, after Dianous chased a force of a hundred Tuareg from the well of Aïn el-Kerma, one of his persecutors, who had hitherto portrayed himself as a secret ally and who had previously given him supplies, slipped him a bag of crushed dates. The gift was devoured avidly.

One of the few plants to thrive in the Sahara is the lettuce-like *efelehleh*. Despite its innocuous appearance it is highly toxic and affects both the digestive and the nervous systems. The crushed dates had been mixed with *efelehleh*. Within minutes Dianous's men were in agonies. They foamed at the mouth, their throats burned and they were devoured by an inextinguishable thirst. Some became paralysed from the waist down; Dianous himself lapsed into semi-coma. Others raved, tore off their clothes and ran into the desert, firing their guns as they went. The Tuareg watched and waited.

On 10 March, some order having been established, thanks largely to the efforts of a few Chaamba cameleers who had suspected trickery and had refused to eat the dates, Dianous sent six men to parley with the Tuareg. They were murdered. With his enfeebled column he then moved on to the next well. Finding it guarded by Tuareg, he at last led an outright attack but was met by bullets from his own captured rifles. Dianous was killed, leaving a wounded and still poisoned Sergeant Pobeguin to lead thirty-four starving men in search of the next well. The Tuareg, having made their point, did not bother to pursue them.

Pobeguin's men ate their remaining food, then their camels and then anything they could find. When they stumbled across a dead camel they ate it – even though the corpse was so old that it had become mummified – and when the camel was finished they started on each other. Again and again they resorted to cannibalism. A group of nine stragglers, who shot themselves rather than die of starvation, were devoured raw. When Pobeguin himself became too weak to continue he was killed and eaten. Finally, on 4 April, the survivors crawled into Ouargla. There were twelve of them: eleven Chaamba, one *tirailleur*, no Europeans. Later, another five *tirailleurs* would emerge from the desert, claiming to have found refuge with a less hostile band of Tuareg. These two clutches of human debris were all that remained of Flatters's optimistic venture.

France's humiliation was complete. Never before had a European power been crushed so thoroughly by a native force. And certainly never by natives whose traditional weapons were sabres and lances and whose only defence against bullets was the long, white, leather shields that they slung from their camels. In Paris disbelief was followed by outrage. 'We march from insult to insult, from defiance to defiance, from humiliation to humiliation,' one newspaper wrote. 'The honour of our name, our legitimate influence, the security of our Algerian enterprise, the grandeur and the economy of our projects in Africa require that we exact a prompt and energetic revenge for so much bad faith, perfidiousness and ferocity.'[16] But of course there were no reprisals that could be taken. Like other developed nations, before and since, France quickly realized the impracticability of pitting conventional forces against an unconventional enemy in an unfamiliar landscape. Nothing was done and, after a few weeks, the clamour subsided.

Nevertheless, neither Flatters nor the Transsaharian was forgotten. Flatters assumed near-mythical status: his death was honoured in subsequent years by explorers who repeatedly erected memorial cairns and by an extraordinary story that he had not been killed but was living in state as a great Saharan chief. The desert, meanwhile, still occupied the French imagination. Although there was a temporary lapse of enthusiasm for trans-Saharan railway construction, the project had not been punctured. Like the memory of Flatters it was packed carefully in the national cupboard and reinflated whenever the needs of colonialism demanded.

In the immediate aftermath of the débâcle, France had two concerns: how to restore its African prestige in a manner that did not involve great loss of life in the Sahara; and how this blow to its invincibility would affect the situation in Algeria. The first question was answered that spring with the invasion of Tunisia. The answer to the second came when Bou-Amama heard of France's military incompetence in the desert and decided to launch his *jihad*. Thus, although Foucauld did not know it at the time, it was the Sahara that prompted his return to Africa.

4

RECONNAISANCE
AU MAROC

Foucauld had at first hoped to be sent to Tunisia. Why, after all, return to a country with which he was familiar when a new land beckoned? 'An expedition of this sort,' he wrote in October 1881, 'is too rare a pleasure to be allowed to pass without tasting it.'[1] But he was not sent to Tunisia. Instead, the Fourth Chasseurs were ordered to patrol the High Plateaux of the Algerian Atlas, an area that was removed from the main war zone and in which conflict was a potential but improbable threat. Expecting the boredom from which he had previously fled, Foucauld was pleasantly surprised by his induction into campaign life. As he wrote in October, 'I have lost nothing much by coming here; in the 3½ months I have been with the Fourth Chasseurs D'Afrique, I have not passed two nights in a house.'[2] Harsh conditions, coupled with the suggestion of excitement, seemed to agree with him. They agreed, too, with Vallombrosa, who had joined the Fourth Hussars at the same time as Foucauld and, as a keen shot, saw the war as an admirable opportunity to hone his marksmanship. Above all, the war pleased another of Foucauld's fellow graduates from St Cyr, a serious-minded young officer named Henri Laperrine.

Two years younger than Foucauld, Laperrine was his opposite in almost every way. Although of aristocratic lineage – theoretically he should have been Laperrine de Hautpol – he refused to accept the title and of all his ancestors was proudest of one whom he described as 'a bad sort', who had ended his life on the gallows. His family had a history of misadventure and what little fortune it once possessed had been wasted by his father, an ex-African army officer who was renowned for his violence and his financial incompetence. In Algeria, Laperrine senior had been famous for provoking duels and after killing several men he had been thrown out of the service. He had then devoted himself to a series of ill-fated financial adventures that emptied the family coffers and left him with only a small chateau in the south, alongside the railway between Carcassonne and Toulouse. Once, when the youthful Laperrine was travelling home on that same track, he fell into conversation with a local lawyer. 'Young man,' said the lawyer, pointing to Chateau Laperrine, 'in all my career, I've never seen anything so absurd as what has gone on there.'[3] He listed a set of misdemeanours so fascinating that Laperrine missed his stop and had to catch the next train back. His father was so memorably incompetent that Laperrine entered St Cyr under a cloud. Marshal MacMahon, one of Laperrine Senior's superior officers, went out of his way to let this be known, remarking at an official inspection, 'Laperrine? Laperrine? Don't I know your father?' Laperrine said he might possibly. 'Well, tell him I've never forgiven him.'[4]

Where Foucauld lounged, Laperrine applied himself furiously. Foucauld was grossly overweight and languid; Laperrine was tall, thin and temperamental. Where Foucauld loved women, Laperrine seemed incapable of love: he never formed a romantic liaison with any member of either sex and lived only for the army. Where Foucauld was oiled and impeccably groomed, Laperrine was a ragamuffin: his beard sprouted in all directions; his uniform did not so much fit as float or hang around him, a collection of pockets arranged in a framework of misaligned belts, buttons and epaulettes; even his hats refused to sit straight, pushed by his hair into an angle that passed for rakish. In photographs he appears manically unfinished, a shop-window dummy awaiting the dressers' return from lunch.

But Laperrine was no dummy. He was a career soldier, an intelligent man, whose devotion to the military was equalled, in time, only by his determination to reform it. At home, the French army conformed to the standard European conventions of display, set-piece grandeur, and spit and polish, with unquestioning obedience expected by an officer class that had little experience of war. In Algeria, however, things were different. When not on parade soldiers threw aside their uniforms in favour of whatever was most comfortable. Baggy trousers and bare feet were the norm. They fought in a manner that fitted no European preconception and obeyed only those who inspired them. It suited Laperrine admirably. The Bou-Amama war gave him a taste for a continent that, bar the odd recall to France, he would not leave until his death thirty-nine years later.

The Bou-Amama war was hardly a war at all – more a series of brief encounters interspersed with the usual atrocities. Bou-Amama's forces rarely met the French troops head on and after a few months chasing hither and thither the conflict fizzled out inconclusively. The 'rebels' retired silently from whence they came, their leader was never captured, and the French announced a glorious victory. The experience, however, created an unlikely friendship between Foucauld and Laperrine. It was Laperrine's first posting abroad and although it was Foucauld's second he had been away for long enough to lose his tan. The two men were thus drawn together if for no other reason than that they were the two palest faces in the regiment. Laperrine, who remembered Foucauld as 'Piggy', was struck by his comrade's enthusiasm for campaigning and by the change it brought about in him. Foucauld took an extraordinary (for him) interest in his men's welfare: when, for example, they dug a well, he would distribute his personal supply of rum to disguise the brackish taste of the water – and also, following accepted wisdom, to sterilize it. He admired their privations and delighted in sharing them. 'The army of Africa is even better than that of Metropolitan France,' he wrote.[5] 'Half the men in my platoon would have made excellent monks.' He admired, too, the Berbers he encountered. Their lives and their faith appeared strikingly self-sufficient, detached almost to the point of asceticism. Part of his wonder may have stemmed from innocence: the way in which they neglected to mend their tents and seemed indifferent to their flocks was more the result of constant military depredation than any inherent spiritualism. But their practice of dropping to the ground at given hours to pray to Allah, without pomp and regardless of circumstance, was an approach to religion that Foucauld had never before witnessed. 'Islam,' he wrote, 'is extremely seductive, and it seduced me excessively.'[6] As the days passed he became noticeably thinner and less attached to material comforts. 'Of the Foucauld of Saumur and Pont-à-Mousson,' Laperrine wrote, 'nothing was left except a tiny pet edition of Aristophanes which was always with him, and just a touch of snobbery which made him give up smoking from the day that he could no longer procure cigars of his favourite brand.'[7]

The last French columns returned to barracks on 15 January 1882 and Foucauld, stationed now in the town of Masacara, once again became bored. This time, however, he did not retire to a life of equal boredom in some European spa but decided to take part in a new adventure. 'I detest garrison life,' he explained to a friend in February, 'I had always intended to leave the military one day or another – and in these circumstances I decided to do it sooner; what's the point of throwing away my youth in a career that does not interest me; I would rather spend it travelling; in this way at least I will be educating myself and won't be wasting my time. My resignation is in the post.'[8] The adventure he had in mind was an overland trip through the Sahara to Cairo. In the month that it took for his resignation to be finalized he underwent intensive tuition in Arabic while poring over maps of the region. By December, however, he had a new goal in mind. For reasons that stemmed from France's annexation of Tunisia, the concomitant tension with Tripolitania and a general unwillingness to let travellers enter Tuareg zones unprotected – in 1881 another two priests had been murdered – the authorities had denied him permission to travel eastwards. Instead, he was steered towards a region that was equally unknown, equally exciting and, to the military, of far greater interest: Morocco.

Since the French invasion of Algeria, the Sultan of Morocco had closed his borders to the outside world. A few major ports such as Tangiers and Mogador were open to international trade and one or two enclaves along the coast had been seized by Spain, who had made in recent years several costly and not very successful attempts to extend their suzerainty inland. In the main, however, Morocco was a poorly charted wilderness whose Islamic inhabitants were – rightly, given the example of Algeria – hostile to any perceived encroachment on their territory. But where did that territory begin? The military, being the military, drew a line on their maps, but it was a hazy demarcation that meant little to those on the spot and which applied only to the fertile regions of the coast. Further south, towards the Sahara, the line petered out. Thereafter, the border between Algeria and Morocco was left to the imagination. Nobody knew at which particular dune either country began or ended. Had a frontier existed it would have been meaningless, because neither the Sultan of Morocco nor the Governor of Algeria exercised the slightest control over the land through which it ran. The French had yet to penetrate that far and the Sultan's authority was restricted to those areas surrounding the urban centres of the north, the so-called *bled el makhzen*. In the *bled el siba*, the 'free' or 'rebellious' country to the south, an area that centred around Marrakech but which extended to the Atlas mountains and portions of the Sahara, most people obeyed local chieftains and had only the vaguest sense of either the Sultan's existence or the fact that they were actually Moroccan. As Duveyrier put it, the *bled el siba* was 'about as much under Moroccan jurisdiction as the Transvaal or the Republic of Andorra'.[9]

This state of affairs annoyed the French even more than it did the Sultan. Tunisia having fallen and the Sahara demanding that it be treated with a new caution, Morocco was the next most obvious target for expansion. But how could one target a place about which one knew nothing and beyond whose frontier (where, and if, it existed) all maps portrayed a blank? If the Algerian military was to move west it needed to know where it was going. It needed to know the terrain, the nature of its inhabitants and the willingness of local rulers to form allegiances with a foreign power; it needed to know which villages

were important, where they were, how much taxable land they had at
their disposal and how they could be reached. Where did Morocco's
roads lead and in what condition were they? Were rivers seasonal or
did they flow all year round? How high were the mountains and who
lived in them? All these questions were of concern to strategists. And
as Foucauld seemed willing to answer them, he was – on Duveyrier's
recommendation – allowed to do so.

In Algiers dwelled Oscar MacCarthy, a man little known today but
respected then as one of the greatest authorities on North Africa. A
monkish figure, of Irish descent, with a close-cropped skull and flowing beard, he had first come to Algeria in 1849, since when he had
travelled widely in the Maghreb before retiring to Algiers, where he
became custodian of the Mustapha Pasha library, whose 25,000 volumes formed the largest and most encyclopedic body of literature on
North Africa. Here he lived in semi-native fashion surrounded by
books, maps, memories and projects. The 'big-headed man' or the
'gun man', as he was known (the latter nickname came from his habit
of travelling with a leather-cased barometer slung over his shoulder)
was one of the city's characters. 'As brown as a white man can
become,' ran one description, 'as thin as can be a man in good health,
he can now affront fatigue, sun, and time itself: he looks as though he
has never been young, and no one will ever see him age or even be
able to guess how old he is. Always fit, dry, alert, and a tireless walker,
he takes no more care of what he calls his envelope than is sufficient
to make it render adequately the services he requires of it.'[10] He
overflowed with indiscriminate enthusiasm – one of his great ambitions, constantly proposed but never realized, was to cross the Sahara
to Timbuctoo: in 1858 he had purchased several tins of biscuits to see
him through the voyage; twenty-five years later they were still in stor-
age – and he welcomed any opportunity to instruct fellow dreamers
about the magic of Africa. It was only natural that Foucauld should
present himself at his door. He spent long hours in MacCarthy's courtyard, imbibing the older man's wisdom while at the same time
perfecting his Arabic. MacCarthy's sixteen-year-old servant girl

recalled of Foucauld that 'Each time I came I found him almost always in precisely the same attitude, sitting on the ground in a *gandourah*, Arab fashion, reading the Koran.'[11] When not in the courtyard, Foucauld and MacCarthy would repair to its balustrades where, sifting through ancient charts and dusty folios, they discussed the perils and potentialities of Morocco.

Foucauld was busier than ever before in his life. 'The only habit I have retained from my old job is that of making time-tables,' he wrote, 'and *ma foi*, they are horribly full: work starts at 7 a.m. and finishes at midnight with two half-hour breaks for meals – everything in between is divided into lessons: Arabic, history, geography and so on.'[12] Where time allowed, he had also to organize the practical aspects of his expedition. In this respect MacCarthy's own wanderings made an excellent example. 'To be safe everywhere,' wrote one biographer, 'he had become insensible to heat or cold, travelled without escort or baggage, his pockets stuffed with notebooks and manuscript cards, heedless of all the conveniences of material life, protected by his destitution itself, according to the Oriental proverb which says: "A thousand horsemen could not strip a naked man."'[13] Foucauld was therefore to travel light. But in what guise was he to do so? He could not enter Morocco as a Christian: that would have meant death, for every Christian was considered a potential spy. Nor was the role of an apostate without risk: in 1880 an explorer named Oscar Lenz had travelled from Tangier to Timbuctoo posing as a convert to Islam, and on entering the Atlas had narrowly escaped being lynched. MacCarthy's solution was that Foucauld should travel as a Jew. Jewish communities were scattered throughout North Africa, including Morocco, and their members visited each other regularly. They tended, too, to be paler-skinned than the Arabs and their religion was tolerated in Muslim communities. If Foucauld could find a holy man, a rabbi, to accompany him, and if he dressed appropriately, did not create a fuss and took notes in a surreptitious fashion, it was very possible that he might return from his mission alive.

The guide on whom MacCarthy eventually settled was Mardochée Abi Serour, an ageing rabbi who had spent much of his life in Morocco and who had once owned substantial business interests in Timbuctoo before falling upon hard times. At first sight, he did not inspire confidence. 'One day, in February 1883,' Foucauld wrote, 'I was in the library talking with M. MacCarthy when we saw coming in a Jew between fifty and sixty years old, but very bent and walking with the hesitancy of a person suffering from bad eyesight . . . His clothes, obviously once costly, were old and dirty, and his whole person suggested a poor and careless person. 'Who is that Jew?' I asked MacCarthy.' To which came the reply, 'He's just what we're after.'[14] After a suitable period of bargaining Mardochée agreed to lead his charge through Morocco for the sum of 247 francs per month. (Not a large sum but, to put it in context, ten francs more than MacCarthy's official pay as librarian. Foucauld later gave him 2,000 francs for trade goods. And Foucauld's sister wrote in secret, offering a bounty if he brought her brother back alive.) He would also instruct him on how to behave, what clothes to wear and how to speak a smattering of Hebrew. Foucauld's timetables became busier than ever. To his original studies were now added Mardochée's lessons, plus a crash course in astronomy aboard a warship in Algiers harbour (the captain was a cousin), where he learned how to use a sextant, compass and barometer. Finally, on 10 June 1883, the journey started.

It was an incongruous mix of African and European cultures, of secrecy and openness. Dressed in 'a long chemise with flowing sleeves, a pair of linen breeches to the knee, a Turkish waistcoat of dark material, a white, short-sleeved robe with a [hood], white stockings, sandals, a red cap and a black silk turban,'[15] Foucauld met Mardochée at his home in the Jewish quarter of Algiers at 5 a.m. The two men slunk through the streets, and then bought two third-class tickets on the first train west. 'There we both were,' Foucauld wrote. 'The weather wonderful, the carriage full of Arab workmen, we left surrounded by gaiety and flooded with sunlight.'[16] That evening, at Oran, they booked into a low-class hotel where Mardochée talked long into the night with a friend from the nearby synagogue. Foucauld revelled in the strangeness of his situation. '[Listening to their talk,] I learned that Mardochée is seeking the philosopher's stone; the other

Jew is a fellow alchemist. For a long time I watched them, feebly outlined by the light of a candle, their shadows casting huge silhouettes
on the wall; I fell asleep on my mattress, lulled by these strange
discourses.'[17]

Foucauld's alias was that of Rabbi Joseph Aleman, a Russian doctor
who had recently fled the pogroms of his native land and was travelling hither and thither 'poor, but confiding in divine providence'.[18] It
was well-thought out: being Russian would explain his bad accent;
and being a doctor would confer upon him a degree of respect while
at the same time providing an excuse if he should be discovered in
the suspicious act of writing in a notebook. How successfully the disguise would go down in Morocco, they had yet to discover. But
Foucauld was delighted, on reaching the border town of Tlemcen, to
see how it fooled his fellow Europeans. '[Mardochée and I] bought
some bread and olives,' he recorded, 'and sat down to eat them on the
ground. Whilst we were thus, a band of officers of the Chasseurs
D'Afrique, coming out of the club, passed at two paces from me. I
know nearly all of them; they looked at me without suspecting who I
was.'[19] One of the band, René de Segonzac, later wrote his own
account of the meeting: 'The officers filed off, heedless or contemptuous; one of them, with a sneer, remarked to his comrades that that
little squatting Jew, eating olives, looked like a monkey.'[20]

On 18 June the two men caught a ship that arrived two days later in
Tangiers. By this time Foucauld was becoming a little weary of his
companion. 'I am very pleased with Mardochée,' he wrote to
MacCarthy. 'He has only one fault, an excessive prudence; he evi-
dently needs a thorough shaking – he'll get it from me!'[21] (The
prudence stemmed from Marie's promised bonus for bringing her
brother home alive. Foucauld, however, was unaware of this.) Then
having described Mardochée's 'only' fault he launched into a cata-
logue of others. 'Actually, his slowness is perhaps excusable, as his
physical condition is truly deplorable; he is almost completely blind,
fairly deaf and walks with difficulty. It's really more astonishing that
he should undertake such a trip in this state than that he should be on
the cautious side; he sees so little I'm surprised he hasn't met with an

accident to date. He blusters a good deal.'[22] When MacCarthy read these words he must have felt a twinge of anxiety. In many ways it was he who was on the expedition; the whole operation had been planned as a re-enactment of his own travels. But those travels were in the past and his advice was based on experience little fresher than his tins of biscuits. Perhaps, in his vicarious participation, he had placed his pupil in danger. It did not ease his mind when, on opening the letter, he found it contained a copy of Foucauld's will.

MacCarthy need not have worried. The journey was a lot less hazardous than expected. Despite Mardochée's insistence that the territory through which he had promised to lead him was too dangerous – he did not know, never having been there – Foucauld bullied him into fulfilling the contract. Travelling in caravans and hosted, thanks to Mardochée's connections, in reasonable comfort whenever they stopped at a town, the two men covered the length and breadth of unexplored Morocco. Foucauld took copious notes. In caravan he was always at the front or the back, a position that allowed him to scribble surreptitiously with a stub of pencil on a notebook fifty millimetres square that he concealed in his sleeve. Whenever possible he departed for a period of private meditation, during which he would sketch the countryside and take celestial readings. At hostelries he would leave the company at noon in order to pray in seclusion on the roof – when in fact he was shooting his position with a sextant. In a boyish way, Foucauld loved the secrecy and adventure of it all. 'What stories were not invented to explain setting up the sextant?'[23] he wrote. Sometimes it was for reading the future in the sky, sometimes it was for transmitting news about dead relatives. In one town it was a preventative against cholera and in another a device for measuring the sins of the Jews. Elsewhere it was accepted as an elaborate form of clock, a weather forecaster or a diagnostic apparatus for gauging the state of the road ahead. His excuses were always accepted, even if they were so contrived that everyone suspected he was up to something. (He cannot possibly have hidden the quantity of his instruments which included, apart from the sextant, a compass, a watch and pocket barometer, a false horizon for taking longitudes and latitudes, two larger barometers, several hygrometers, a chronometer and maximum and minimum thermometers.) But without clear evidence that he was a spy, his companions allowed him to continue.

That he was able to do any of this was thanks to Mardochée's assistance, but Foucauld did not see it that way. 'He is feeble-spirited beyond belief;' he wrote, 'he does nothing but whine and sometimes he just bursts out weeping. At first it was funny; it has finally become a bore. On the road he complains of the sun or his mule; in a town he grumbles at the fleas and bugs. And then the water is tepid, or the food is poor. No doubt these little details *are* sometimes hard to bear, but then he shouldn't have bothered me in Algiers to take me with him. I must admit that if I were not so determined to keep to my itinerary and not to return without accomplishing something, I would have thanked him and let him go a month since and would have come back to Algeria to look for someone more active, enterprising and virile. But I don't want to come back at any price without seeing what I said I would see, and going where I said I would go.'[24]

Where he went, he liked what he saw. The people were welcoming, even if, from convention, they tended to curse him for being a Jew and occasionally threw stones – and the countryside was beautiful. 'Algeria is a desert compared to Morocco,'[25] he wrote. On entering the Rif mountains, he was enchanted. His journal reads like a hot-weather equivalent of those describing the discovery of the Alps one hundred years before: 'Streams flow on every side, tumbling in cascades amidst ferns, laurels, figs and vines growing wild along the sides. Never and nowhere else have I seen such an air of prosperity, such a generous earth, nor such hard-working inhabitants. All the way to Chechaouen it is the same: the names change but the landscape remains the same.'[26] His disguise, however, was by now so thin that local rulers would offer him a telescope and a chair by the window so that he could survey his next day's journey. 'It is difficult to express the terror in which the population live; so they think only of one thing – the coming of the French,' Foucauld wrote. 'How many times have I heard the Mussulmans exclaim: "When will the French come . . . when shall we live in peace?" They pray that that day might come soon; they have no doubt as to its arrival: in this respect they share the common opinion of a great part of Eastern Morocco, and nearly all the upper classes in the Empire.'[27]

Foucauld liked Morocco's ruling class. Seeing him as an emissary of France, its members whispered inducements: clothes, slaves, women, anything he wanted was his for the taking, provided he sent back a favourable report. Which he did. 'Do they dread this expected French domination?' he wrote. 'The great lords, the traders, the groups oppressed by the Sultan or by powerful neighbours would accept it without displeasure. To them it represents an increase of riches, the establishment of railways (a thing very much desired), peace, security; in a word, a regular and protective government.'[28]

He disliked, however, the everyday specimens with whom he had to deal for most of his journey. 'Extreme cupidity and, as companions, robbery and lying in all their forms, reign almost everywhere,' he wrote. 'Brigandage, armed attacks are, in general, considered as honourable actions. Morals are dissolute ... With the exception of the towns and some isolated districts, Morocco is very ignorant.'[29] Ungratefully, he also took against the Jews, whom he described as savages. 'To live constantly with Moroccan Jews – people, apart from rare exceptions, despicable and repugnant among all others – was utterly intolerable. They spoke openly to me as a brother, disclosing their base feelings. How often I regretted my hypocrisy!'[30] As one Moroccan said (and Foucauld did not disagree), they were 'insincere people, rascals to be unceasingly on one's guard against'.[31]

From the Rif his route took him south through the sterner valleys of the High Atlas and thence into the semi-arid regions bordering the Sahara. '[Here] one steps into a New World,' he wrote. He was beguiled by the oases which, with their forests of palm trees, their irrigation canals and their neat, square fields, struck him as positively Arcadian: 'I am in a new climate; there is no winter . . . the air is never cold; above my head the sky is blue.'[32] They were, he said, 'made for none but the happy'. That the oases seemed to him magical was due partly to their novelty: hitherto he had travelled through landscapes that were not so very different from those of southern Europe; here, on the other hand, was something alien and exotic. What truly impressed him, however, was the waterless desert that gave the oases meaning and which he viewed now for the first time in his life.

Foucauld's journal of his trip is a dry, and at times tedious affair, concerned mainly with facts and figures. It is a record intended for geographers and the military, containing none of the romantic elaborations that were then fashionable and offering few insights save into the youthful prejudices of its author. It could have been written by no other explorer of the age – a Stanley, Livingstone, Nansen, Peary or any other adventurer would have turned it into high drama. Foucauld simply described what he saw and what he did, his aim being to impress an official rather than a popular readership. Sometimes, however, a guarded sense of excitement creeps into his account. One such moment comes when he first sees the desert. Looking south from the oasis of Tisint, he described 'an immense plain, now white, now brown, with its stony solitudes stretching far away out of sight; an azure streak limits it on the horizon and separates it from the sky . . . This burned expanse contains no other vegetation than a few stunted gum-trees, no other relief than the narrow chains of rocky and broken hills twisting about like fragments of serpents.'[33] Barren in the scorching sun, the desert assumed a different character under the stars. 'In this profound calm, in the midst of this fairy-tale country, I had my first real taste of the Sahara,' Foucauld wrote. 'In the contemplation of these nights one understands the belief of the Arabs in a mysterious night, *leila el qedr*, when the heavens open, when angels come down to earth, when the waters of the sea become sweet, and when every inanimate thing in nature bows down to worship its Creator.'[34]

What he saw was not the Sahara proper, merely its outer fringe. But it was enough both to intrigue him as to what lay beyond and to assure him that he had reached the limit of his travels. To go further would have meant a voyage into uncharted lawlessness. He had already been concerned by the state of the Atlas – 'a country in which the authority of the Sultan is nil'[35] – and the desert seemed even more dangerous. He had set himself the task of exploring Morocco and, having reached a geographical boundary, he felt his task was complete. At Tisint, therefore, he turned west and headed for the Atlantic port of Mogador, where the Sultan's authority did prevail and where there was even a small community of Europeans. He had no intention of stopping there: he still planned to make the return trek overland to Algeria; but in order to do so he needed to replenish his funds and Mogador was the only place in this part of Morocco where he could do so. Accordingly, leaving Mardochée in Tisint, he departed for the coast on 9 January 1884 (at night to avoid brigands) and by the 28th had nearly reached his destination. It took him three and a half hours to negotiate a 'vast forest overshadowing immense grazing fields', and then he was in Mogador. He went straight to the consulate and announced himself: 'I should like to see the French Consul, to cash a cheque on the Bank of England,' he said. 'I am the Vicomte de Foucauld, officer of the French Cavalry.'[36]

The Consul's secretary did not believe him. 'Go and sit outside with your back to the wall,' he said, 'You can't see him dressed like that.'[37] So Foucauld sat against the wall. After a while he asked to be shown a place where he could wash and change his clothes. The secretary directed him to a small hut, then, prompted by a sudden curiosity, peered through a crack in the door. As Foucauld undressed there fell from his pockets and folds in his clothes instrument after instrument – sextant, hygrometer, compass, barometer and chronometer. This, the secretary realized, was no ordinary tramp. Minutes later he was ushered into the Consul's office.

While waiting for the money to come through, Foucauld busied himself with his journal and with correspondence. 'From the geographical point of view, my journey goes on very well,' he wrote to his sister. 'My instruments are in good condition; none of them got out of order; I have visited new countries, and bring back, I believe, some useful information.'[38] On reviewing the experience, however, he admitted to a terrible sense of solitude, one that extended not just to the past eight months but his whole life. 'From a moral point of view, it is very sad; always alone, never a friend, never a Christian to speak to . . . If you knew how much I am thinking of you, of our happy days in the past with grandfather . . . It is, above all, Christmas and New Year's Day which seemed to me so sad. I remembered grandfather and the Christmas tree, and all the good times of our childhood.'[39] He distracted himself with work: 'I am up to my neck in my longitudes. I work from morning to night, and then a part of the night. This is a hundred times more thrilling than the journey itself, for therein lies the result.'[40] He also found diversions of a less technical nature, one of which could be found at the home of the Anglican missionary. 'At present a very handsome young English lady is there who speaks French perfectly,' he noted. 'I find it very pleasant to go from time to time and spend the evening in this house.'[41] But even here, as he listened politely to the piano recitals and songs (in French) that were laid on for his entertainment, he was overcome by loss. '[They] remind me of a very happy time; but it is already far away . . .'[42]

He left Mogador on 14 March and returned to Tisint, where he rejoined Mardochée for the trip home. It was not an easy trip: no caravan would accompany them through the border territory to the north-east that Foucauld wished to map, so they were forced to make a detour through the Atlas, hiring local protection as they went. By this time Foucauld was becoming weary: of his 429-page journal less than one hundred pages cover the journey home and few of them are written with much enthusiasm. The one incident that stands out is that of 12 May 1884, when his four-man escort decided 'from the whiteness of my clothes and the good look of my mule and also, it appears, from the gossip of the Jews, that I was laden with gold'.[43] Accordingly, they mugged him. As he recorded, 'At half-past twelve, as I was riding at the head of the caravan, making my notes, I suddenly felt myself pulled backward and dragged off my mount; then my hood was pulled over my face and the two men searched me – one held me up, the other felt me methodically all over.'[44] They took his baggage and his money (a disappointingly small sum) and then strapped him across his donkey while they continued north, arguing over his fate. Mardochée came to his rescue but was driven off at sword-point. 'It was a strange situation,' Foucauld wrote, 'to hear for a day and a half one's life or death discussed by so few people and yet to be unable to do anything in one's defence. I was unarmed: I had a revolver in my baggage but it had been taken. Had it been left, I would not have used it, for what could I do alone in the desert, in the midst of tribes for whom any stranger is an enemy?'[45] At length, the escort decided their reputation could survive a theft but not a murder and dumped their prisoner at the town of Debdou, from where it was but a few days' journey to the safety of French North Africa. On 21 May 1884, at 10 a.m., Foucauld crossed the border between Morocco and Algeria. 'Shortly afterwards,' he wrote, on the last page of his journal, 'I arrived at Lalla Marnia, and thus terminated my journey.'[46]

His arrival was as much a surprise to the officers of Lalla Marnia as it had been to those of Mogador. From within his robes Foucauld produced a visiting card which he handed to the Commandant's servant, adding as he did so that if the man didn't deliver it he would complain to divisional headquarters. It was raining, one witness recalled, the Commandant and his officers were drunk and bored; they decided to inspect their visitor. 'There we saw a native of medium height, wearing a light cloak over his dirty, white woollen robe; his head was covered by the black bonnet of Moroccan Jews. His arms were crossed on his chest; he was stooping in an attitude of great humility. The Commandant offered him coffee and a chair, but he refused to sit in one, as he said he had not done so for a year. He wouldn't talk; all he would say was that he was the Vicomte de Foucauld and that the Paris Geographical Society and M. Henri Duveyrier had sent him to Morocco.'[47] Only when one of the junior lieutenants recognized him as a fellow officer with whom he had served in the Bou-Amama rebellion, did they believe the stranger's story. The 'rabbi' was carried to the officers' mess where he was given a cripplingly festive homecoming.

The sudden reintroduction to European life came as a shock. For almost a year Foucauld had lived on the lower rungs of Moroccan society (even during his interlude at Mogador he had stayed in Jewish hostels) and he grown accustomed to a mendicant's existence. Also, he had had a taste of the Sahara. Like many other explorers, Foucauld was attracted by the desert's emptiness and stillness; he was engaged, too, by the manner in which human beings managed to survive its sterility, picking their way from well to well in temperatures that ranged from 50 °C at midday to below freezing at midnight. Its physical purity impressed him in the same way as had the spiritual purity he had perceived among Algeria's Muslims. He liked it. When later asked which day had been the worst of his entire trip, Foucauld replied, 'the day I got back'.[48]

Foucauld's journey had taken him eleven months instead of the six he had envisaged and, with Mardochée's wages, the cost of food and accommodation for both of them, bribes, protection and various other expenses, it had cost him 6,000 francs. (By the end of his travels he was penniless and could only afford the last stretch by selling his donkeys and continuing on foot.) But it had been an overwhelming success. He had covered more ground, and had spent a longer time in the *bled el siba*, than any other European. Only once had he been in danger, and to only four individuals had he felt it necessary to reveal that he was a Christian. He had returned with numerous astronomical readings – forty-five longitudes, forty latitudes – and had measured 3,000 new altitudes. He had retraced 689 kilometres of his predecessors' tracks, correcting their observations as he did so, and had added another 2,250 kilometres of his own. He had investigated the terrain, the habits and physiognomy of its inhabitants and the political inclinations of their leaders. And he had not spent a centime of government money.

Of those who had helped Foucauld achieve these results, Mardochée sank swiftly from sight: he retired to his home in Algiers, where he spent his time and earnings in search of the philosopher's stone, and died within two years from mercury poisoning. But Oscar MacCarthy, the other protagonist behind the expedition, penned a eulogy that made its way to a friend in the Ministry of War. 'M. de Foucauld,' he wrote, 'is now back from a marvellous voyage of exploration covering 3,000 kilometres of Morocco. What he has to tell us shows how much we erred in everything we thought we knew about this great country. Pray confer on [him] the honours of the

Geographical Society of Paris; he deserves them on every count; rarely, very rarely, has anyone worked so long and so well. If you possess a big gold medal, never did anyone merit it more!'[49] There was no such award at present, but MacCarthy's friend made sure that there soon would be – and that Foucauld would receive it.

At a meeting held on 24 April 1885 at the Société de Géographie de Paris, the oldest geographical society in the world, no less a figure than Henri Duveyrier spoke in praise of Foucauld's achievements: 'Sacrificing far more than his personal comfort, having made and maintained to the end more than a mere vow of poverty and misery, having renounced for almost a year the title and respect of his rank in the army, he has delivered a mass of precise intelligence that revolutionizes, quite literally, our geographical and political knowledge of almost the whole of Morocco.'[50] In Duveyrier's opinion Foucauld's trek was a welcome antidote to the Flatters disaster, an example of all that was most magnificent in the national character. 'You must see,' he said, 'that we have to thank M. de Foucauld for opening what is indeed a new era, and one does not know which is to be most admired, these fine and useful results, or the self-sacrifice, courage and ascetic abnegation, thanks to which this young French officer has obtained them.'[51] He ended his speech with the announcement that Foucauld was to be awarded the Society's first ever gold medal.

More plaudits were to come. When Foucauld's *Reconnaissance au Maroc* came out in 1888 it was received rapturously. Nothing like it had ever been written before. Speaking in 1902, a British geographer said that '[It relates] the most important and most remarkable journey that a European has for a century undertaken in Morocco. No modern traveller has approached M. de Foucauld, from the double point of view of the precision of his observations and the preparation for his journey. Besides the work accomplished by him, the attempts of other travellers have been but child's play.'[52]

Foucauld did not receive his gold medal directly. His cousin's husband, the Duc de Bondy had to accept it on his behalf because, except for two months between mid-July and mid-September, Foucauld was in Algiers, alternately writing up his journal and preparing for another voyage of exploration – the Saharan trip he had been planning before he left for Morocco. With a horse, a few mules and an Arab servant, he departed in September 1885 on a route that led to Tunis via the northern oases of El Goléa, Ouargla and Touggourt. It was a dangerous itinerary: officers of the Bureau Arabe had infiltrated every major centre, but the region remained insecure, with no garrisons and irregular post. Outside the oases it was impossible to guarantee a traveller's safety. Travelling south, Foucauld joined a caravan containing Commandant Didier of the Bureau Arabe, who carried with him several coops of homing pigeons. These birds, Didier confided, were the key to Saharan communications. He planned to erect dovecotes at El Goléa, Touggourt and other oases throughout the desert, from where his birds would carry news faster than any camel or railway. When they reached El Goléa, Foucauld left Didier to his project* and continued his journey alone. He cared little for the prospect of peril. Comparisons with other portions of North Africa would be helpful in completing his description of Morocco, he said, and after his recent expedition he felt he could cope with anything. However, neither justification was valid: hardly anywhere in *Reconnaissance* does Foucauld draw parallels between conditions in the Moroccan Sahara and the desert further east; nor, as he must have known, did his experience of Moroccan banditry equip him for the violence he could expect in Tuareg country. Luckily, the desert was quiet – thanks, probably, to the disruption to trade caused by France's annexation of Tunisia – and Foucauld reached his goal not only intact but in a state of Duveyrier-like enthusiasm. On 18 November, midway between the oases of El Goléa and Ouargla, he wrote a letter pooh-poohing the desert's reputation for danger. 'Those times are in the past,' he said. 'For the last three years the region has been safe: liberty, equality and, above all, fraternity, reign here as much as they do in France.'[53] In the same letter he detailed his plans for the future. He would become an explorer, basing himself in Paris but spending time now and then

*Didier did create a dovecote at El Goléa, but the pigeons were eaten by falcons and the sergeant he left in charge deserted soon after.

with relatives in the country; during these fallow periods his invest-
ments would multiply until they produced an income sufficient to
send him back to the desert. He had it mapped out. It would take him
two or three years to accumulate enough cash for the next journey,
and while he waited, he would 'learn to draw a bit, speak English a
bit, and brush up my Arabic'.[54]

In 1886 he returned to Paris and sank into a life of masterful inac-
tivity. During the afternoons he worked on his manuscript,
occasionally popping over to ask advice from Duveyrier, and then,
sociable as ever, he dressed in formal clothes for a night on the town.
For a brief period he became engaged to a woman he had met in
Algiers. Yet, however hard he tried, he was unable to settle. This was
obvious to anyone who visited his apartment. Although small, it was
decorated in the manner one might expect of a wealthy young traveller – fine pieces of furniture, trophies and weapons from Algeria,
family portraits, sketches and watercolours of Morocco, rare editions
in the bookshelf – but there did not seem to be a bed. There was
none. When Foucauld returned from an evening out, he discarded his
finery, put on a *gandourah*, and slept on the carpet.

The shallowness of Parisian society bored him. During his expeditions he had found, if not faith then its precursor – an admiration of
those who possessed it. He had met various *hadji*, who had made the
pilgrimage to Mecca (they had not travelled on foot, taking, against
precept, a ship from Tangiers) and had returned with a wisdom and
tolerance that, combined with the *ad hoc* worship he had seen during
his service against Bou-Amama, filled Foucauld with admiration. He
wanted to recreate a similar purity in his own life. But Catholicism, as
he knew it and as it was practised in Paris, disappointed him. For a
while he considered converting to Islam before rejecting the religion
as 'being too material',[55] – no doubt cultural taboos influenced him
too. Therefore, following the pattern of his past, he drifted, waiting for
a chance to steer him in a new direction. Duveyrier, with whom
Foucauld had formed a close friendship (he called him 'the greatest of
the Tuaregs'; Duveyrier called him 'the greatest Moroccan') noticed
that he was becoming increasingly depressed. 'I feel a very real affection

for M. de Foucauld,' he wrote, replying on their joint behalf to a dinner invitation, 'his is a most distinguished nature, and I very much fear that he is a man attacked by a fatal malady or very gravely injured in his affections. [Nevertheless] he is worth humouring.'[56] Foucauld made no secret of his dilemma. 'I am seeking the light,' he admitted, 'and do not find it.'[57]

Illumination came one summer evening at a dinner party given by his far-from-spiritual aunt, Inès Moitessier. Amongst the guests was Abbé Huvelin, a wizened priest similar in many respects to Oscar MacCarthy but with access to a different set of maps. Physically, Huvelin was just another old man: his 'head leant upon his shoulders, and his face was full of wrinkles; walking was often a torture'. In the pulpit, however, he was astonishing, 'a man of digressions, parentheses, exclamations, and unexpected flashes – above all a man with a long experience of the world and of mercy'.[58] His message was one of teaching by example – 'One does good much less by what one says or does,' ran one of his maxims, 'than by what one is.'[59] Huvelin's brand of Catholicism was new to Foucauld. It reminded him of Islam but without the drawbacks. In October 1886 he visited Huvelin's confessional and became once again a member of the Catholic church. Huvelin, he wrote revealingly to Duveyrier, was 'a real father to me, who lost my own in infancy'.[60]

The new believer carried on as before – he continued to party, to save money for his next exploration, to prepare his journal and to sleep on the floor. By 1888 *Reconnaissance* was ready for publication and Foucauld had enough funds for a new voyage. It was not, however, the voyage his friends had been expecting. Instead of renewing his African travels he sailed, on 2 November 1888, for Palestine. He assured his family that it would be a short visit – a few weeks at most. In mid-December he reached Jerusalem where he visited the holy sites, climbed the Mount of Olives and spent Christmas in Bethlehem. He hired a donkey and rode to Galilee. The few weeks became months. By New Year he was still in Nazareth. He did not come back to Paris until March 1889, and when he did it was to leave almost at once for a tour of France's monastic centres. He spent Easter at

Solesmes, the home of the Benedictines; over Trinity he was with the Trappists, at whose spiritual headquarters in the Languedoc, Notre-Dame-des-Neiges, he spent a further week's meditation in October; then came a stay with the Jesuits at Clamart. He did not take to the Benedictines, nor to the Jesuits, but La Grande Trappe seemed appealing.

Huvelin, like MacCarthy, guided him throughout. On his prompting Foucauld came to a decision about his next journey. 'I have at last,' he wrote to his sister, 'in great security and great peace, on the formal counsel of the Father who directed me, taken entire and without reserve the resolution of which I have been thinking for a long time.'[61] By the end of 1889 the debauched cadet turned lacklustre officer and promising explorer had become a Trappist monk.

5

SENEGALESE
HOOLIGANS

While Foucauld was engaged first in his geographical and then his spiritual explorations, Henri Laperrine was establishing himself in North Africa. After a short period with the Fourth Chasseurs in Tunisia, he returned to Algeria where, in 1885, he was promoted to Lieutenant in the First Spahis. Garrisoned at Medea, in the south, he became intrigued by the wastes that lay beyond the Atlas. Already interested in the Maghreb – like Foucauld he had learned Arabic and studied Islamic practices – his curiosity was further stirred by reports of desert life that he received from officers of the Bureau Arabe who passed occasionally through Medea. One of his most regular informants was a man named Gaspard Cauvet.

Ever since the Flatters disaster, when it became clear that the Tuareg could never be conquered by overt military force, France had adopted tactics similar to those employed by the Ottomans – distant stick and surreptitious politicking. The stick could not be used, merely waved in the air, but its threat enabled agents from the Bureau Arabe to inveigle their way southwards. Cauvet was one of those agents. An old St Cyrien, who had been a member of the Bureau since 1881, this small and rather remarkable lieutenant had

accompanied the first Flatters expedition as far as Ouargla and had
since become notorious for his abilities, which were not only exten-
sive (as was expected of any member of the Bureau Arabe) but
eccentric. Many officers in his position filled their spare time by
studying archaeological remains – it was an accepted perk of the job.
Cauvet, however, took to hydrology, saddlery and the study of rep-
tiles. He investigated the water systems of Ouargla, invented and
tested a new form of camel harness and acquired a disturbing intimacy
with the desert's most poisonous inhabitants: while talking he might
juggle idly with a scorpion or allow a horned viper to wind around his
arm. This last skill (which, according to one source, he passed on to
Laperrine) had a mesmerizing effect on audiences. In the words of
one queasy acquaintance, 'He had an extraordinary hold over the
natives.'[1]

Laperrine disliked garrison life – it was one of the few points in
which he did resemble Foucauld – and before meeting Cauvet he had
already enrolled for a year's training in France as a cavalry instructor.
But now his interest in Africa was refreshed. In August 1887, his
course completed, he rejected the well-paid and easy life that might
have been his and returned instead to Medea. Cauvet was no longer
there, he had been posted to Ghardaia, but Laperrine put the empty
evenings to good use by writing a manual for officers serving in
North Africa. Not published in his lifetime, its contents were radical
for the time, displaying a remarkable degree of common sense and a
fine attention to detail. One of his main points was that if something
went wrong the fault lay not in the way a soldier obeyed orders but
in the manner in which his officer delivered them. 'Living in equality
with one's subordinates requires a degree of tact,' he wrote. 'Every
commanding officer must, as a point of honour, accept responsibility
for the orders he has given. Treat your inferiors in the same way as
you would wish your superiors to treat you . . . Avoid blaming
people. Learn to praise, even when it is only half merited. Praise is
a much more effective tool than criticism. It is the only way you will
make your subordinates work with spirit, loyalty and good heart.' If
things went wrong then the commander was to gather his officers and

NCOs and say, '"I probably expressed myself badly when giving the order; this is how I would like it to be . . ." Everyone will understand you far better than if you had raged, sworn, and threatened them with punishment.' He gave useful tips on how to sleep in the desert, how to protect the body against cold, the head against heat and the eyes against sand. He was strict on personal hygiene: 'Every man must be told that they should not change their underwear only on Sundays and Thursdays but everytime it is dirty; and in summer that means seven times a week.' Nobody, though, should wash their face in daytime because water magnified the sun's rays and broiled the skin; all cleansing should be done at night, in a canvas-lined bath dug into the sand. Soap was never to be used in the wells. Food must be given without stint, medicine likewise, and everyone was to dress as smartly as possible – which, despite his instincts to the contrary, Laperrine tried to do. Above all, he emphasized the need for independent action. 'Control the results, direct the accomplishment; never ask for an account of how it is done,' he advised. 'Initiative does not mean indiscipline.'[2]

It was as well that Laperrine's journal was not published, as this last comment, combined with other acute observations on the responsibilities of African command, was precisely what the establishment didn't want to hear. Initiative very often *did* mean indiscipline as far as many members of government were concerned. Algeria's budget was an annual reminder of what Bugeaud's 'initiative' continued to cost France. The establishment, however, was in Paris and Laperrine was in Africa, where European traditions were irrelevant, where officialdom was far distant and where he intended, therefore, to stay. What with his unorthodox views and his informal training under Cauvet, he would have made an ideal candidate for the Bureau Arabe. Instead he chose to go to war. In March 1889 he joined the Senegalese spahis.

Darkest Africa (as Victorians liked to call every non-coastal region about which they were totally ignorant) was being illuminated rapidly. But the people who gave it the dubious lustre of European religion, laws, bureaucracy and trade, were for the most part not French: they were British. The Scottish doctor David Livingstone had probed the Zambezi and Limpopo rivers, opening a vast region to exploitation by the British. The Welsh-born Henry Morton Stanley had traversed the continent east to west, an arduous task that earned him the nickname 'Bula Mutari' ('Breaker of Stones')*. During this expedition he 'discovered' the stupendous natural wealth of the Congo. Samuel Baker, Richard Burton, James Grant and John Hanning Speke had jointly and severally travelled to the sources of the Nile, thereby alerting Britain to another area worthy of colonization. Elsewhere, in South Africa and on the belly of West Africa, British influence was seeping remorselessly inland. There were other culprits apart from Britain: Portugal, Spain and Germany had all joined the scramble for Africa; so had King Leopold II of Belgium, who wangled matters so ingeniously that the entire Congo became his own personal fiefdom. But Britain was the most successful scrambler, and the one that worried France most.

The problem for all nations involved in the colonization of Africa was that they did not know where they were meant to stop. Zones of influence had long been agreed for the territory surrounding coastal trading stations. Inland, however, anyone could wander anywhere, return with a few sheets of paper on which tribal leaders had signed away their sovereignty (knowing nothing of the European laws under which their signature was henceforth binding) and claim yet another addition to this or that country's foreign possessions. Europe, tiny in comparison with the continent it sought to master but disproportionately powerful, depended for its stability upon legalities and when African rulers continued to act as if they were not bound by law (which they did) there could be only one answer: military intervention. But this brought another difficulty, for as much as it relied on law, Europe was accustomed to boundaries in which its laws could be enforced. Lighter though Darkest Africa may have become, it lacked

---

*One eminent Africanist has suggested that 'Breaker of Balls' would be an apter description.

frontiers in the accepted European sense. There arose, therefore, a situation in which the forces of colonialism were bound to clash and the inevitable consequence, which everyone was keen to avoid, would be war in Europe itself.

The Conference of Berlin, in 1885, went some way to avert that possibility, agreeing certain frontiers and regulating the manner in which nations were to behave when appropriating territory outside those borders. It was no longer sufficient for European nations to say that a portion of Africa was theirs simply because a flag had been raised or a document signed. To claim ownership of an area they had to colonize it properly, with soldiers, settlers and some form of administrative apparatus. The Conference, however, dealt primarily with squabbles affecting the profitable regions of Africa – King Leopold's Congo in particular. The Sahara had not been mentioned on account of its worthlessness. Still, France feared that Britain might yet thwart its ambition of uniting its West African colonies with those of the north – and might, for some inexplicable reason, decide that its interests would be served by an incursion into the desert. Diplomatic representations were made and on 5 August 1890, the Anglo-French Convention agreed a minor reshuffling of African geopolitics. The most obvious change was that France swapped the valuable trading island of Zanzibar for the larger, but economically unattractive, British-owned island of Madagascar. In compensation for what seemed a one-sided deal, Britain also said that France could have the Sahara. A huge block of land running south from Algeria and Tunisia, to a line drawn between Lake Chad and the town of Say on the Niger, was France's to have and to hold from that day forth, and with it the French could do as they wished.

Paris was delighted. All that now remained was to conquer the territory, build a railway and exploit the vast economic potential of the desert. For, contrary to appearances, the desert *was* wealthy. According to government propaganda it contained whole reefs of minerals that waited only upon the rap of a geologist's hammer to reveal the cornucopia within. A story gained credence that before his death Flatters had discovered a field of emeralds. It was carefully not denied, despite its lack of foundation. The propaganda concealed a kernel of truth: the Sahara did have mineral deposits, but they would not be discovered for many decades and when they were, their extraction proved to be as cost-ineffective as those of Algeria. As for its oil-bearing strata, for which it would become famous, they were of little importance to a coal-driven world. Nevertheless, in terms of opportunity, Paris considered the Anglo-French Convention a coup. 'Without any great effort, without any real sacrifice . . . with a single treaty, we have secured the recognition by Britain (the only power whose rivalry we need fear) that Algeria and Senegal will in the near future form a single domain. Today the government can tell the nation that this vast African empire is no longer a dream, a distant ideal . . . but a reality.'[3]

Britain saw it differently. Lord Salisbury, who had arranged the Convention, told the House of Commons that the territory ceded was 'what a farmer would call "very light land"'. Triumphantly – gleefully – he announced that 'We have given the Gallic cockerel an enormous amount of sand. Let him scratch it as he pleases.'[4] This statement, as tactless as it was accurate, stuck in France's craw. A pressure group – the Comité de l'Afrique Française – was formed to promote the conquest of the Sahara. Alphonse Duponchel demanded that a United States of Europe be formed to thwart British colonialism worldwide and to throw Britain out of Africa in particular. (To which Duveyrier replied that much as he agreed with the sentiment it was, perhaps, a trifle hasty.) And the Governor of Algeria, Jules Cambon, wrote: 'Well then, we shall scratch this sand, we shall put rails on it, plant telegraph poles, make wells spring from the soil. From every casbah in every oasis the Gallic cockerel will crow at its loudest and most cheerful.'[5]

How, though, was this to be achieved? The Tuareg still ruled the Hoggar and although France had extended its control to the northernmost Algerian oases – Touggourt, Ouargla, El Goléa and Beni Abbès – these were many hundreds of kilometres from the Hoggar. Possibly a strike might have been made at the Tuat, a string of oases that pearled into the Sahara from the Moroccan Atlas and whose southernmost settlement, In Salah, was the last stop for caravans before they entered the wastes leading to the Soudan. (In Salah's name, given by travellers who reached it from the south, meant 'Thank God'.) But the Tuat was nominally ruled by the Sultan of Morocco and although Britain had grandly given the Sahara to France the Tuat had not been included in the gift. As was the case with so much of his southern Empire, the Sultan of Morocco exerted no jurisdiction whatsoever over the Tuat. But his claim was recognized by Britain, which made its conquest by France diplomatically impossible. Moreover, the people who commanded the Tuat in reality were the Hoggar Tuareg against whom, as France knew, there was very little it could do. Jules Cambon proposed one solution: a form of siege in reverse, in which by seizing a few strategic points he hoped to deny the Tuareg access to supplies. Describing the Sahara as an ocean of sand, he pronounced that 'It is sufficient to occupy the ports of this sea to be its master.'[6] By the ports he meant In Salah and other Tuat oases where the Tuareg came for food and supplies. The result was the establishment of two outposts, Fort Miribel and Fort MacMahon, on the northern routes from Algeria to the Tuat. Described by the Saharan historian, Douglas Porch, as 'a combination of penal colony and military disaster',[7] Miribel and MacMahon were a reversion to the ineffective tactics that had hampered the early stages of France's conquest of Algeria. Wretched mud stockades placed on a plain of utter desolation, they 'might have been taken straight out of *Beau Geste*, except that even the Foreign Legion declined to garrison them'.[8] The native *tirailleurs* to whose unhappy lot that task fell were ineffective, their reach extending only as far as they could walk and for as long as their supplies lasted. Meanwhile, the cumbersome columns that provisioned them from the north were prey to any determined group equipped with camels. Cambon had succeeded admirably in his intention to create a state of siege – unfortunately it was his own men who were being besieged.

If the Sahara could not be taken from the north, as appeared to be the case, there was always another option: to advance through the Soudan, that lay to its south. This appealed to imperialist factions. It also appealed very strongly indeed to the military in Senegal whose officers, the sweepings of St Cyr, described by colleagues at home as 'a collection of hooligans',[9] welcomed any opportunity for adventure. Not that they needed permission to seize it: bored, headstrong and even further from metropolitan France than were their colleagues in Algeria, they acted with sublime indifference to orders from Paris. They followed the Bugeaudesque ethos of do-and-damn-the-consequences that had since been civilized to extinction in Algeria. For years they had picked quarrels, made petty war and pushed Senegal's frontier steadily outwards. As the colony expanded, terrible acts of bloodshed ensued, often perpetrated by men who were semi-lunatics. Laperrine became part of the madness. From 1890 he flung himself into battle after regional battle. His bravery – increasingly reckless, and in apparent disregard of the considered principles he had previously espoused – earned the respect of his fellow officers. On 5 August 1892, on their recommendation, he was awarded the Légion d'Honneur. Thus garlanded, he became part of the 'hooligans'' maddest adventure.

On 26 December 1893, Lieutenant Colonel Eugène Bonnier led 204 Senegalese *tirailleurs*, thirteen French officers and nine NCOs, equipped with two eighty-millimetre cannons and a small flotilla of canoes, up the Niger to occupy Timbuctoo. This city of fable, the Eldorado of early African explorers, containing magnificent palaces, rare libraries and streets that were paved with gold, had long since been revealed as the dull, mud-brick trading-post that it was. Bonnier did not care. Neither did his myrmidon, Lieutenant H. Boiteux, who preceded him upriver with two gunboats. Both of them wanted to be associated by conquest with the mythical name of Timbuctoo. Two days after Bonnier's departure Laperrine followed him in a force commanded by Major Joseph Joffre (who, as a General, would achieve notoriety in the First World War) that comprised 400 infantry and cavalry, 700 porters, 200 mules and a battery of field artillery. The plan was that Joffre and Laperrine would catch up with the Bonnier–Boiteux expedition and reinforce it with the necessary food, men and munitions for a campaign deeper into the Soudan – or as Joffre put it quaintly, to support Bonnier in 'organizing the region'.

Boiteux took Timbuctoo and Bonnier, angry that he had been fore-stalled by a subordinate, left him in charge of the town while he forged north with 150 *tirailleurs* and his two pieces of artillery. He was entering dangerous territory. Those few adventurers who had visited Timbuctoo had warned that it was a perilous place, in thrall to the Tuareg. Major Gordon Laing, the first white man to reach it, had been murdered; René Caillié, the second, had escaped by the skin of his teeth. Bonnier, however, was confident that Timbuctoo and the area of the Soudan that surrounded it was completely safe – or at least that he and his little army could manage whatever difficulty came their way. He shared the opinion of Henri Schirmer, a Saharan specialist who, although uncertain as to the desert's worth as a colony, was certain that its inhabitants offered no threat. 'Several hundred Europeans,' said Schirmer, 'would have nothing to fear from 1,200 to 1,500 Tuareg warriors armed with lances and with flintlocks.'[10]

In a fit of common sense, the Senegalese authorities ordered Bonnier to desist. Similar instructions were sent to Joffre. Both men ignored the order: Bonnier because he felt like it; and Joffre (appar-ently) because of a confrontation in which Laperrine insisted that if his superior officer was so cowardly as to retreat then he would con-tinue alone with his spahis. And so both columns carried on. On 12 January 1894, his first day out of Timbuctoo, Bonnier raided a Tuareg camp, seizing more than 500 sheep, cattle and camels. On 14 January his men constructed a square laager of thorn bushes, outside which they tethered their captured stock and then, propping their rifles against the thorns, prepared to spend the night in what they thought was an impregnable camp. At 4 a.m. the Tuareg attacked. They arrived on camels, dismounted a safe distance from the stockade and then, according to some accounts, wormed their way under the ani-mals, stampeding them as they did so, until they reached the thorns. While the camp was in disarray they broke through the thorns and started on their business. Bonnier, eleven other officers, two NCOs, a native interpreter and sixty-eight *tirailleurs* died in the assault. By chance one officer, Captain Nigotte, managed to escape and, with a few other survivors, brought the news home. They were not hunted

down only for the reason that the Tuareg had already started to squab-
ble over the spoils.

Joffre and Laperrine, Bonnier's comrades in insubordination, were
the ones who picked up the pieces. 'In a clearing, at the foot of a thick
bush,' Joffre wrote, 'was a mass of corpses, probably those of the
tirailleurs, while in the middle and to the south, other bodies lay in
various positions.' He collected the bodies of Bonnier and the other
white men for burial in Timbuctoo and then, 'We left the place with
a sense of disquiet and powerless rage which is extremely trying.'[11]

That Bonnier and Boiteux had raised the *tricouleur* over Timbuctoo
was the only positive result of a hasty, mismanaged expedition.
Needless to say, the army considered Timbuctoo a splendid prize.
One Lieutenant Bluzet, who had assisted in its capture, described
it to the Geographical Society of Paris as a positive 'Bourse', so
tremendous was the volume of trade that passed through it. 'Is it an
addition to our colonial wealth?' Bluzet asked. 'Assuredly, yes!'[12] But
the trade was conducted at far lower levels than Bluzet liked to think
and comprised basic goods – salt, millet, goat skins and iron – that
were of little interest to France even had there been a railway to carry
them. In theory the town might have had a certain strategic worth, situated as it was on the upper Niger and being one of the few centres
linking tropical Africa with the Sahara, but this was undermined by
the fact that its exposure put it at the constant mercy of the Tuareg.
Timbuctoo's ramshackle condition made its conquest not so much a
result as an incident; an incident, moreover, whose few positive
aspects were far outweighed by the negative effect of Bonnier's massacre. His failure to conquer even a tiny portion of the wider Soudan
had spoiled the ambitions of his superiors and, more importantly, had
dealt yet another blow to France's prestige. Until now, the Senegalese
'hooligans' had enjoyed a reputation for heavy-handed invincibility,
their superior arms and disciplined native troops allowing them to
swagger through the ill-equipped locals who opposed them. After the
massacre, everybody knew that the French were not supermen. They
knew it in the Soudan and they knew it, worst of all, in Paris where,
after the official report on the disaster was published in March 1894,

newspapers vilified the manner in which Bonnier had brought France into disrepute. Mud was flung widely and indiscriminately. The press accused the authorities of incompetence, the Senegalese army of indiscipline and Joffre of disobeying orders. The military and its right-wing defenders railed against what it called an 'odious campaign', and said that if the Senegalese army was at fault it could only be because it had fallen under the influence of Jews and, not long afterwards, announced Joffre's promotion to the rank of Lieutenant Colonel. Amidst the ruckus, some level-headed people raised the point that France already had sufficient colonies to maintain without adding more to the list, especially ones of such dubious value as the Sahara and the Soudan. But this was an old chestnut, and the colonialists treated it with disdain. The important question was how the Bonnier massacre was to be avenged and how France was to acquire Lake Chad, the easternmost point granted to them under the Anglo-French Convention.

Like Timbuctoo, Lake Chad had acquired a mystique far exceeding its reality. Little more than a big, swampy soak-away, it had become in the imagination of French colonialists a glittering inland sea of vast economic importance. The innumerable (and, typically, unnameable) benefits that would accrue from its conquest were too great to be ignored. In the view of locomotive enthusiasts it was also essential to own Lake Chad because that was where the Transsaharian would go, and without a terminus there was no point building a railway that led towards it. Circular arguments, false enticements, and a feeling that France was letting things slip, fuelled the imperialist urge. One writer, Pierre Vuillot, encouraged his readers to contemplate 'the mysterious Sahara, a terrible minotaur that has devoured so many courageous travellers, so many intrepid explorers, around which a noose is being tightened daily; no time should be wasted in crushing the obstacles that oppose the advancement of civilization and science'. He went further, declaring: 'Secure the Saharan trade routes, direct towards our possessions – Algeria, Senegal, the southern rivers, the shores of Benin – all the commerce of the Soudan, from the Niger to the Chad. This should be the true, the only objective of France, one from which it should not be diverted. Too many unfortunate people, martyrs to a noble but chimaeric ideal, have strewn the Sahara with their bones; too many explorers, soldiers and educated men have watered the Saharan plains with their blood; and still their goal has not been achieved. They have given their lives to the cause of France, to the glory and prosperity of their country . . . Hear their call; follow their example; like them, continue to the end and realize, at last, their dream: A FRENCH AFRICA FROM CHAD TO THE ATLANTIC, FROM ALGERIA TO THE SOUDAN.'[13]

Separating bombast from reality were the 1,600 kilometres between Timbuctoo and Lake Chad. This stretch of territory, where not occupied by hostile black kingdoms, was in submission either to the Hoggar Tuareg or to their equally bellicose relatives, the Tuareg of the Adrar des Iforas in northern Soudan. Its conquest would require massive force of arms and, before that, a show of ferocity to demonstrate that Bonnier's massacre had not been forgotten. Laperrine lacked the authority and materiel for the former, but a display of ferocity was within his capability. So too was a degree of diplomacy – some would call it cunning – that had been conspicuously absent from the Senegalese army's policy to date. Following the events of January 1894 Laperrine had led his spahis on a number of *razzias* that were of little importance in the grand scheme but in which much enemy blood had been spilt and thousands of head of livestock either seized or slaughtered. His actions had secured Timbuctoo's perimeter and also gained him the confidence of the area's semi-nomadic tribesmen who, although not true Tuareg, survived in a similar fashion. He befriended their leaders, luring them so successfully with promises of pillage that eventually they joined him on his excursions. During his raids he gained an insight into the nature of the Tuareg. According to one biographer, 'He was impressed by the nobility of these veiled men, by their gestures and by their stature; he had an instinctive sympathy for their bravery.' This, however, 'did not prevent him treating the redoubtable pillagers in the manner they deserved'.[14] In March 1896, when the Hoggar Tuareg made one of their habitual raids on the Soudan, Laperrine was there to meet them. With a force

of spahis and Soudanese cameleers he rode after the enemy. By night-
fall on the first day he had not located the foe and by rights – by
orders, too – should have given up the chase. Instead, he continued.
The result was a mirrored version of the Bonnier massacre. The
Hoggar Tuareg had camped within a circle of thorns, at a spot called
Aken-Ken, certain that the French were far distant, when out of the
darkness came Laperrine on his horse. Jumping the barricade, he laid
about him with sword and revolver while the spahis and Soudanese
surged in his wake.

Laperrine's victory was conclusive, brutal and significant. Those at
home who followed these things were enraptured by the romance of
his strike: the brave captain riding through the cold night at the head
of his tiny force, the brilliant African stars overhead, the measured,
spongy thud of the camels' hooves contrasting with the faster rhythm
of the spahis' horses as they raced on their mission of fire and retribution. The minor scale of the raid – not even a raid but a
counter-raid – did not diminish its popular appeal, neither did the fact
that Laperrine had directly disobeyed orders by straying so far into
enemy territory. With great éclat, Laperrine had added another cliché
to the annals of African warfare: that of a lone European leading loyal
natives against the forces of evil. Eulogists would later study his tactics in wonder, describing his ability to ride, 'silent as the desert
itself',[15] in pursuit of Tuareg who 'rose like a cloud on the horizon'.[16] Actually, Laperrine had introduced little that was new: all
European nations relied on native soldiery to enforce colonial rule,
and the *razzia* and counter-*razzia* were by now old-hat in military
terms. Such novelty as the action could boast was in the success with
which Laperrine had suborned indigenous peoples to the French
cause. In the future this would have far-reaching consequences. But
for the moment, Laperrine's triumph was that he had struck a daring
blow against the enemy and had done so at a time when the military
badly needed glamorous deeds to restore public confidence in colonialism. In 1894, Lieutenant Bluzet had railed against those who
favoured a retreat from the Soudan, 'It would be criminal to even
dream of abandoning the country,' he wrote. 'If nothing else, the

honour of the flag, consecrated by the blood of our comrades, demands that we stay there.'[17] Laperrine's minor but symbolic avenging of Bonnier's death had given the backsliders something to chew on. It had also earned him a rare citation for valour and made him something of a legend.

The military had no intention of abandoning the Soudan, whatever the public or the ever-changing government in Paris might say. So afraid was it that Britain might get there first that it made incursions into the British colony of Nigeria. The convention of 1890, it appeared, had not allocated ownership in a proper fashion. 'We soldiers know only that there are territories in Africa which ought to belong to us and that the English and Germans are in the process of appropriating them,' wrote Lieutenant Colonel Joseph Gallieni in 1891. 'We are trying to beat them to it.'[18] Britain responded by increasing its Nigerian forces to unheard-of levels and then, before full-scale war broke out, signed in 1898 (wearily) yet another convention with France. The new agreement delimited a frontier between Nigeria and French territories that lay to the north. It did not, however, say anything about Lake Chad, probably because, in British eyes, there was nothing more to be said about such a useless piece of marshland. France became worried. Did this mean that perfidious Albion had designs on Chad? If so, it would be disappointed. In that year France launched a three-pronged pre-emptive strike: one column was to march north from the Congo; a second would advance east from Timbuctoo; and a third would plunge south from Algeria. God willing, all three would meet at Chad.

Laperrine took no part in the operation. Perhaps alone amongst France's headstrong officers he remembered that one of the original reasons for seizing the Soudan was that it would enable them to take the Sahara. He realized the fallacy of this argument: the Tuareg could never be displaced so long as they controlled the oases of the Tuat; and it was there that France should turn its attention rather than fool around with Lake Chad. In his view, the military were engaged in a gold rush that had gone astray. Besides, he was no longer interested in the Soudan. It was the desert that drew him. Although capable of socializing, Laperrine was essentially a solitary man. The raucous atmosphere of Senegalese officers' messes had lost whatever appeal it may have had when he first moved to West Africa; in addition, the business of organized soldiering had become too humdrum for the hero of Aken-Ken. What Laperrine wanted was a posting that offered simultaneously solitude, the prospect of irregular fighting, and a real chance to conquer the Sahara. Fort MacMahon satisfied all these requirements.

The situation in the Tuat and In Salah was much the same in 1898 as it had been in 1890. France was still in a diplomatic straitjacket, the oases continued to be controlled by the Tuareg and Forts MacMahon and Miribel were as unpleasant and ineffective as ever. There was, however, one small difference: in 1894, the governor of Algeria had ordered a force of spahis to be stationed at Fort MacMahon; innovatively, these spahis were to be mounted on camels instead of horses. The idea appealed to Laperrine. The spahi cameleers were not the wild tribesmen he might have preferred but they had potential. The Tuat was, in his opinion, the most strategically important region in the Sahara. And nobody could dispute Fort MacMahon's claim to be one of the loneliest military outposts in the world. On 6 November 1897 his transfer was approved.

The move was not in any way comparable to the epiphany experienced by Foucauld; nevertheless, consciously or unconsciously, Laperrine had taken the same step as his comrade. When he sailed for Algeria, carrying papers that confirmed his appointment as second-in-command of the spahis at Fort MacMahon, he was heading for a life of dutiful discomfort as far removed from ordinary existence as was possible. He had not taken monastic orders – but he had accepted the nearest the military had to offer.

6

THE MONK'S FRIEND

Despite its relatively long gestation, Foucauld's decision to become a Trappist monk fell upon his friends and relatives with terrible suddenness. The man who had a few months before been partying with the best of them, made an abrupt and almost hysterical disappearance from society. 'Twenty-four hours is so little,' he wrote in January 1890 to a cousin to whom he had spoken the previous day, 'I have not yet realized that I have said farewell to you for always . . . Still, it is the truth, I know it, I wish it and I cannot believe it . . . But I must draw strength from my very weakness, use this weakness itself for God, thank Him for His sorrow, offer it to him that this sacrifice may comfort Him, He who accepts that of a contrite and humbled heart, in order that this sacrifice may do good to all His children and above all to you: I ask Him with all my heart to increase my sorrow if I can bear a greater weight, in order that He may be a little more consoled and that His children and you, above all, may have a little more of good . . . I am sure that He wishes it.'[1] Comparing his sufferings with those of St Bernard, he wrote, revealingly, of his orphan status: 'I have lost infinitely more than St Bernard, I have lost as much as it is possible to lose; may the dear God, therefore, not take away my sorrow, which it would be very sad for me to lose.'[2]

From his correspondence it is impossible to separate Foucauld from the parents he knew only as an infant. Again and again he refers to his loss, to past memories, to despair. While his withdrawal from the world undoubtedly had solid spiritual foundations, it was a retreat from life in every sense of the word. Throughout his teenage and adult years he had battled to rebuild himself but had found no situation in which he felt truly comfortable. His answer was to remove himself from life (inasmuch as he could) and devote his years to the contemplation of its opposite – effectively, an attempt to hasten the moment when he would be reunited with his parents, or, as some psychologists suggest, to punish himself for their absence. Many have discovered peace, purity and beauty in monasticism, and for this reason it would be wrong to dismiss it as a lifestyle. Foucauld, however, seems to have approached it with a morbidity verging on the self-indulgent. For him it was not a means to appreciate life, but a form of anti-life, a black hole into which he fell with relief. He wanted not joy but sorrow; he sought not to rebuild his life but to become a passive participant in its crumbling. It is hard not to diagnose him – as Duveyrier had, in 1886, in so many words – as a man undergoing some form of breakdown.

On the morning of 27 June 1890, having spent an introductory period sweeping floors at Notre-Dame-des-Neiges, Foucauld boarded a steamer at Marseilles, his destination the monastery of Akbès in Syria. 'It seems,' he wrote, 'that I will feel every one of the waves which, one after the other, will bear me further away. It seems to me that my only resource will be to think that each one is also one step towards the end of my life.'[3]

Akbès was a suitable staging post along that route. Constructed in 1882, as a possible refuge in case the Trappists were forced to leave France, it was a sorry collection of thatched huts set in a distant mountain valley. The nearest town of any importance was eighteen hours away by mule; the area was prone to cholera and plague; brigands presented a continual threat; and the winters were icily cold. The surrounding fields were cultivable but transportation costs meant that produce could not be sold at a profit, and as a result the monastery was never self-supporting. It contained some twenty monks and a slightly smaller number of orphans to whose needs the monks tended when not praying or tilling their unprofitable fields. It was hard to imagine a site chosen more deliberately for its awkwardness than Akbès – even if, as Foucauld wrote, the views to the east were splendid.

For two years Foucauld wallowed in abasement. He laid the fires, swept the floors, cleared the fields, picked potatoes, gathered grapes, harvested cotton, pummelled laundry and mended the orphans' clothes. Come winter he discarded his shoes and chopped wood in the snow until his feet were ruined. While recuperating he rang the bells and put the library in order. 'One has so much pity for all who work when one shares their toil,'[4] he wrote. It was a well-meant statement but a patronizing one: Foucauld did not really share a worker's hardship, he merely acted a part. In fact, his whole life as a monk smacked of the theatrical; his suffering was a matter of need rather than necessity. He shared nothing with those whose experiences he sought to emulate, and his humility expressed itself at times in wildly extrovert deeds. With certain qualifications, it could be said that Foucauld's new persona was not very different from the old one.

Foucauld's entry into Trappism required a sloughing of his past. He took a new name, Brother Marie-Albéric, and transferred what was left of his money to his sister. He resigned his reserve commission in the army, cancelled his membership of the Paris Geographical Society and renounced all connection with his previous life. His disavowal was a slight charade. Although he called himself Brother Marie-Albéric, most people still knew him as Charles de Foucauld. He had no hesitation in contacting his family when he needed money. And far from severing contact with his friends, he kept in touch with everybody he had ever known, despatching at regular intervals missives of jubilant discomfort. One of his correspondents was Duveyrier, to whom he divulged all the details of his new life. But, apart from one early letter in 1890, Duveyrier did not respond. When next Foucauld heard of him, two years later, it was in a letter from a cousin to announce his death. Ever since his expedition, Duveyrier had been unwell. The cause of his illness was uncertain, but everyone was sure that it could be traced to his time in the Sahara. The strain of being an authority may have been a contributory factor; approached at every opportunity to adjudicate upon a subject of which he had no clear memory, Duveyrier must have been exhausted. Whatever the cause, he went into his garden one April morning, lay down, unpinned his Légion d'Honneur and placed it carefully beside him. Then he shot himself in the head.

'Far be it from me to judge severely one I loved so tenderly,' Foucauld wrote on hearing the news. 'To love and to pray is our destiny, not to judge.'[5] It was a slightly pompous adieu to an old friend but perhaps Foucauld could be forgiven for he was riding a new wave of purity; two months before Duveyrier's death he had taken his first vows as a monk. On 3 February 1892, he wrote, 'Since yesterday, I have belonged wholly to Our Lord. About seven a.m. I pronounced my vows; about eleven a few locks were cut from my hair in church, then my head was shaved leaving the crown. And now I do not belong to myself any more in any way at all.'[6] Having said that, he almost immediately began to assert his individuality. Trappism, he decided, might not be for him. The hardship did not worry him; on the contrary, he found the regime too soft. 'I am a little uneasy,' he wrote to Huvelin in June. 'Holy poverty is so little loved around me, austerity is so little loved . . . I am sometimes afraid that I may also lose my esteem for these blessed virtues or else lose my esteem for those around me or else lose both.'[7] For the moment he took no action – 'Being in a boat, I am afraid of jumping into the sea'[8] – but he became famous for the severity with which he applied his vows and was very disappointed in November when suspected tuberculosis turned out to be nothing worse than a fever. 'I haven't a hope of dying this time,' he wrote, 'but to say I don't wish to would not be true.'[9]

As he pondered his withdrawal from Trappism, Foucauld stiffened his resolve with the knowledge that he was on the brink of something great. By personal example, he wanted to attract multitudes (or a decent handful at least) into a life of denial comparable to that led by

Jesus. He had no immediate chance of doing so – a request to settle as a hermit in a nearby grotto was rejected by his superiors – but he lived in hope. In his opinion he had an indisputable priority when it came to fathoming the Almighty's wishes. As he wrote to his St Cyr comrade, Vallombrosa, 'It is an infinite grace which God gives me.'[10]

By coincidence, Vallombrosa received Foucauld's letter at a time when he was in similar turmoil. His problem, however, was of a political rather than a spiritual nature. How, Vallombrosa, wanted to know, was the Sahara best to be conquered? His solution had an indirect but powerful influence on France's race for Lake Chad.

Antoine de Vallombrosa, Marquis de Morès, had been an enthusiastic but not very good cavalry officer when Foucauld last saw him. Since then he had moved on. Resigning his commission after the Bou-Amama rebellion, he had married Medora Von Hoffman, the daughter of a New York financier, and in 1883, with every anticipation of wealth and excitement, had accepted his father-in-law's gift of a 10,500-hectare ranch in North Dakota. Here, in the so-called 'badlands', he embarked upon an ambitious money-making scheme. Reasoning (rightly) that the Chicago meat-packers were taking a huge profit, he decided (wrongly) that he could cut out the middle-men and sell his meat direct to the market. At great expense, therefore, he purchased several hundred thousand head of sheep and cattle, built his own meat-packing plant, formed his own freight company and bought a fleet of refrigerated railway cars. The meat-packers needed somewhere to live, so he built first a brick factory and then a town, that he named Medora after his wife. The town needed a mail service so he set up his own stagecoach line. The stagecoach line needed a stopover on its 150-odd kilometre route to Rapid City, the nearest large centre, so he built another small town – De Morès. Recognizing that his empire needed some form of headquarters, Vallombrosa also constructed a small chateau overlooking Medora. From this twenty-six-room summer residence, staffed by twenty servants (it is still there, a memorial and museum to its extraordinary owner), he galloped forth to shoot bison, inspect his livestock and admire the many kilometres of barbed wire with which he had fenced his perimeter. He was not a good farmer. Nor was he a good neighbour. Neither could it be said that he was a good businessman, quarrelling constantly with everyone upon whom his livelihood depended. He was, however, a very good shot and his talents as a duellist allowed people to ignore his shortcomings in other departments. During the course of his reign he killed at least one opponent and offered to fight countless others. To one Theodore Roosevelt, for example, who had had the temerity to buy an adjoining stretch of land, he wrote: 'My principle is to take the bull by the horns . . . If you are my enemy I want to know it. I am always on hand as you know, and between gentlemen it is easy to settle matters of that sort directly.' Roosevelt replied bravely that 'I too, as you know, am always at hand, and ever ready to hold myself account-able.'[11] Their imaginary differences, described by one newspaper as those between 'two very big toads in a very small puddle',[12] were eventually settled, but the spat did nothing to endear Vallombrosa to his fellow landowners.

In 1886 North Dakota was hit by a drought and then, the following year, by a winter so severe that three out of four steers perished. These natural disasters, combined with his tempestuous business arrangements, drove Vallombrosa to bankruptcy. He left the prairie without regret. He was a society man at heart and Dakota had always bored him. In 1887 he returned to Europe, taking the scenic route via French Indo-China (where he spent an enjoyable period touring the countryside of Tongkin) and India (the tiger shooting was excellent) before arriving in Paris in 1888.

Once on home territory, Vallombrosa made up for time wasted in the States. He flung himself into a round of gambling, drinking, duelling and debauchery that would have been familiar to anyone who knew him from St Cyr. Indeed, his family were so shocked by his expenditure that they reacted in the same way as had Foucauld's, appointing an official guardian to prevent him dissipating his entire fortune. Vallombrosa responded by damning their eyes. If he could not be part of the smart set then he would be against it. He came out as a 'republican and socialist',[13] and embarked on a single-handed crusade to reorganize the world. Unfortunately, his proposed reforms were very similar to those espoused by the class he affected to dislike. Already anti-Semitic, he embraced a prevalent hatred of Jews and was peripherally involved in the Dreyfus affair of 1896. He also embraced an anti-British chauvinism that had been gaining ground in France ever since the Napoleonic Wars. He was unable, however, to find a political party willing to accept his theories and in 1893 he travelled to Algiers where he gave a lecture on 'International Relations and the Monetary Question'. Later he published a pamphlet on 'The Secret of Finance'. Vallombrosa knew nothing about monetary questions and next to nothing about any finances except his own, but he did have an instinctive feel for an audience.

Despite ever heftier injections of government money, Algerian settlers were still impoverished, insecure and predominantly urban. They were heartened to learn, therefore, that they owed their plight not to mismanagement, corruption and local resentment, but to an Anglo-Jewish conspiracy whose leaders were, in Vallombrosa's words, 'masters of gold' and 'corrupters of the Latin spirit'.[14] When Vallombrosa delivered a similar speech in Tunis, three years later in 1896, he attracted a crowd of 2,000. He called, as Duponchel had, for a grand alliance to turf Britain out of Africa. However, where Duponchel had spoken of a European alliance, Vallombrosa supported a Franco-Islamic uprising that would deliver French Africa from the Anglo-Saxon menace. Such an alliance, he said, would create the longed-for union between Algeria and the Soudan; it would also push Britain out of the Upper Nile, a region it had dominated in the name of the Khedive of Egypt ever since the Mahdi uprising of 1884–5. It might even enable the French to take control of Egypt itself – and surely, since France had been the first European nation to invade Egypt, this could only be just. His audience reacted with an 'enthusiasm which bordered on delirium'.[15]

Vallombrosa's reference to the Upper Nile was not based on an idle pipedream. It was, in fact, part of French colonial policy to oust Britain from the area. This did not mean that it was necessarily government policy, more that of an influential cross-party body of

lobbyists. But the colonial faction put their case strongly and succeeded in persuading an unstable cabinet to take a stance on a subject
about which it knew little save that it sounded popular. Not that it
really mattered what the government decided, for the military already
had things in hand. In the same year that Vallombrosa made his
speech in Tunis, an expeditionary force of 300 Senegalese *tirailleurs*,
led by Captain Jean Baptiste Marchand, marched east from the mouth
of the Congo, to assert France's 'historic rights' over the Upper Nile
and Egypt. Marchand's task was nigh impossible: without back-up he
was to traverse Africa, establish himself on the Upper Nile and then,
with what remained of his puny force, challenge the massed ranks of
the British Empire. It took him two years, but he did it. In 1898, after
one of the longest and most astonishing treks in military history, that
involved cutting a trail through 5,000 kilometres of fever-ridden and
inhospitable terrain, Marchand raised the *tricouleur* at Fashoda, on
the Upper Nile. All he achieved was national humiliation. British
troops encircled his camp and threatened France with a war for which
it was unprepared and which it could not afford. After a token rattling
of sabres the French government realized belatedly what had been
going on behind its back and surrendered its claim to the Upper Nile.

The Marchand expedition was one of the most preposterous scram-
bles in the history of African colonization, outstripping in brazenness
even the Jameson Raid of 1895–6, in which Rhodesian frontiersmen
failed embarrassingly to start a war between Britain and the Boer
Republics of South Africa. There was, however, a widespread admiration for Marchand's audacity and nowhere was this more heartfelt
than in France's North African colonies on the eve of his departure.
Antoine Vallombrosa, Marquis de Morès, with his waxed moustache
and itchy trigger-finger, seized the moment.

Already, in 1896, Vallombrosa had tried to penetrate the Sahara
from Algeria, declaring that his life had been wasted and he now
sought 'a useful and glorious death'[16] in the service of France. He had
been blocked by garrison commanders in the oases. They suspected
he was mad – which he probably was – and feared that he would disrupt their carefully nurtured relationship with the Tuareg. He had

better luck in Tunisia. Drawing on local subscriptions and funds from home, he organized a small caravan to carry him through the Sahara to the Upper Nile where he would assist Marchand in ridding Egypt of the Anglo-Jewish scourge, before continuing west to Lake Chad. He hired a Tuareg guide, an interpreter and a number of servants to see him through the desert, he loaded his camels with valuable gifts, and he packed eight repeating rifles and a pistol with which to blast through any opposition. One or two officials still tried to thwart him: on the eve of his departure two of his men were arrested on the grounds that their papers were out of order. Vallombrosa was having none of it. Striding into the responsible officer's room he told him that if his men were not released in two hours, he would demand satisfaction. The men were released and Vallombrosa continued on his way. He did so with an added sense of paranoia: a rumour had reached him that the same obstructive bureaucrats had arranged for his caravan to be ambushed by Tuareg should he try to cross the Algerian–Tunisian border.

'The best I am able to do is succeed,' he wrote to his wife on 12 May 1896. 'I see more and more the importance of reaching my objective, and I sense that I am being watched everywhere by people ready to profit from my errors or weakness . . . My enemies are around me, behind me, here and in Paris, but not in front . . . My expedition has taken on an importance which I did not expect. It has become a national affair. It must succeed.'[17] He saw himself as a Flatters, a Flatters unfettered by government or colonial say-so, who would probe the unknown with a skill and verve that Paris could not command. Surprisingly, he expected also to encounter the man upon whom he modelled himself: the rumour of Flatters's survival had been resurrected and Vallombrosa, the man of so many moments, was amongst its adherents. On a map of his proposed route he scrawled the words – '*Toujours en avant avec l'aide de Dieu* – Morès'.[18]

When Vallombrosa left the Tunisian port of Gabes on the morning of 14 May 1896, it was in confusing circumstances. Some officers, it appeared, actually wanted him to cross the Algerian border in order to bring about an alliance with the Tuareg and had encouraged local commanders to give him every assistance. Others warned that his wealthy but lightly armed caravan was an invitation to bandits and that the course he planned was not only diplomatically unwise but suicidal. Vallombrosa's philosophy was equal to the occasion. He wrote to the *Mouvement Antisémite de Constantine*, advising its members that if he died in the desert it would be the fault of the Jews, against whom they should take immediate reprisals. Then he marched south. 'Life,' he announced, 'is but a battle and a passage. Life is only worthwhile through action! Too bad if that action is fatal!'[19]

He did not cross the Algerian border but skirted instead towards Tripolitania – an area he had been warned repeatedly to avoid, lest he disrupt relations with the Ottoman Empire – and by 30 May, having reached the town of Djenaien, he was in the highest spirits. 'My dearest Medora,' he wrote to his wife, 'We have made friends all along the route, and if you pass this way you will find them. It is a second Far-West, full of wonders if ever so little you enter into the spirit of the country and in harmony with the native people . . . We are in the process of opening a route, and, if I am able to say, creating great excitement in the desert.'[20] From Djenaien, however, matters took their predictable course. On 1 June a group of Tuareg joined the caravan, promising both to supply Vallombrosa with fresh camels (those he had purchased in Gabes were of poor quality) and to escort him through the dangerous regions ahead. Vallombrosa greeted them as fellow warriors. Two days later he was still impressed by their devotion to the cause and, interrupting a conversation that he could not understand but which concerned the time and manner of his death, he invited them to a meal of couscous and tinned fish. Afterwards, the Tuareg prostrated themselves for evening prayers while Vallombrosa remained standing to say his own. He was proud to be part of such a reconciliation. 'The camp was magnificent,' he wrote. 'It was a reunion of two worlds.'[21] On 4 June, Vallombrosa sent most of his dud camels home in anticipation of their replacements. He liked the Tuareg more and more. They were, he wrote, '*de veritables hommes*'. On 5 June, he distributed a few trade gifts in appreciation of their services. On 6 June, a band of Chaamba arrived with the offer of camels, an offer he rejected because he had already concluded a deal with the Tuareg. On 7 June, as the Chaamba joined the Tuareg in discussing the means of his despatch, Vallombrosa sensed something was awry. When he arose on the morning of 8 June he discovered that the Chaamba had fled with his prize white camel. The Tuareg sold him an ancient and dilapidated replacement. That night their servants stole a chest of papers from his tent. On 9 June, Vallombrosa reassessed the character of his companions. Rising before daybreak, he ordered the caravan to head north, back to the safety of Djenaien. Confident that his orders would be obeyed, he did not bother to check his compass, and, as one biographer wrote, 'indifferent to danger, he left his coat of mail in his baggage'.[22] When light came he realized that the caravan was continuing south, into Tuareg territory. He rode to the head of the column and turned it around.

There are conflicting reports as to the initial stages of Vallombrosa's demise, but the process probably began at 8 a.m., or thereabouts, on 9 June 1896. According to some accounts his rifle was snatched from his saddle and he was brought down by Tuareg tugging on his pistol holster. According to others, he tried to escape on his camel and then, frustrated at its slowness, shot it with his revolver, realizing only when the beast fell that his rifle was trapped beneath it. Thereupon the stories converge. Vallombrosa was struck on the head by a sabre but was saved from fatal injury by the heavy, felt cowboy hat he usually wore. He killed three of his assailants before staggering, half-blinded by a scalp wound, against a tree. The Tuareg retreated to a safe distance and peppered him with inaccurate fire for two hours. At 10 a.m. Vallombrosa was still alive and the Tuareg sent an interpreter to negotiate a truce. Vallombrosa held the man hostage for a while and then, when he tried to escape, shot him. Shortly afterwards, the battle reached its inevitable denouement. Vallombrosa was hit in the neck and, although he managed to wound several more of the attackers as they closed in, was eventually despatched by knife. The Tuareg removed his money and his clothes and then, having tied a rope around its ankle, dragged his mutilated corpse into a thicket of bushes. They then killed those of his servants they could find.

One man escaped the murderers' clutches and brought the news of Vallombrosa's death back to Gabes, from where it was telegraphed to France, Britain and the United States. Each nation reacted differently. The *New York Herald* ran the story under the headline, 'SLAIN BY HIS NATIVE ESCORT', and took proprietorial pride in Vallombrosa's gun-slinging abilities – as it revealed, 'no less than 18 attempts were made on his life in Dakota'.[23] The British, who had experienced similar empire-building setbacks, were admiring: 'If he had been English,' the soon-to-be King Edward VII, is reported to have said, 'I would have made him a Viceroy.'[24] In France, Vallombrosa's death was greeted with fury. *La Patrie*, which had supported Vallombrosa's aims, called for 'a crusade against England'.[25] More to the point, but no less angrily, a military spokesman said that France should 'kill as many Tuareg as possible'.[26] In Tunis, where Vallombrosa's remains were laid out for a funeral mass – one reporter said that his body had twenty bullet holes – the Archbishop delivered a sermon that spoke as much to his thousands-strong congregation as it did to the colonial party at home: 'In his Saharan expedition, the Marquis de Morès was not pursuing the seductive shadow of glory for himself. He wanted, in the highest sense, to devote his efforts to his country, to win over a people through good works, and he had undertaken this rash but sublime enterprise in a Christian manner.'[27] The Archbishop may not have been correctly informed as to the nature either of Vallombrosa or his expedition, but he was quite certain about the manner in which his death should be avenged: 'France, who in 1830 purged the Mediterranean of the Barbary pirates, must now eliminate the pirates of the desert.'[28]

Retaliation was not, actually, what the North African authorities wanted. Such a move would disrupt the policy of appeasement that had been pursued ever since the Flatters disaster and which, although unglamorous, had allowed France to extend its commercial tentacles into the Sahara far more successfully than any military operation. In recent years it had even been known for explorers to penetrate Tuareg territory and return alive – accompanied, of course, by a suitably large escort. For this reason, and because Vallombrosa was no more important than anyone else who had died in the desert, the consensus amongst those in command was that his murder should be hushed up. His mission had been of his own devising; it did not reflect official policy; he had been warned of the perils; and steps had been taken to prevent him leaving for the desert. If he were made a martyr, his death would require a retribution that experience had shown to be impossible. Best, therefore, to keep things quiet – especially as further investigation would reveal that some elements of the military had abetted Vallombrosa in his quest and others had, possibly, colluded in his death.

Events did not proceed as the authorities wished. Acting on their own initiative, enthusiastic Algerian officers vowed to bring the guilty parties to account, returning after several raids with three Chaamba suspects who had given themselves up on the promise that they would receive a pardon (which they did not). And Vallombrosa's wife set in motion an inquiry to examine the role that Tunisian officials played in her husband's demise. M. Jules Delahaye, a newspaperman and ex-politician, was her investigator and mouthpiece, whose task was to 'prove, if not with the impartiality of judges, at least with the proofs in her possession, that Morès was indeed a victim or a martyr'.[29] The process took years and involved a messy investigation into internal politics. According to the *New York World*, 'the Marquis possessed personal knowledge of many of the undisclosed secrets of the Dreyfus case – knowledge menacing the peace of men high in the army and the government. In order that those secrets might be buried forever, the Marquise and her friends say, he was first packed off to Africa and there assassinated.'[30] Delahaye's findings seemed to support this. Having spoken to the three prisoners, he wrote that, 'All stories hitherto given to the world about the murder are lies invented by French officials. It has been stated that the caravan was composed of brave men, devoted to their master. We can prove, on the contrary, that the caravan was organized expressly to lead de Morès to his death. It has been the boast of the chief assassin that he was entrusted with the work of conducting the unlucky Marquis to the place where he was to meet his fate.'[31] He singled out the military attaché at Tunis,

Lieutenant Colonel François Rebillet, as the culprit. Rebillet and Vallombrosa had quarrelled violently – it had been Rebillet who detained two of his men – and from this Delahaye extrapolated a scenario in which Rebillet was a corrupt official with money invested in the Saharan caravan trade, who, fearing that Vallombrosa's expedition would upset his business arrangements, had tried to stop him first by legal means and then by underhand methods. Delahaye was unable to prove that Rebillet was a Jew or an Englishman, but he was the next worst thing: a Freemason.

Like all conspiracy theories, Delahaye's was based on rumour, circumstantial evidence and the odd nugget of unexplained truth. There had, indeed, been something strange in Rebillet's delaying tactics, and in the apparent support of local officers for Vallombrosa's crossing of the Algerian border. Why, too, had Vallombrosa found himself in the company of a guide who, by Delahaye's reckoning, had already been involved in the murder of fifty-nine other people? These and other points Delahaye raised before the inquiry that was held at Sousse, in Tunisia, in 1901. But the judge refused to adjudicate in his favour, and the upshot was that the three prisoners were found guilty of murder and one was eventually executed (one had already died in captivity and the other, on the Marquise's urging, had his sentence reduced to hard labour for life). Another seventeen men were also found guilty and sentenced to death but, as they had failed to appear in court and nobody knew where they were (nor, very probably, who they were) the penalty was meaningless. Delahaye retorted that the inquiry had been a whitewash and continued his campaign. Rebillet responded vigorously. By all accounts a brilliant but flawed officer – 'a weak appearance but very tough,' wrote one of his commanders, 'tireless, well turned out and an excellent horseman; an excitable nature, energetic, impressionable and strongwilled'[32] – he had been asked to resign because of the scandal, and on taking Delahaye to court for defamation was awarded 5,000 francs. Delahaye replied with a three-volume opus on the Morès affair from which everyone was able to deduce that the man whom he called X was in fact Rebillet. The Marquise, meanwhile, passed the legend of her husband's martyrdom down the family line. In 1970, Vallombrosa's grandson told a biographer that 'My grandfather was killed in the Libyan Desert by Tuareg paid by his political enemies.'[33]

Whether or not the authorities were complicit in Vallombrosa's death remains uncertain. Rebillet may well have been involved in a bit of under-the-counter profiteering, and if so he would have tried to stop Vallombrosa. In doing so he would have been acting according to the nation's will. In colonial terms, France prided itself on going native, and if taking a profit was the norm, its representatives were equal to the challenge. But it is unlikely that Rebillet ordered Vallombrosa's murder. The Tunisian press probably had it right when they said, 'Monsieur de Morès was assassinated by natives who, in very good faith, thought they were doing a favour to the governors of Tunisia.'[34] What is certain, however, is that the military had good reason to keep it quiet. They wished to play down an event that gave an insight into the way France's colonies were mismanaged and that drew unwelcome attention to their unaccountable activities in the Sahara. In this they were unsuccessful.

Vallombrosa became a *cause célèbre*. Despite his anti-Semitism, or perhaps because of it, and his unattractive propensity for shooting people he disliked, he still had about him an unsavoury romance. The image of a nobleman who had held his own against the roughnecks of the Wild West, who had launched a personal crusade to further his country's imperial aims, and who had died in the desert, pistol in hand, fighting his murderers to the last, was the very essence of popular fiction. His funeral at Montmartre was a well-publicized occasion, attended by mourners from all classes of French society, the largest block comprising the butchers of Paris, who turned out to pay their respects to the late meat-packer. Vallombrosa's death did more than tug at sentiments; it also brought the colonial question to the forefront of the national consciousness and reminded people that France was not doing very well with its overseas possessions. There were constant insurrections in Indo-China; a rebellion in Madagascar had recently been put down with much difficulty and great loss of life; there had been the Bonnier débâcle at Timbuctoo; the Marchand expedition was lurching towards Egypt on a quest that could result only in an unwinnable war with Britain or a humiliating retreat; and now there was this shameful episode in the Tunisian desert. The Vallombrosa affair was in no way comparable to that of Flatters but it transmitted a similar message of impotence. Among the colonialists it was determined that France should act immediately. There would be no half-hearted dithering of the kind that had prevailed hitherto. France must seize control of the Sahara and the Soudan and exert authority over the region it had claimed so vehemently as its own. This was music to the ears of Jules Cambon who, in 1897, was coming to the end of his tenure as Governor-General of Algeria. In an outgoing speech, he urged France 'to avenge our compatriots and take up their unfinished work'.[35] His successor, Julien Laferrière, was pleased to be in a position to assist. A man whose ambitions for the Sahara were almost as aggressive as Cambon's, he too welcomed the day when the Gallic cockerel would crow over every casbah. One Lieutenant Émile Hourst, who had just returned from exploring the Niger, put the prevailing mood on paper: 'With the fullest conviction of my soul, I say France ought to acquire . . . colonies,' he wrote in his journal. 'Through them alone will she recover her commercial ascendancy, which has been so seriously jeopardized; through them alone will her *social position become assured* . . . The Sahara is closed to us, more completely closed than when Duveyrier visited it . . . Forward, for the sake of old France!'[36]

In the government's eyes it *was* going forward. Had it not authorized three expeditions to strike at the Soudan from three separate directions? One group, the Central African Mission, was already primed to advance from Timbuctoo; the second, the Congo Mission, was waiting only for a ship to take its leader, Émile Gentil, to the Congo; as for the third, and most important, which was to travel south through the Sahara, preparations were well in hand. They had already chosen a commander: Major François Lamy.

A well-groomed but short-tempered officer, Lamy had served in the Algerian desert, Madagascar, the Far East, and had also spent time in the Élysée as an aide to the President. He was instructed to take his pick of volunteers and once his force was complete, to march from Algeria to the Soudan and there join the struggle for Lake Chad. According to Lamy the response was avid: when he approached the First Algerian *tirailleurs* all 400 men applied for service, and 'we were obliged to lock some of them in the barracks to prevent them all from volunteering, and this included the officers and all of the NCOs'.[37] When he completed his selection he had 212 *tirailleurs* and thirteen spahis, among them two French doctors, and thirty-one French NCOs. His force was armed with rifles – repeating and single-shot – plus two pieces of field artillery with 200 shells for each. To transport this army and its supplies he requisitioned every camel for kilometres around. The final tally of beasts came to 1,004, making Lamy's one of the largest caravans to attempt a trans-Saharan crossing in recent times.

Curiously, despite such an unheard-of assemblage, Lamy's great enterprise was one that hardly dared proclaim its purpose. Amidst the internecine politicking of the Third Republic, it was simple to declare a policy but often very difficult to implement it. Thus, while the War Ministry allowed Lamy to take his pick of troops, it refused to fund the venture for which they had been chosen. Perhaps this was because so much had been spent on the other two expeditions; perhaps it was because Flatters still cast his doleful shadow across the desert; perhaps it was a gesture to placate the doubters who wanted France to stay out of the Sahara. For whatever reason, Lamy had to find private investors. The only non-governmental body willing to support his trip was the *Société de Géographie de Paris* but, unfortunately, the *Société* had already allotted 300,000 francs to one Fernand Foureau for an expedition of the very kind that Lamy was proposing. Lamy sought out Foureau and persuaded him to join his force; and then, after persistent appeals to the government, managed to secure another 500,000 francs for what was billed less as a military expedition than as a scientific investigation of the Sahara. On 20 September 1898, at 5.45 a.m., Lamy put his soldiers on the train that would take them from their garrison at Blida to the oasis of Biskra.

Situated at a point where the Atlas mountains dropped to the desert, Biskra was one of the southernmost termini of Algeria's railway system and as such had become a combination of tourist resort and military marshalling yard. It was here that troops assembled before departing for the Sahara. It was here, too, that tubercular Europeans came to benefit from the dry, healthy climate. Biskra's architecture was an incongruous mix of barracks and sanatoria – in the words of one Briton, 'a combination of Brighton and Aldershot'.[38] Travellers were compelled by its contrasts. Soldiers trudged through the dust, trains of camels yawed to and fro, long-robed Chaamba tribesmen mingled with Arab merchants, and distanced from the mêlée, well-heeled patients wandered through the palm trees or gazed motionless from hotel verandahs, surveying both the desert and the activities of those who would soon enter it. The place was quite surreal – which made it the perfect point of embarkation for an expedition that was itself to take on an increasingly bizarre aspect.

7

FROM ALGIERS TO
THE CONGO

Described by Duveyrier as, 'the man most capable of leading a successful expedition to link Algeria with the French Soudan',[1] Fernand Foureau was a colourful figure. In 1876, aged twenty-six, he had moved to Algeria to pursue a career as a farmer but had rapidly abandoned agriculture in favour of Saharan exploration. By 1898, he had made no fewer than eleven expeditions into the desert (nine of them under the auspices of the Ministry of Public Instruction) and was regarded as the world's pre-eminent Saharan specialist. Photographs show a tall, scrawny, sun-baked man, clad in a pale uniform of tight-shouldered, round-collared jacket, impossibly voluminous trousers, drawn in sharply at the ankles, and a wide-brimmed hat pulled slantwise over his brow. Arms crossed, chin jutting, moustache waxed into a horizontal rapier, he stares majestically into the distance. The effect would be comical, almost a parody, were it not that Foureau was the genuine article. He had one goal in life and he pursued it to the exclusion of all others. 'From the very first,' he wrote, 'my aim has been to attack the continent from the north, to cross the Sahara and to reach the Soudan.'[2]

By 1898 he had traversed 21,000 kilometres of sand and rubble,

9,000 of them hitherto untrodden by French foot, had mapped large sections of unknown territory, taking in the process half a thousand latitudes and longitudes, and had struck deep into Tuareg territory. But, accompanied only by a small escort, he had never been able to penetrate as far as he would have liked. Although his force was strong enough to prevent him being killed, it was too feeble to impress the Tuareg. Every mission ended with the nomads asking him to go home.

In 1894, for example, he had travelled to the Adjer. The inhabitants jeered openly at his, and his nation's, ambitions. 'Do you believe,' asked one chieftain, 'that there is anything to be gained in the Soudan? Do you think that there is any trade to be had from the country? Why do you – you who have mountains of gold and silver, you who have only to take the metal and make it into money – want to invade a land where the people are poor and the only living is made at the point of a lance?'[3] The man was even more expressive on the subject of the Transsaharian. Throwing out his arm towards the rocky plateau that lay to the south, he said, 'You see that mountain? It is the Tassili. No European has yet crossed it; and no European will put a railway over it as long as there is one Adjer Tuareg still alive.'[4] Then, displaying a sound grip of engineering, he added, 'Besides, you can see for yourself how difficult it would be; there is no man in the world who could carry off such an enterprise.'[5] Foureau replied that he did not himself want to build a railway, merely to walk over the mountains to see what was on the other side; and would welcome a guide to lead him to the Soudan. He was told to go away.

Foureau's problem was one of finance. As he saw it, there was no point trying to sidle peacefully through the desert on a low budget because such a thing was impossible. After long experience he sided with one General Arnaudeau, who had said of the Flatters expedition, 'You may say that you want to be peace-loving. You can be as peace-loving as you like. But what is the good of having yourself assassinated peacefully?'[6] Arnaudeau had been ignored at the time and for years thereafter. Now Foureau was advocating a return to the old methods.

He proposed crossing the Sahara with an immense force, one so strong and self-sufficient as to obviate the need for Tuareg protection. As he wrote, 'it is necessary to show that I have the means to make them respect me, to prove that I am independent and that I have my own escort'.[7] Such an army, however, would require money that Foureau did not possess. The colonialists came to his rescue.

In 1874, M. Renoust des Orgeries, Chief Engineer for Roads and Bridges, and ardent imperialist, died. During his lifetime he had amassed a considerable fortune and the Paris Geographical Society was the sole beneficiary of his estate. In his will, Orgeries left specific instructions as to how the legacy was to be spent: 'to bring peacefully under the influence or protection of France those countries still independent within the African interior so that a homogenous unity might be created between Algeria and our possessions in Senegal and the Congo'.[8] After consultation with executors and trustees, and having taken advice from various belligerent aristocrats, the Society voted that Orgeries's legacy be given to Fernand Foureau. The sum in question was 300,000 francs, large enough to furnish Foureau with the 150 riflemen he deemed necessary for his journey, and large enough, too, to draw the attention of Major François Lamy. On being introduced by a mutual friend, the two men agreed to unite their funds and mount an expedition so powerful that it would never need to fire a shot in defence. Which was why, on 23 October 1898, when the Foureau–Lamy expedition left the oasis of Ouargla it comprised not the 150 men that Foureau had requested, nor the 212 that Lamy had initially raised, but a total of 381 well-armed troops.

Their departure was chaotic. More than 5,000 cases had to be loaded, containing everything from food to tobacco, candles, soap, ammunition and scientific equipment. There were boxes of personal effects, sacks of potatoes and large metal water-tanks that were saddle-bagged on either side of the camels. There was even a wind-up gramophone that Foureau had brought along to 'seduce the natives'.[9] The process was hampered by sandstorms and plagues of mosquitoes, 'which do not leave us alone for a minute'.[10] But, come dusk, the mosquitoes disappeared and the expedition leaders were able to relish the splendour of the environment. They did not draw the same Koranic comparisons as Foucauld had done but they experienced the same wonder. Lamy ran out one evening just to watch the heavens. 'The nights are marvellous,' he wrote, 'the sky is a deep blue, sprinkled with thousands of stars.'[11]

The instructions given to Foureau, the expedition's titular leader, were vague: 'Explore the Sahara between Algeria and the French Soudan.' He assumed that the requirements of topographical exploration could be satisfied simply by the expedition's passage over the 2,500 kilometres that separated Ouargla from Lake Chad; but, in deference to his orders, he had also employed some 'scientists' to take observations en route. There were four of them: Noel Villatte, astronomer; L. Leroy, photographer; Jacques du Passage, naturalist; and Charles Dorian, politician. None of them were particularly effective. Passage was sent home a few days into the desert on the grounds that he was too young and Leroy took many photographs but was later obliged to leave most of his glass plates behind.* Dorian had no qualifications whatsoever, other than a desire to take part and the possession of a smoking jacket that he thought would add a touch of class. Exploration, however, was not the expedition's primary motive. No matter how Foureau tried to dress it up, this was a mission of revenge. According to the Paris Geographical Society, Foureau was leading 'a national expedition, to correct . . . the legend of impotence created by Flatters [and to] efface this lugubrious memory . . . The Foureau–Lamy mission [is] the Flatters expedition, renewed and reconstituted.'[12]

As Foureau and Lamy had anticipated, they met no resistance from the Tuareg on their march south to the Soudan. This may have been because of their strength; it may also have been because the Tuareg

---

*The majority of images that later appeared in the expedition's journal were exposed by Foureau himself. He wrote venomously of the hours he had to spend under a dark cloth, clad only in underpants and streaming with sweat, while waiting for the pictures to develop.

knew they needn't bother. In their efforts to present an invincible face, Foureau and Lamy had ignored the primary laws of desert survival: to carry little, move fast, and travel in small groups that would not strain the Sahara's meagre resources. The Foureau–Lamy expedition was large, slow and heavily laden. It was also, despite the careful preparations, poorly organized. Their main problem was the camels. Not only did none of the men know how to handle them – a few Chaamba cameleers were pressed into service, to little avail – but there were too many of them. The desert's sparse forage could not feed such numbers and its wells (polluted and stinking of sulphur) could not water them. The camels deteriorated steadily. So did the men they were meant to be supplying. While Foureau and Lamy had taken too many camels for the terrain, they had, conversely, taken not enough for the job. Although heavily burdened, the camels carried insufficient provisions to feed the swollen army that eventually left Ouargla, an inadequacy that was exacerbated by the increasingly arduous conditions the expedition encountered.

Struggling through the rocky landscape, the men began to complain about the paucity of their rations: 200 grams of flour per person per day plus an allocation of dates did not satisfy their appetites. Foureau and Lamy had arranged back-up caravans from Ouargla to replenish the expedition's provisions, but these caravans never seemed to arrive when they were needed. They had also hired twenty Chaamba sharpshooters to bring in fresh meat but, for the same reasons that there was little for the camels to eat, so there was little for the Chaamba to shoot. Twenty-three days into their trek the Chaamba had killed a single antelope and sixteen gazelle.

Despite these difficulties, the expedition reached the foothills of the Hoggar, where Foureau insisted on seeing the site of the Flatters massacre. With a small group of men he rode through fields 'of barren schist and granite, a landscape that leaves an impression of infinite sadness',[14] to visit the infamous well. He found little to mourn. Reports would later claim he had discovered a hole in which the Tuareg had made a pyre of the French bodies. In his journal, however, he mentioned only a number of unidentifiable bones, the remains of a European shoe and, at a distance of 800–1,000 metres to the north-west of the site, a humerus he thought might have belonged to one of Flatters's officers, Captain Masson. He built a cairn, sent a message to Ouargla, advising the commander to come and collect the remains, then rode back to rejoin his force.

The expedition continued southwards, instilling fear wherever it went. A group of thirty Hoggar Tuareg approached their camp and assured them that 'As long as you are with us, you have nothing to fear; you are in our land and between you and us there shall be peace. But if you go further we cannot be responsible for your safety.'[15] Foureau and Lamy laughed. They had no need of Tuareg guarantees; they could look after themselves. The expedition emerged from the Hoggar without having fired a shot in self-defence and with no greater loss than the occasional, opportunistic theft of a camel. The mountains, however, had provided them with little food and their provisions were now running low. As one Sergeant Charles Guilleux said, 'We began to know what hunger is. Yet had we known what the future had in store for us, we would have thought ourselves very lucky.'[16]

Before them lay the worst part of their journey: the Ténéré, a fea-tureless, monotonous expanse of rock and sand, whose traverse necessitated a forced march of at least seven days. The camels were simply not up to it. Starved and mistreated they began to die. 'This is a terrible desert,' Foureau recorded, 'desolate, deceiving and dis-couraging for us malnourished souls. The road is strewn with the skeletons of camels, whose number we augment incessantly. A camel stops, we push it, it bows down on its legs and sits there. There is nothing we can do but unload it and continue. The poor animal rests, motionless as a statue, a rigid, brown silhouette, getting smaller and smaller as we move on. Eventually it is a small black dot between the purple ground and the blue sky, peering in the direction of its com-panions in misery. The next day it is stretched out on the gravel, yet another milestone on this implacable and devouring path . . . I had already seen similar things on previous expeditions, but never on a scale such as this.'[17] Every dead camel meant the abandonment of the provisions it carried and as the expedition progressed the men became hungrier and hungrier. Foureau and Lamy pushed them faster, rousing them at 3 a.m. and not letting them stop until 9 p.m. For breakfast they boiled a kettle of tea; lunch was a handful of dates; and then in the evening they would eat, inevitably, one of their newly dead camels. But soon the camels were dying faster than they could eat them. 'Our losses, over the last seven days, have risen to more than 140 animals,' Foureau wrote in his journal. 'In the conditions in which we find ourselves, these numbers are terrible and alarming. It has to be said that, in the middle of the desert, a group of men who see their caravan, or their animals, disappear, is irrevocably lost; nothing can save them; there is nothing left but to lie down in the shade of a boulder and wait for the final deliverance, that is to say, death.'[18] One night they were woken by rifle fire: a *tirailleur* had shot himself.

They did make it safely to the other side of the Ténéré, but the camels continued to die and by the time the expedition reached the relative prosperity of the Aïr, in northern Soudan, it was weakening rapidly. On 24 February 1899, at the village of Iferouane, with only 585 camels remaining, it ground to a halt. Unable to go further without new beasts, Foureau found himself having to renounce his prized independence by bargaining for replacements. Unfortunately, the people with whom he was forced to bargain were Tuareg; and as he had feared, they took his dependence for weakness. Five hundred fresh mounts were promised but failed to arrive. On 8 March, two of Foureau's men were murdered. Then, four days later, the Tuareg launched an all-out assault on the expedition's feebly barricaded camp.

At 6 a.m. on 12 March, a few minutes after reveille, Lamy became aware of 'a great rumour, piercing cries [and] an indescribable brouhaha'.[19] Peering out of his tent he saw 'an immense cloud of dust . . . rising from the valley some 300 to 400 metres from our camp.'[20] It was hard to see precisely what was happening – the dust and the morning haze obscured everything beyond 200 metres – but it wasn't hard to guess. Out of the haze came 400–500 Tuareg, armed with swords and lances, sweeping forward on their camels, accompanied by a yelling mass of black foot-soldiers, some of whom hung from the beasts' tails, goading them on with knives. Here, at last, the soldiers had a chance to do what they had been trained for – and to use in action for the first time the two artillery pieces they had dragged across more than 1,800 kilometres of desert. Lamy eyed his enemy with disdain then ordered thirty men to take position and instructed the artillery to load grapeshot. When he gave the word they fired. Bodies dropped *en masse*. 'It caused a moment of stupor and hesitation,'[21] he wrote sardonically. From a distance of 200 metres, and possessing no firearms, the Tuareg did not have a chance. Their bravery took them to within fifty metres of the French defences but there they stopped. By 6.25 a.m. the battle was over. The ground was covered with dead Tuareg and their camels. Not one of Lamy's men had been injured.

Lamy's victory gave his men a much-needed boost of morale and cleared the staleness of their dreary trudge across the Sahara. It did not, however, solve the pressing problem of transport. When he sent his troops to secure the area, they managed to bring in a few stray camels whose owners had died in the battle, but this was far from the number they needed. For ninety days the expedition waited at Iferouane, trying in vain to buy more animals. The locals promised much but delivered little, and all the time the expedition's stock continued to dwindle. 'The rate at which our camels are dying is perfectly dreadful,' Foureau wrote. 'Wax models placed by a fire could not melt away faster.'[22] After lengthy discussions, Foureau and Lamy agreed that if no one was willing to help them, they would have to help themselves. Throughout the last weeks of May and the first of June, in a series of *razzias* they pillaged the countryside for camels and, when no camels were to be found, for donkeys and bullocks. Their success was limited: a few score beasts were eventually mustered but these gains were offset by continuing deaths amongst their original herd. By 5 June there were only seventy-five camels left of the 1,004 that had set out from Ouargla.

During their long wait Foureau and Lamy had managed to extract a donkey-train of millet from the ruler of Agadez, to the south. With these donkeys and the other beasts they had mustered, they decided to break out of Iferouane and complete their march to Lake Chad. Baggage was stripped to a minimum. Food, ammunition and medicine were the only loads permitted. Excess provisions were consumed in a final orgy and those that remained were burned. 'It was a complete disaster,'[23] Foureau wrote mournfully. Lamy was incandescent: 'It was heart-breaking for all of us to have to destroy [everything] which we had dragged so far with such difficulty; and to know that we had to make this sacrifice solely because of the ill-will, the inertia, the malice and the stupidity of the people of Aïr.'[24] The men had hoped to save their personal belongings but these too went into the flames. Stripped almost to the skin, the Foureau–Lamy expedition departed for Agadez on 10 June.

The countryside was bleak and mountainous; there was little vegetation for the camels; their guides, seven local women, were unsure of the way, often leading them in the wrong direction; their clothes fell to pieces, their boots wore out and, above all, there was not enough food. Exhausted and starving, the men were on the point of mutiny. 'They no longer feared punishment,' wrote one sergeant, 'nor death.'[25] When the expedition reached Agadez on 28 July, after marches of twenty-five kilometres and more per day, only its weaponry proclaimed that here were soldiers of the French army; otherwise the outfit could have been mistaken for a horde of tramps. They were all barefoot, including the officers; a few people possessed trousers, fashioned from old date sacks; one or two officers had made hats out of palm leaves; and their 'uniform' tops consisted of whatever coloured material they had left. Foureau, for example, was clad in a purple vest and Charles Dorian wore his smoking jacket, the only item remaining in his wardrobe.

After all they had come through, Agadez seemed a veritable haven of prosperity and order: it had minarets, palaces and fortifications; it had houses, a market, and a ruler who controlled the activities of its many inhabitants. Lamy set up camp outside its walls, blew a bugle and fired a cannon shot to announce his presence. The sultan rode out in person to greet him, and said that he would find the supplies the expedition needed – but it would be difficult; the town was very poor at the moment. Rejecting this as a mere ploy to raise prices, a delighted Lamy waited for Agadez to unleash a cornucopia of food and camels. But Agadez was a town of hollow promise. Once a trading centre of importance it had become a vassal city in thrall to the Tuareg. Its walls were broken and useless; its market was a rubbish-strewn strip of dirt; and its sultan was a Tuareg-appointed puppet. In fact, the sultan they had met was not even the sultan but a turbanned proxy who had been sent to inspect the foreigners while the genuine article hid inside his crumbling palace. On 31 July, having heard nothing, Lamy sent 200 *tirailleurs* to occupy the mosque. The sultan persuaded them to withdraw with a gift of millet and two cows. Lamy waited until 9 August for the promised camels and then lost patience. Training his artillery on the town he sent word that unless he received some form of transport very soon, he would fire. The sultan hastily sent a quantity of donkeys plus a guide, with which he hoped his troublesome visitors would be satisfied. Lamy was far from satisfied. Nevertheless, he accepted the animals, ordered the sultan to raise the *tricouleur* above his palace, and the next day left for the town of Zinder, some 480 kilometres to the south.

He was soon back, and in a vile mood. The wells had been dry; hordes of donkeys had died, forcing him to abandon valuable cases of food and ammunition; the guide had led them north instead of south; Tuareg had shadowed his column at night, spooking his guards so badly that they fired on each other (one man died in the crossfire); and most days their only fluid was one cup of coffee per person. On 17 August, with their reserves down to a quarter-litre of water per person, Lamy had turned the column around. Covering in three days the distance it had taken them eight to cross, they were almost at their goal when, as Foureau recorded, 'we were struck by a tornado bigger than I could possibly have imagined'. The first sign was a blast of wind from the north-west. Looking up, he saw 'vast, towering clouds of dust, of a sinister copper colour and topped by wild plumes . . . covering a good quarter of the horizon. They advanced with fantastic speed and swept over us with a force that nothing could resist . . . blinding everybody, blowing the baggage from the camels' backs, knocking over the mules. It was impossible to turn your back to it. Sand and gravel flew from every direction. We could not see farther than a few metres.'[26] They cowered for five and a half hours until the storm cleared. On 19 August they reached the outskirts of Agadez, where a raucous party held in celebration of their departure came to an abrupt halt.

'This march,' Foureau wrote, 'made under a high temperature by men heavily loaded, without a drop to drink . . . has hardly a parallel in the history of exploration.'[27] Lamy agreed entirely. Having already shot the guide who had misled them, he was now restrained only with difficulty from blowing Agadez to bits. He and Foureau then settled down to weeks of 'interminable discussions' with the town's ruler. It soon became clear that Agadez had nothing to offer. A dribble of provisions issued forth – 'just enough so that we do not die of hunger, but little enough that we suffer'[28] – but the sultan produced no camels. Lamy suspected that this was because he would not hand them over. More likely, though, it was because he *could* not: he had no need of the things, controlling only the beasts of burden that satisfied the town's immediate requirements. It was the Tuareg who kept camels and, after the massacre at Iferouane, they were in no hurry to sell them to the French. Towards the end of September, Lamy lost his temper once again. He ordered his men to occupy the wells and announced that until he had his camels Agadez could have no water. It worked. On 17 October the Foureau–Lamy expedition was once more on its way with a motley assortment of beasts that, to be fair to the sultan who must have paid dearly for them, did include a number of camels, but which comprised mostly donkeys and bullocks. In the interim rain had fallen, the wells were now full and, moving at a smart clip of forty kilometres per day, the column hastened towards Zinder.

It reached its destination on 2 November, 'looking more like a collection of bandits than a mission made up of honest men'.[29] Their wretchedness was emphasized by the splendour of their welcome. The sultan of Zinder rode out in person to greet them, accompanied by a group of brightly dressed horsemen who skittered through the dust, firing rifles into the air. A mounted orchestra swelled the throng, producing an exuberant cacophony with the aid of bells, drums and trumpets three metres long – 'most remarkable,'[30] Foureau wrote. And, most wondrous of all, marching alongside the Zindermen was a detachment of uniformed Senegalese *tirailleurs* with a Frenchman, Sergeant Bouthel, at their head. As the cavalcade made its way back to town – 'a moving and inspiriting spectacle'[31] – where Bouthel equipped them with fresh uniforms and introduced them gently to the comforts of civilization, some men began to cry.

During their battle with the desert, Foureau and Lamy had considered only briefly the part they were playing in France's broader colonial strategy. The first reminder that they were part of a three-pronged strike towards Lake Chad had come at Iferouane, where they learned that a French force had left the Niger and was heading into the Soudan. They had paid little attention to the report, being occupied at the time with more immediate concerns. Then, on 20 September, they had received a strange letter from a lieutenant belonging to the Central African Mission, that told of mutinies among the men and illness among the officers. He referred to a previous missive that explained matters in greater detail, but this had obviously gone astray. 'Naturally, we could not understand what he was talking about,' wrote Foureau. 'We could only make hypotheses, and the events to which he alluded remained a sad but unfathomable mystery.'[32] The first letter did, eventually, reach them at Zinder. By then, however, Sergeant Bouthel had already brought them up to date. His tale was an unpleasant one.

In November 1898, while Foureau and Lamy were less than a fortnight out of Ouargla, Captain Paul Voulet and Lieutenant Charles Chanoine left Koulikoro, a small town about 640 kilometres upriver

on the Niger from Timbuctoo, in command of the Central African
Mission. Their objective was Lake Chad, which lay more than 1,500
kilometres of unconquered and inimical territory to the east. On
paper, the Central African Mission was a small force: its core comprised nine French officers and NCOs, plus a mere fifty Senegalese
tirailleurs, twenty Sudanese spahis, and thirty native interpreters and
guides – far fewer than had been employed by Foureau and Lamy.
Voulet and Chanoine, however, were not men who paid much attention to paper; they were known sadists with a reputation for cruelty,
Senegalese hooligans of the worst type, who acted as they wished
whenever they were given the chance. Their orders gave them every
scope for doing so. 'I will neither pretend to indicate to you which
route you must follow,' wrote a distant functionary, 'nor the way to
conduct yourself with the native chiefs and the native population.'[33]
On this say-so, Voulet and Chanoine stocked up for a campaign whose
extent they could not determine but which, they were sure, would
involve satisfactory levels of violence.

In addition to their regular troops they hired a band of 400
Soudanese auxiliaries who were offered a monthly wage of fifteen
francs plus all the pillage they could get. They also conscripted 800
porters to carry a ferocious amount of weaponry: 450 rifles, fifty car-
bines, 180,000 rounds of ammunition, and an eighty-millimetre cannon
with 100 shells to feed into it. Like Lamy, however, they were so
keen to present an invincible face that they forgot to pack enough
food. When Voulet reached Timbuctoo, the garrison commander,
Lieutenant Colonel Jean-François Klobb, was welcoming but also
worried. 'I am anxious,' he wrote. '[He] seems to be heading off without knowing what he is doing.'[34] This was not quite true. Voulet did
have a firm intention of visiting the 'barbarians and savages' of Lake
Chad with fire and sword and of crushing the region's most powerful
leader, Rabih Zubair, who had recently annexed the territory south-
west of Lake Chad and who was (naturally) suspected of being in the
pay of the British. Where Voulet fell down was in provisioning his men
until they got there. Never having campaigned in arid conditions, he
assumed his column would be able to live off the land. But although the

Soudan was more prosperous than the Sahara, its pickings were by no means rich. In Senegal, the column might have been able to forage successfully, leaving a gap that would close behind it. In the Soudan, where margins of survival were tighter, its passage caused devastation.

The Central African Mission devoured everything in its track: food, men and animals alike. When their demands were not met, Voulet and Chanoine used force: resistance was crushed brutally, villages burned and their inhabitants slaughtered. Sometimes they used force, apparently for the sheer joy of it. 'I gave them everything they asked for,' one chieftain later complained. 'They told me to provide them with six horses and thirty cattle in three days. I did it, and they killed everyone they could: 101 men, women and children were massacred.'[35] Through the first months of 1899 Voulet and Chanoine hacked grimly on, leaving a trail of smouldering settlements and severed heads on stakes. If they had hoped to terrorize the country into submission their tactic failed; soon, the land was emptying before them as people 'fled with all speed at the mere sight of the tricoloured flag'[36] – and an empty land was one that did not contain the manpower or food that the expedition required. There was no need for the populace to adopt a scorched-earth policy. Like an advancing dragon, the Central African Mission did the job for them.

If conditions were bad for those who opposed the Mission they were little better for those who were part of it. As recorded by Douglas Porch, who in 1985 became the first English-language chronicler of this desperate episode in French imperialism, Voulet and Chanoine treated their men with appalling brutality. The porters were treated as dispensable scum: when they fell ill they were denied medical attention; if they tried to escape they were shot; if, through lack of food, they became too weak to go any further, they were decapitated (to save a bullet); even if they were able-bodied and willing to continue, they might be shot on a whim. Cruelty became almost institutionalized – one *tirailleur* was executed for shooting a porter rather than bayoneting him. And as food became scarcer, the soldiers turned in frustration on their guides for leading them into barren ground. 'We would hang them,' wrote one officer, 'and most of them, hanged very close to the ground, had their legs devoured by hyenas, while the rest were left for the vultures.'[37]

In April, rumours of the Central African Mission's atrocities reached Paris. Even by the standards of the day – which were broad enough to accommodate almost any form of violence in the name of Empire – Voulet and Chanoine were perceived to have overstepped the mark. Klobb, the conscientious commander of Timbuctoo, was ordered to investigate. Travelling light, with fewer than a hundred men, he moved swiftly in Voulet's wake. From evidence he encountered along the way – dead guides swinging at crossroads, villages burned and abandoned, thirteen women strung up here, two children there – it became clear that he was chasing no ordinary Senegalese zealots but men who were seriously unhinged. Confirmation came on 10 July when, only a few hours behind the column, he sent a courier to inform Voulet that he was relieving him of his command. Voulet's response, in so many words, was that he would like to see him try it. Klobb, he said, was a hostile conspirator who sought the glory of conquering Lake Chad for himself; he, Voulet, knew this for a fact, and was going to continue on his appointed path. He would never submit. 'I am resolved to sacrifice my life rather than submit to the humiliation which you have been ordered to impose upon me,' he wrote. 'But also, I prefer to gamble everything and above all not to abandon my place to an intriguer of your ilk by a stupid suicide.'[38] The Central African Mission moved on. So did Klobb.

On 13 July, having slaughtered 150 women and children in reprisal for losing two *tirailleurs* in a raid on a village, Voulet sent word to his pursuers: 'Tell the colonel that if he tries to catch up with my column, I will attack.'[39] Klobb pressed on. Voulet sent another warning on 14 July: 'If you come one step closer, I will fire. I will fight to the death.'[40] Klobb did not take him seriously and continued to advance. That same day, he at last caught sight of his quarry. At a distance of 150 metres he unfurled the *tricouleur*, drew his men into a line, and then walked out to parley with the madman. True to his word, Voulet ordered his men to open fire. Klobb was wounded by the first volley and killed by the second. His men fled when Voulet's troops atacked them with bayonets. Among the wounded was Klobb's second-in-command, Lieutenant Octave Meynier, whom Voulet attended personally, dressing his wounds while indulging in insane 'diatribes against France, against the government, against the Colonel, at times broken by a little remorse and then a return to rage, an unsettling madness'.[41]

Voulet revealed the extent of his madness that evening when he informed his officers that he was no longer beholden to Paris. 'I am an outlaw, I renounce my family, my country, I am no longer a Frenchman, I am a black chief,' he said. Describing his plans for the column's future, he sketched an outline of delirious grandeur. 'We are going to create a strong empire, impregnable, which I shall surround with an enormous bush without water. To take me, it will require 10,000 men and 20 million [francs] . . . If I were in Paris, I would be master of France.'[42] He encouraged his black NCOs with promises of power. 'My country is over there in the east,' he said. 'We are going to conquer it. You are no longer sergeants. You are great black chiefs!'[43] Terrifyingly, his proposals were not so far-fetched. Men like Rabih Zubair had carved themselves a slice of Africa (so, too, had men like Cecil Rhodes and King Leopold of Belgium); why should not Voulet, with his overwhelming firepower, do the same? The white officers and NCOs, who hesitated to accept their commander's proposal, knew the answer. To do such a thing required at the very least a disciplined body of troops and a vestige of sanity. Voulet, by now, had neither.

Voulet and Chanoine left the doubting whites behind and marched on with the *tirailleurs* and black irregulars towards a glorious destiny. Within a few days their men had mutinied and the two madmen were both dead. The remaining officers took shaky control of the column and proceeded to Zinder from where, having shot another forty-five mutinous *tirailleurs*, they proceeded towards Lake Chad. A hundred-strong garrison was left at Zinder and it was these men, under the command of Sergeant Bouthel, who greeted the Foureau–Lamy expedition with such sympathetic warmth when it staggered out of the bush on 2 November 1899.

Foureau and Lamy were worried by Bouthel's story. Their own *tirailleurs*, who had already come close to mutiny, were now being entertained by *tirailleurs* who *had* mutinied. The Central African Mission was rambling on its ruinous course; they had not themselves reached Lake Chad, which was their appointed goal, and the dry season was upon them. No matter how hospitably Bouthel had arranged their billets, the leaders of the Trans-Saharan Expedition felt it was time to move on. First, however, there were one or two things to be done. The bodies of a French officer and his interpreter were fished out of a well and given a decent burial. Then Lamy led a party to retrieve Klobb's remains for interment at Zinder. While he did so, Foureau investigated the town. He was impressed by what he saw. It was 'large and fine', with a 'pleasing aspect', and was dominated from outside its thick, seven-gated walls by a Tuareg fortress placed upon a towering pile of granite rocks. This edifice (which had been 'presented to France', as Foureau coyly put it) doubled as a warehouse and he wandered, marvelling, through its pungent depths. 'I saw, in the midst of cottons, silks, ostrich feathers, spices etc., a variety of unexpected articles, such as French scent-bottles, Arab bon-bon boxes, bottles of Hunyadi Janos water, and cages of live civets, from which the musk is extracted weekly.'[44] He liked, too, Zinder's market, which occupied the space outside one of its seven gates. It was 'formed of rows of sheds divided into little shops. A little of everything, from cottons to tobaccos, jewels, salt, kola-nuts, etc., is sold here by negresses seated in parallel lines.' But he oversold Zinder's attractions when he compared the vultures that scavenged its streets to 'the various kinds of turtle doves [that are distributed] throughout the whole country'.[45]

Foureau may have been describing an Arcadia; Lamy saw only a rotting town at the centre of a rebellious region. When he returned from fetching Klobb's remains, he went on a mission 'for the purpose of enforcing the obedience of certain recalcitrant chiefs'.[46] He came back with 300 horses and a hundred camel, which was just enough to put the expedition back on its feet. This, combined with a telegram addressed to Foureau, that had made its way from the Minister for Public Instruction to Zinder, 'authorizing me to choose my own route for the return journey',[47] gave them confidence to lead their troops towards Chad. They departed shortly before New Year 1900 and almost immediately encountered familiar difficulties. 'Our wretched animals were still strewing their bones along the road,' Foureau wrote, 'their only food being dry grass, which supplied very scanty nutriment; and in regard to food supply, our situation became daily worse.'[48] Even when they passed into more forgiving territory their problems did not cease, for the whole area had been scorched by warfare. Foureau placed the blame on Rabih Zubair, who may indeed have been the culprit. But the Central African Mission had also passed this way. Whoever the agent, the destruction was terrible. 'All the villages . . . had been pillaged and burned,' Foureau wrote, 'and heaps of human bones lay whitening on all sides.' Of Kuka, the capital of Bornu, that had once contained 100,000 inhabitants, nothing was left but 'a melancholy heap of ruins. Crumbling walls, already covered with creepers, trees growing up in the interior of the houses, thousands of earthen jars, broken or whole, are all that meets the eye.'[49]

When they reached Lake Chad on 21 January 1900, Foureau was enraptured. 'It is really it, this long hoped for lake, this goal of our efforts for these long months, this goal of my dreams for more than twenty years! Before us, a scintillating expanse of water stretched to the horizon, which we saw through the spaces between the numerous islands of reeds which grew near the edge.'[50] The water was fresh, and good to drink. Best of all, the countryside was rich enough to support both men and animals. 'Game simply swarms,' Foureau wrote. There were giraffes, lions, elephants – 'which showed themselves very tame' – and, 'on one occasion the troops of antelopes occupied more than ten minutes passing our encampment'.[51]

Foureau spoke as if he were the first white man to visit Lake Chad. He was not. Britain's Clapperton–Denham–Oudney expedition had reached it in the 1820s; the German explorer Barth had been there in the 1850s; and within the last decade an entrepreneur had been puttering across it in a steam boat that he transported in sections from the Gulf of Benin. Also, Lake Chad was not as enticing as Foureau made out, comprising a relatively small stretch of water surrounded by gelatinous mud flats. Only on its western shore was life good; everywhere else it was surrounded by small sand dunes beyond which lay a maze of swamps and little lakelets. Foureau, Lamy and their men trudged around this gloomy pond until, by the banks of the River Chari, which flowed into Lake Chad from the south, they met the Central African Mission. With not so much as a nod to its recent history – Foureau described its lieutenant as 'full of spirit and dash, bold and adventurous, above all a charming and gay companion'[52] – they joined forces. Two French armies were bad enough, as Rabih Zubair found on 2 March when they overran the town of Kusri – 'the enemy losing heavily, both in men, arms, and supplies'.[53] But on 20 April they were joined by a third, when the long-forgotten Congo Mission, the third prong of France's assault on Lake Chad, arrived at the Chari. Led by the young naval ensign, Émile Gentil, the Congo Mission had been battling towards its goal since 1897; it had endured great privations and had lost many of its men, but in April 1900 it arrived proudly at its destination. It was clear to the Soudanese and Saharan veterans that its journey had been as unpleasant as theirs. 'What a strange procession,' wrote one man. 'There are blacks of all races, men and women, all hideous, without a stitch of clothing to cover their bodies. From time to time a soldier walks by looking exhausted. They also suffered to get here!'[54] All three columns then combined to exterminate the enemy.

The enemy, of course, was the African countryside as much as Rabih Zubair, but he was a convenient scapegoat and they hunted him down as if he were personally responsible for their past humiliations and hardships. They caught up with him on 22 April, in a fort by the Chari and proceeded to destroy him. The battle was violent and very, very bloody. 'Bodies were everywhere,' recorded a French sergeant, 'the wounded got up to shoot their last bullet at us. Disembowelled horses lay across the streets. The straw huts were on fire and grilled our flesh . . . Everywhere men were fighting hand to hand. We bellowed, we fought, we tore into them like ferocious lions.'[55] Rabih Zubair's men were good, but they could not match the pent-up ferocity of Lamy and the practised butchery of the Central African Mission. The last cornered troops were shot down at point-blank range as they tried to escape over the walls. 'It was a terrible atrocity which I will never forget,' wrote one of Lamy's officers. 'This mass, which swarmed and jostled, the men stepping over the bodies, climbed over each other to reach the top of the rampart, where a bullet would bring them tumbling back down . . . Not one of them escaped and a mound of cadavers gradually piled up from which rose a sickening and insipid stench of hot blood. I turned away to be sick.'[56]

Hundreds of Africans had been killed against twenty-five *tirailleurs* dead and another seventy-five wounded. Lamy was among the invalids. Struck in the chest by a bullet, he lived long enough to see the head of Rabih Zubair brought to his bedside before he, too, died. Zubair's body was then dragged into a nearby village where 'men, women and children, everyone trampled on it, shouting their wild cries, so that tomorrow morning nothing will be left but a shapeless jelly'.[57] And thus ended the conquest of Lake Chad.

Foureau had not participated in the massacre. He had left on 2 April and, using canoes and porters from the Congo Mission, which he met en route, eventually reached Brazzaville, in the Congo, from where he travelled to the coast and 'took ship for France, happy in the thought that my work was now accomplished'.[58] He arrived in Marseilles on 2 September 1900. 'The circle is closed,' he wrote, 'the work is done, the dream pursued for so long has been realized! Farewell, African soil, be kind and hospitable to those who come after us!'[59] What, though, *had* Foureau accomplished? He had undergone many tribulations and in crossing the Sahara from Algeria to the Congo had fulfilled a long-held personal ambition. He had collected zoological and entomological specimens, had recorded the nature and composition of the terrain and had made anthropological observations of varying objectivity. (Of the women of Zinder: 'Their glossy bronze busts are, on the whole, of irreproachable design.').[60] But much of his route had already been pioneered by others, his so-called scientific mission was really an imperial one, and while he had passed through the Sahara he had failed to conquer it. If anything, his mission had reassured the Hoggar Tuareg of their invincibility; they sneered at the Europeans' helplessness. 'The mission has just traversed the

Sahara like a ship on the sea, leaving behind nothing but a wake which closes immediately,' wrote one Algerian officer. 'No treaty, no claims, no vigorous act showing that we are the masters. Pass through, pass through quickly, that seems to be the goal.'[61] All Foureau had done was help bring carnage to the Soudan.

French expansion into the Soudan and the Sahara was supposed to benefit the mother country's commerce. That had been the message promulgated by imperialists for more than forty years and on which the Transsaharian dream was based. Whether the Transsaharian was the right means of extracting the wealth of those regions remained as uncertain as ever. Foureau's assessment was negative: 'As a business concern, which will tie up enormous amounts of capital, I have very mediocre expectations of any return given the paucity of the trade I have witnessed.'[62] Still, railway or no railway, the official line prevailed: these colonies were valuable and there was money to be made. Unfortunately, the forces of capitalism took a diferent view. As a merchant named Ferdinand Laurens noted, French entrepreneurs appeared to have absolutely no interest in the Soudan. In the 1900 edition of the *Bulletin de la Société de Géographie Commerciale* he published an analysis of the goods on sale in the Soudan and the countries from which they came. The cotton was from England and Austria, the tea from Malta, the sugar from Austria, the glassware from Italy or Austria, the ironmongery from Germany or Austria, the jewellery from Germany, Austria, Italy and America, and (a gross insult) the perfume came from Bulgaria. He was able to find just one French company, Lemmonier of Rouen, that supplied a small amount of cloth to the Soudanese; apart from that, everything originated in other countries.

What was the point, Laurens asked, in building a trans-Saharan railway when French business could not be bothered to use existing avenues of trade? In fact, France's incursions into the desert had damaged national interest by driving commerce elsewhere. All the goods he mentioned had reached their destination if not by sea then by caravans from Morocco and Libya. None had passed through Algeria. Why waste money and lives, he asked, when the only result was that 'our African colonies constitute an outlet for foreign products'?[63] He published names and addresses that might be of use to French exporters – Mohammed el Hadj of Ghat, Mohammed el Alouad el Khadamsi of Ghadames, Boura el-Arbi, Mevorah Hassem, Raphael Hassoum and Ricardo Cesar of Tripoli – but he did not expect his advice to be taken up. Ruefully, he agreed with the opinion, held at home and in other countries, that France lacked decisiveness and initiative in its imperial programme. 'It is time,' he wrote, 'that our businessmen, if they cannot deal directly on the shores of Lake Chad, at least make arrangements with those who can. Perhaps then, it will not be solely on behalf of foreigners that Gentil, Foureau, Lamy and their comrades will have fought for this mysterious lake. We have so often plucked chestnuts from the fire that have been eaten by others; now we should pull some out for ourselves. But there is no time to lose because, if we hesitate, there will be no place for us around the fire.'[64]

Laurens spoke to the point. However, he still believed the imperialist propaganda that conquest fuelled commerce. Those in the field knew otherwise. The light had already dawned on Foureau who, having dismissed the Transsaharian's commercial usefulness, added, 'But, if you look upon it as an *instrument of domination* (some call it an *Imperial Railway*, which is the same thing), then, for this purpose alone, it will be a splendid project, smoothing over many difficulties and removing many obstacles. Its apostles defend it with vigour and hope ardently that its construction will be the first affirmation of 20th-century enterprise.'[65] In different ways, Foureau and Laurens were saying the same thing. The only fire around which their nation sought a place was that of imperial grandeur. Everything else could be dismissed. France was conquering Africa just for the sake of it.

The Transsaharian remained an enticing project. But despite the support of figures such as Ferdinand de Lesseps, the man who had engineered the Suez Canal – and who would have supported a trans-Saharan clothes-line if it gave him the chance to use heavy machinery – it remained low on the list of colonial priorities. All France wanted to do was to raise the *tricouleur* over as many African lands as was possible. It had already reached its limits under the accord signed with Britain – in itself a monumental expanse – yet there was one blank that still defied the mapmakers' pen. It could be found where Laperrine and others had always said it would – in the Tuareg heartlands of In Salah and the Hoggar.

8

'THINK THAT YOU
ARE GOING TO
DIE A MARTYR'

In 1900 a report was published in the *Journal of the Royal Geographical Society* on the state of French Africa. It covered less than two pages and was hidden among the back pages, alongside 'Dr. Kandt's Surveys in the Lake Kivu Region', and 'Pendulum Observations in German East Africa.' The first sentence read: 'Recent news shows that French activity in the Sahara, south of Algeria, has entered a new phase.'[1] Given the activity of the past few years, a French reader might have assumed this was an example of British understatement. Quite the opposite. Although the Royal Geographical Society journal was capable of stinging sarcasm, on this occasion it was being perfectly open. It was uninterested in the conquest of the Soudan; the names of Foureau, Lamy and Gentil did not appear once; neither was there a mention of the Central African Mission. Instead, the article singled out for 'special mention' Captain Henri Laperrine.

Since 1897, far from the massacres of the Soudan, Laperrine had been accustoming himself to life in Fort MacMahon. It was an eremetic existence. Sometimes a supply train might blow in from the north, but this hardly constituted a social life. In fact, the arrival of these columns, battered as they were by raiding Chaamba tribesmen, reinforced the sense of isolation. They emphasized how far Fort MacMahon was from Western civilization, how tenuous was its existence. As a man who sought solitude but conversely enjoyed company (by nature he was a raconteur) Laperrine adapted stoically to the situation. Most days he could be found in his quarters, staring silently at the whitewashed walls. Sometimes, however, the sirocco might strike, afflicting the black garrison and its two white officers alike with the *cafard*. 'One is fidgety,' Laperrine wrote, 'one becomes irritable without knowing why. The slightest joke is taken the wrong way, one becomes insupportable.'[2] On these occasions he would erupt from his reverie to hurl objects around the room or excoriate the black soldiers for misunderstanding his Arabic, which, although fluent, was spoken with a French accent that became thicker and more incomprehensible as his anger mounted.

In between the sirocco and the silence, Laperrine found ways to combat the tedium of desert service. The troops of MacMahon had little to do – and what they did do, in the way of attacking raiders, had little effect – so Laperrine donned his rakish kepi and led them on expeditions of reconnaissance. He mapped the immediate surroundings and then probed further into the Sahara, heading always for In Salah. He described where wells and pasturage could be found, which routes were best suited to an invading force and the nature of the people he met along the way. During these journeys he also had an opportunity to gauge the effectiveness of the camel-mounted spahis with which Fort MacMahon had been equipped since 1894. He was not entirely happy with their performance.

Introduced to Africa from Asia in about the first century BC, the camel is a unique example of nature's engineering, adapted like no other beast to desert conditions. Its feet are spongy and do not sink into the sand. It stores its energy as fat in its hump, the size of which provides an accurate measure of its vitality. (When pushed to its limits, the hump disappears.) Its stomach holds 200 litres of water and when those are exhausted it can survive for two or three days on the moisture left in its body tissues; moreover it can lose more than a quarter of its body weight in fluid with no ill effect and make it up again in a few minutes. The camel's blood does not thicken in heat, as happens to other animals, so it does not suffer from heatstroke. It can eat almost anything, from grass to the leaves that grow on the desert acacias, known as camel-thorns. And it travels at an energy-efficient pace: trotting, it manages maybe six kilometres per hour; when pressed it will go to nine; and in emergencies it will move at twenty, but for only a few minutes. Rarely it can be provoked to high speeds: there are tales of camels covering more than 300 kilometres in two days. But, although capable of great endurance, its stamina is unpredictable: it does not flag like normal beasts but keeps up a steady pace until, without warning, it keels over: 'When it is at the end of its tether, it suddenly stops, cowers down and dies with considerable dignity and a far-away expression, as if its thoughts are elsewhere. It has a slightly roguish look, as if it is about to play one splendid, final trick on its master.'[3] And therein lies another trait of the camel for, although normally docile – Arab legend tells of a camel tethered by a jerboa that dragged its reins down its burrow – it is notoriously dismissive of those who try to ride it.

France had an unsuccessful history of adapting camels to military service. At the dawn of the nineteenth century, Napoleon had tried to form a camel corps in Egypt. Expecting them to perform like horses, he had been disappointed by their plodding nature and obstinacy. There was also the difficulty of finding men to ride them, for their yawing stride made life in the saddle uncomfortable. Soldiers complained of sea-sickness, upon which Napoleon replaced them with marines. But it made no difference. They were experimented with once more, during the conquest of Algeria's southern oases, but were rejected for the same reasons. Thereafter, although soldiers were occasionally made to travel on them – officers usually went on horseback – they were relegated to the role of carrying burdens or, when supplies failed, of food.

Laperrine knew about camels. He had ridden a few and had learned much from his contacts in the Bureau Arabe. Onlookers were amazed by the way he could leap aboard the hump and then, seizing the reins with his bare feet, direct the animal with a twitch of his toes. His MacMahon spahis, however, could not do the same. Recruited mostly from Algeria's highlands, they were magnificent on horseback but floundered when faced with camels. The seat was uncomfortable and the ride unfamiliar. Despite training, they were oblivious to the finer points of camel maintenance – they did not know how to tether them, feed them, dress their sores, or to tell when they needed rest. In modern terms they were like learners driving a car for the first time: they knew what to do with the accelerator, the brake and the steering wheel, but they had a hazy knowledge of gears and no idea whatsoever of what lay beneath the bonnet.

Laperrine made the best he could of this amateur force. Each sortie filled in yet another slice of the unknown and within two years of his arrival he had completed a map of the area between MacMahon and In Salah. Admittedly, it wasn't a very accurate map, having been drawn under constant fear of attack and with the use of no finer instrument than a compass, but it could be followed by anyone willing to conquer the Tuat and thence In Salah. Laperrine very much wanted to be that person, but he was denied the pleasure. In 1899 he was promoted, recalled to France, and sent to a training school in Sampigny, a small village in the Vosges, from where he watched impotently as events unfolded in the Sahara in exactly the way he had foreseen.

The Foureau–Lamy expedition had concluded in 1900 in a barrage of back-slapping. Even before the applause began, however, more astute members of the colonial faction realized that a simple traverse of the desert would not deliver the gains they sought. They needed the Tuat and In Salah if they were to control the Sahara. How, though, were they to seize these strategic areas? Morocco still claimed that it owned the Tuat, and Britain still supported its claim. The Sultan of Morocco could be ignored, for he had neither the means to defend the Tuat nor much intention of doing so. But the British were notoriously protective of their foreign clients and an invasion of the Tuat might lead to war. This, France did not want. In 1899, fortuitously, Britain was fully occupied with the Boers of South

Africa. Anticipating an easy victory it had already struck medals to commemorate the campaign – the obverse bore a winged victory clutching a laurel wreath, above it the date 1899 – but the war took longer than expected, and while the Royal Mint was scrubbing the date off its medals France judged the time to be ripe. There was still a niggling fear that outright invasion would be ill-received in diplomatic circles, so the military advanced, as it had done with the Foureau–Lamy expedition, under the guise of science. One M. Flamand, a geologist from Algiers, was invited to survey the Tuat. Naturally, he could not go there without protection. Thus, when he departed from Ouargla on 28 November 1899, he carried a small hammer for picking at rocks and was accompanied by an artillery detachment and almost 150 soldiers, whose task was to ensure that he could wield his hammer in peace.

A black comedy of errors ensued. As the military knew would be the case, the inhabitants of the Tuat – not Tuareg but settled oasis-dwellers – resented the approach of an armed column and defended themselves vigorously. Flamand's escort responded with measured volleys and accurate cannon fire. One by one, the fortified villages of the Tuat were broken down but, not entirely confident of success, Flamand's men sent for the spahis of Laperrine's old commanding officer, St Germain. The spahis performed wonderfully but when the action was over they suddenly discovered that they had brought insufficient food to see them back to Fort MacMahon. As In Salah was the nearest reprovisioning point, it was deemed necessary to take it; which they did, almost without resistance. Then, in an unforeseen chain of events, more than 1,500 raiders crept down from the Moroccan Atlas to snatch back the Tuat. Flamand sent a courier to Ouargla, asking for reinforcements. They came, saw, reconquered and departed, leaving behind a small garrison that immediately felt threatened and once more called for reinforcements. An infantry force supported by artillery, cavalry, sappers, 1,579 camels, and accompanied by a flock of more than 2,400 sheep, marched hurriedly south from El Goléa. Upon their arrival the French felt they could finally call the oases their own.

The overkill was remarked upon even in Paris. As one journal put it, 'the whole affair resulted from the excursion of a peaceable geologist, M. Flamand, who had been breaking stones with his little geologist's hammer a little too close to In Salah, and had been attacked by its wicked inhabitants. The government was forced to protect M. Flamand [and then] to protect detachments which had gone to each other's assistance after the first detachment had gone to assist the original geologist. Thus, the whole policy of our country in the Sahara would appear to have been nothing but a rescue operation in several stages.' It scoffed at the minister responsible – 'Like a child before its elders, he swears he did not do it on purpose.'4

Purposely or not, the deed had been done; and, as was the nature of these things, it could not be undone. The French therefore found themselves in possession of yet another piece of the Sahara. It was a more productive bit of desert than some – which wasn't saying much: its annual turnover was described as roughly the same as that of 'a grocery store in a large town'5 – and it was certainly an important gain if the Transsaharian was ever to be built. (Predictably, there was renewed interest in the project.) All the same, most French men and women remained indifferent to the Sahara's charms. By 1901, when at last the *tricouleur* hung limply but triumphantly over the Tuat, the only people who cared whether it stood or fell were the military, the railway projectors and a rebellious monk named Brother Marie-Albéric.

In 1897, when the Foureau–Lamy expedition left Biskra, Charles de Foucauld was already – in his mind at least – preparing for a return to the desert. In a spiritual sense, the last few years had been disappointing. Although spartan, conditions at the Trappist monastery of Akbès were not as abstemious as he would have liked. There was, for example, the papally sanctioned introduction of butter to the diet: 'We no longer have our dear cooking with salt and water,' Foucauld wrote, 'but they put I don't know what greasy stuff in our food . . . A little less mortification is a little less given to God; a little more expense is a little less given to the poor . . . and then where will it stop? Down what slope are we sliding? May God preserve us.'6 And then, to compound his distress, the once remote monastery of Akbès found itself at the heart of international affairs.

While France and other West European nations sought glory abroad, Turkey bolstered its authority with domestic mayhem. In 1896 Abdul Hamid II, Sultan of the Ottoman Empire and titular Caliph of the Islamic faith, launched a pogrom against the Armenian Christians scattered throughout his realm. It was an exceptionally bloody extermination, in which Kurdish auxiliaries were employed to slaughter hundreds of thousands of Armenians. Foucauld witnessed just a part of it. 'All around us were horrors;' he wrote, 'many of the Christians were really martyrs, for they died voluntarily without defending themselves rather than deny their Faith. There is frightful misery in this unfortunate country. The winter is very hard . . . By the Sultan's orders, in a few months nearly 140,000 Christians were murdered. At Marache, the nearest town to us, 4,500 Christians in two days. We, at Akbès, and all the Christians within two days of us ought to have perished. I was not worthy . . . Pray that next time I shall no longer be thrust back from the already half-open gates of heaven.'[7] As an erstwhile man of the world he could not help but add a commentary on the diplomatic situation that allowed the atrocities to proceed. 'It is a disgrace to all Europe; with a single word she could have prevented these horrors. The Turkish government has bought the press and given huge sums to certain papers to publish only *their* communiqués. But the governments know the truth from their embassies and consulates.'[8]

Privately, Foucauld sympathized with the Ottomans; he damned the Armenians as troublemakers and appreciated the troops that were sent to guard Akbès against the Kurds. The pogrom, however, was yet another signal that Akbès could not deliver the nullification he sought. He pondered the idea of retreating to some distant place and there creating a monastic order of his own, one that would be harsher and purer than any other, one that took denial to its limits. He wrote to Abbé Huvelin, describing the abstinence he had in mind. Huvelin's response was negative. 'I am heart broken,' he wrote, 'Your rule is absolutely impracticable . . . The Pope hesitated to give his approbation to the Franciscan rule; he found it too severe . . . But this rule! . . . To tell you the truth, it scared me! Live at the door of a community, in the abjection you wish . . . but I beseech you, don't make a rule.'[9] Foucauld followed his advice. In 1897 he left Akbès – 'where I have by no means found what I was wanting,' – and travelled to Nazareth where he enrolled as general handyman with a community of Poor Clares.

Foucauld's idea had been that he would 'live there without anyone knowing who I was, as a workman living by his daily labours'.[10] Unfortunately, this was not how things turned out. His 'labourer's' costume, which consisted of turban, sandals and blue cotton pyjamas wrapped around with a wide leather belt from which hung an outsize rosary, made him an object of instant curiosity. (Gratifyingly, he was able to horrify a young European woman: 'I am so scared of vermin,'[11] she said to her husband, as Foucauld drew nigh.) The Poor Clares soon discovered who this curiously dressed man really was. And it became rapidly apparent that his labouring skills were minimal: having witnessed his attempts at wall-building, carpentry and gardening, the Poor Clares assigned him to sweeping (Saturdays) and fetching the mail (Thursdays and Sundays). His own description of life in Nazareth hardly conformed to any recognizable image of labour: 'Very often I draw little pictures for the Sisters. If there are any small jobs I do them, but this is rare; generally I spend the whole day doing little things in my little room.'[12] Nevertheless, he believed he had broken successfully into a working man's existence. He wrote triumphantly of how he had arrived 'without any papers but my passport, and on the sixth day I found not only a means of earning my living but of earning it under just the conditions I had been dreaming of for so many years; it seemed as though this place was waiting for me, and indeed it was waiting for me, for nothing happens by chance, and everything that happens has been prepared by God; I am a servant, the domestic, the valet, of a poor religious community.'[13]

The Poor Clares treated him with benevolent respect. They did not demur when he turned down their offered accommodation and opted instead to sleep in a small tool shed overlooking a paddock. Nor

did they insist, beyond a delicate suggestion that a bowl of soup might
be fortifying, that he accept any more than the dry bread, twice a
day, which he asked as his wage. They maintained his own pretence
that he was a simple nobody and did not mind when he seemed
unable to do anything beyond the most trivial chores. There were
occasions, however, when outsiders were surprised by Foucauld's
behaviour. A visiting bishop became intolerant at his continual fawn-
ing and demanded he be sent back to work; another was amazed at his
attempts to cut his own hair and assumed he had ring-worm; a third
was bewildered when, on asking why he looked so happy, he received
the answer that children had thrown stones at him in the street. His
confessor, the only person he saw on a regular basis other than the
Poor Clares, remarked that 'He is a very good boy, but not one of the
most intelligent.'[14]

If Foucauld seemed unintelligent it was probably because his confessor judged him by conventional standards. Foucauld was perfectly
rational, he could make incisive political comments when he felt like
it, and he retained enough military expertise for the Poor Clares to
give him a shotgun to defend their hen-run. But he was not interested
in rationality, politics or guns. His self-declared aim was 'a deeper
dispossession and a greater lowliness so that I might be still more
like Jesus'.[15] In his little room he prayed, pondered God, flagellated
himself daily – 'not hard, never till I draw blood, but for a fairly long
time'[16] – and wrote long, abnegatory tracts in his journal. One particular entry revealed the extent of his morbidity: 'Think that you are
going to die a martyr, stripped of everything, stretched out on the
ground, hardly recognizable, covered with blood and wounds, violently and painfully killed . . . and wish it to be today . . . Think of this
death often, prepare yourself for it and judge things at their true
value.'[17] Whatever his confessor may have thought was of sublime
indifference. So was the fate of the Poor Clares' hens, all of them
eaten by jackals while their guardian contemplated the Almighty.

Foucauld still cherished the idea of forming some kind of order and
by 1899, despite Huvelin's advice to the contrary, he had completed
a first draft of a rule for 'The Little Brothers of the Sacred Heart of

Jesus'. He went no further than that, but the very act of putting his thoughts to paper was an indication that, yet again, he was becoming dissatisfied with his present existence. An even stronger indication was the bizarre plan he hatched the following year: he would buy the Mount of Beatitudes for the Franciscans and build there a sanctuary in which he and possibly one other priest would spend their lives in worship. 'There on the mountain,' he explained, 'lonely, isolated, among hostile Arabs I shall need every instant a firm faith; here, at Nazareth, on the contrary now, I lack nothing. Therefore it is there that my faith will get most exercise ... Here, more distractions are offered by my surroundings; there, I could spend much more time in front of the Blessed Sacrament. Here, face to face with myself, I am superior to my condition; there, as a priest, ignorant and incapable, I shall be profoundly below it.'[18] The idea that the Mount of Beatitudes might be bought and sold like any other piece of property may seem extraordinary today. But there it was, on the market like any other piece of land, and it was being offered for 13,000 francs. Foucauld immediately wrote to his family for the money. His plan had flaws: even if he bought the hill and built the sanctuary, the Franciscans could not afford to maintain it; nor could they guarantee to supply him with a spare priest; and there was no certainty that the site he wanted to buy was indeed the Mount of Beatitudes. Foucauld was undeterred. 'Offering myself in a strange habit, asking to live a particular kind of life, to establish a tabernacle in a holy place whose authenticity is doubtful, I shall be, from the first day, the object of every mockery, rebuff and contradiction. Alone in a desert, with a native Christian, who will be absolutely esssential, in the midst of savage and hostile populations, I shall find more opportunity to exercise my courage.'[19] As an afterthought, he mentioned that the Mount might be a good place to start his new order.

'I am horrified by your projects,' Huvelin replied. While accepting reluctantly the purchase, he was appalled by Foucauld's idea of establishing an order. 'I can see nothing but objections, and I fear the stubbornness of character that underlies your devotion and piety ... If you can withdraw, pray do so.'[20] Foucauld did not withdraw.

Instead, he walked to Jerusalem to ask permission of the Patriarch to establish a community of Little Brothers under his jurisdiction. He did not make a good impression: his trousers, worn away at the knees from prayer, were patched with paper; and his sandals, having like-wise given out, were replaced by blocks of wood tied to his feet with string; his face was red and swollen from sunburn. The Patriarch liked his proposal no more than he liked his appearance. 'He sent me away quite quickly,'[21] Foucauld recorded. Still, he persisted. When the money arrived (along with another letter from Huvelin: 'Don't get yourself involved in financial transactions. I absolutely forbid it.'),[22] Foucauld duly paid 13,000 francs for the freehold of the Mount of Beatitudes. He never received the deeds. When the deal was completed he discovered that the vendor had already sold the property to someone else.

It was a blow, but perhaps a predictable one. Ever since the death of his parents, Foucauld had existed on a cocktail of impulse, innocence and optimism and had suffered the inevitable disappointments. Working towards a goal whose attainment he had yet precisely to fathom, he had arrayed himself in a variety of masks all of which had, after an initial bout of enthusiasm, proved to be inadequate. When this latest venture peeled off like a false moustache, it gave him a disheartening glimpse of reality. Suddenly he appreciated that life with the Poor Clares, which he had previously listed as one of the milestones on his spiritual path, was a sham. 'My stay with the Poor Clares cannot continue indefinitely,' he wrote. 'If I were unknown, if I had been unknown when I came, if I had been useful, with a well demarcated job of work, perhaps it would have been possible. But I was known before I entered, and I was received because I was known (without being told), and though I try honestly to gain my bread, I feel I am not in my place . . . Moreover (which is more serious), to follow the crucified Christ I must lead a life at the cross, and here it is a life of delights. It is rest, peace, enjoyment, it cannot last; I must not fall asleep among these pleasures but must suffer with Jesus.'[23]

He left the Holy Land for Europe in August 1900. He was unsure where his road might take him but he knew, for certain, that he could not belong to any branch of organized religion. If he was to achieve the anguish he believed to be his destiny, and if he wanted the death for which he prayed but which was consistently denied him, then he would have to seek it on his own and without constraint. He still hoped to establish an order but his main wish was to lead the life of Jesus (as he interpreted it) and if possible to take it to a similar conclusion. Others were welcome to join him – he hoped fervently that they would – but they would have to live not by instruction from above nor with the aim of proselytizing the faith. They would have to be, like himself, passive in the face of hardship, contemptuous of comfort, teaching only by example.

During much of 1900 he did not demonstrate such an example. In France he resumed a Western lifestyle, dressing in the accepted mode, lunching with Huvelin and other friends, visiting his family, travelling here and there by train. In September, however, he returned to the Trappists of Notre-Dame-des-Neiges where he fell into a kind of ecstasy. 'He behaved like an automaton,' wrote one man, 'his spirit was soaring in continual prayer.'[24] Axiomatically, he now accepted the strictures that had caused him to leave first Akbès and then Nazareth. He stayed with the Trappists for more than eight months training to be a priest and finally took orders on 9 June 1901. But although he accepted priesthood he was, once again, working to his own agenda. As he later recalled, 'The divine Banquet of which I was becoming minister must be offered, not to the relatives and to the rich, but to the lame, the blind and the poor, that is to say, to souls lacking priests.'[25] Where would he find these people? Coincidentally, in the one place where he could also be guaranteed the sparsest living available to any priest in the world. 'In my youth I had travelled all over Algeria and Morocco,' he wrote. 'In Morocco, as big as France, with 10,000,000 inhabitants, not a single priest in the interior; in the Sahara, seven or eight times as big as France, and much more inhabited than was thought earlier, a mere dozen missionaries. No people seemed to be more abandoned than these.'[26]

On 9 September 1901 he boarded a ship at Marseilles. He reached Algiers the day after, carrying a quantity of tent canvas, some empty sacks to serve as rugs, forty-five metres of rope and a bucket (for wells), plus a small number of books and the fittings for a private, desert chapel.

9

BENI ABBÈS

Algiers had changed since Foucauld had last seen it. It was still white, the roses and bougainvillea still blossomed in the suburbs of Mustapha, and the streets were as crowded by day and as sinister by night as they had been when he first arrived in the colony. But it had filled out in the last twenty years, becoming less a statement of colonial intent and more a working city complete with all the labour disputes and petty political squabbles that epitomized its French counterparts. In fact, it was quite an exciting place to be; and in 1901, the year in which Foucauld hauled his hermit's baggage up the steps that led from the quay to the seafront esplanade, aided by a bishop and archbishop from the order of White Fathers, it was more exciting than usual.

The city had two problems in 1901, of which its Mayor, M. Max Regis, was the most immediate. Regis belonged to an anti-Semitic party of the kind that, since the Dreyfus affair, had lain low in France but was still active in Algeria. On 21 April, stones were thrown and shots were fired when Regis delivered one of his more virulent speeches. Nine days later he got into an argument with two newspaper proprietors, during which M. Tallhouidée of the *Nouvelles* drew a revolver and shot him in the head, while M. Labardesque of the *Revanche des Peuples* 'assisted'. It was a glancing wound. That same night Regis retired to a chemist's shop where he, along with two of his cohorts who had also been injured, had his wounds dressed. All three then returned to the café in which they had been attacked, wrecked it from top to bottom, and marched back to Regis's office, singing loudly. Regis blamed the Prefect of Algiers, an innocuous liberal named Lautaud, for trying to orchestrate his death. He also blamed M. Jonnart, the Governor-General of Algeria, who had been appointed only the previous October, for being too soft on the natives. And then he sacked three police commissioners for having insufficiently protected his person. Jonnart retorted by placing a ban on all public gatherings, and Lautaud ordered the dissolution of all anti-Semitic committees as a menace to the peace. Regis promptly held several more public gatherings in which, to cheers, he distributed anti-Semitic pamphlets denouncing his superiors as poltroons. Exhausted by the struggle, and in ill-health, Jonnart resigned his post. His successor from 22 May, Paul Revoil, an ex-journalist and erstwhile Minister to Morocco and Brazil, assumed control of the police, the magistrates, the military and such civil servants as Algeria possesed, effectively stripping Regis of his powers. On 3 July, Regis resigned in order 'to be able to continue with more acrimony his campaign against M. Lautaud the Prefect, and against the Jews'.[1] On 15 July, Lautaud, 'wretch, robber and assassin', also quit his post – with some relief, for he had announced his departure three months before. On 17 July, Regis was stabbed in the neck, causing a scuffle in which thirty people were arrested. And so it all went on. French newspapers reported events with censure but no great surprise. This, they had come to learn, was how colonists conducted their affairs.

Algiers' second and greater problem, however, was that it was still an alien enclave surrounded by hostile North Africans. Outwardly, it was a bustling capital, filled with people of every skin colour and religious persuasion. It was raucous with life – an eclipse of the sun on 1 June caused the hubbub to subside only slightly –

and its industrial facilities were so advanced that when French dock-
ers went on strike so did those of Algeria, African and European
alike. It remained a popular spot for tourists and those suffering
from respiratory diseases: General Sir Donald Stewart, a stalwart of
the British Empire, had died there of asthma only the year before. It
controlled more than 120,000 hectares of vineyards, whose produce
enabled France to reject the cheap, Spanish brands with which it
diluted its second-grade wines. Between Algiers and Oran there
were whole cliffs of phosphate, enough to fertilize all Europe for the
rest of the century. Prospectors in South Oran had discovered oil
strata that would fuel the world's automobiles for an indefinite
period: twelve companies were already clamouring for concessions.
Its wheat and barley yields were multiplying satisfactorily. The population was increasing at the rate of 5 per cent per annum. With luck
and application, Algeria would soon meet many of France's import
requirements at a very satisfactory price and have enough left over to
become an international exporter. When one considered these advantages – which Paris did, loudly and often, during 1901 – Algiers shone
like a jewel amongst colonial capitals.

Yet, for all its apparent prosperity, Algiers was still a rough-and-
tumble frontier town, as the Regis affair proved. Moreover, the
population that it governed did not enjoy the country's wealth in
equal measures. According to the census published in November
1901, Algeria contained 4,774,000 inhabitants of whom 291,000 were
French, 292,000 were non-French Europeans (mostly Italians,
Maltese and Spaniards) and the rest were Africans. Comparatively,
this was perceived as an excellent percentage of black to white. No
other nation was as successful as France when it came to planting
white settlers in an African colony. But no other nation had striven so
indefatigably to achieve this goal. As far as most colonizing countries
were concerned, Africa was a supplier of raw materials and a market
for manufactured goods. White settlers were encouraged to occupy
the newly available land, but they came in relatively small numbers
and were an adjunct to conquest rather than its motivating force. In
Algeria, however, settlement was a priority. Native farmers were

pushed aside in favour of a competing class of white smallholders whose land-grabbing was enforced by an ever larger army. (The 1901 census recorded that the increase in Algeria's French population over the last five years was due mainly to an injection of 40,000 troops.) Even in outlying districts, where displaced Algerians had once been able to make a living, French colonists had started to encroach upon their independence. The 'mixed commune' system, for example, was intended to harness African labour to European skills with the aim of introducing the work force to the concept of supply and demand, bringing them within a framework of taxes and benefits, and thereby allowing them better to appreciate the joys of capitalism. In reality, it meant that a few colonists exercised tyrannical powers over pockets of up to 30–40,000 Algerians, occupied their land for so-called municipal purposes, and spent the taxes they levied on an infrastructure (forts, and the roads and bridges leading to them) that was beneficial only to their own increased security. Such small steps as the Algerians took towards financial independence were damned by agencies over which they had no control – in 1901, for example, the British market for Esparto grass bottomed, destroying the liveli-hoods of the Atlas highlanders who gathered it. The Parisian newspaper, *Le Temps*, had nothing good to say about the system: 'Taxes, injustice and insults – that is about all the natives have.'[2] *The Times* of London was no less damning: 'The natives pay the majority of the taxes and receive little enough in exchange . . . They are placed in a situation in which they must choose between resignation to utter misery and revolt.'[3]

The revolt started in the Sahara, on 2 July 1900, when five Italians of the Foreign Legion were decapitated near the Tuat and Lieutenant Lan of the 1st Algerian Spahis was speared to death, and then spread north. On 28 April 1901, the village of Marguerite, population 150–200, eighty kilometres from Algiers, was attacked by 400 angry tribesmen. Very few people escaped. A few days later a goods train was derailed. A detachment of gendarmes, sent to investigate, was murdered to a man. Not long after, a coach was ambushed, the driver critically wounded and a priest outraged by a bullet that passed through his cassock. Almost daily, throughout the spring of 1901, colonists received news of fresh atrocities in the countryside – an incursion here, a farmer and his wife killed there – to which they responded with demands for military assistance and, when the assistance did not immediately appear, with outbursts of violence. Some blamed English missionaries, who had 'diffused contempt and hatred for France from one end of the country to another'.[4] Others said it was the work of Regis's anti-Jonnart faction, who were trying to subvert the Governor-General's liberal programme with acts of deliberate sabotage. Jonnart himself blamed Regis's riots. 'It would be childish,' he said on 30 April, 'to conceal how contagious and deadly may be in this colony the example of our civil discords and the madness of the persecution of races'.[5] The real cause of the uprising, however, had nothing to do with internal politics, nor with British missionaries. (The government later retracted the accusations and sacked the Prefect of Constantine who had made them.) It stemmed instead from France's actions in the Sahara.

In conquering the Tuat and In Salah, the French had acted with the aim not only of tightening their grip on the desert but of preparing the way for an invasion of Morocco. For a long time politicians had been saying that the imperial programme in Africa was pointless and costly. In November 1900, a retired diplomat named D'Estournelles got up and said it again: 'France has a tendency when she has obtained one possession to try to extend it, as though every colonial possession, however useless or onerous, is an advantage, at the risk of provoking the most dangerous conflicts . . . These imprudencies should be arrested.'[6] But for an equally long time it had been obvious that the only reason Morocco remained independent was because nobody could decide who should have it. Britain, France, Germany and Spain were all interested in the country. So, in a fantastical way, was Russia. Yet no one (with the exception of Spain, whose armed incursions were so feeble that everyone ignored them) had been willing to risk the balance of European power by offending the others with a blatant show of force. France saw its chance. Proceeding on the assumption that Morocco should long ago have been part of the

French Empire, and that therefore the arguments against expansion did not apply, and reasoning that where straightforward invasion might fail, an engineered 'provocation' might be successful, and taking into account Britain's continuing engagement in South Africa, it might be possible to get away with a small amount of force, and considering the undelimited boundary between Algerian and Moroccan desert, the French colonial faction decided it was time to strike. Therefore, when the various contingents that came to Flamand's rescue occupied the Tuat, they also seized, in March 1901, the north-western oasis of Igli.

In the grand scale of imperial design, the occupation of Igli was an innocuous event: it was a small oasis and its inhabitants surrendered without firing a shot. To the military, Igli's capture made perfect sense: situated at the head of the river which fed the Tuat oases it was a logical extension of their previous conquests. Also, it was a notorious troublespot, being the nearest point of pillage for Atlas tribesmen, who targeted the trans-Saharan caravans and over whom nobody seemed to have any control: in 1894, Morocco's Sultan Moulai Hassan had led an expeditionary force to extract taxes from them; he had been driven back and had died ignominiously during the retreat. Obviously, therefore, a French presence in Igli was desirable. Unfortunately, the French had no right to be in Igli. When the Moroccan–Algerian frontier had been agreed in 1845, both parties had decided it was pointless to include the desert; broadly, however, it was accepted that if one drew a line south of the accepted demarcation, which stopped at a point between Aïn Sefra (Algerian) and the town of Figuig (Moroccan), everything to the west belonged to Morocco and everything to the east to Algeria. Since then, strange things had been happening on French maps. With every decade, the frontier seemed to shrink northwards until, by 1900, Aïn Sefra and Figuig, both of whose status had been defined in 1845, now appeared as undetermined points in the desert. Even so, it was still possible to draw a line south and from whatever point one drew it, Igli was approximately 200 kilometres to its west.

Moulai Hassan's successor, Abd el-Aziz – a twenty-year-old, bicycle-riding Anglophile, famous for a love of gadgetry so overwhelming that he installed an elevator in his one-storey palace – addressed the situation with greater tact. He approached all the Great Powers of Europe, complaining that his country's interests were being damaged and pleading for assistance to reverse this injustice. But he was a young man and his Vizier, an experienced diplomat who might have been able to help, had just died. Indeed, his pleas rebounded against him, for they gave France the opportunity to present the world with their 'provocation'. In 1900, acting suspiciously counter to their previous policy of keeping individuals away from the border area, the Algerian authorities had given a French traveller permission to enter Morocco. Predictably, he had been killed by bandits. France pointed out that if the Sultan could not control his own domain then someone had to do it for him, so it was just as well they had conquered Igli; and while the Sultan was to hand, perhaps he should consider some compensation. The affair was put in the hands of Paul Revoil, whose appointment as Governor-General of Algiers was postponed so that he could deal with it, and the Sultan backed off in disarray, accepting at the same time a loan of 7.5 million francs from the Banque de Paris et des Pays-Bas. (America and Germany were also expecting compensation for similar 'provocations' and the Sultan's income was small.) In incremental stages, the French had begun their occupation of Morocco.

In Paris, many saw this as an unwelcome development. Georges Clemenceau, the bullish statesman who later won notoriety as an architect of the 1919 Treaty of Versailles, and whose defence of France's interests earned him the nickname 'The Tiger', could see no advantage. 'Morocco is a mere wasp's nest,' he declared. 'We might, to be sure, take possession of it, but at what a cost of blood and treasure . . . [if] the pretext of the French intervention lies in the inability of the Sultan to reduce the rebel tribes to submission, we shall have to undertake this responsibility. This is not a small business. In any case, the taxpayers will do well to provide themselves with small change for an eventuality which seems near at hand.'[7] Clemenceau was mistaken only in his estimate of time: it was 1912 before France finally succeeded in establishing a protectorate over

Morocco. Meanwhile, taxpayers continued to pay their francs and the military continued to spend them more or less as it saw fit. Some of the money went to completing the conquest of the Sahara; more of it was spent in preparing for an advance on Morocco. From the South Oran to the Tuat, garrisons swelled as Foreign Legionnaires, Algerian *tirailleurs* and spahis were ordered to the Moroccan border. The troops were stationed in barracks of rudimentary sophistication, of which Beni Abbès, thirty kilometres south of Igli, was one of the more remote.

Occupied on 3 March 1901, Beni Abbès did not, officially, belong to the Tuat; but its human and topographical composition made it indistinguishable from those oases that did. Containing some 1,500 people, it lay on the dried bed of the Souara (a river that rose in the Moroccan Grand Atlas and had once run overground but now appeared only at infrequent points along its course) and comprised a three-kilometre-wide forest of 7,000 palm trees in whose shade grew strips of barley and orchards of apricot, peach and fig trees. At its heart lay a fortified town of covered streets, home to the Berber farmers who worked the surrounding groves. On its outskirts were two villages: one, a collection of tents, harboured a small group of nomads; the other, a rudimentary slum of shacks, housed the slaves who worked both for the farmers and for the nomads. Meanwhile, on a plateau outside the oasis, gleamed the newly built *bordj*, or redoubt, of the French army. To the north and east, the *bordj* looked onto the Western Erg, whose pink dunes, up to 180 metres high, rippled into the distance. To the west, a hard, flat pavement of rocks reached out towards Morocco. To the south lay hundreds of kilometres of black rock and shale. And to the south-east the Souara flowed, intermittently, through the regions of Gouara, Tuat and Tidikelt, that together made up the Tuat complex, before vanishing beneath the Sahara. It was beautiful but it was solitary: the nearest point of supply for its 800-strong garrison (three companies of Algerian *tirailleurs*, one of French light infantry, and a handful of spahis) was the rail-head at Aïn Sefra, several hundred kilometres away in South Oran. It was

also dangerous, for the threat of attack from Morocco had not subsided. In short, Beni Abbès was about as remote and uncomfortable
a spot as anyone could wish for.

'It is decided,' wrote Foucauld, 'that I shall establish myself in a French
garrison which is called Beni Abbès. It is an important Saharan oasis
situated on the Moroccan frontier. I am to carry the Blessed Sacrament
further into the south and to the west than it has ever been in all
probability, and certainly since the time of St Augustine, to sanctify the
infidels by this divine Presence and to carry the consolations of religion
to our dying soldiers; this is a very great, very fine mission, but one
which requires much virtue . . . I shall be actually alone as a priest; the
nearest colleague will be some 450 kilometres away.'[8]

When Foucauld said it was 'decided', he really meant that he had
arranged it. Shortly after his ordination, and before he had even sailed
for Africa, he had begun pestering his military contacts for assistance.
He had first written to Henri de Castries, a fellow campaigner from
the Bou-Amama days, to ask his help in finding a remote spot for a
'little foundation'.[9] Castries had passed him on to the Director of
Native Affairs in Algiers, another old St Cyrien named Major Lacroix,
who was only too pleased to facilitate his desire to be placed in 'some
solitary oasis between Aïn Sefra and the Tuat'.[10] To Castries, Lacroix
and others, Foucauld was frank about his intentions: 'to found on the
Moroccan frontier, not a Trappist house, not a big monastery, not a
centre for agricultural development, but a sort of humble little hermitage where a few poor monks could live on fruit and a little barley
harvested with their own hands, in narrow enclosure, in penance and
adoration of the blessed Sacrament, not going outside their enclosure, not preaching but giving hospitality to all comers, good or bad,
friend or foe, Muslim or Christian.'[11] When seeking permission of
the religious authorities, however, he explained himself in more conventional terms, using the argument that French soldiers were dying
in the desert without the benefit of the last rites. 'The memory of my
companions who died without sacraments in the expeditions against
Bou-Amama twenty years ago, in which I took part, impels me to

leave for the Sahara,'[12] he wrote. And he added a rider that he knew would appeal to all parties: 'This is evangelization, not through words, but through the presence of the Most Blessed Sacrament, the offering of the divine sacrifice, prayer, penance, the practice of evangelical virtues.'[13]

Evangelization was the mortar that imperialists hoped would turn the desert from conquered territory to complaisant colony. The conversion of Muslims to Christianity was encouraged not only for the souls it would save but for the very real saving it would make in the cost of policing the Sahara. For a long time the Church had worked towards this goal, the most obvious manifestation of its intent being the creation in 1873 by Algiers' Archbishop Lavigerie of the White Fathers, a group of missionaries whose task was to pacify the Tuareg with their divine message. (A similar order of nuns, the White Sisters, was established to provide spiritual continuity in the White Fathers' wake.) Unfortunately, the White Fathers met with a hostile reception – which was not surprising for they were a grim bunch of crusaders. White-robed and bearded (the clothes and facial hair were obligatory), they established themselves in Algeria and later in Tunisia before descending on the Sahara. 'Algeria is nothing but a door opened by Providence to a barbarous continent of two million souls,'[14] the Archbishop exhorted. Stern and authoritarian, clearly the emissaries of a colonial power, they marched forwards. In 1876 Lavigerie wrote: 'At this moment three of our missionaries are with the Tuaregs en route for Timbuctoo. They are resolved to establish themselves permanently in the capital of the Soudan or to give their lives in the cause of eternal truth.'[15] They were cut to pieces. At the White Fathers' next convocation they all sang the *Te Deum* and swore to avenge their comrades, 'who had fallen on the field of honour of the Apostolate'.[16] Meanwhile, Lavigerie sent stinging messages to those in the field. 'The Protestants,' he wrote in 1877 to one missionary, 'have sought a route through the Sahara for less time than us and they are succeeding. And you, who have the support of the Good Lord, you who have a mission to go forward, are doing nothing. You are leading us nowhere. I do not understand you at all.'[17] In deference to Lavigerie's wishes three missionaries went to the Adjer, where they were duly murdered. Lavigerie died in 1892, and his zealotry went with him. By the turn of the century the White Fathers had established themselves only in areas that had already been occupied by the military, a stigma that reduced still further their standing amongst those they sought to convert. In 1901, when Charles Guérin, an ascetic White Father in his twenties, was appointed Bishop of the Sahara, he was very aware that while his diocese may have been the largest in the world it also contained the smallest number of Christians.

Guérin was excited by Foucauld's plan: where instruction had failed, maybe example would succeed. Moreover, Foucauld's mystic version of Christianity was a kind that many Muslims respected. Everyone with whom he corresponded on the matter offered encouragement. Dom Henri, prior of Staouëli, the Trappist monastery outside Algiers, wrote that, 'He walks with giant steps along the road of sacrifice, and has an insatiable desire to devote himself to the redemption of the infidel. He is capable of everything . . . His mere presence is an eloquent sermon, and, despite the apparent oddness of the mission to which he believes himself called, you may receive him with total confidence.'[18] Abbé Huvelin was similarly enthusiastic: 'Nothing bizarre or extraordinary, but an irresistible force that impels, a strong implement for rough tasks. Firmness, a desire to go the limit in love and giving; never discouragement, a little harshness formerly, but that has been tempered! Let him come at his own risk, see him in action, and judge.'[19] Here, perhaps, was the breakthrough the White Fathers needed. Guérin left Ghardaia, the oasis in which his bishopric was based, and travelled to Algiers where, on 10 September, accompanied by Archbishop Livinhac, he welcomed his new apostle to Africa.

Like so much that went on in North Africa, Foucauld's mission was not sanctioned by the French government. In fact, the strongly anti-clerical administration would probably have forbidden it had they had any say in the matter. But Paris's influence was so minimal in North Africa and that of Foucauld's allies so strong that, from the day of his arrival, it took less than a month for him to be issued with the documentation he required for his journey. 'All the difficulties have been ironed out, one after the other,' Dom Henri wrote. 'Protectors and friends appeared as if by magic.'[20] On 15 October, armed with a multitude of permits, Foucauld boarded a train that took him, via Oran, to Aïn Sefra.

The rickety, narrow-gauge track that ran through the Sud-Oranais carried Foucauld into a landscape of infernal inhospitability. His diaries give no description of what he saw through the window of his third-class carriage as his train rattled slowly south on its narrow-gauge track, but the Swiss-born traveller Isabelle Eberhardt, who made the same journey in 1903, left a vivid portrait:

> An immense chaos of broken stones, tumbled about, rolled down, as though cut off from the soil by a terrible cyclone. Sharp needles stand one above the other: a monstrous lacework stretched across rocks; and across the clay hillocks, over narrow trenches cut deep like corridors, enormous rocks rest in hazardous balance, ready at any moment to detach themselves and crush the passing train. We pass through an enormous flow of lava, cast up by dark peaks which cut off the horizon; the lava has become cold after invading the valley and has hardened around much older and harder masses, thus forming a puffed crust; the skeleton of a city destroyed by the fire of heaven. On this rubble an un-heard of spectrum of colour is displayed – all the reflections of fire; a dull leaden pink of clinkers hardly extinguished, every tint of rust and of greenish ochre, deep violet and dark carmine. All this on the cold clay with its bluish-grey protruding veins. All the stones are covered with a glossy black polish, as though having retained the traces of the fire and of the original smoke. [It is] A dark and splendid setting of a petrified furnace; a lunar landscape of helpless desolation and of tragic grandeur, but under a smiling sky.[21]

At Aïn Sefra, where the railway came to a halt, the scenery was only marginally less bizarre. On a black plateau of rock and shale lay a single, golden dune, 1.2 kilometres long and half that distance wide, beyond which rose a craggy mountain. Nobody knew how this dune had come into being, but there it sat, an exotic intruder in the wilderness, constantly shifting but always retaining its approximate shape. In between the dune and the mountain stretched a sandy river bed that, after the rains, reverted briefly and at infrequent intervals to the torrent it once had been. On one side of the river bed, the one that lay beneath the mountain, a sprawling shanty town housed the 200-odd nomadic families that made Aïn Sefra their base. On the other side, beneath the dune, the French garrison lived in a drab cluster of buildings that included the railway station, the *bordj*, the ubiquitous post office, one or two bars, a dusty hotel and a few other houses made of mud and corrugated iron. In a central square, a stand of imported trees struggled against the odds to recreate the atmosphere of metropolitan France. To quote Douglas Porch, '[it] was a dreadful place, more dreadful than most of the dreadful towns which the French constructed in Algiers'.[22]

Again, Foucauld does not mention Aïn Sefra's lack of appeal. The aesthetics of colonization probably did not bother him – they patently did not bother anyone else. What did bother him was the fact that the officer-in-charge gave him a bed to sleep in – he slept instead on the floor – and then provided him with a horse and an armed escort for the journey to Beni Abbès, a distance he had intended to cross alone and on foot. But he soon recovered from the disappointment. At every stage on his way south he was treated as a VIP. On approaching Taghit, a garrison that lay halfway between Aïn Sefra and Beni Abbès, the Arab Bureau officer Captain Susbielle rode out to greet him, dressed in white and wearing a sky-blue kepi. He was accompanied by fifteen Arab horsemen, whom he had previously warned: 'The man you are going to see is a French marabout. He is coming to live among you and the poor people of the desert, to stay here always. Receive him with honour!'[23] They did as he commanded. One by one his escort dismounted and knelt to kiss the hem of Foucauld's robes. It moved Foucauld to tears. That day, to celebrate his acceptance by the noble savages of the desert, he held his first Mass in the Sahara.

He then moved on to Beni Abbès, where he was greeted with displays of equal affection.

To what extent Foucauld saw himself as a pawn in the colonial game is uncertain. He was clearly aware that evangelization would help the imperial cause; and he acceded happily to Guérin's request that he reconnoitre en route to Beni Abbès various oases that might be suitable for occupation by the White Fathers. Throughout his stay in the desert he provided a stream of information about the state of the populace and how they could be persuaded to accept French rule. Occasionally, he expressed himself in terms that might have been used by the most ardent supremacist and which sat uneasily with his dogma of equality before Christ. In all likelihood, however, he used the military as much as they used him. He knew that he needed their permission to settle in the Sahara and if the quid pro quo was intelligence then he did not mind supplying it, so long as it was to the advantage of the faith; and the interests of Christianity and colonialism were so closely intertwined that he saw little difference between the two. As for his racist outbursts, they were a product of his upbringing and of his time. He was a man whose personal mission took precedence over everything else.

On arriving at Beni Abbès, Foucauld began the construction of his hermitage. He had already written to his family for the money to purchase a nine-hectare plot between the *bordj* and the oasis (it cost 1,070 francs, which was far more than it was worth), and with the help of the garrison, who renovated two disused springs, cleared a couple of wells, planted 250 palms, some figs, some olives, a strip of barley, and then built a chapel for the hermit to live in, he entered yet another stage of his tortured existence.

The chapel was small, devoid of all facilities, and stifling: in summer, for three months, the thermometer registered up to 48°C. 'The roof is horizontal,' Foucauld wrote, 'made of big beams of unhewn palms; it is very rustic, very poor, but harmonious and pretty. To hold up the roof there are four vertical palm trunks.'[24] After a period of sleeping like a dog in front of the altar, Foucauld retired to an adjoining 1.5-metre-long sacristy that provided greater discomfort.

When asked why he did so, he replied that, 'On the cross, Jesus was not lying down.'[25] His existence was cloistered in the most literal sense: he surrounded his chapel with a ring of stones beyond which he refused to venture, seeing no apparent conflict in ordering a self-sufficient plot and then constructing a perimeter that refused him access to it.

The garrison gave him ample provisions but Foucauld preferred to live off a bland gruel of barley and figs, supplemented by a small amount of grain that he ground into flour before baking it on the stones of his fire. The rest he distributed as alms to the poor and needy of Beni Abbès, who quickly realized they were onto a good thing and trampled over his cloister wall in droves. 'I want all the inhabitants [of Beni Abbès], Christian, Moslem, Jew, and idolator, to regard me as their brother,'[26] he wrote. But soon he was experiencing less a sense of brotherhood than one of distress: he had come to the Sahara to be alone, to meditate, to pursue the life of Christ; instead he found himself handing out food, medicine and advice to all and sundry. His original idea had been to rise at 3 a.m. and divide his day between charitable and physical work (seven hours), prayers (twelve hours) and sleep (five hours). But this proved impracticable. As the number of supplicants swelled to 200 per day, he found himself dealing with their problems until midnight. Then, at 4.30 a.m., the first of the next morning's contingent would knock at his door. 'Every day the same thing,' he wrote to Huvelin, 'the poor and the sick, one after another; I reproach myself for not devoting enough time to prayer: in the day, they do not stop knocking on my door.'[27] Between 5 a.m. and 9 a.m., and from 4 p.m. to 6 p.m., his chapel was 'a beehive'.[28]

It wore him down. Nevertheless, in his first months at Beni Abbès, he found time to compose reports on its inhabitants. The farmers, he wrote, were fine and industrious folk: 'Very pleasant. After dreading the arrival of the French, they seem pleased by it and recognize that for the first time in generations they can gather in their crops, which the pillagers used to appropriate.' He was less happy with the nomads: 'By nature harsh and cruel, at heart very ill-disposed to the French, obstinately Muslim but practising their religion feebly.'[29] The slaves were his despair. Expecting to make immediate converts among them, he wrote instead that they were 'soup Christians',[30] who had no interest in any faith and only came to him for the food he distributed.

He was not blind to the cause of the slaves' apathy and inveighed against a policy that allowed them to remain in bondage. 'It must be made known to whom it may concern: "this is not legal",' he wrote. 'It is hypocrisy to put on stamps and everything else, "liberty, equality, fraternity, human rights," you who fetter slaves and condemn to the galleys those making a lie of what you print on your banknotes; you who steal children from their parents and sell them publicly; you who punish the theft of a chicken and allow that of a human being.'[31] He detailed horrible instances of bludgeoning and starvation; he was outraged when, on one occasion, some slaves sought refuge with the French only to be returned to their masters who then sliced their tendons as an example to other would-be escapers. 'Voices must be raised so that France will know of this injustice and thievery. I have informed the apostolic prefect.'[32] But Guérin could do nothing about it: 'It is through an *order of General Risbourg*, confirmed by Colonel Billet, that slavery is allowed to continue.'[33]

Foucauld also complained to Castries, who assured him that he would look into the matter. But the military had no interest in emancipation. As far back as 1853 Governor-General Randon had outlined France's policy towards the Saharan tribes: 'We do not wish in any way to interfere with your interior affairs; you will retain all your customs as heretofore: we will interest ourselves in your actions only when they concern the peace and the rights of those tribes who have made their submission to us.'[34] Long since made redundant by the march of French colonialism, Randon's declaration still provided a rule-of-thumb for those officers who gave not a fig for moral enlightenment and all the other claptrap that comprised the so-called 'White Man's Burden'. These officers, who were by no means in the majority, but whose assessment of imperialist goals was brutally clear-sighted, were interested only in territorial acquisition. Risbourg and Billet, who had led the occupation of Beni Abbès and who had been rewarded with high-ranking posts in Oran, were among them. Slavery was eventually abolished in 1904, followed four years later by Risbourg's suspension for excess rigour in the course of duty. For the moment, however, the words of Randon prevailed. Risbourg, Billet and others saw no reason why they should destabilize their conquests by alienating local rulers for whom slaves were as much a status symbol as a source of free labour. Castries's inquiries fell on closed ears.

'Nothing has changed,' Foucauld wrote to Guérin on 28 June 1902. 'Not only do those enslaved remain so, but slaves are being bought and sold every day with the full knowledge of the Arab bureau ... which consider themselves obliged to accept such an attitude because of discipline and orders received ... The authorities will always overlook what happens inside tents in the Erg. They say: slaves are necessary in this country, for without them the oases would perish. That is inaccurate. Many prosperous oases have not one slave ... The only people with large contingents of slaves are the nomads and marabouts, who *never work*, who spend their whole lives in idleness and who rise up against us at every opportunity. Freeing their slaves would force them to work a little, which would improve them ... The slaves must be liberated.'[35] Guérin's response was pragmatic: 'we must consider carefully the circumstances in which we find ourselves and take care that we do not have taken from us the means through which we can do a little good by making grand gestures that can have *no* result.'[36] He warned Foucauld against an excess of zeal, and told him to toe the party line. 'Without actually speaking of enfranchisement, try to impress upon [the slaves], the divine rewards that come from hard work.'[37]

Guérin's caution came from a recent trip to France in which he had seen the extent to which the government was pursuing its anti-clerical agenda. One religious institution had been forced to dismiss 2,000 of its members. Fearing a similar purge in Africa, Guérin advised Foucauld to keep his head down. 'Given public opinion on the subject of converting the Mussulmans, it is best not to attract the attention of those who surround us.'[38] When Foucauld questioned him again about slavery, Guérin's response was curt: 'We must . . . never contemplate making an official denunciation of what happens in these countries.'[39] Foucauld continued to denounce it all the same until 15 December 1904, when he was at last able to write to Castries: 'by common accord, the chiefs attached to the oases have taken measures to abolish slavery. Not in one day, that would not be prudent, but gradually.'[40]

Slavery was not his only concern. Without going so far as to condemn colonialism, he railed against the manner in which it was undertaken: 'there is only cupidity and violence, with no thought for the good of the peoples.'[41] He had a poor opinion of Beni Abbès' garrison. 'It is deplorable to send lightweights here,' he wrote to Lacroix, 'you know the kind I mean, and you can guess what contempt they inspire in the natives; on the Moroccan frontier we must have troops that do us honour and not men who inspire universal contempt. Europeans are represented in these parts only by lightweights and by the Foreign Legion.'[42] According to one biographer, 'he became the conscience of France in Algeria',[43] a role that won him many enemies. Foucauld was oblivious to the animosity. Within his ring of stones – which, after months of labour, he transformed into a tiny, ramshackle wall over which everyone stepped, despite the addition of barbed wire – he was at an infinite distance from Paris, Algiers and even Aïn Sefra. His daily regime was so harsh and so deeply absorbed in the adoration of Christ that political machinations in far-off places were irrelevant. How could any authority seriously expect to discipline a man who lived on barley, bread, dates and water, who despised comfort, and whose one wish was to die as soon and as painfully as possible? Besides, there were many who still supported his cause: his family, specifically his cousin Marie de Bondy,* provided a regular

---

*Marie de Bondy was the daughter of Inès Moitessier and, according to some biographers, the object of Foucauld's frustrated sexual desires. A fervent Catholic, she gave money whenever he needed it and was the recipient of his most intimate correspondence. The two became so close that her son later described his father as a spiritual cuckold.

income; a collection among the garrison at Beni Abbès produced forty to fifty francs per month; the Poor Clares of Nazareth sent him pressed flowers, clothes pegs, a wooden spoon, a mousetrap, and a piece of white calico (which he gave away immediately); and from Dom Henri of Staouëli came a robe, two shirts, twelve towels, a blanket and a cloak – but only on loan, 'so that I can't give them away'. Officers of the Bureau Arabe supplied other little gifts of blankets and clothing. 'So you see,' he wrote to Marie de Bondy, 'I am very well off.'[44] Sympathy and material aid, however, were not what he wanted. His most ardent desire was to create a brotherhood of fellow sufferers, and in this he was to be eternally thwarted.

Although the soldiers of Beni Abbès called his hermitage 'The Fraternity', it was not a fraternity in the way Foucauld wished it to be. He yearned for someone to share his burden, to accept his order and to abase themselves as he did. On 28 April 1902 he received a letter from Guérin that filled him with joy. 'At last,' he wrote, 'I am authorised to found a new religious family under the Rule of St. Augustine with the name Little Brothers of the Sacred Heart of Jesus; their object will be perpetual adoration day and night of the Blessed Sacrament exposed, combined with a life of poverty and manual work.'[45] But official sanction produced no tangible result; the rooms he built to house his would-be assistants remained stubbornly empty. He tried to combine his desire for companionship with his emancipating instincts by buying several slaves whom he later freed in the hope that they would become Christians. He converted only one, an ancient, blind woman who was not entirely in her right mind. None of the others listened. One ran away, another was sent to Algiers for further instruction (he was 'too lazy'), another, a three-year-old, was also sent to Algiers, and a third returned to his family. A fifteen-year-old named Paul Embarek, purchased on 14 September 1902, hung around in a half-hearted fashion, assisting as a catechumen when Catholic dogma required the presence of more than one person for the celebration of Mass, but refused resolutely to accept Christianity. 'A very sad fellow,' Foucauld wrote to Huvelin. 'Unless his faults become criminal I shall keep him with me, remembering that Christ kept Judas.'[46]

Guérin informed him that he should stop it at once. Although more than a decade Foucauld's junior, he chided him as if he were a schoolboy. The transportation of his younger slaves to Algiers, he said, was very trying for the officers involved, not to mention costly for the White Fathers who then had to pay for their board and education. 'Is this the best use of the mission's limited resources? I think not.'[47] Again, he emphasized the White Fathers' perilous political situation. *'I advise you very insistently to act with great prudence – and I beseech you not to take any steps that might be construed as being of an official nature.'*[48]

These minor, and not very successful attempts to subvert official policy may have given Foucauld some consolation but they did not advance his cause. The Little Brothers he hoped to attract had first to receive permission from Guérin and others in the religious hierarchy, and permission was not readily forthcoming. Perhaps, given Foucauld's reputation in some quarters as a troublemaker, they feared the attention he might attract. Content that he spread the Gospel and lead a life of example, they may not have been so happy with his proposed community of ascetics. What if the contagion spread? Suppose the desert was overrun by hermits whose rebellious doctrine brought down the wrath of Paris and spelled an end both to military and to ecclesiastical expansion? Fortunately, they did not need an excuse to stop Foucauld's madness: he provided it himself. Nobody, however eremetically inclined, could match his capacity for self-denial; as Dom Henri wrote to Lacroix, 'His life is so austere that those among the superiors of our order who have the most sincere affection for him, judge him more admirable than imitable and fear to throw into discouragement the disciples they could procure for him. Therefore he will probably have to live alone or recruit little by little the elements of his future community on the spot.'[49] Dom Martin, of Notre-Dame-des-Neiges, was more forthright. In a letter to Guérin, he said, 'The only thing [about Foucauld] that surprises me is that he doesn't work miracles . . . But I have to admit to having reservations regarding his prudence and discretion. The intense singlemindedness that he imposes upon himself and would impose on his disciples, seems to me so superhuman that I fear he might drive a disciple mad by excessive mental concentration before killing him by excessive austerities.'[50]

When four Trappists inquired about a position in his Fraternity, Foucauld replied that his rule was 'harsh and strict', and that they would have to '1) be ready to have their heads cut off, 2) be prepared to die of hunger and 3) to obey him in spite of his unworthiness'.[51] They did not accept the offer: unworthiness they could cope with; insanity they could not. By the summer of 1902 his raging fanaticism brought him nearly to the point of death. Reduced to decrepitude by malnutrition – his diet, at this point, consisted of bread, barley porridge and tea – he had become a wreck: his teeth were falling out and his hair was going the same way. Captain Regnault, the Bureau Arabe officer attached to Beni Abbès, reported that, 'In spite of the repeated entreaties of the officers of the garrison he never will vary his diet: the vegetables he is sent from the mess are generally given to the poor or his passing guests.'[52] Huvelin was appalled: 'My dear child, sustain yourself!' he wrote. 'Do not deprive yourself too much – eat a bit – find time for the sleep you need to carry on your work.'[53] Foucauld replied: 'I am lazy and gluttonous.'[54] He slept and ate even less; as his immune system gave way he retired to the floor of his sacristy, where he lay crippled by rheumatism and intermittent bouts of fever. In the end, he persuaded himself to live. Marie de Bondy seems to have provided the necessary encouragement. 'My cousin sends me ten francs a month on condition that I use them to *eat* . . . I have accepted both the money and the conditions,' he wrote. 'My menu is: at noon, couscous or bread with condensed milk; in the evening bread and black coffee. At the garrison, the officers . . . are very kind to me and overwhelm me with attentions.'[55] Hardly a feast, the new regime nevertheless brought him slowly back to life.

As his mind and body recuperated, Foucauld drew strength from the desert. 'It is so good,' he wrote to Castries, 'even though one prays with all one's heart for the human beings who are on this poor earth, to lift one's eyes very high above it, up to the big sky, image of the infinity for which we are created.'[56] Sometimes he was joined by officers of the Bureau Arabe. Captain Susbielle recorded visits to

Foucauld's fraternity, when 'We would sit down on the ground in front of the brotherhood, contemplating the great sand dune and the great silence of the Sahara. And there we would pass hours I found too brief.'[57] Best of all, however, were the small hours when nobody was present and Foucauld could indulge himself. 'The evenings are so calm, the nights so serene, this immense sky and these vast horizons dimly lit by the heavenly bodies are so peaceful as they silently sing the eternal, the infinite, and the beyond; one could pass whole nights outdoors in contemplation. I cut them short, however, and go back inside to the tabernacle; nothing is anything compared to the Beloved.'[58]

Despite his oddness, Foucauld remained popular with the garrison and with most of the military in the Sahara. They gave him food when he was ill, provided orderlies to help with the housekeeping, helped decorate his chapel and installed a bell, sent to him by Marie de Bondy in a wine barrel, with which he could call them to Mass. They might have done this out of duty and because he was their official chaplain, but they did not. They did it because they considered him to be one of them. 'We loved Father de Foucauld above all because he had remained a soldier,' explained one officer, 'because he thought as a soldier, and because he judged us all as a soldier.'[59]

When not starving himself or praying, Foucauld was, indeed, a remarkably militaristic monk. He wanted to lead his order into unconquered Muslim territory, possibly as a precursor to armed invasion, and Morocco seemed to him as tempting a plum as it did to the army. On 13 April 1902, he wrote to Lacroix, giving an estimate of the French army's position on the Moroccan border and promoting the seizure of Tabelbalet, an oasis 400 kilometres south-west of Beni Abbès, which was both a trade centre and a doorway to the Dra, one of the many regions in southern Morocco that lay outside the Sultan's control. It had recently been reconnoitred by Captain Regnault and Foucauld was excited by its potential. 'I wish to point out to you the extreme importance of the recent exploration of the oasis of Tabelbalet by Captain Regnault,' he began. 'A brief glance at the map shows the remarkable situation of this place, but what the map does not show is that it is possible to go there and install oneself without a single blow . . . A company of infantry from the garrison of Beni Abbès (who are bored with having nothing to do) and a squadron of Saharian spahis, under cover of a march, of a military manoeuvre, or of a simple reconnaissance, can install themselves just as easily as they already went there . . . Our present possessions would be in complete security, and come the day when we wish to advance towards the Dra and the Tafilelt [in Morocco], not only will Tabelbalet be our capital, but, by our pacific relations strongly established there, new conquests will be greatly facilitated.'[60] Lacroix had no authority to order such a thing and passed the letter to his superiors. Foucauld then took a more personal approach. 'Please,' he begged, 'have me given the necessary authorization and the promise of moral support in case I make a private journey (without anything official about it) to the Dra or elsewhere in Morocco. You will render a great service to France, to civilization, to Almighty God, and to your old friend.'[61] He approached Guérin in more circumspect tones. In December he wrote, 'Oh! What a wonderful New Year's gift it would be if you ordered a prayer *For the Propagation of the Faith!* I cannot stop thinking about those ten million Moroccans – on our doorstep, almost touching us – who are without a priest, a missionary, an altar, or a tabernacle, and for whom Christmas night will come and go without a mass! What sorrow and mourning!'[62] Later, he would ask in an offhand way, 'Should there be any major reconnaissance towards the West, and if I am allowed to be part of it, ought I to go?'[63] Guérin approved in principle: 'Morocco is your special calling. Pray that at last the good Jesus opens it to the light of the Gospel. And if weapons can pave the way for the arrival of missionaries, then let them be used to such a glorious end.'[64]

    Although the military used Foucauld as a sort of freelance spy, they tended to ignore his strategic recommendations. Like the complaints he made to the White Fathers on the subject of slavery, they were usually shelved for being 'imprudent' – an adjective that shadowed him wherever he went. In this instance, however, the army did have an interest in what he had to say. Paul Revoil, the Governor-General of Algeria, summoned Captain Regnault to discuss the matter of Tabelbalet. He also invited another, more forceful personality to his office. News of this meeting provided Foucauld with his hoped-for New Year's gift. On 31 December 1902, he wrote excitedly to Guérin, 'I have just learned this moment that Commandant Laperrine has been summoned to Algiers.'[65]

10

LAPERRINE'S
COMMAND

In June 1901, three months before Foucauld landed in Algiers, Laperrine too returned to North Africa. He was destined not for the Moroccan border but for the Tuat, where a situation was developing that threatened to undermine the whole colonial impetus. The problem stemmed, as always, from the impossibility of applying traditional military methods to Saharan conditions. Already, the army had realized that its strategy of hurling huge, unwieldy columns over the desert to squash every African who defied them was unsustainable. It might work in the short term for capturing settled areas, but it was quite ineffective against a mobile enemy such as the Tuareg. Moreover, the oases could not support the number of men required to defend them without a constant stream of expensive (and vulnerable) supply caravans. A railway would have solved things but, despite the publication of several books promoting the advantages of the Transsaharian, no visible steps were taken towards its construction. Paradoxically, the Transsaharian could not be built until the Tuat was firmly under French control, and the Tuat could not be controlled until the Transsaharian was in place. The army was in a tight spot and it knew it – worse still, so did the government.

The conquest of the Tuat had been appallingly expensive: the bill for the year 1900 came to twenty million francs; for 1901 it was thirty-three million. And all those millions had been spent in a largely wasteful manner. The 1901 budget, for example, was for the camels involved in the campaign. In total, 35,000 beasts had been requisitioned from the Algerian oases, 25,000 of which had died from thirst and ill-treatment. In one striking instance, of more than 9,000 camels assembled at El Goléa, some 40 per cent had died before they even left the place. 'I do not think that there has been a massacre comparable to that of 1901,' wrote one Saharan traveller. 'For thousands of kilometres the desert tracks were marked by carcases set more closely than telegraph poles on a European road. During the early months a blind man could have guided himself by the stench. The jackals and the vultures along the way were overwhelmed with the immensity of their task.'[1] Such images did not go down well with the public. Worst of all was the knock-on effect the loss of so many beasts had on the local economy. Deprived of their livelihood the tribesmen had little option but to revert to banditry and the most tempting targets were, clearly, the villages of Algeria (hence the disturbances of 1901) and the supply columns for oasis garrisons. Occupation of the Tuat had produced nothing but expense and disruption and the only foreseeable return was more of the same. In every respect – financial, political, military and civil – it was a millstone around France's neck. As a report made clear in March 1901, 'until now [it has] cost us dearly in men, money and camels to conquer a country which is unhealthy, miserable, hardly able to nourish its inhabitants, producing only dates, uninhabitable for European troops, in a word, not worth the sacrifices made.'[2] The government stated forthrightly that unless the military cut their expenses they would have to withdraw from the region.

To retreat was unthinkable; such an act would be a disgrace without parallel in the history of French imperialism; it would also ruin the dream of joining Algeria to the Soudan. And so, with the newly created title Commander of the Oases, Laperrine was despatched to sort things out. Based in Adrar, the administrative capital of the Tuat, he was charged with organizing a new force for controlling the Sahara: a camel corps that moved through the desert in the same manner and at the same speed as the enemy. Since neither French nor Algerian troops had the expertise, such a corps would have to be recruited among the desert-dwellers themselves. The idea was not a new one. 'If we want a real fighting unit it must be a mobile one,' one Major Victor Pierron had written in March 1900. 'I believe the Saharian troops should be neither spahis nor *tirailleurs*, but a troop which combines the two, trained to fight as infantry, but transported on camels without which soldiers in the Sahara are unable to move and are useless. But there is no gainsaying that such an organization is difficult to realize and will be worth as much as the commander in charge.'[3] Laperrine, with his record for bravery and leadership, and his experience of camel troops at Fort MacMahon, was chosen for the job. As one subordinate said, '[The army] quickly realized that he was the right man for the Sahara – the only man, in fact – and so they recalled him.'[4]

The composition of Laperrine's force was laid out for him: it would comprise three companies of 300 native troops, with a sprinkling of European NCOs and officers to command them. Stationed in Gouara, the Tuat and the Tidikelt, each company would be recruited from their respective local populations and would consist of 230 infantry, plus a small body of seventy camel-mounted nomads. If Laperrine had ever expected his task to be easy, he was soon disabused. Recruits were hard to find, particularly in the Tidikelt (two years after his arrival so few men had been mustered that the three proposed companies had to be reduced to two), and the size of the camel contingent was, in his view, quite insufficient. Not, however, that Laperrine had any intention of restricting his role in the Tuat to that of up-market recruiting sergeant. He wanted to show the Tuareg exactly who ran the Sahara, and was confident that he could do so with conventional forces. Before the first company of Saharians had even been formed he was drawing up plans for a comprehensive sweep of the desert. In Beni Abbès, Foucauld wrote that his ambitions included a strike against the Hoggar, a traverse of the desert from the Tuat to Timbuctoo and the seizure of Tabelbalet. This was exactly what the government did not want him to do. As the size of his corps suggested – and as the war minister was at pains to point out – Laperrine was only a policeman. He could patrol the Tuat, he could maintain a vigorous presence in the conquered territories and he could defend the oases against enemy incursion. But he was not, under any circumstances, to initiate aggressive action of the kind that had recently caused Paris so much embarrassment and expense. His appointment had been approved on these conditions and these conditions alone, a fact that the authorities expected him to appreciate, which he did, but in traditional colonial fashion: by March 1902 French troops from In Salah were already marching on the Hoggar.

When Laperrine reached Adrar he was dismayed. Far from bringing the Tuareg to their knees, as was the original design, the occupation of the Tuat had merely stirred them to further bellicosity. The *amenoukhal*, or chief, of the Hoggar tribes had recently died and his successor was Attici ag Amellal, the man who had supervised the Flatters massacre and who had been elected to his post for the very reason that he hated the French. (His name translated as 'leopard amongst the whites'.) Caustically, Laperrine judged the situation as 'not glittering'.[5] A tour of the Tidikelt in 1901 confirmed his judgement. Accompanied by the lieutenant in charge of the In Salah garrison, he heard nothing but stories of caravans pillaged and trade disrupted. The Tuareg he met in the Tidikelt markets 'were rude, and ignored us. This made a bad impression on me. I told the lieutenant in question that these stories, and everything I saw, did not tally with the optimism of his official reports and I instructed him to react vigorously at the first sign of aggression.'[6] The lieutenant (whose name Laperrine did not give) reacted more vigorously to the implied criticism of his leadership than to the threat of the natives. A few days later, he mounted a *razzia*, during the course of which he went mad, shot the leader of his native troops, wounded a friendly chieftain, and did no harm at all to the Tuareg before returning to In Salah where he was evacuated north for medical attention.

Laperrine invited Captain Cauvet, his old friend from the Bureau Arabe, to take charge of In Salah. On rummaging through the departed lieutenant's papers, Cauvet discovered evidence of 'an excessive spirit of conciliation'.[7] In a sealed chest there were copies of letters between the lieutenant and Attici, in one of which Attici had written, 'If you come to the Hoggar, I will destroy you by force or cunning; if you prevent my people from revictualling at the markets I will cut down every palm tree in the Tidikelt.'[8] Laperrine was angered by the threat. He became even angrier when he learned of the lieutenant's reply. '[Cauvet found] a draft that the madman had made . . . [It] was couched in the most extravagant terms but, reading between the lines, there seemed to be a contract of peace. To quote: "I do not see why the eagle on the rock and the lion on the plain cannot live happily together." . . . This quasi-guarantee was a great impediment to me, because it was obvious that, in the eyes of the Tuareg, we had become ridiculous.'[9] He and Cauvet decided to respect the lieutenant's promises in principle but, 'at the first aggression, at the first sign of insolence',[10] they would close the Tidikelt markets and attack the Hoggar.

Attici ag Amellal immediately gave them an excuse for doing so. In March 1902, one of his chieftains attacked a Tuareg noblewoman and stole three of her camels. On its own, this was a minor incident – Laperrine described it as 'quite unimportant'[11] – but it had wider political implications, for the woman came from In Rhar, an oasis fifty-six kilometres west of In Salah, and was therefore deemed to be under French protection. Moreover, as well as stealing her camels and ordering his slaves to beat her with sticks, her assailant had used strong language: 'This is what happens to Tuareg nobles who accept the yoke of those filthy French infidels,'[12] he is reported to have said. (That was Laperrine's version; Cauvet translated it more colourfully. Without question, this was an act of aggression. It was also abominably insolent. 'These words, spoken by one of the leading Hoggar chieftains,' wrote Laperrine, 'showed very clearly that [although said to the woman] they were aimed at us.'[13] No further provocation was needed. On 23 March 1902, a troop of 130 *goumiers*, or local recruits, left In Salah under the command of a single Frenchman, Lieutenant Gaston Cottonest. Their destination was the Hoggar. According to

Cauvet, the expedition was cautionary rather than aggressive: 'I think the Hoggars will avoid him, but it will be a good result if we can promenade in the heart of their country.'[14] He also used the threadbare excuse, so beloved of colonialists, that it would be fruitful, 'if only from a geographical point of view'.[15] Laperrine was more honest: 'The officer's mission . . . was to give a sharp lesson to the tribes involved in the recent pillage.'[16]

Responsibility for the sortie, which ran against all instructions from Paris, was later disputed. Cauvet said, 'I had no orders. There were none at In Salah. I even avoided asking Laperrine who might have received some or who would have felt obliged to ask for some. Therefore I did not overstep my orders. The distinction is perhaps a trifle subtle, for I know exactly what the reply would have been if I had proposed to send my people on a tour of the Hoggar. But it exists nevertheless.'[17] So, too, existed the possibility that Laperrine turned a Nelsonian eye to Cauvet's campaign and that Cauvet – the same Cauvet who was Laperrine's friend and who, as an officer of the Bureau Arabe, had introduced him to desert life – reciprocated by taking responsibility for an action that might have cost Laperrine his command. From Laperrine's own writings it is clear that he saw Cottonest's foray not only as a long-overdue poke in the eye for the Tuareg but as a testing ground for the native troops who might later serve in his camel corps. Whoever gave the order, by April 1902 Cottonest was proceeding towards the Hoggar while two other forces – definitely ordered by Laperrine – were probing south and east to prevent neighbouring tribes coalescing to block his advance.

Apart from an inconclusive skirmish with a Tuareg raiding party on 3 May, Cottonest reached the Hoggar unopposed and on the afternoon of 7 May he was encamped at Tit, an oasis to the south-west of the massif. Here, he sent patrols to guard against a possible attack; and here, with an innate sense of the terrain, 300 of Attici's Tuareg rose suddenly from behind an embankment to split his force in two. At first, Cottonest hoped the slow-moving, camel-mounted mass that came towards him might be coming in friendship – he hoped it very much for, to his dismay, the Tuareg carried rifles as well as swords, shields and lances – but when they dismounted and began attacking him, he was forced to reconsider. Outnumbered and outflanked, he retreated to a stony outcrop on which he, and the seventy men he had with him, prepared to make their last stand. The Tuareg were poor shots and low on ammunition, but Cottonest's exposed position gave them the advantage. Slithering from rock to rock, they crept closer and closer, one man coming to within twenty-five metres of the French position, from where he succeeded in wounding Cottonest. An hour into the battle, the French detachment's ammunition was running low and it looked as if it was doomed; then, miraculously, two of Cottonest's patrols arrived on the scene. Caught between fires, the Tuareg fled, leaving almost a hundred dead and wounded – the latter were slaughtered by Cottonest's men. Satisfied with the outcome, Cottonest buried his three dead, loaded his ten injured onto their horses and went back to In Salah where Laperrine rode out with a squadron of spahis to escort him home.

In Paris, colonialists cheered this latest advance for the *tricouleur*. The government was less enthusiastic. It transferred Cottonest back to France, and gave Cauvet early retirement. It would probably have liked to have punished Laperrine in some way too, were it not that Cauvet had taken responsibility for the raid and that it would appear ungracious to censure such a senior figure for what had, after all, been a French victory. It contented itself instead with repeating its earlier warning: 'As for the Commander of the Saharian Oases,' the war minister said in July 1902, 'he must adopt a purely passive role of local defence, from which the government had decided he must not deviate, and for which the Saharian companies were specially created.'[18] Laperrine's situation could not have been stated more clearly. Nevertheless, he thought it was imprecise enough to allow a show of initiative.

Tit was the worst and most humiliating defeat the Hoggar Tuareg had ever suffered. Apart from the loss of men – which although small numerically was a large percentage of their fighting population – it seemed incredible that they, the masters of the desert, should lose a battle against outsiders on their home territory. Neither in their lifetimes nor in their legends had such a thing happened. Many refused to believe it. Two days after the battle a great number came to see the evidence for themselves. They disinterred Cottonest's three men, and raised small pyramids of stones over the bodies of their own before returning to spread the news that they had, truly, been defeated. Six months later, doubters were still visiting the site to ascertain whether these wild allegations were true. Yet even though they had been beaten, they saw no reason to abandon their traditional lifestyle. By September 1902, as the Tidikelt caravans continued to be pillaged, Laperrine decided it was time for another display of force.

On 1 October, Lieutenant Guillo-Lohan marched south with 200 men on a 'tour' of the Hoggar. No aggression was intended and, apart from the capture of the odd village, the shooting of three terrified Tuareg, and the seizure of several camels and the women who tended them (both later released, as a gesture of goodwill), none took place. It was, for once, just a display. But it was a mighty satisfying one. On 25 November Guillo-Lohan reached Tit. '[It] resembles a real charnel house,' he wrote. 'The ground is littered with the bodies of camels and horses, above all in the depression where the convoy was located.'[19] He peered between the chinks of the Tuareg's stone burial mounds and saw the dead, 'stretched out completely clothed, just as they were on the day of combat'.[20] Despite the desert's desiccating properties, he could almost touch the smell of decomposition. 'It has been six months since the battle, but this cemetery still reeks of an insupportable stench.'[21] Happy that the Tuareg 'are now convinced of the reality of their defeat, which wounds their pride more deeply than their hearts',[22] he led his men into the Hoggar itself.

The Hoggar has been described by Douglas Porch as 'a land of jagged peaks and necks of rock, trenched and broken by volcanic eruptions of past geological epochs. From a distance, it appears as desolate as a desecrated graveyard. The dark towers of rock are stripped of vegetation and the valleys filled with the slag of petrified flows of lava. [It] offers a tableau of frozen violence, a vision of Hell or, at the very least of a land which has incurred the wrath of God, an appropriate home for devils and demons.'[23] Guillo-Lohan, the first white man to see this fabled land, felt much the same. 'We traversed a tormented region, a blend of ravines and arid bluffs, of stony plateaus and fleshless hillocks.'[24] Rain had just fallen, and had he come a few weeks later he would have seen the Hoggar in its full flowering, carpeted with green and dotted with Tuareg encampments. But the greenery was for now absent and as he led his troops up the Hoggar's narrow, serpentine paths he nearly faltered. 'Our progress was slow,' he wrote, 'hampered by the column that stretched out hopelessly behind us. Continually, we had to stop to allow the rear to catch up. The camels suffered from the rain, and the consequent drop in temperature, and struggled over rocks that cut their hooves to the quick. Many, too exhausted to continue, lay down and refused to move. We cut their throats so that they could not be used by the Tuareg.'[25] When he attained the plateau, Guillo-Lohan was flabbergasted. For a distance of eighty kilometres there stretched nothing but gritty wasteland, from which colossal needles of black rock rose into the sky. It was 'magnificently sinister',[26] – and also a touch disconcerting. How best was he to assert dominance over this sere and wind-blasted wilderness? Leading his troops deeper into the plateau was a prospect he did not relish: apart from its apparent lack of water and wildlife (actually, had he continued he would have found both) there was no settlement to impose upon, no chieftain to impress, no tribe to attack. He chose a topographical option: he would scale the highest mountain he could see, a sharp obelisk that his guides told him was called Ilaman.

Guillo-Lohan's decision was very much of its time. At the turn of the century, mountaineering was one of Europe's most popular amateur pastimes: from every nation, men in tackety boots sallied forth to conquer the world's ranges; it was not at all unusual for army officers to find themselves at the foot of a foreign hill and, with time on their hands, scramble to its peak. But, surely, no mountaineer had ever approached a challenge in the way Guillo-Lohan did. Fearful that his native troops might desert in his absence, he ordered them to accompany him (announcing improbably that he needed to meet a group of Tuareg who were encamped on the summit). And so 200 men, with their baggage and their camels, proceeded up Mt Ilaman. They climbed 1,850 metres before the slope brought them to a halt. Thereupon, Guillo-Lohan ordered the column to stay where it was and continued with one French corporal and four African *tirailleurs*. As the others shivered below, Guillo-Lohan's team struggled towards the summit. 'It was a terrible climb, over almost perpendicular slopes, and the difficulties were far greater than expected. Every handhold had to be tested because the rock was crumbling. Constantly, the tyro alpinists grappled with sheer walls that they overcame only by the strength of their arms.'[27] Eventually, the six men reached a point where they could go no further. Straddling a ridge, Guillo-Lohan 'made several useful observations in the teeth of an icy wind and admired a splendid view of all the mountains',[28] then descended to rejoin his men and lead them out of the Hoggar.

Guillo-Lohan's adventures did not last much longer. When news of the operation seeped back to Algiers, the Governor-General ordered its immediate return. But, by the time his order reached Guillo-Lohan, at the base of the Hoggar, the 'tour' was already at an end and had achieved everything Laperrine had hoped it would. Together with the Cottonest expedition, it had shown that a small, well-armed group could defeat the Tuareg hordes, that French troops could travel through Tuareg territory with impunity, and that resistance was futile. It had also produced a feat of mountaineering so unorthodox and secretive that not even the Alpine Club, the London-based arbiter on all such matters, reported.* Predominantly, however, it had destroyed Attici's pretensions to power, forcing him to retreat to Ghat, in Ottoman-controlled Tripolitania, where he remained a malign but impotent presence on the Algerian border. His flight left a gap in the Hoggar Tuareg hierarchy and Laperrine had his eye on a man who might fill it.

---

*It would be 1935 before a pair of Zurich climbers completed Guillo-Lohan's ascent.

In the election that had made Attici supreme leader of the Hoggar tribe, a youthful also-ran named Moussa ag Amastane had espoused friendship with the French. On that occasion, it had been a losing ticket; but now, with Attici gone, a new election was held and this time Moussa was the victor. His first act as *amenoukhal* was to send an embassy to In Salah to sue for peace. Laperrine was delighted. 'From the moment that he is my servant,' he wrote, 'I will see that he is as influential as possible.'[29] He reopened the Tuat markets to the nomads and announced his decision to award Moussa the title, Amenoukhal of the Confederation of Hoggar Tuareg. But he recognized that to make Moussa his true servant, and to stop the Tuareg reverting to their old ways, he needed to do more than restore trading rights and distribute meaningless honours. Laperrine had to proceed with a conflicting mix of violence, diplomacy and intrigue – to maintain a constant show of force, to demonstrate that French rule was essentially peaceful, and to keep an eye on the Hoggar without contravening the legislation that forbade him to establish new garrisons south of the Tuat. His Saharian companies could answer the first problem. But how to solve the second and third? Foucauld sprang immediately to mind.

11

A TOUR OF THE INTERIOR

Laperrine was scathing about Foucauld's vocation. 'That wretched Huvelin, in five seconds turned my friend Charles inside out and made a monk out of him,'[1] he wrote. But, disappointed as he was at losing a military comrade, he saw the advantage of having a monk on his side. In April 1903 he sent a subordinate, Captain Nieger, to roust Foucauld from his nest. 'Go to Beni Abbès, and see Foucauld,' he told Nieger. 'He's playing at being a mason and has built himself a hermitage. He never leaves it; he eats nothing; he lives off charity and yet still finds the money to buy slaves coming out of Morocco. He is obsessed with Morocco. There's nothing for him in that direction, but he's dull-witted and plagued by memories of his youth. He must be persuaded to come here and join us. He will become the Tuareg's priest and will be a great help to us.'[2]

Laperrine was correct in his estimate of the Moroccan situation. By 1902, after a campaign that had taken longer than expected and had enfeebled its reputation and resources, Britain had finally won the war in South Africa. Once more it was able to reassert itself as the protector of Morocco. France, whose troops had been mustering flamboyantly along the border – Colonel Hubert Louis Lyautey of Aïn

Sefra, for example, rode about in a gold and purple burnous, wore pistols holstered in tiger skin and occupied a tent complete with oriental carpets, scarlet ceiling and a door guarded by two of the most imposing spahis in his command – could no longer rely on its neighbour's indifference. This did not stop Lyautey and his kind parading as ostentatiously as before, but it lent a hollowness to their bravado, as was evident when one of Foucauld's many requests to Lacroix for an invasion of the Dra was 'momentarily refused out of fear of England'.[3]

The situation was resolved in 1904 when France and Britain put aside their traditional enmity by signing the Entente Cordiale, amongst whose many clauses was one in which France agreed to renounce its claims to Egypt if Britain withdrew its support for the Sultan of Morocco. As France had no means of enforcing its claims in Egypt, and Britain had little interest in Morocco, the agreement suited both sides. Unfortunately, no sooner had Britain abandoned its last interest in North Africa than Germany stated its determination to become the Sultan's protector, a move that momentarily left France as helpless as before. Rumours of the impending diplomatic shift and its likely consequences had already reached the Sahara by the time Laperrine sent his man to Beni Abbès.

Nieger met Foucauld on 19 April 1903. Neither man recorded what was said during the meeting, but the message that Nieger delivered (hopefully in more tactful terms than the original) seemed to have an effect. Three days later, Foucauld wrote to Guérin, suggesting that a colony of White Fathers be established in the Tuat – he, however, would wait on the Moroccan border. Laperrine had foreseen this tactic. Like most of his colleagues he disliked the White Fathers and wished to have nothing to do with them. He gave the following reasons: '1st: they cause the military trouble wherever they go; 2nd: although brave they are clumsy and tactless, meddling in affairs that are no concern of theirs; 3rd: they are useless.'[4] He needed a cleric who might be useful, a rebel like Foucauld whose Christian practices accorded with some of the more esoteric aspects of Islam. Suspecting that Nieger might have been insufficiently persuasive, he sent a letter whose arrival Foucauld recorded in his diary on 21 June. Its contents oozed manipulation. There was, Laperrine wrote, a Tuareg woman named Tarichat who had succoured the surviving members of Flatters's expedition. She had refused Attici entry to her tent, had seen the men back to health and then assisted them back to safety. She was now forty-three years old, famed for her good deeds and, surely, ripe for conversion. She was, he added almost as an aside, extremely influential. Foucauld took the bait Laperrine dangled before him.

'Is this soul not ready for the Gospel?' he asked himself, 'Should I not write and tell her that we know of, and thank God for, the charity she showed twenty-two years ago, when she collected the wounded, tended them, protected them and then sent them safely home?'[5] Immediately he drafted a letter. It started well. He described the love that God had for humankind, how all men were brothers in His eyes, how He recognized her charity and loved her for it (just as the French did), and how she would be rewarded in heaven for her actions on earth. But Foucauld's enthusiasm soon got the better of his pan-religious sentiments. By the end he was abjuring her to pray for his soul, telling her that she was a kindred spirit, directed as he was by Christ to serve the suffering mortals on this planet. 'Glory, blessing, honour and praise be to Him, now and for ever,' he concluded. 'Amen.'[6] Later, he decided it was better that Guérin write the letter.

Guérin did not write to Tarichat. He wrote instead to Foucauld, apologizing that current circumstances forbade any evangelization by either himself or the White Fathers. The Saharan command seemed to have an antipathy towards his men which he did not understand but which he could not fight. And he was still fearful of drawing attention to his order: according to Cardinal Livinhac the future looked gloomy for religious institutions in France and its colonies. 'It is possible that *none* will be tolerated.'[7] Foucauld replied that if Guérin's hands were tied, his were not. He would like very much to visit Tarichat and, while he was there, to visit all the Tuareg. He thought it would be good if, in a convenient oasis near the Hoggar, he built a small cell – and he meant small: the building he had in mind measured two metres by two metres – where he could live a life of poverty (but not a cloistered one) and, between periods of prayer, learn the Tuareg language (Tamacheq), translate the Bible into its written equivalent (Tinifar), and travel throughout Tuareg territory as well as making an annual tour of Adrar, In Salah, Beni Abbès, Taghit and anywhere else a French garrison might need the services of a priest. He was comfortable with this gargantuan workload because, 'a friend from the oases' had offered to help him. Guérin advised him to stick with Morocco, but Laperrine was more persuasive. The door to Morocco was closed so why not use another one, the door that led to the Sahara? Foucauld hovered uncertainly and then plumped for Laperrine. He was aided by the sluggish postal system that reached Beni Abbès once a fortnight. When Guérin told him not to leave, his letter crossed with one from Foucauld saying that he would leave unless he heard from him. On receiving Guérin's letter, Foucauld wrote that he would do whatever the Monseigneur wished, which crossed with Guérin's response that he act however he saw fit. Foucauld said he wanted to go to Morocco; Guérin told him that he might as well go to the Sahara. Then Huvelin leaped into the fray, with a letter saying that Foucauld should go wherever his calling led him, which prompted a spat of epistles from all three parties.

The clerics scribbled ever more furiously, begging each other's indulgence, permission and pardon, examining the minutiae of Foucauld's proposal, dissecting his character, wondering if the Vatican might allow him to hold Mass on his own (the answer, which entailed further letters, was no), and beseeching God to guide them. Increasingly, as they went off at tangents and forgot what they had written the day, week or fortnight before, they began to repeat themselves. Laperrine wasn't having it; he informed Algiers that he was taking Foucauld under his command. 'You may count on him as a perfect instrument of pacification and moralization', wrote a helpful Trappist. 'He will do, wherever he is, in a small way for French influence what the great Cardinal [Lavigerie] did in Tunisia.'[8] Then he told him to pack his bags for a tour of the desert. 'I believe there is a great deal of good to be done,' he wrote enticingly, 'because if we cannot hope for instant converts, or make [the Tuareg] accept the *dogma*, we can at least spread Christian *morals* through example and by daily contact.'[9] He offered him a choice of convoys: there would be one leaving Beni Abbès on 6 September and another on 15 October. 'I count on leaving on the 6th,' Foucauld wrote in his journal.

He did not catch Laperrine's column. The Moroccan border had deteriorated – as it tended suddenly to do – and in mid-August Captain Susbielle was besieged for four days in Taghit by a force of 9,000 Atlas tribesmen. Hardly had he driven the enemy away than a group of 300 raiders attacked a column of spahis and Foreign Legionnaires at the convoy halt of El Moungar, to the north of Taghit. They killed both officers and all the NCOs as well as making a murderous inroad into the soldiery. The battle took less than six hours and by the time Susbielle galloped to the rescue, thirty-six men were dead, forty-nine were wounded, and only twenty were still standing. No Moroccan corpse was found. Susbielle dug a mass grave for the dead soldiers then carried the officers' bodies and the wounded back to Taghit, from where he sent for Foucauld.

Foucauld had given the succour of French troops as one of the reasons for coming to Beni Abbès; therefore, when he received the call, he could not ignore it. (He called Susbielle's defence of Taghit 'The finest deed of arms in Algeria for forty years.')[10] Abandoning his Saharan tour, he arrived at Taghit on 6 September to provide spiritual comfort for the wounded and to bless the graves of the dead. The emergency forced him to reconsider his plans. If the situation worsened he could not justify a trip to the Tuat. By December, however, when the fear of attack had diminished, and the last of the wounded had recovered – none of them died, which made some clerics wonder if he had performed a small miracle – he began to think again. Maybe he should go to the desert after all, since no other priest seemed able to do so? Then he got cold feet at the prospect of deserting his Fraternity for the unknown, deeper Sahara. 'The countryside is excessively unpleasant,' he wrote to Huvelin. 'I shudder – I am ashamed to admit it – at the thought of leaving Beni Abbès, the calm at the foot of the altar, and embarking on travels for which I now have an extreme horror.'[11] Yet, a few lines later, he wrote, 'Inside, I feel myself increasingly impelled to make the journey.'[12] He employed similar back-and-forth arguments with Guérin, who replied with equal equivocation. Their correspondence threatened to become as convoluted as before, until Laperrine cut it short. There was a convoy leaving Beni Abbès on 10 January 1904 and he would like Foucauld to join it. Foucauld bowed to the pressure. 'I will leave on 10 January,' Foucauld wrote faintly to Huvelin, 'unless I hear from you otherwise.'[13] Three days after his due departure date he was still waiting for a reply when Laperrine's men picked him up and carried him off to the Tidikelt.

Foucauld was slightly indignant. He did not mind going to the oases but he had hoped to walk there, accompanied by his long-suffering assistant and ex-slave, Paul Embarek, with just a donkey to carry their possessions. Laperrine, however, had provided him with a horse for himself and a camel for his water, a tent, an altar, wine, bread, and everything he needed for twelve months' Mass in the Sahara. (Paul Embarek, presumably, was expected to go on foot, a situation that Foucauld did not comment upon.) In this manner the monk and his assistant reached Adrar, where Laperrine was waiting to begin his tour. From that moment, according to one of Laperrine's biographers, Foucauld became 'his friend's confidant, often his advisor, always a faithful interpreter of [his] thoughts and plans'.[14] Foucauld would never have thought of himself as a spy, but that was what he had become. And Laperrine was shaping up nicely as a spymaster. He took an obvious pleasure from working on the fringe of officialdom and from conducting operations that stretched his remit to the limit. He excelled in fieldwork and did not care if his actions were not immediately sanctioned from on high. Like a latter-day Bugeaud, he wrote, 'I authorize Foucauld to come to the Tidikelt. I have no right to do so, but I hope to get away with it, as usual, with several threatening letters and a few menaces from the sub-division, backed by all the higher-ups. It is curious how one gets acclimatized to kicks in the pants . . . They have now practically not the slightest effect. I simply keep a special folder for them in my archives.'[15]

Since the battle of Tit, Laperrine had devoted himself seriously to the recruitment of his Saharian companies. His first requirement was that they be cheap, his second was that they be utterly professional. He was ruthless in his selection of officers. Volunteers he had in plenty, who came from every Algerian cavalry and infantry regiment, all of them attracted by the promise of action. He chose only the most capable and best educated. If they did not already know Arabic he gave them six months in which to learn it; after that, if they still could not speak the language, he threw them out. NCOs, traditionally the backbone of every military unit, were graded with exceptional severity. Laperrine refused to take anyone who did not have a clean service sheet, whose training was not perfect and whose education showed the smallest defect. They had also to surrender their stripes, which they could only win back on merit, a point on which he was 'pitilessly strict'.[16] His priorities were clear: he wanted every Frenchman to be capable of both attacking the enemy and talking to them. As for the native soldiers, they were to fund themselves. He offered them four to five francs per day on which, be they infantry, spahis or *méharistes*, the elite camel troops, they were expected to pay for the upkeep of themselves and their mounts. The foot-soldiers and cavalrymen soon faded away, leaving Laperrine with a core of *méharistes*, drawn from the only group that had the same desert skills as the Tuareg: the Chaamba.

These Berber nomads, who called themselves *Habb er Rih*, 'breath of wind', were like the Tuareg, masters of the desert. Their ability to find their way through what to most Europeans looked like featureless landscape was matchless. They could read the stars like a map, divining their course at any given hour by the positions of the constellations; by day they steered according to the sun, human compasses travelling with utter certainty at the heart of a featureless bowl of horizon. Their tracking skills were as impressive as their navigational ones: a glance at a camel's hoofprints could tell them

how old it was, how long it had been since it passed by and, sometimes, even the name of its owner. They were also inured to the
rigours of desert life. Mounted on their fine-boned *méhari*, or racing
camels, they could travel immense distances fortified by nothing more
than a handful of dates. Indeed, they prided themselves on their
toughness and would rather die – sometimes nearly did – than admit
they had gone without food or water for a few days less than some of
their acquaintances; over camp fires they swapped exaggerated tales
of the hardships they and their ancestors had seen. Based in the oases
of southern Algeria they had initially been an irritant to the French,
but as the occupying power tightened its grip, Chaamba aggression
became more and more sporadic, and the two sides often reached an
accord. Chaamba nomads had assisted Laperrine at Fort MacMahon
in the first fruitless attempt to create a camel corps; they had also
served as guides and trackers for many of the late-nineteenth century
excursions into the Sahara and numbers had taken part in the
conquest of the Tuat and in Guillo-Lohan's sortie to the Hoggar. True,
they had done so for money, not through love, but as opportunities for
traditional raiding became rarer and more hazardous, so enlistment in
Laperrine's Saharian corps seemed an attractive alternative. They
would be fighting, which they enjoyed; they would be fighting the
Tuareg, who sneeringly dismissed them as Arabs, and with whom
they had a long-standing rivalry; and, best of all, they would be paid
for doing so.

Laperrine's tour of 1904 gave him an opportunity to see how his
Saharians operated as a military unit. It also afforded a chance to see
Foucauld in action. He was more than satisfied with both. The
Saharians coped smoothly with a task that was well within their capa-
bility. No combat was required; all they had to do was escort
Laperrine over tribal territories that had already acknowledged
French dominance. On their back, Laperrine swam through Tuareg
society with shark-like diplomacy, always moving, always powerful.
While greeting elders with a haughty respect, he paid menacing atten-
tion to children. As he wrote, 'Nothing is more amusing and less
compromising than to talk to the young, make them some tiny gifts.

Their mothers are watching. When you pass by their tent they smile, they say something pleasant, the father greets you, and before you know it he comes to see you to thank you for what you have given the children. The ice is broken. And, moreover, the child is the future. A tribe where the youngsters love the French officers and treat them as fathers is glad to welcome them near their tents. In ten years you have a group of young men devoted to our ideas, our way of life, and the whole tribe is ours.'[17] His officers called him 'the children's general'.

Foucauld, meanwhile, was performing very satisfactorily indeed. 'He's working hard at his [Tamacheq],' Laperrine wrote to Regnault on 19 February, 'and has ransacked my archives.'[18] Foucauld saw his studies as a way to promote Christianity. Laperrine saw them as a way to spread French rule. The speed with which his pet monk picked up Tamacheq pleased Laperrine greatly. 'He is quite aware that the fulfilment of any dream must be preceded by a thorough knowledge of the language; the Arab is the hereditary enemy; we are the interlopers, the unknown, but the Tuareg hate us less than they do the Chaamba. Time will show.'[19] He was pleased, too, by the way Foucauld returned to the military fold: 'I've been very glad to have a few days with him. Face to face with the adventurous life, the de Foucauld of Morocco finds himself again: he misses his sextant, copies his maps, etc.'[20] He was enraptured by Foucauld's ability to travel light – 'His packing is a miracle of neatness. He'd make a sailor jealous'[21] – if exasperated at his insistence on walking rather than riding a camel. And he enjoyed his participation in the column's evening meal. These dinners, cooked under the Saharan stars, saw Laperrine at his most casual. En route he could live off a few dates and a bite of bread. When relaxed he became gluttonously expansive. He would eat a whole haunch of gazelle at a sitting and, between mouthfuls, entertain his messmates with tales of the past. If anyone had the nerve to suggest that they had heard these tales before, Laperrine would roar, 'What the ****!, I tell it for *my* enjoyment not yours.'[22] He liked having Foucauld by his side – 'He eats with us and makes excellent company' – and he hoped that the bonding would be beneficial. 'I am sure that he will find time between his charities, his distributions of medicines and prayers to make a very interesting study of the country and its inhabitants,' he wrote. 'If my rounds don't allow of my leaving him in Tuareg country, I will deposit him at Akabli [an oasis that Foucauld saw as a possible site for a hermitage] or at the camp at Tidikelt, but I'd rather have him far away from us, so that people will get used to seeing him without any bayonets around.'[23] He dreamed of glorious things: 'I hope to make him the first priest of the Hoggar, Moussa's chaplain, perhaps even head of a village.'[24]

The first Tuareg Laperrine intended visiting were those in the Adrar des Iforas, based to the south-west of the Hoggar. From there he would strike north to the Hoggar itself and thence back to In Salah. It was a perfectly rational route, encompassing all the tribes who came under Moussa's control and were therefore in need of pacification. Less rational was the projected detour Laperrine tacked onto his itinerary: after he had finished with the Iforas, and before moving on to the Hoggar, he thought he might as well take his men through the Soudan and spend a few days in Timbuctoo. There was some tiny justification for straying into the Soudan, in that the Iforas Tuareg sometimes raided the country, but none at all for continuing to Timbuctoo. It was purely a matter of vanity. Laperrine had watched the Foureau–Lamy expedition cross the desert but had not been able to participate in it. He had watched his Soudanese comrades march north to Chad but had taken no part in their adventures. Now, he wanted to do what everyone else seemed to have done: travel from Algeria to Timbuctoo. But he wanted to make the traverse in style, without the use of artillery or baggage trains, and without slaughtering anyone en route. This would be the supreme test of his Saharians. It would also prove that, at last, Algeria really had been united to the Soudan and that the French could pass from top to bottom of their vast empire in peace. It never happened.

It wasn't the Iforas Tuareg who were the problem. Impoverished and enfeebled – 'it is not rare for them to *die* of hunger,'[25] Foucauld wrote – they deputed their most antagonistic marabout to surrender with face-saving surliness, then deluged the column with demands for food and medical supplies. Foucauld, who had previously recorded every encounter with the Tuareg, now stopped doing so. As he explained in his diary, it would save paper if he just noted the days when he did *not* see them. No, the Iforas Tuareg were harmless. It was the French themselves who stood in Laperrine's way. On the evening of 16 April 1904, his column reached the wells of Timiaouine on the as-yet-undemarcated border between Algeria and the Soudan. A group of soldiers clad in dusty, wrinkled uniforms were waiting for him. They were a detachment of twenty-five Soudanese *tirailleurs*, accompanied by ten auxiliaries, under the command of Captain Jean-Baptiste Theveniault.

When it suited them – as with the Cottonest and Guillo-Lohan expeditions – Saharan officers bemoaned the slowness of communication between the Tuat and France. It could take forty days for a letter to reach France from In Salah and they could not be held responsible for any infringements of official policy that might arise from such a laggardly postal system. Clearly, however, news could move a lot faster when it needed to. Between Laperrine's departure from Adrar in February and his arrival at Timiaouine in April – a period just sufficient for a return post between the oases and Paris – news of his excursion had reached the Colonial Office, had been transmitted to Senegal and then to the Soudan, with time left over for Theveniault to organize an expedition and march north to Timiaouine. Within the same space of time the commanding officer of Timbuctoo had written an order that the Commander of the Oases should not enter Soudanese territory. Theveniault now brandished this letter in Laperrine's face.

During the heated exchange that followed, several facts became clear: the Saharians had no authority to travel this far south; the Iforas Tuareg roamed across Saharan and Soudanese territory and although they had surrendered to Laperrine they had not yet surrendered to the Soudanese authorities; the Soudanese authorities, as a matter of *amour propre*, wanted to deal with the Tuareg in their own way; the Soudan fell under the jurisdiction of the Colonial Office, whereas Laperrine was a mere servant of the Governor-General of Algiers;

and if Laperrine wanted to make anything of it, Theveniault was ordered to fight back. 'If you intend to press on further with your men, I shall adhere to my orders, which are to make the rights of the Soudan respected,' runs one account of Theveniault's speech, 'and I shall not be answerable for what happens.'[26] Laperrine had once been a West African 'hooligan' himself and very nearly accepted Theveniault's offer. Only the chaperoneship of Foucauld stopped the two men embarking on an intra-service civil war – that, and the realization that neither of them knew where Algeria stopped and the Soudan began.

Their meeting epitomized the shambles that was French Africa. Everywhere, whether in Algeria, Senegal or the Soudan, soldiers seemed to be going about their business without any cohesive strategy. Their disorganization reflected Paris's ambivalent attitude towards colonialism: its desire to be seen as a major player and its fiscal abhorrence of such a role; its appreciation of republican values and the nagging suspicion that its current programme was not the best way of propagating them. In military terms Africa was a superb training ground – most of France's First World War generals served an apprenticeship there – but politically it was a minefield. Wisely (and perhaps with Voulet and Chanoine in mind), Laperrine and Theveniault decided that this problem required governmental intervention. Over a frosty dinner at Timiaouine on the night of 16 April 1904, they agreed to return whence they came, neither man interfering with the Iforas Tuareg until their superiors had drawn a boundary between the two territories.

On the morning of 17 April, Laperrine ordered his Saharians to ride for the Hoggar, and Theveniault marched back to Timbuctoo. Their compromise had defused a potentially explosive situation, but it left Laperrine angry. The encounter had offended his sense of honour: the Iforas Tuareg had surrendered, yet Theveniault had treated them as enemies, *razzia*-ing brutally even when the two parties were encamped together. It had dented his pride: as Commander of the Oases he was the Tuareg's protector but he had been unable to protect them. And it had damaged France's standing: the sight of their conquerors preparing to fight each other did not make a good impression on the natives. Foucauld, too, was shocked by the Soudanese approach to colonialism: 'At every turn we learn of a new act of brutality or theft.' He had shaken Theveniault's hand on meeting him but he did not shake it when he departed. 'I shall leave without saying goodbye, because I do not want to enter a compact with infamy,' he wrote. 'I will not make any reproachful comments because, 1) it would do them no good, 2) it would distance them from religion, 3) it would create a rift between their officers and ours.'[27] That said, he reproached Theveniault in his diary. 'What I see of the officers of the Soudan saddens me,' he wrote. 'They come across as pillagers, bandits, filibusters. I fear that this great colonial empire, which could and should give birth to so much good – moral good, true good – is presently only a cause of shame. It makes us blush before the savages, and leads them to curse the name of France and, alas, the name of Christianity. All we are doing is making poor people even poorer.'[28] Captain Theveniault was 'a brigand. But we, we have nothing but good, pure, fraternal intentions.'[29]

The journey north to the Hoggar was hard. The rains had been intermittent and the springs of Tinherhor, which they reached on 7 May, greeted them with a muddy seepage. It took more than three days to water their 300 camels and when the column departed, at 5 p.m. on the 11th, its water containers held as much grit as fluid. Laperrine sent two lieutenants and a guide to scout for wells, but the guide ran off, leaving the Frenchmen to flounder through the desert in the middle of a sandstorm that not only prevented them navigating by the stars but also obliterated their tracks. It was mostly by luck that Laperrine's men caught up with them and brought them safely to Tinef at the edge of the Hoggar.

Here, after the setback at Timiaouine, Laperrine began his pacification afresh. Declining to ascend the massif itself, he skirted through the Hoggar's western oases, taking submissions as he went. Foucauld was his ever-present aide. He assisted the expedition's 'scientists' (unqualified officers who recorded with mystification the readings on their barometers and thermometers) by making sketches of the surrounding countryside. When Laperrine received each chieftain's formal submission, Foucauld was there, sitting cheerfully at his feet. At each oasis he distributed alms in the form of money or goods (usually lengths of cotton) to demonstrate to the people the generosity of their new overlords. And in his diary he amassed information that he hoped would be of value to the colonial programme.

Its tiny pages (135 millimetres by 88 millimetres, covered in diagrams and vertical annotations, scrawled in a mix of pencil and either black or violet ink) portray him as an indefatigable pathfinder for the Faith. They are peppered with endless, and often repetitive lists of advice to future evangelists: how to organize their day, when to say their prayers, how to make a water-skin, what clothes to wear and how to treat the natives. They give precise details of what camels to use: missionaries, Foucauld said, should never choose a *méhara*, because they were too fast for a man to walk alongside them in contemplation; neither should they go for the cheapest option, the pack camel, for these were too plodding and awkward to handle; they should purchase a cross between the two, the *demi-méhara*. They describe what alms to distribute: francs if need be, but preferably cotton, flour, wheat, barley or dates, the last being most desirable. Foucauld also noted that all kinds of fruit and vegetables were in short supply and should a traveller have space he should pack chillies, tomatoes, carrots, cucumbers, beetroot, turnips, onions, pumpkins and water melons, as well as a few date, fig, apricot and peach saplings; Japanese medlars were also popular. His diary gives a ready reckoner of the prevailing exchange rate: two francs were equivalent to four metres of cotton; a *qsaa* (2¼ litres) of wheat was worth one franc twenty-five cents; and the same measure of barley was worth one franc; when dealing in dates, missionaries should double their order because the haulier charged half the cargo. They tell how much to distribute and to whom: between fifty cents and one franc per poorest person per visit, perhaps more if they were to be visited less than twice a year; and for every projected month of his stay the missionary should also carry trade goods to the sum of 130 needles, fifty handkerchiefs and a pair of scissors. They also list the dispensary every missionary should carry: zinc sulphate for eye conditions, mercury for syphilis, potassium iodide for rheumatism, quinine for fevers, bismuth for intestinal complaints and a number of unspecified remedies for the other most common complaints, gonorrhoea, bronchitis, hernias and snake bites.

Revealing as it is about the practicalities of desert evangelism, Foucauld's diary is slightly skewed. He kept it only because Guérin told him to do so – all White Fathers were required to keep similar journals, which they handed in at regular intervals for inspection – and it was written with Guérin in mind. Despite his decision to go to the Sahara, Foucauld hoped secretly that there might yet be an opening for him in Morocco and, therefore, he wrote his reports with an air of insouciance, perhaps fearing that too overt a display of enthusiasm might damage his prospects in the West. But his keenness for the Sahara could not be suppressed. He surveyed every oasis for its potential as a hermitage, annotating the richness of the soil, the amount of pasturage and the sweetness and longevity of its wells. When excited by a particular site he drew sketch maps of its situation, pinpointing grottos in which a religious community might find shelter and bluffs on which its buildings might impose to greatest effect. And when he spoke of the men who might inhabit these spots, he spoke as if he would be their leader.

Foucauld was tantalized by the Hoggar. On first seeing it, from Tinef, on 17 May 1904, he wrote of his desire 'To found in the heart of Tuareg country the sanctuary, the fraternity of the Sacred Heart of Jesus ... I offer my life for the conversion of the Tuareg, the Moroccans, all the people of the Sahara, all the infidels.'[30] Again and again, he saw sites that might be suitable. 'I will settle in the Hoggar,' he wrote to one of Laperrine's underlings, Lieutenant Besset, 'Come with me. The Tuareg love you. Laperrine will give you a command there. One of my friends, a Trappist in Staouëli, is a physician. He will join me. He will minister to the bodies, I will take care of the souls, and you will exercise temporal power.'[31] His proposed kingdom of the soul was a joke – but only just. On 26 May Laperrine's column reached Tit. Superficially, Tit was a splendid place for a fraternity. The water was fresh and reliable; the soil was rich and cultivable. A band of monks could live there in complete self-sufficiency; and because Tit was on one of the main trade routes they would be able to display their faith to every passer-by. But Tit was also the worst place to settle. It was pungent with symbolism. For a Frenchman to set up camp on the site of the Tuareg's greatest humiliation would be grossly undiplomatic. Only an insensitive fool or the most domineering colonialist would consider it. Maybe Foucauld was both. In his diary he wrote, 'Tit seems to me the most suitable place to establish a mission since it is the true heart of the Hoggar and of all the Tuareg country . . . I'm formally asking Laperrine permission to stay here. I expect his answer tomorrow or the day after.'[32] Laperrine said no.

He led Foucauld instead to Tarichat, the Tuareg widow whose good-heartedness had lured Foucauld to the desert 'She is between forty and fifty, distinguished, silent and modest,'[33] Foucauld wrote. But she did not seem interested in Christianity, nor to have received a letter from Guérin, and Foucauld's speeches about the benefits of French rule elicited only the memory of a *tirailleur* named Amer, 'whom she had saved and repatriated and who had promised he would send her weight in cash'. Foucauld was innocently indignant: 'He has never sent her a penny!'[34] Laperrine hurried him on.

On 12 June, the column split in two. One half, under Captain Roussel, would proceed with the tour while the other, under Laperrine, would return to In Salah. After two days' deliberation, Foucauld chose to go with Roussel. When Laperrine assented, Foucauld was overjoyed: 'he gave his whole-hearted permission and himself told Roussel, if he sees Moussa to negotiate with him my immediate and definite establishment in the Hoggar. He then left me after having for these past five months showered kindnesses of every kind upon me . . . and said that he hoped to see me again in the Hoggar.'[35] To Cauvet, Laperrine wrote, 'I'm leaving Foucauld in the Sahara. He's studying Tuareg and he has medicines and two camels. If Count de Foucauld, hussar, ex-explorer, breakaway Trappist, becomes chaplain to Moussa or someone else of that rank, it will be no small thing.'[36]

Moussa did not show himself – he apparently had, at the time, neither the clothes nor the escort grand enough for a display of hauteur – and so for the next three months Foucauld and Roussel travelled through the settlements of the Hoggar in a mundane succession of meetings. They visited 300 villages in all, some at sea level, others perched high in the mountains, whose leaders greeted them with a mixture of pomp, pride and petulance. At Bou Ali ('tolerable welcome') the chief demanded a gift of tea; at Tiouririn ('incomparable welcome') it was twenty sous; at Anzeglouf ('good welcome'), 'a passing marabout from Zaouia Reggan (accompanied by a so-called lunatic who wanted a thousand things) commanded me to give him matches, coffee and a candle.'[37] Almost every stop seemed ripe for an evangelical community and Foucauld employed Roussel to petition the local chieftains on his behalf. His petitions always failed. On 29 July, for example, at Ideles ('Altitude about 1,000 metres. Very favourable spot . . . Srir ag Bedda gave us a good welcome'), he emphasized in his diary, '*M. Roussel asked him if I could stay at Ideles. He said: no.*' It was the same on 4 August at Tazerouk ('about 2,000 metres above sea level; cold; often rains; snows'.): '*M. Roussel asked Si Mohammed ben Otman if I could stay at Tazerouk. He replied: no.*' The refusals exasperated Foucauld. In his diary, he called Si Mohammed ben Otman a vain, stupid young windbag. To his cousin Marie de Bondy, however, he was more pragmatic: '[Their welcome] is not sincere; they cede to necessity. Will they be able to distinguish between soldiers and priests and see in us universal brothers?'[38]

On 20 September Roussel, Foucauld and their Saharians reached In Salah. They had travelled more than 5,000 kilometres and were exhausted. But Foucauld still burned with feverish energy. He applied at once for permission to return to the Hoggar and when it was not forthcoming he marched with Paul Embarek to El Goléa and from El Goléa to Guérin's headquarters at Ghardaia. The White Fathers who came to meet him almost mistook him for a mendicant dervish: 'We could never have distinguished the European from the native, for both were burnt the same colour by the sun, had it not been for the red cloth heart on Father de Foucauld's gandorah and the rosary tied to his leather belt.'[39] Parched and scraggy, he was carried back to Ghardaia like a hot coal.

12

TOWARDS THE HOGGAR

As 1904 drew to a close, three figures could be discerned on the dusty track that ran from Ghardaia to El Goléa. They moved slowly and in a rough arrow-formation. The rearmost two were mounted on camels while, in the van, a lone individual plodded on foot, one hand hooked in his own camel's reins. As they padded through the sand, the couple at the back maintained a desultory conversation. The pedestrian recited Hail Marys. At every o'clock one of the riders would strike the hour on a mess tin hanging from his saddle. Without breaking his stride the man in front would turn, nod his thanks, and then resume his litany. Charles de Foucauld (who had forgotten his watch) was guiding two White Fathers to El Goléa.

On New Year's Day 1905, the tinkling caravan reached its destination, where Laperrine came forward to greet it. Since parting from Foucauld in July the previous year, Laperrine had been busy. The tour of 1904 had not been an unqualified success. A number of Tuareg settlements had been 'pacified' and the Saharians had performed seamlessly. However, his efforts to place Foucauld in the Hoggar had failed – standing orders said that no priest could live in the Sahara unless they were near a garrison; and the same orders forbade the installation of a garrison south of the Tuat. Had Moussa invited him to stay, then that would have been a different matter. But Moussa had not appeared, which was in itself another problem, for Laperrine wanted very much to receive his submission on his own territory. Then there was the embarrassment at Timiaouine. In order to clear his name, sort out the status of the Iforas Tuareg and clarify the position of missionaries in Tuareg territory – also to have a holiday – Laperrine had gone to France. Expecting to be roasted for disobedience, he received a mild condemnation before being promoted to Lieutenant Colonel and told to keep up the good work. Now he was back in the Sahara with unfinished tasks in mind.

At El Goléa, and on the road back to Adrar, Laperrine painted sweeping pictures of political and religious conquest. There would be another tour of pacification in 1905, this time commanded not by himself but by a new man he had installed at In Salah, Captain Jean Dinaux. He assured his companion that Dinaux was extremely capable and just the man to locate Moussa and find Foucauld a home in the Hoggar. Once settled amidst the Tuareg, Foucauld would become a magnet for other evangelists. White Fathers, White Sisters: all were welcome. They would flock to the place once they knew Foucauld was there. And the authorities had no objection to his settling in the Hoggar. It was all arranged! But best not to talk of these things openly, lest word reach the ears of those who did not share their dreams. The two men ambled towards the Tuat in a roseate glow of conspiracy.

Before he went anywhere near the Hoggar, Foucauld wanted a restorative period at his Fraternity in Beni Abbès. He also needed to consult Guérin, a process that involved the usual exchange of letters and which was muddled still further by Foucauld's decision to transmit his messages in code. Fortunately, Guérin shared Foucauld's Laperrine-inspired obsession with secrecy (though from his correspondence he seems to have spent more time worrying about the fate of the White Fathers than the souls of his would-be converts), and he adapted quickly to the simple, eighty-two-word substitution system. It was worth the effort, for Foucauld sent him uplifting news. Kaddour

(Laperrine) expected several sacks of wool (White Sisters) to be in the Hoggar within eighteen months to two years and had already drawn up a list of oases in which they could be settled. When they arrived he wanted them to be able to speak Tamacheq, teach the Tuareg French, and play a musical instrument – a skill valued highly by Tuareg women. The sacks of flour (White Fathers), with their reputation for obduracy, were more problematic. Nevertheless, Laperrine was sure he could find something for them to do, even if it was a roaming curacy, distributing medicine, alms, gifts and sermons, helping orphans and doing the occasional odd-job. This tremendous advance for the faith was accompanied by one caveat: the White Fathers would have to fund it themselves. 'Do not even speak of money!' Laperrine warned. 'On no account will it be given; to ask for it will only attract unwelcome attention.'[1]

Laperrine was being duplicitous. He knew perfectly well that the White Fathers' tiny budget could not support missions to the Hoggar. Anyway, he didn't want them there. What he wanted was a monk with military training who could report on the Tuareg while bringing them within the Christian fold. He wanted Foucauld. And he intended to get him, even if it entailed giving false promises to the priesthood.

By this time, Foucauld had achieved a measure of fame. Disagree as they might with his religion – and there were many who did – Frenchmen serving in the Sahara admired his diligence and his toughness; they respected the manner in which he had adapted to desert life but retained his essential Europeanness, how he had gone native without going all the way. Also, unlike other meddling clerics, he was an ex-officer, and therefore 'one of them'. In the coarse milieu of garrison life, Foucauld was looked upon with fondness. He had become, in a way, the mascot of the African Army. Nor was he admired by the soldiery alone. Word of his mission had spread across France, where it served as a beacon for the persecuted faithful. A pious woman from Lyons wrote that she had offered her life as an oblation to him – an offer that Foucauld accepted – and until her death in 1912 he remembered her daily in his devotions. So great was his reputation that General Lyautey, of Aïn Sefra, decided to pay him a visit. He had met him once before, in 1903, but, intrigued by the talk of his officers – 'who have a cult for him'[2] – he wanted another look at the man.

When Foucauld reached Beni Abbès on 24 January 1905, he closed the doors of his Fraternity. He wanted to stretch his spiritual limbs, to adore Jesus in solitude and to ask His advice on the forthcoming Saharan tour. The only people he allowed in were Paul Embarek and Marie, the old, blind black woman whom he had baptized and who had been awaiting his return for more than twelve months. Four days later, Lyautey burst into his meditations. Dragging Foucauld over to the *bordj*, he and his entourage treated the monk to a raucous, wine-sodden dinner. Afterwards, Lyautey played a selection of lewd songs on the Beni Abbès phonograph. Mischievously, he awaited Foucauld's departure. But Foucauld surprised him. 'I was watching de Foucauld,' he wrote, 'and I said to myself, "He's going to leave." He did not leave, he even laughed!'[3] The next day, at 7 a.m, Lyautey took his officers for Mass at the Fraternity. 'A hovel, that hermitage! His chapel, a miserable corridor on columns covered with rushes! A board for the altar; for decoration, a piece of calico with a picture of Christ; tin candlesticks; a flattened sardine tin with two bottles that once held mouthwash, for cruets and tray! Our feet on the sand. Well, I've never heard Mass said as Father de Foucauld said it . . . It was one of the greatest impressions of my life.'[4]

Curiosity apart, Lyautey had a practical reason for visiting Foucauld. He wanted to size him up for a prospective trip to Morocco – *Reconnaissance au Maroc* was still, by far and away, the most authoritative text on that unknown country and, as Lyautey said, 'We never grow tired of calling upon his documentation.'[5] But when he saw him in his hermitage he realized that Foucauld's calling lay to the south. 'Past the humble earthen walls,' he wrote, 'there was a vision of the Saharan vastness, of that Sahara whose sands came like waves to beat at the chapel door, a Sahara where he truly ruled through the strength of that prayer.'[6] He did not especially like Laperrine, and was indignant at the way he disregarded orders, but he admired his efficiency and shared his goals. He told Foucauld to forget Morocco and to concentrate instead on Laperrine's mission in the Sahara. After a long discussion, in which the two men found much common ground, Lyautey left Beni Abbès with a profound respect for his army's mascot. 'He is the most lofty spiritual figure I have ever encountered,' he wrote. 'I have no doubt that Foucauld will have a significant place in the order of the world.'[7]

Tormented by doubts – Guérin was advising him to stay at Beni Abbès – Foucauld fell ill and retired to his cell. He could not decide which was best: to live the life of Nazareth, quietly and in a cloister; or to pursue a more active existence in the Sahara. He wrote to Huvelin and Guérin, explaining his dilemma. The Tuareg needed him: they had no priests and he was the only man whom the authorities would allow in the area; it was his duty to go. But Beni Abbès was his home, his vocation, the site he had chosen for his order. As the letters flowed back and forth, none of them providing any real satisfaction, Foucauld lay back on his bed, nursing his toothache, fever and neuralgia, while he waited for God, Guérin, Huvelin, Laperrine or *anyone* to tell him what to do. Laperrine got there first. 'The Tuareg have no priest,' Foucauld wrote, 'and no priest has yet been allowed to go there. Yet, not only have I been given permission but I have actually been invited . . . Only I can go there. Should I refuse?'[8] On 3 May he caught a convoy to meet Laperrine's protégé Dinaux in the Tuat.

If Foucauld was becoming something of a cult, so too were Laperrine and his Saharians. They had achieved an enviable reputation for free-thinking and straight action. As an elite corps they far outstripped the Foreign Legion, which at this period was little more than a band of desperate and low-paid thugs, who undertook whatever act of violence their officers deemed necessary. If a man was after a bit of adventure, if he wanted to escape the drudgery of garrison duties and the tedium of the Moroccan border – which would soon become lively enough – then he applied to join the Saharians. One recruit wrote, 'I am free to follow my ambitions in a country where healthy adventure is still possible. I command and I organize. I do not have to make any reports until the end of an expedition. Post is rare – thank God! I don't want to hear anything about Europe, where I would be a tiny stick in the current. Here I am one of the first in an epoch where everyone is starting off under a new adminstration.'[9] Another put it more intellectually: 'The style of a Saharian is not that of a *roumi* [the African word for a French settler], it is to have none of the prejudices of the provincial petit bourgeois and above all to be shocked by nothing.'[10] Lieutenant Guy Dervil was seduced by these very arguments.

Beni Abbès was to Foucauld a source of solace. To Dervil, in 1904, it was the fount of ultimate boredom. A young spahi officer, who had recently been posted from Aïn Sefra, Dervil could not stand the place. 'Hour follows hour, sometimes broken by the alert of a *rezzou* always pursued in vain, or the periodic arrival of a supply convoy,' he wrote. 'Each day, a little before sunset, I go to stretch out on the sand at the end of the wall and, inevitably, I look toward the south until it is too dark to see. My relatively inactive life bores me. A passionate wish tortures me; to go over there, beyond the horizon, further, always further. I dream of long patrols, of razzias, of pursuing Tuareg, the "Men of the Veil", and in my mind I turn over one thousand plans to escape from this prison.'[11] When a Saharian corporal came into town, demanding his unit's wages, Dervil was entranced. The man was shaven-headed, had a tangled beard, was shoeless and had a dagger stuck into the belt of his *gandourah*. Yet he spoke perfect French and was very firm in his desire to collect the money. Dervil offered to count it out for him. Two and a half hours later he had sifted through 4,000 francs of miscellaneous metal weighing more than thirty-four kilograms. 'I did not realize what I had volunteered for!' he wrote. 'There are coins there of every calibre, of every epoch, from every country, of every value: Marie-Theresa dollars (Bou Tyr), doubloons, duros, four-franc pieces (Bou Medva, with crossed cannons), three-franc pieces, two-franc fifty, two-francs, one-france twenty-five, one franc: 18, 14, 10, 8, 5, 4, 2 and one sou: some of the coins were cut in half to "make change!"'[12] The romance of the money and the quiet

authority with which the shabby corporal received it decided Dervil.
He had an interview with Laperrine, who asked him two questions:
was he fluent in Arabic? and did he have any charges against him?
Dervil replied yes to both. Laperrine laughed and said there was a
vacancy for him in the Tidikelt. 'You won't get up to much mischief
there.'[13] Dervil went to the Tidikelt as requested and in May 1905
was asked by Captain Dinaux to accompany him on a tour of the Hoggar.
Before they started, however, they had to wait at the wells of Ouan
Thora for Foucauld to join them.

Dinaux recorded the monk's arrival on 8 June 1905: 'Charles
walked fast, bent almost double, pulling along one of his baggage
camels, while Paul led the other. His emaciated face, with a straggly
beard which he trimmed himself with a pair of scissors, was illuminated by his deep-set eyes, with their penetrating regard, and by his
big smile . . . He wore sandals made of camel skin, of his own making,
which he fastened, as did the Saharan shepherds, by a thong between
his toes.'[14] Dervil, who had met Foucauld in Beni Abbès but had
never seen him in the field, gave a penetrating description: 'He is on
the small side. A short, greying beard frames a face upon which the
prominent cheekbones accentuate the thinness. He is mostly bald in
front. In deep sockets, beneath thick eyebrows, his dark eyes wear a
curious expression, a mixture of modesty and authority, of intelligence and self-effacement. I judge them to be capable of firmness,
even of harshness.'[15]

This tour was different from the one of 1904. It comprised not
only military men and Chaamba camel troops but four civilians
whose job was to survey the terrain for a trans-Saharan telegraph
link. There were two geologists, Professor Gautier and M. Chudeau,
both of whom were experienced desert hands and reasonable men.
And there was M. Etiennot, an inspector of telegraph poles, and his
assistant. Detested by all, Etiennot was an incompetent surveyor,
who was forever borrowing the officers' maps so that he could copy
them as his own. He resented his mission and consoled himself
with bottles of absinthe, which he shared with nobody. He was a fat,
overbearing man with strong anti-clerical views, and when not

bullying his assistant he liked to pick on Foucauld, whom he called Brother Charles (to the Saharians Foucauld was always Father). When one day he strode up to the monk and said, 'Well, Brother Charles, you don't say much do you?'[16] Foucauld replied, 'That's because I have a horror of garrulous people, Monsieur.' The officers tittered at the rebuff.

It was the comfort-loving Etiennot's great misfortune that Laperrine had ordered Dinaux to make his tour in midsummer. This was a time when most garrisons were silent, their officers taking cold showers, playing the odd game of tennis, and whiling away the afternoons in the company of 'wives' they had chosen from the local women. (At In Salah, Dervil kept a thirteen-year-old, half-Tuareg 'wife' who had cost him 300 francs. He explained that she gave him Tamacheq lessons. Foucauld, who spent a lot of his time organizing care for the illegitimate offspring of French NCOs, told him, 'I have only one piece of advice to give you. Avoid having children.')[17] However great the financial temptation, no trade caravans crossed the Sahara in midsummer. Even the Tuareg kept to the shade of their tents and remained as immobile as the state of their pastures permitted. Only a madman would venture into the searing heat of the Sahara's worst season. But Laperrine wanted to show Moussa that his Saharians were equal to any enemy, climate included. The French could go wherever they wanted whenever they wished.

The column moved south at a speed of forty kilometres per day, Foucauld striding alongside it with manic determination. 'The stages of our journey were for him a test of mortification,' Dinaux recorded. 'The pace of a detachment of camel troopers is considerably faster than that of a walker. The priest continued to follow us on foot to the point of exhaustion, telling his beads and reciting litanies. He forced his pace when the terrain was difficult. From five o'clock in the morning, the sun beat down mercilessly, and the temperature in the shade varied from 40 to 50°C. Each of us downed from nine to eleven litres of water a day, and what water, bucketed from ponds in which livestock had been splashing. And the father followed along at a rapid pace.'[18] In Dervil's opinion, Foucauld's daily routine was barely human.

He rose fifteen minutes before everyone else, in order to say Mass, then after a day's hard walking he would spend several hours on his paperwork, of which he seemed to have an endless amount. En route from Beni Abbès to In Salah he had finally completed his Tamacheq translation of the Gospels and now he was working on a Tamacheq lexicon (a Tamacheq grammar and a French–Tamacheq dictionary had been published in the 1890s but Foucauld thought them insufficient) as well as transcribing every scrap of Tuareg legend, poetry and oral history he could persuade the nomads to recite.

Foucauld, who was not by nature a scholar, gave two reasons for his diligence, the first of which was admirably far-sighted. He foresaw a time when the industrial values of Europe and America would dominate the world, swamping fragile societies such as the Tuareg. Before this happened he wanted to put Tuareg lore on paper, creating a culture-bank that would withstand the onslaught to come. Conversely, his second motive was to spread the westernization that he sought to keep at bay. Having seen how sullenly the Arabs accepted French rule, he had grown to detest them; he wanted to separate the Tuareg from their influence, to distance them from an Islamic faith that they practised only half-heartedly and to inculcate them with the glories of Christianity. To him, the Tuareg teetered between nobility and savagery and only French missionaries could swing the balance. In order to perform effectively evangelists needed to know the language and history of their evangelized, and Foucauld hoped that his compilations would be of assistance.

Foucauld admired the Tuareg's noble savagery but, in reality, he did not like them much more than the Arabs. 'Like the Arabs, they are only subjugated by *force*; like the Arabs, their ignorance is extreme, and, like the Arabs, they have a violent character and violent habits that only force can control.' Yet he had hopes: 'With instruction and laws they would become civilized more quickly than the Arabs; they are far less closed in their characters, are livelier and more curious. What keeps them from us is their extreme ignorance; they call us simply "pagans" (which, alas, it is only too often true that we are) and consider us savages with murderous and bloody habits. They have the

most monstrous preconceptions about us, and there are extraordinary
stories current about our customs. They think themselves the most
civilized and perfect people in the world . . . Still, they really *are* barbarians because they are ignorant *and* barbarians . . . They are the
descendants of Cham, look like ancient Egyptians, are thin, tall, very
white, with much national pride and a language of which they are very
proud. . . . What is needed is to enlighten their souls, to soften their
habits and to make them gentle and humble of heart, for is not humility the truth, and is not pride the brother of ignorance?'[19] Politically,
this translated into a desire for a Saharan colony devolved from the
mess that Algeria was rapidly becoming – which was what Laperrine
had in mind when he made Moussa head of the 'Confederacy of
Tuareg Tribes'.

Professor Gautier, an explorer in his own right, rode alongside
Foucauld for a chat. His first impression was that 'Nothing about him
betrayed his military origins. He was a monk from head to toe, all self-
effacement and humility.'[20] As they crossed an increasingly bleak and
horrible landscape, Foucauld did nothing to dispel that impression.
On passing a mountain, which Gautier thought was one of the most
forbidding things he had ever seen in the entire course of his life,
Foucauld sighed: 'How beautiful it is!'[21] But then, a few minutes
later, Foucauld began to reminisce about the past. He wondered what
had happened to various figures from his youth. 'You don't know what
has become of them?' Gautier asked in disbelief. Foucauld replied
that he didn't even know if they were dead or alive. Gautier filled him
in. Foucauld's old history teacher was now the Minister of Education
and his foreign languages professor was a member of the Académie
Française. They also talked about the actress Sarah Bernhardt. 'I saw
her several times and used to enjoy seeing her,' said Foucauld. 'You
mean to say that she is still alive, still acting?'[22] Gautier assured him
that she was in fine fettle and still going strong on the stage, despite
being sixty and having a slight limp. Foucauld digested the news in
silence. 'Really!' he said at last.

Dinaux's column followed, more or less, the same route as
Laperrine's in 1904, travelling directly south to Timiaouine, then

north to the Hoggar. It moved in military fashion, camping each night in square, defensive formation, the sentries changing guard every few hours. (Foucauld was allotted the quietest corner where he prayed in peace until 2 a.m.) But their aggressor was not the Tuareg: it was the Sahara. The first leg of the journey proved how hazardous it was to travel in midsummer. The wells, never very productive at the best of times, were even less so and the column soon ran dry. As the first camels started to die, Etiennot waxed furious. 'Posterity will learn of this,' he raged at Dinaux. 'If we escape death I will tell everyone that it was your fault that we almost died.'[23] Foucauld offered him the last of his water, a tepid gruel tasting of tar, which Etiennot downed without thanks. Dinaux managed to calm him, but he was as worried as Etiennot about their prospects. He ordered the men to halt and sent six Chaamba ahead to scout for wells. Then he sat down on a camp chair and awaited their return.

For almost two days the camp sweltered, immobile on the sand. As the thermometer rose to 54 °C in the shade, the interpreter, an Algerian Jew, became delirious. Dervil, whose mouth was so dry that not even the old trick of sucking a pebble could produce any saliva, felt certain they were going to die. Even the Chaamba cracked under the strain: two of them wandered vaguely into the desert until Dinaux dragged them back and ordered his sentries to shoot anyone who tried to escape. Dervil recorded one man lying on the ground completely naked, 'his ribs so prominent that he looked like a skeleton'. When at last the six scouts returned, having located the wells of In-Ziza – less by their own skill than by their camels' nose for water – there was a riot as the men fought over the bloated water-skins. Eight hours later the column was at In-Ziza. In normal circumstances, the French officers would have laughed if anyone had described this stagnant, green pool, awash with camel excrement, as a well. Nevertheless, they flung themselves into it, jostling with each other, their men and their camels for a mouthful of fluid. None of them had travelled so far south or spent so long a time in the desert. As an initiation to life in Laperrine's camel corps, In-Ziza was something they would not forget.

On 15 June, at In Ouzel, they finally met the elusive Moussa. Foucauld's first impression was: 'very good, very intelligent, very frank . . . wishing to do the right thing as a Muslim liberal but at the same time ambitious and fond of money, pleasure, honour. To sum it up, Moussa is a good and pious Muslim, has the ideas, the way of life, the qualities and the vices of a logical Muslim and at the same time is as open-minded as he can be. He very much wishes to visit Algiers and France.'[25] Foucauld liked Moussa for his honesty and respected him as a potential ally. But he was also wary of him, suspecting that he would desert the French at the slightest sign of their grip weakening on the Sahara. He had grounds for caution: Moussa was an adroit politician and one of the reasons he had not shown himself during Laperrine's tour of 1904 was that he had been in Tripolitania, negotiating with Attici and his displaced band of warriors. His excuse that he did not have the right clothes to meet Laperrine stemmed from the negotiations – one of Attici's henchmen had pillaged his baggage – and this dagger to his pride was responsible as much as anything for his acceptance of French rule. If Attici was against him then he would side with the foreigners who were against Attici. Eleven years later Foucauld was still unsure how far he could trust him. 'He has an inveterate habit of using deceit and lying,' he wrote in 1915, 'with many other faults, including that of trying to make a good thing for himself out of every occasion.'[26] But maybe Foucauld was being too harsh on the man. Moussa remained loyal to the French for the rest of his life (he was awarded the Légion d'Honneur) and if he did so only because it was in his own interests then that was no reason to castigate him. When Laperrine met him, he delivered a much kinder judgement: 'He does not hesitate when one asks him to speak his mind frankly even when his views do not conform to ours. He is very deferential, specifying that he only speaks his mind because we ask and not to oppose us . . . [He] is on the one hand very greedy for money and honours and on the other amuses himself like a child as soon as he feels at home. For the legend of the majestic and impassible Touareg receives a knock as soon as one makes these nomads relax.' All in all, he was 'very superior to the immense majority'.[27]

Moussa gave immediate proof of his loyalty. At Timiaouine, on 10 July, Dinaux bade farewell to the civilians. Etiennot returned whence he came, to the immense joy of his fellow travellers, wobbling northward on his camel without bothering to say goodbye, followed by his long-suffering assistant who, unbeknownst to his superior, carried a letter signed by every officer testifying to the wretched manner in which he had been treated. Gautier and Chudeau, meanwhile, continued south. It had been expected that a Soudanese escort would be there to guide them. But the Soudanese had not appeared and so Moussa volunteered three of his own men to act in their stead. The two geologists reached Niger unharmed which, for Dinaux and Laperrine, was both a splendid triumph over the Soudanese and a testimony to Moussa's trustworthiness. It was also, though neither Frenchman realized it, an added inducement for Moussa to side with the French. A few weeks before his surrender, Paris had drawn a border between Algeria and the Soudan and, like almost every African border settled in Europe, it paid no attention to the Africans. This one sliced through the middle of the Iforas territory, separating their desert camps from the monsoon-fed pastures of Soudan. Moussa had been angered by the decision, for his people depended on these pastures during those seasons when the Hoggar dried up completely. By sending his men through the Soudan, he had proved to his supporters that if France could cross the desert as and when they liked, then he too could cross their arbitrary boundaries in the same fashion – but only with the support of Laperrine. Moussa was learning to play colonial politics with the same skill as he played those of his homeland.

When Dinaux suggested that Foucauld might like to settle in the Hoggar – for he was a man who liked solitude and wanted only to study Tuareg language and customs – Moussa had no objections. Indeed, he welcomed him with open arms. To have a Frenchman living in the Hoggar would be further proof of his good faith. It would also give him a hostage if the relationship soured. He knew the perfect place for 'the Christian marabout': an impoverished village in the middle of nowhere, named Tamanrasset. It was the first time

Foucauld had ever heard the name but he reacted as if he had been given directions to the Holy Grail. By some peculiar instinct – maybe a God-given one – he recognized Tamanrasset as his destiny. His letters, which had always displayed some sign of equivocation, now showed a firm intent. 'Right away I shall build a hut there,' he wrote to his cousin, 'and I shall live a poor and retired life, trying only to imitate the divine worker of Nazareth.'[28] Five days later, on 11 August, Dinaux's column reached Tamanrasset.

13

'I CHOOSE TAMANRASSET'

According to Tuareg mythology, God had created the world's mountains by throwing stones at the globe as it spun by. Eventually, tiring of the game, he had emptied his hand into the desert: the resultant jumble of rock was the Hoggar. At some later date a passing giant had taken a swipe at the Hoggar with his sabre, leaving a deep gash in the southern foothills. And when, at an even later date, humans arrived in the Sahara, they had been thankful for the giant's action, for this gap provided them with a gateway to the cool highlands. Passing through it, travellers from the south encountered a threadbare plateau surrounded on all sides by hills. To east, south and west, rose the red granite of the Hoggar's lower ramparts; to the north, mountain upon mountain climbed towards the massif itself, culminating in the 3,000-metre obelisk of Mt Ilaman. Running north-east, south-west across the plateau was a dried-up waterbed, in whose ravines and pools water collected during the rainy season. The Tuareg considered the plateau to be no more than a watering hole, but a few *harratin* managed to scratch a subsistence from the land. Usually they could harvest a crop of wheat and in good years a crop of vegetables; but it was an uncertain existence, dependent as was everything in the

Sahara upon the weather. Unlike the nomads, who simply decamped to better pastures when times were hard, the *harratin* were immobile. In periods of drought they could only wait and pray. The pools were deep and when they ran dry, water could be obtained by digging in the river bed. But there was only enough to keep a small population alive for three or four years. After that, if no rains came, the *harratin* would die. The spot was called Tamanrasset.

'I choose Tamanrasset!' Foucauld wrote in his diary. 'Deep in the mountains, in the heart of the Hoggar, away from all major centres . . . it does not seem destined ever to have a garrison, a telegraph, or Europeans, and it will be a long time before it has a mission. I choose this *forsaken* place, and here I will stay.'[1] With the help of Dinaux's men he built a *zeriba*, or cabin, of palm branches for his immediate shelter and then embarked upon the construction of a more permanent hermitage whose walls were of stone, held together by mud. Made to his own design, it measured twenty-three metres by two and protruded like a rectangular sphinx amidst the *zeribas* of Tamanrasset. It comprised a single room that served as bedroom, dining-room, office, library and storeroom, separated by a partition from a minuscule chapel with an altar made from a packing case that visitors tended to sit on until Foucauld shooed them to their feet. Its windows were mere holes, without curtains or glass, over which he placed a board to keep out the sun and the wind. Its one doorway was punched halfway up the wall in order to deter snakes and scorpions. He called it his 'frigate'. Later Foucauld would add a two-metre-square reed hut that doubled as kitchen and guest quarters, plus an outside corridor in which he sometimes slept because it was more uncomfortable, and a small warehouse for grain and dates. 'It's a bit strange,' he admitted, 'but very convenient.'[2]

Near the frigate, in an elaborate ceremony, Moussa surrendered formally to Dinaux on 25 August 1905. He was awarded a scarlet burnous, fifteen rifles, a yearly pension of 5,000 francs and the vague promise of a holiday in Paris. In return, he offered to pay taxes, uphold French law and look after Foucauld. For Laperrine, far away in In Salah, it was a momentous occasion. He had at last received the

Tuareg's submission and could now claim the Hoggar as French territory. For Dinaux, it was a moment of doubt: could he trust Moussa? Could he leave Foucauld in his care? Could he be responsible for abandoning a Frenchman alone in the Sahara? Tamanrasset was 700 kilometres, or sixty days' travel from the nearest French garrison; post would reach it possibly once a month; there was no chance of the Saharians being able to rescue Foucauld if anything went wrong. With these doubts in mind, he left on 4 September to continue his tour. When he returned on 15 October for a final check, however, he found Foucauld glowing with fervour and determined to stay. Reassured, he continued on his way. 'We left him on the doorstep of his little hermitage of straw and mud, alone with his piety, his goodness and silence!' wrote Dervil. 'For many months I had lived in the ambience of a saint, without realizing it, I must admit. It was only now that I saw the greatness of a character so perfect that its perfection was not obvious.'[3]

From In Salah, Dinaux sent a report to the Governor-General of Algeria outlining the results of his tour. In it he wrote, 'Father de Foucauld's reputation for sanctity, the results he has already obtained in healing the sick, will do more for the extension of our influence and the rallying of the tribes to our ideas than a permanent occupation of the country.'[4] Laperrine's plan had worked. The Sahara had fallen to France – or, at least, the part of the Sahara he was interested in – and if the *tricouleur* did not yet fly physically over the Hoggar, it soon would. For the flagpole was in place.

In their attempts to distance Foucauld from the colonial programme his apologists have claimed repeatedly that his interest in the desert was purely spiritual: he relished the Sahara first for its solitude and second for the number of potential converts that it contained. The argument has inherent contradictions: the Hoggar Tuareg were small enough in number for Foucauld, over time, to know most of them by name; but the intimacy that he hoped would lead to conversion militated directly against the solitude he craved. These contradictions do not destroy the argument, however, for they mirror

Foucauld's own confusion over his destiny. At one moment he wanted to be left alone in contemplation; at others he felt impelled to go forth and spread the Word. It was a paradox he would struggle with for the rest of his life. To state that Foucauld was concerned only with religious matters, however, is not entirely accurate. He retained enough of the explorer's instinct to send Lacroix a detailed rebuttal of Etiennot's telegraph survey and suggest a more practical route (which was adopted). Outside the hermitage, on Tamanrasset's only tree, he hung a selection of barometers and thermometers, whose readings he took daily for the benefit of scientists in France. And, from almost his first day in residence, he applied himself to the task of subjugating the Tuareg.

His journal entry for 23 October – the first entry after Dinaux's departure the preceding week – is a compendious list of ways in which the inhabitants of the Hoggar should be 'civilized'. In divisions and sub-divisions, as was his habit, Foucauld described his ambitions for Moussa's subjects. He wanted the children to be educated in French manners and the French language. He suggested that model communities of French farmers be imported to instil European values of hard work amongst the men, and that women be sent from southern Algeria to teach the wives how to weave wool, camel- and goat-hair. He wanted the Hoggar to have a *jardin d'essai*, to hold annual markets, to have agricultural shows and competitions, with prizes awarded by the French government, to have French-speaking merchants and to develop a community of artisans manufacturing saddles, small leather goods and wooden bowls. (The fact that Tamanrasset had one tree, and he was using it, did not dim his expectations for the wood-turning industry.) There should also be a resident doctor to revive the Tuareg when they wilted under the unaccustomed toil. For these plans to be implemented it was vital that Moussa remain loyal to the French and that his power and influence not be allowed to diminish. Moussa, he said, must make frequent, educational trips to France; he must reform his people gradually, not through dictat but by rewarding handsomely those who showed promise; and he must remain strong, with an army capable of defeating an attack from without and quashing a rebellion from within – more rifles would be a good start. Above all, Moussa had to realize that from this point forth, only one man mattered in his life: Laperrine.

Foucauld's entry for 23 October 1905 ends with a heading: 'Miscellaneous Observations'. Far from being miscellaneous, this extraordinary A to Z is concerned exclusively with Moussa's conduct *vis-à-vis* Laperrine. Had the Commander of the Oases written it himself, he could not have put it better.

A – The best way for Moussa to win the colonel's affection is to open his heart to him as if to his brother, as if he was the one person in the world whom he loved the best and in whom he had the greatest confidence.

B – Truly, whether among Muslims or Christians, he has no better, more faithful, more reliable and more selfless friend than the colonel. He can have complete confidence in him.

C – I advise him to give the colonel a demonstration of his friendship and a demonstration of his trustworthinesss. The demonstration of friendship is to meet him as he would an old friend he longs to see, that is, as soon and as speedily as possible. The demonstration of trustworthiness is to explain at once why he did not meet him the previous year.

D – I advise him to . . . stay a long while with the colonel, to open his heart to him, to swear eternal friendship, because the colonel will never leave [Adrar] until he dies and until that time will be more and more in a position to protect and benefit the Tuareg.

E – All matters concerning Moussa are controlled by the colonel; even in Algiers, even in Paris, nothing happens without consulting the colonel – who knows better than anyone what is best for the Tuareg and whom everyone trusts implicitly. Everything is done either by the colonel, or at his request, or on his advice. All business should be conducted through [Adrar]; there is nothing to be gained from any other avenue, not from Algiers nor from Paris. Even if Moussa asks of Algiers or Paris something that seems reasonable, they will not say yes or no without writing to the colonel and they will not give a decision until they have received the colonel's reply and acted on his advice.[5]

The list continued. F) was an invitation: Moussa must come to France and meet some decent Christians. G) was a warning: the French disliked greed, so Moussa should never ask for anything for himself but only for his people. H) was a threat: the more willingly Moussa and his tribe displayed their servility then, 'the more smoothly will everything go with Moussa and the Hoggar, the less we will visit the Hoggar, the less we will intervene and the more everything will be left in Moussa's hands.' I) was an order: Moussa should *never* prevent Frenchmen coming to the Hoggar. J) was a reminder: who were Moussa's best friends? They were Foucauld and Laperrine, 'I who love him because God has ordered me to, and the colonel who loves him because he is good.' K) was a washing of the hands: 'I have no contact with anyone in government: the marabout is *dead* to the world and lives only for *God's will.*' L) explained the chain of command: if Moussa was unable to contact Laperrine then he should ask for Lieutenant Nieger, 'because M. Nieger will rise swiftly in rank and will always be interested in the Tuareg . . . He is an intimate friend of the colonel, he is very nice, Moussa can be completely honest with him, have every trust in him, and if need be, ask his advice as if he was his brother.' At M) Foucauld ran out of things to say. Even for such an indefatigable list-maker the alphabet was too great a task when it came to Moussa. He left a blank space to be filled in at a later date and proceeded to Z) 'The three things that seem to me most important for the Tuareg are *education*, the habit of *work*, and *solid family values.*'[6]

Foucauld was to be disappointed. Certainly, Moussa became a reliable puppet ruler who feared with utmost sincerity the Great Power with its flying columns of *méharistes* that now occupied the Tuat. He respected Laperrine and accepted Foucauld as his deputy. His people, however, were less trusting. Initially suspicious, they soon became accustomed to the strange Christian marabout who wandered uninvited into their camps and they responded by visiting his hermitage with demands for food and medicine. But they were wary of a man who had been placed in their midst by the enemy. They tolerated him only because he was protected by Moussa and fled at the first sign that he was about to speak of Christianity. Foucauld's dream of making the Hoggar a copy of provincial France was doomed. The schools, the markets, the artisans, the agricultural shows, the prizes – none of these would come to pass. There was no likelihood of his making converts. Even the amenable Moussa refused to speak of any God other than his own. No word came from Laperrine. Foucauld felt nervous and abandoned. 'Consider me dead and buried here with Christ in his life of Nazareth,'[7] he wrote to Huvelin as early as 26 October. By Christmas he was seriously depressed. In a letter to his sister he lapsed into nostalgia: 'How far are the Christmasses and New Year's Days of childhood! Through what a haze we see them! What sorrows have since passed over us!'[8] He was no better in July 1906, when he told Huvelin that 'I am cowardly and cold . . . very half-hearted in my prayers, on the point of mortification. My life is pedestrian, lukewarm and empty. Prayer is difficult for me. Barely have I begun than I must do battle with sleep or unbearable thoughts. This difficulty is constant.'[9]

Foucauld was no more immune to the *cafard* than any other Frenchman. But in his case it was aggravated by the solitude of his position. In Beni Abbès he had had the comfort of a garrison. In Tamanrasset he had no companion – nobody, that is, but Paul Embarek, the redeemed slave who assisted him at Mass. Little is known about this enigmatic figure who trudged in his master's footsteps. In Foucauld's letters and diaries he is portrayed as a useless layabout, a necessary encumbrance – 'I am, as it were, manacled to him,'[10] he wrote to Marie de Bondy. Contemporary memoirs give the same impression. Gautier, who had met him on the tour of 1904, remembered him as a doltish *primitif*, 'walking behind the baggage camels, a cudgel in his hand, intoning something that, if one listened carefully, could be discerned as scraps of the Catholic liturgy'.[11] He had an admirable capacity for eating anything put in front of him, however unwholesome, which to Gautier signified not only an iron constitution but an absence of religious conscience. 'Paul did not recognize the dietary restrictions of developed religions, nor even the taboos of fetishism. He had no religion at all, which was peculiarly unnatural in the Sahara. I imagine he had broken through the boundaries of Christianity and Islam into neutral territory.'[12] (Paul's absence of dietary conscience may, of course, have had much to do with the absence of anything decent to eat, the responsibility for which lay with the same people who served him rubbish and then mocked him for devouring it.) According to Gautier, Foucauld refused to baptize him because it would defile the sacrament and suffered him only because he had to: Mass needed to be held, and it could not be held without an assistant. 'This little villain has no idea of the trouble he causes me,'[13] Foucauld told Gautier.

Yet for all the short shrift Foucauld gave him, Paul Embarek must have been a man of exceptional qualities. Stolen during a raid on the Soudan, enslaved in Beni Abbès, freed by Foucauld (though 'freed' is maybe not the right word, given the conditions of his service), then dragged hither and yon over the desert by a master who would not accept him into the religion he expected him to obey, Paul's life was one of constant dislocation. It was also one of punitive hardship. When Foucauld chose to walk through the Sahara rather than ride, Paul walked with him; when Foucauld rose at 2 a.m. to say Mass, Paul also rose; when Foucauld woke for his early morning devotions, Paul woke too. He shared his master's every tribulation and was rewarded by a daily wage of half a *qsaa* (1,100g) of wheat, or 12½ sous – if possible the former, for Foucauld considered cash an invitation to sin. He observed a discipline harsher even than Foucauld's – harsher because he had not chosen it and because, in many ways, his life would have been easier had he remained a slave – and in return he received nothing save the daily measure of grain and Foucauld's condemnation for being non-specifically 'immoral'. On 17 May 1906, he walked out.

It would be nice to say that Foucauld appreciated Paul's companionship once he had lost it. But he did not. Although he prayed for Paul's soul he felt more the lack of a servant than a friend. 'Paul left the fraternity this morning,' he wrote in his diary. 'May God help me celebrate the Holy Mass.'[14] On 3 June he was saved by the arrival of Adolphe de Calassanti-Motylinski, a French officer whom he had met during the Bou-Amama campaign and who had since become a famous linguist. As Professor of Arabic at Constantine and head of the city's *medrassa*, or Islamic school – run by the Algerian government – Motylinski had come to the Hoggar to study Tuareg dialect. He was willing and able to assist Foucauld at Mass – which was handy, because the day of his arrival was Whit Sunday: 'The good God has sent him here just in the nick of time,'[15] Foucauld sighed. He was also in a position to help him with his French–Tamacheq dictionary. More than anything, he was good company – and, with his escort of Chaamba *méharistes*, he provided a certain security.

Foucauld had already decided that he would not reside solely in Tamanrasset but would, whenever possible, spend a period of each year in Beni Abbès, visiting en route the outlying Tuareg territories and the Tuat. This accorded perfectly with Motylinksi's own plans and so, in July, the two men embarked on a three-month tour of the desert that would ultimately lead them to In Salah. Foucauld's spirits rose immediately. 'I find this desert life profoundly, deeply sweet,' he wrote. 'It is so pleasant and healthy to set oneself down in solitude, face to face with eternal things; one feels oneself penetrated by the truth.'[16] Together, Foucauld and Motylinski compiled an admirable body of ethnological research the results of which were published in 1908 under Motylinski's name (Foucauld refused to share in the glory). They took notes on anything and everything. They annotated the Tuareg's physical idiosyncrasies: one tribe had blue eyes; another had hair that was red or fair. They recorded their superstitions: to dream of teeth was an omen of death; if you scratched your feet you would soon be on the move; a shooting star heralded the death of a chief; owls over a camp were a bad omen; travellers should depart on Monday, Thursday, Friday afternoon or Sunday; if your beard itched it meant you were going to eat butter; if rain fell while the sun shone, then jackals were having a wedding. They noted that the Tuareg had five different names for a sword, and that a decent blade sold for fifty *mitqals* – which was half the cost of a male slave and a quarter that of a pretty female. They described the fast of Ramadan, which to the Tuareg, already strapped for food, was known as 'the black month'. Eating cheese in summer caused fever; hot butter was good for wounds. They delved into their migratory habits: 'Like noble women, goats do not have enough strength to cross the desert.'[17] And they detailed their descriptions of wildlife: 'wolves, that are best left alone; mice that are the colour of troubled water.'[18]

On 11 August 1906, during a brief retreat to Tamanrasset, Foucauld was about to climb over the snake-proof doorstep to his hermitage when he was bitten on the foot by a horned viper. He fell insensible but was aroused when one of Motylinski's Chaamba applied a hot brand to the wound. It took a month and three blood-lettings before he was able to walk again. But this little difficulty did not stop him proceeding to In Salah, which he reached on 5 October and where he and Motylinski parted company, Motylinski returning to Constantine and Foucauld continuing to Beni Abbès where he was welcomed by all. Old blind Marie, his single convert, came out to meet him in tears. The garrison held a dinner in his honour – he refused the invitation – and his chapel was shovelled free of the sand that had almost smothered it during the year he had been away. From Beni Abbès he travelled to Aïn Sefra where he caught the train to Algiers, had interviews with Livinhac and Guérin, then retraced his steps, taking in Ghardaia and El Goléa before he reached In Salah and then Tamanrasset.

Wherever he went, Foucauld created a sensation. Burnished by asceticism, he glowed strangely amidst the dusty communities of French Algeria. In an age of hair-oil and tooth powder, of steam loco-motion and machine-guns, of great powers and grand designs, when every newspaper gave daily intelligence of advances in science, diplo-macy, warfare and heavier-than-air flight, when the coal-fired kitchen range had reached new heights of sophistication and the workers who fuelled it were at last beginning to demand better working conditions – when, in short, the world seemed to be moving forwards – Foucauld was a man who seemed to be moving backwards. Balding, gap-toothed, increasingly blind, with no obvious interest in great events and none at all in the everyday joys of domestic progress, he was an anachronism. He was, however, a very exotic anachronism. In Britain, Rudyard Kipling entertained the public with mystic tales of India; the French had no such orator, nor did they have India; but they did have the Sahara and they had Foucauld. Amid the stream of indignant and self-congratulatory journals published by officers in every corner of France's African empire, Foucauld stood out for his silence. He was a real man doing real work. People liked him for that. They also liked him because he perpetuated the Catholic faith. In 1906 the French government had made a definitive split between Church and State, withdrawing all subsidies to clerical institutions and forcing the ecclesiastics to fend for themselves. For his complete indifference to it all, Foucauld had, in certain circles, become a hero.

He was hero enough for Lyautey, the brutal lounge-lizard of French imperialism, to greet him in person at Aïn Sefra with a guard of fifteen officers. Lyautey described him very much as Laperrine had done, more than twenty years before. 'I found him poor and neglected, though he used to be so refined. And that was intentional. Nothing was left of the former Foucauld. Yes, something: his eyes, which were beautiful, illumined. The officers adored him. He rode with them, barefooted. I had given him a room . . . He slept on the floor.'[19] At El Goléa, the White Sisters adored Foucauld even more. Shocked by his cadaverous state, they fed him, mended his clothes, wove leather laces into his sandals – they had been held together by palm leaves – and taught him how to bake wafers for Mass. In ecstasy, Foucauld let the wafers burn. When the White Sisters found him, he was smiling contentedly in a smoke-filled kitchen.

Foucauld smiled because, at last, he had a companion. For some time now it had seemed as if this, his greatest desire, might be fulfilled. During the past few years a number of candidates – to whom Foucauld referred universally as 'Gérard' (or occasionally 'Félix') in his coded letters to Guérin – had put themselves forward for admission to his brotherhood. But the 'Gérards' had either been refused permission, or they had changed their minds when they discovered what the job entailed, or they had been given such an arduous course of preparation that they had lost interest and drifted away. In 1906, however, Guérin had a man on his staff who seemed an ideal 'Gérard'. He was a young Breton named Michel, who had done a stint in a Zouave regiment and who, having served three years with the White Fathers, now sought a life of greater seclusion. Guérin considered him too unreliable for his own needs, but as he seemed tough and determined, and as he had been smitten by the apparent romance of Foucauld's calling, Guérin thought he might be of assistance to his friend. He discussed the new 'Gérard' with Foucauld during his visit to Algiers and when the monk was enthusiastic, Guérin penned a note to Michel: 'I think I have an opportunity for you . . .'[20]

Michel was in bed when he received the invitation, recovering from what would appear to have been a bout of malaria – despite a comprehensive drainage programme there were still enough marshes to make the disease commonplace in certain areas of the Algerian Tell – but he threw aside his blankets and accepted the challenge. Dressed in Arab robes, he and Foucauld left Algiers in a third-class railway carriage that rattled slowly but successfully to the new terminus of Colomb-Béchar and then travelled with a small escort to Beni Abbès. Michel soon became disillusioned. He did not like Colomb-Béchar – 'At the station the French officers of the garrison again came to seek my venerated Superior, who received hospitality at the house of one of them, whilst I went and lodged, as agreed, in a modest hostel.'[21] He did not like the man whom Foucauld hired to lead their camels – 'a drinker and stubborn, vain, a liar, lazy and greedy, repulsively dirty, and without any religion'.[22] And although he was excited by the three-day journey to Beni Abbès – 'We entered the desert, escorted by five or six African privates under a sergeant. The soldiers were always a few paces ahead of us, searching carefully every bush, every bit of cover in the land, to see they did not conceal any caravan robbers,'[23] – he did not like the accommodation Foucauld offered

him when they arrived. 'The cells . . . were so low that a man of ordinary stature touched the roof on raising his hands a little above his
head, so narrow that in stretching out one's arms in the form of a cross
one could touch the wall on right and left. No bed, seat, table, or
prie-dieu to kneel on; one had to sleep, fully dressed, on a palm mat
spread out on the floor.'[24] (He noted, ruefully, that there was a splendid and very empty room set aside for visitors.) Also, Foucauld having
decided to economize on candles, they lived by the hours of the sun.
Their meals were drab and monotonous: 'we sat on our mats around
the saucepan placed on the ground, just off the fire, the Father, our
black servant and myself, and we ate in the greatest silence, fishing
food out of the dish with a spoon, and drinking water out of the same
vessel.'[25] The menu was bland: couscous boiled in water or, exceptionally, condensed milk, with a few vegetables and a jam of crushed
dates. There were no napkins, tablecloths, plates, knives or forks
and each meal took a maximum of twenty minutes including a prolonged grace at either end. But there were compensations: on
Christmas Day, for example, Foucauld lit his carefully hoarded candles and invited the officers and soldiers from the *bordj* to celebrate
Midnight Mass. They filled his tiny chapel and spilled into the surrounding enclosure. While Foucauld conducted the rites in his
candle-lit hovel, more than a hundred men intoned the responses
beneath the bright, winter stars.

Life became noticeably harder for Michel when he and Foucauld
left Beni Abbès on 27 December 1906 and went deeper into the
desert. By day the temperature was a comfortable 15 to 20°C. But at
night it dropped below freezing. 'In the morning we sometimes found
frozen water in the cruet, and the ground covered with a thin coat of
ice. From time to time a violent wind blew and made thick clouds of
dust, driving sand into our eyes and small pebbles into our faces.'[26]
Sometimes they found shelter in a village; more often they slept
'under the canopy of heaven, without any fire, in a hole large enough
to lodge a man's body, which we ourselves hollowed out with our
hands in the sand, and which served us as a bed. Benumbed with
cold, rolled up in our camp blankets, we turned and turned again and

again on our mats all night, to warm ourselves and induce sleep, but without succeeding.'[27] One day, for a joke, Foucauld invited the officers of his escort to share his midday meal. 'They accepted the challenge,' Michel wrote, 'but during the whole meal they appeared very ill at ease, ate with extreme repugnance, and were soon satisfied: they had no wish, I presume, to accept a second invitation to such a feast.'[28] He recorded with faint horror his master's obsession with economy: he could understand some aspects, such as the recycling of old packing cases into bookshelves and the use of old letters and envelopes as writing paper; but he was slightly disturbed when Foucauld cut up his old robes and invited him to use them as towels and handkerchiefs. As for Foucauld's appearance: 'He loves, he seeks affronts, derision and insults by an outward get-up that he strives to make extravagant. He always walks in rough sandals, his feet bare and chapped by the cold. He wears an unbleached linen robe, always too short and often stained and torn. He cuts his own beard and hair without using a glass. How does it matter what people say and think about him? Provided he pleases God, he is not going to put himself out for what men think of him.'[29]

Michel tried valiantly to share his master's lifestyle. 'In the depths of silent nature, in this dead land, where never had human being fixed his abode, it was easy for us to lead the life of solitude and contemplation. The Father did not once miss celebrating the holy Mysteries on a portable altar at sunrise, generally in the open air, only three or four times in the tent we had pitched the evening before, so as not to suffer from the gusty squalls.'[30] But when they reached In Salah he couldn't take it any more. 'Already anything but well at our departure from Algiers, I felt seriously ill a little more than two months after our departure from Beni Abbès, and I felt incapable of continuing so toilsome a journey on foot in the sands. I was obliged to stop at In-Shallah.'[31] He approached the garrison doctor, who issued him with a docket that absolved the bearer from all further exploration and went home with 'a good sum of money and abundant provisions and . . . two trustworthy men'.[32] Foucauld professed not to be surprised. 'From the start of the journey . . . I saw that he could not stay with me,' he told Guérin. 'I am sending him back to you not because of his *very real* physical weakness but because his spiritual weakness is too great for him to make the necessary progress . . . He is a good child, full of *good intentions*, but excessively obtuse, with no understanding of his own character.'[33] In other reports he wrote: 'He lacks intelligence and formation to an exceptional degree;'[34] 'His weakness of body and soul are a heavy burden;' 'Very limited mind. Very little that is open in his character. I will have in conscience to send him back unless he makes serious efforts.'[35]

Michel, who later gave a full account of his travails, said that Foucauld was to be congratulated for his 'ardent zeal . . . his charity towards his fellow-men . . . his spirit of faith, his firm hope . . . [and his ability to practise] to an heroic degree the three theological and the four cardinal virtues.'[36] But there were aspects of his character that unsettled him: 'his complete detachment from worldly goods . . . his terrible mortification,' and his dictatorial nature. 'To tell the whole truth, I ought, however, to point out one imperfection . . . that I perceived in my worthy Superior. From time to time, when things did not go as he wished, he displayed a sign of impatience.'[37] Reading between the lines, what made Michel turn back at In Salah was not the hardship of desert life (though he did not, admittedly, appreciate it one jot), nor the idea of monastic seclusion (he would later join an order of Carthusian monks, whose regime was by no means easy and which he observed until his death in 1963), but the impossibility of living alongside such a fanatical taskmaster.

Foucauld's long years of selflessness – or, some might say, selfishness – seemed to have made him incapable of forming a working, human relationship. He could handle people only in the abstract, when viewed through the prism of his faith. The Tuareg, for example, to whom he distributed alms and medicine, were not so much individuals (though he dutifully recorded their names in his diary) as pawns in his personal religious game. Likewise, his relations with the French military, although good, were somewhat distant. He was happy to further the ends of men such as Laperrine and Lyautey but only if it helped his own cause – which, fortunately, it did. Even his closest friendships were conducted mostly by letter. His idea of a new rule was neither impossible nor beyond the bounds of human endurance: after his death the order of Little Brothers would flourish (and still does), but he was too singular to act as any more than its founder. During Foucauld's lifetime, Michel was the only man who showed more than theoretical interest in becoming a Little Brother of Jesus.

Nevertheless, Michel's departure depressed Foucauld. So did the news, delivered to him at In Salah by Laperrine on 14 March 1907, that Motylinski had died of typhus in Constantine at the beginning of the month. There was also a message from Guérin, announcing that yet another 'Gérard' had changed his mind. When he reached Tamanrasset, having taken the long route via Timiaouine, assisting a trans-Saharan expedition under Captain Édouard Arnaud and Lieutenant Maurice Cortier, he became even more depressed. In his absence Moussa had shown how much he appreciated Foucauld's role as Laperrine's representative by making Tamanrasset his capital. The little huddle of huts that Foucauld had left was now a sprawling conurbation of tents. New wells had been dug and major tillage works were underway. Moussa also had plans to create a market and shops. 'Must I flee to a more deserted place or see the hand of Jesus extending my influence more easily?'[38] Foucauld wondered. In the end he opted to stay – he could hardly not, being the man who had advised Moussa to build markets and improve his agriculture in the first place. But he was uncomfortable with parallel developments that Moussa had put in hand. Eager not to be seen as a complete puppet, and in order to reassure the anti-French elements amongst his people, Moussa had embarked on a programme of Islamization. Foucauld wrote indignantly to Guérin that, 'Taking advantage of our organization of the Hoggar being so far rather nebulous and uncertain, rather that of a little kingdom, self-governing but paying tribute, than of a country directly governed by us, he hastened to organize it as a Mussulman country.'[39] Worst of all, Moussa was building a mosque and school in Tamanrasset and, using the tax-raising powers devolved on him by Laperrine, was planning to raise a religious tithe to support both institutions. 'It is most serious,' Foucauld wrote. 'Up to the present the Tuareg, not being very fervent Mussulmans, easily made acquaintance with us, becoming very familiar and frank. If once this bad, narrow, close spirit of the Tuat and Tidikelt, which is so full of antipathy towards us, takes hold . . . it will be very different, and it is to be feared that in a few years the population of the Hoggar may be much more hostile than today. Today, it is distrustful, fearful and wild; in a few years, if the Mussulman influence of Tuat gains the upper hand, it will mean a deep and lasting hostility.'[40]

Adding to his misery was the fact that, without an assistant, he was unable to say Mass. Either side of New Year 1908, his diary entries are full of remonstrance: 'No Mass, for I am alone' is a recurring complaint. Guérin and Livinhac had been working on this. On a sheet of choicest vellum, they wrote a petition, asking for Foucauld to be given the same privileges that were accorded to priests in prison. The petition was never presented but a White Father who happened to be passing through Rome raised the subject with the Pope and on 31 January 1908, Laperrine told his friend that permission had been granted. '*Deo Gratias! Deo Gratias! Deo Gratias!*,' Foucauld sang. 'O God, how good thou art! . . . Tomorrow I shall be able to say Mass. Christmas! Christmas! Thanks, my God!'[41] But the mental strain of losing an acolyte and then finding his hermitage overrun by Muslims had already pushed him over the physical limit. In January, he wrote guardedly to Guérin of 'a big hitch in my health'.[42] There was 'first of all an overwhelming fatigue with complete loss of appetite, then something in my chest, or rather heart, which made me pant so much at the slightest movement, that one might think the end was near.'[43] He wrote, too, to Laperrine, asking for a consignment of condensed milk.

Laperrine knew immediately that something was amiss. 'Reverend Father,' he wrote to Guérin on 3 February, 'This letter worries me very much, because if he admits he is worn out and asks me for condensed milk, he must be really ill . . . I am going to tell him off, and get your authority to tell him that penance to the point of suicide is not permitted.'[44] Eight days later, after three camel-loads of food had been despatched to Tamanrasset: 'A few lines at the gallop, to give you news of de Foucauld . . . He has been more ill than he admits; he had fainting fits and the Tuareg who took great care of him are anxious. He is better. I sent him a lecture, for I am strongly of the opinion that his exaggerated penances have a great deal to do with his weakness, and the overworking at his dictionary did the rest . . . I think it indispensable that on his approaching return to the north, you put your grappling-irons on him and keep him a month or two at Ghardaia or Maison Carrée, so that he may fill his hump again – pardon the Saharan expression.'[45]

By March, Foucauld had recovered sufficiently to pen a gleeful report that Moussa's campaign of Islamization had come to naught. The mosque had not been built and the man he put in charge of its tithes had absconded with the money, thereby making the project an object of derision. 'His efforts have totally and piteously failed; not only failed but produced an inverted effect . . . only the recollection of a disagreeable adventure and the horror of . . . tithes remain. Let us pray and do penance.'[46] In June, however, he discovered that Moussa was building a home for himself at Tamanrasset. It was an important home made of mud bricks and several of his relations had plans to imitate him. Again, Foucauld could not condemn Moussa for his desire to create a permanent settlement, for it could only lead to the economic virtues he wished to inculcate. But it made him uncomfortable. He was beginning to realize that he was not cut out for the programmes he advocated. While 'civilization' was nice in theory – as was his order of Little Brothers – in practice he preferred it as an ideal rather than a reality. He was, at heart, a romantic, who cleaved to the dream of the noble savage and who wished to preserve the solitude he had found in the Hoggar. When the fruits of his labour threatened both his solitude and the perceived nobility of his savages, he turned his mind to wildernesses further afield. He did not especially want to leave Tamanrasset now he had settled there – 'I am getting old,' he admitted in 1907 – but he thought it would be good to move around a bit. 'This corner of the earth, which is as it were my parish, is 2,000 kilometres from north to south and 1,000 kilometres from east to west.'[47] Questioned on the worth of travelling through the world's emptiest zone, he replied, 'No doubt the Sahara is not one of the most inhabited countries but, after all, the oases, including the Touareg, contain 100,000 people who are born, live and die, without any knowledge of Jesus . . . He gave his blood for them and what are we doing?'[48] Then, as was his custom, he began to list things that the White Fathers could do. He wanted them to create a body of under-cover priests, who would wander the land in civilian clothes, surprising the natives with acts of goodwill. He also wanted them to found a propaganda machine, 'a sort of Third Order', devoted to chris-tianizing the infidel, for 'the rapidity of communications, and the exploration of the entire world, now give comparatively easy access to all'.[49] More conventionally, he wanted them to fire mixed-sex bundles of missionaries into the desert and other idolatrous regions to sow the seeds from which Christian communities might grow. 'They might be gleaned either here and there, or grouped in order to give them a common preparation.'[50] He agreed that his plans were not yet perfect, 'But certainly there is something to be done . . . It is not with ten, fifteen, twenty or thirty priests, even if you were given them, that you will convert the vast Sahara. You must therefore find other auxiliaries.'[51]

As he recovered from his illness Foucauld explored once more the peripheries of Tamanrasset. Laperrine, who visited him that summer with a column of *méharistes*, was impressed. 'He is very well, and glow-ing with health and gaiety . . . On 29 June he came galloping into my camp like a sub-lieutenant at the head of a group of Touareg riders. He is more popular than ever among them, and appreciates them more and more. On the other hand he has very little esteem for the negroes settled here, who are all lazy and nothing but parasites.'[52] Laperrine shared Foucauld's itchiness about life at Tamanrasset, for he himself was experiencing something similar in Adrar. He cared less how many houses the Tuareg built, whether they started farms or remained nomadic. He was concerned only with their allegiance to France. He was happy with Moussa's progress – in Foucauld's opinion, the *ame-noukhal* had become fat and self-satisfied – yet he was uncertain how far he could rely upon him as a law-enforcer. There was, for example, the regrettable incident that had occurred less than a year after Moussa had formally sworn his allegiance.

When Foucauld and Motylinski had made their ethnological tour in 1906, they had offered the Tuareg a sou for every legend received. Ever obliging when shown money, the Tuareg had provided history by the handful. They gave it, however, with no regard to timescale. Alongside tales of the distant past, came accounts of raids and pillaging that had occurred within the last few weeks. The latter were irrelevant to the Frenchmen's purpose, but they recorded them all the same. One day, however, their studies were interrupted by a member of their Chaamba escort, who staggered into camp in a terrible state. He was naked, he had severe head injuries and he had a spear through his chest. Remarkably, he went on to make a full recovery. Even more remarkably, a man arrived a few days later to give the two Frenchmen details of the attack. While searching for firewood the *méhariste* had met a Tuareg who invited him to shoot a distant gazelle. As he drew a bead, the Tuareg struck him from behind so forcefully that the lance ran through his body. Then, with the lance still in place, the two men fought with hands and teeth until the Tuareg finally beat his opponent on the head with a rock, and continued beating him until he looked as if he was dead, before stripping him of his clothes, his rifle and his ammunition. Most remarkable of all, Foucauld and Motylinski then paid the informant his sou, thanked him for his trouble and added his story to their compilation.

Their philosophy seemed to be, 'these things happen'. Laperrine disagreed. In a pacified desert, these things should not happen. He wanted to show the Tuareg his fist and he could not do so by sitting in Adrar. More forceful tours were required; tours that would show his determination to bring the Sahara to heel. His philosophy was direct, as he explained in a letter to Cauvet: 'I have, perhaps, been preceded by a reputation for ferocity, as a man with an iron fist. But I also have a reputation for keeping my word, whether it is a threat or a promise, whether it is given to a Sofa of Samory or to a Touareg. *Hé bien*, it has served me well in the past, and I am relying on you to help me maintain it. Here is what I have said to the Touareg every time they come to size me up: forget everything that happened in the Tidikelt before France occupied it; remember only the tricks you have played since and the vengeance, swift or slow but always certain, that has followed; above all remember what has happened since I arrived in 1901. I expect to travel freely through the Sahara how and when I please . . . If people show a smiling face I promise to treat them as friends. If they are hostile I promise to smash their noses.'[53] While Foucauld and Motylinski pottered around the Hoggar, Laperrine had been applying his principles.

14

WHITE MARABOUT

In 1906, concessionaries scrambled for access to Algeria's mineral wealth, new evidence of which was being discovered every year. But the Sahara remained as yet inviolate. A few far-sighted geologists suspected that it would yield even greater profits than the lands to the north – as it eventually would – but their reports were pigeonholed. The region was too distant and too unstable to attract investors and the French government refused to undertake the task itself. There was, however, one mine that was already functional and needed no extra funding. It lay in the middle of nowhere, several hundred kilometres west of the Hoggar and the same distance south of Adrar. It was reasonably accessible if one was prepared to organize the caravans. Its name was Taoudeni and it produced salt.

Taoudeni was one of the desert's greatest commercial assets. Few purer deposits of sodium were to be found in Saharan Africa. There were other and bigger salt markets – Bilma, for example – but their produce was contaminated. Foureau recorded that Bilma salt gave him violent indigestion and that most of his officers would not touch it, even though they suffered muscular cramps as a result. Trains of camels, thousands-strong, had for centuries made a twice-yearly pilgrimage from the Soudan to Taoudeni to collect the precious lumps of salt and bring them back to Timbuctoo, where they were exchanged for gold dust, ivory, slaves, ostrich feathers, tobacco, carpets, leather goods from Morocco and dates from the Tuat. It was exaggerated reports of this trade that had given rise to Europe's perception of Timbuctoo as an African el Dorado whose streets were paved with gold. As Laperrine and everyone else who had visited it knew, Timbuctoo was a drab entrepôt indistinguishable from any other in the Soudan. But the town still retained its links with Taoudeni and salt remained its most valuable commodity. For as many centuries as caravans had been sent to Taoudeni, Soudanese and Moroccan forces had fought for control of the mine. Soudan had usually won. By 1906, however, the situation had altered.

Although Taoudeni fell theoretically within the boundaries of the new French colony of Soudan, in practice it belonged to nobody. In the period of disruption following France's occupation, Taoudeni had been left to fend for itself – which it did, inasmuch as it continued to produce salt. But, deprived of its customary protection, it had fallen prey to Moroccan raiders, who attacked the salt caravans with impunity. Laperrine made Taoudeni his next object of pacification. The authorities in Algiers forbade him to go there. He did not care. He told them that he was making a tour and would await their permission in due course. Then he summoned three officers and seventy-five *méharistes* and told them to prepare for a long trip. The detachment left Adrar on 26 March 1906, with 140 camels and provisions to last ninety days. Each man carried 500g of flour, eighty of sugar, fifty of coffee, thirty-three of butter and twenty of salt. Meat, it was hoped, they could shoot along the way. In addition there were two pigskins of water per person, enough for four days' travel, plus eight metal tanks containing a reserve of 350 litres in case the wells were dry. And the second-in-command, Lieutenant Nieger, carried barometers, compasses, sextants and other equipment for charting their route. Led by two trustworthy Tuareg guides, Laperrine's *méharistes* sloped south-east from Adrar towards the Hoggar, where they turned south-west for the Soudan.

Laperrine had already crossed the Soudanese border when he received a flustered message from Algiers: if he really wanted to go to Taoudeni then he had permission to do so, but he should be warned that the Soudanese authorities had decided to pacify Taoudeni themselves and were probably there already. Also, the message continued, the geologist Chudeau, whom he had taken south two years before, was accompanying the Soudanese and would appreciate an escort from Taoudeni to the Tuat and then to Algiers. Laperrine was irritated. Not only had the grand object of his tour been snatched from him, but he was reduced to acting as nursemaid for a man who was making, for the second time, the crossing that he, Laperrine, had yet to make once. Balefully, he refuelled and headed north-east for Taoudeni.

It was a terrible journey. The desert was drying up. Rain had not fallen for many years and the pastures, if they could be called that, were mostly barren. Every well they met was either empty or undrinkable. The men's pigskins were old and shoddy. Most were leaking and many had to be thrown away. The metal tanks that contained their reserves were in no better shape: four of them were so rusty that they had to be abandoned; of the remaining four only two were sound and the other two were dribbling water. Their camels were flagging. On 20 May, within a few score kilometres of Taoudeni they reached Hassi Guettara, a well that gave them clear water and had, miraculously, a patch of pasturage. But as they recuperated, three of their outriders spotted a small group of men, their outlines shimmering on the horizon. Was it a caravan, in which case they could barter for new water containers? Or was it the enemy? In the event, it was neither. As the group drew nearer, Laperrine's scouts made out the distinctive conical hats and ostrich plumes of a troop of Soudanese *tirailleurs*.

This bedraggled detachment, under the command of Lieutenant Cortier, was on the eastward leg of a polygonal tour that mirrored Laperrine's own. Cortier's original plan had been to meet the Saharians and guide them to Taoudeni, thus effacing the memory of 1904 with a display of unity that would demonstrate how seamlessly the branches of French colonialism worked together. However, the desert had been his undoing. The Soudanese lacked the Saharians' expertise and had left Timbuctoo in such a hurry that they had forgotten much of their baggage. Food, scientific instruments – even Chudeau – had all been left behind. What provisions they did carry had mostly been consumed at Taoudeni where, after waiting ten days for Laperrine, the commanding officer had retreated to more hospitable climes, leaving Cortier to welcome the Saharians. But as Cortier apologized, his men had neither the strength nor the supplies to double back to Taoudeni and still regain Timbuctoo. In fact, if the Saharians had any food to spare he would be most grateful for it. Laperrine became angry. For Cortier this was a new and memorable experience. 'The Lieutenant-Colonel expressed his impatience,'[1] he wrote nervously. But once Laperrine had calmed down, the two columns were allowed to mingle. They spent two days together, during which Laperrine showed himself at his most hospitable. 'At every meal, the Colonel presided over a table comprising Europeans from both detachments; the *tirailleurs* and Chaamba . . . [meanwhile] did their best.'[2] Never for a moment, though, did he leave any doubt as to who was in command. 'The two camps arrayed themselves about the well,' Cortier wrote. 'To the north were the Algerians with their big, airy tents, their massive convoy, their long file of camels, amidst which the Chaamba strode arrogantly, clothed in their big white shirts and red sashes crossed with bandoliers of ammunition, a sight at once picturesque and dashing. To the south were the Soudanese, humiliated in their narrow, little camp, without baggage, almost without food . . . the *tirailleurs* dressed in khaki drab, their pride saved only by their red leather hats decorated with a double row of curled ostrich feathers.'[3] All the same, 'the greatest cordiality reigned',[4] and when the two contingents parted company on 22 May, Cortier leading his men south to Timbuctoo and Laperrine continuing for Taoudeni, they drank farewell toasts and fired volleys into the air. Their meeting 'was a magnificent example of energy and endurance', wrote one of Laperrine's more ebullient biographers, 'a fine display of French faith and enthusiasm, the likes of which can hardly be matched in our colonial history'.[5]

Laperrine did not see it that way. The Soudanese had beaten him to his primary objective and deprived him of his secondary taste. He had nothing to pacify, no geologist to escort to Algiers, and he was sitting in a waterless, foodless desert with seventy-eight men and their camels. There was one way, however, to salvage his honour. Between Taoudeni and Adrar lay the rolling dunes of Erg Chech. No Frenchman had ever crossed the Erg before, and its traverse would be an impressive demonstration of his *méharistes'* capabilities. It would also be the first time an expedition had left the Tuat from the east and returned from the west, thus proving conclusively that the French were masters of the desert. But when he reached Taoudeni at the end of May, he became doubtful. Of the 140 camels with which he had started, only fifty were healthy; the rest were either dead or on the point of death. His food supplies were low, his water containers were battered and leaking, and his men were tired. 'Our situation, without being critical, is not brilliant,'[6] Laperrine confessed. He could, if he wished, retrace his steps via the Hoggar, but that involved a journey of thousands of kilometres over land that he knew was short of both water and pasture. Alternatively, he could sprint north over the few hundred kilometres of the Erg Chech where, according to his guide, the main well of Tnihaia had a reputation for making people bloat. The safest route was unarguably the one he had just covered: if the wells were poor, at least they existed; the same applied to pasture for the camels; and if his food ran out there was game to be shot. On the other hand, he estimated it would take only ten days to cross the Erg Chech; he had enough food to last that long and if the wells were good – he would have to take a chance on Tnihaia – then he could return home in glory. Erg Chech was a risk, but he decided it was one worth taking. They filled their water-skins from the wells of El Biar, just outside Taoudeni, and left for the Tuat on 2 June.

'A very hard day, torrid heat, no pasturage,'[7] Laperrine recorded. It was the same for the next three days. The Chaamba, who vied with each other to see who could go longest without water, began to faint. Laperrine ordered them to march at night and sleep by day to conserve moisture. When the camels lagged, Laperrine told his men to eat them. 'It was a question of sacrificing men or animals. I did not hesitate.'[8] By 5 June they were sixty kilometres from Tnihaia and their water was running low. They jettisoned everything that was not essential and dashed for the well. They kept only seven days' food and a litre of water apiece, while the officers retained a small reserve for emergencies. The remains of their provisions, their ammunition, the empty iron water containers, 'and all the impedimenta'[9] – including Nieger's instruments – were buried until they could reclaim them. After an eleven-hour forced march they reached Tnihaia at 5.35 on the morning of 6 June.

Laperrine warned his men to be careful, but they drank from the pool regardless. What they drank was almost pure chlorine. 'We had not been misled about the quality of water at Tnihaia,' Laperrine wrote in his official report. 'It was disgusting; like detergent . . . Everybody had their face, hands and feet swollen, to a greater or lesser degree; some were afflicted especially badly.'[10] In a later account that he sent to the Geographical Society of Paris, he tried to make light of the occasion: 'The effects on the human organism were very unpleasant but also very curious . . . Frenchmen and natives alike swelled to exaggerated proportions. It was a highly entertaining spectacle to see the astonishment with which everyone examined their comrades after a night's rest.' He also described the manner in which the water dried on the faces of those who drank it, leaving them with a 'thick covering of pure, white salt'. What he did not mention to the Geographical Society, but did include in his official report, was that the water was so caustic that it burned their clothes.

He would have liked to have left the place at once but he needed to send the camels back for the supplies they had abandoned the previous day. Then, when the animals returned, they had to be fed. For four days they camped at this insufferable spot, while the animals fed on a meagre strip of pasture. When they finally left on the evening of 11 June, the *méharistes* lolled about like rag dolls, almost insensible from thirst and chlorine poisoning. 'This stage was terrible,' Lapperine wrote. 'Parched, and still suffering from the [chlorine], the men rode completely naked. Some, almost at the point of delirium, refused to go forward and fell to the ground, saying they would rather be left to die where they were. We had to strap them to their camels and sometimes even beat them until they came to their senses.'[11] Four days later they reached a well that was pure, but it had no pasture so they had to move on. After another three days, they came to a well that had pasture but whose water was almost as foul as that of Tnihaia. They spent three thirsty days amidst the stink of chlorine and saltpetre while the camels fed. Their next stop, Bir el Hadjhadj, was the last before they came to the Tuat. They reached it on 1 July. Normally, Bir el Hadjhadj provided excellent water from a well that was fifteen metres deep. But it had been a long time since a caravan had travelled that way, and the well had collapsed. In searing heat, they dug for twenty-eight hours until at last they struck a fresh source.

By this time they were starving as well as thirsty. Since Tnihaia Laperrine had halved his men's rations, then quartered them, and now they had nothing to eat. Accordingly, he ordered them to slaughter the weakest camels. Accustomed to a diet of dates and couscous, they could not cope with the rush of protein. 'I had nothing but meat to give them,' Laperrine explained, 'they were ravenous and and ate without any moderation . . . almost all developed dysentery.'[12] Two *méharistes* died. The guide and a young recruit seized an unwashed camel stomach and dropped it over the fire before devouring it. Both men became so ill that they could not move for more than a week. Finally, on 8 July, the column limped into the Tuat village of Zaouiet Sidi Abdelkader, and on the 9th it arrived at Adrar. The journey from Taoudeni had taken not ten days but more than a month.

Laperrine was suitably chastened – though not so chastened as to prevent him from claiming the tour as a complete success. Taoudeni had been freed of its oppressors, the meeting of the two French forces had had an 'enormous moral effect'[13] upon the natives, they had explored an unknown stretch of desert, and Nieger had plotted the positions of many wells, thus reducing their future dependency on guides. On paper, his situation looked excellent: he was master of the oases and of the whole Algerian desert to their south. But paper was an ephemeral substance. In 1904, the Geographical Society of

Paris had published Nieger's report that: 'The Tuareg question can be considered more or less at an end . . . with a bit of patience we expect all the complications attendant on their recent submission to resolve themselves peacefully.' Three years later, that particular bit of paper carried as much authority as a spill for lighting fires.

Since 1904 the renegade Tuareg chief, Attici, had made repeated incursions into Algeria, raiding French columns when he could find them and despatching marabouts to invigorate Moussa's sagging Muslim subjects. He had had great success. By 1907 French forces on the Tripolitanian border were feeling harried and the Hoggar, previously an area of semi-anarchy, was – as Foucauld reported – on the verge of becoming an organized Muslim kingdom. Laperrine replied with a statement of intent: 'The tactic is straightforward. When we threaten and bother these people, they leave us alone and we regain the moral high ground. We must continue, continue until they beg for mercy. On the other hand, we must welcome those who make the first gesture of peace, so that others will be tempted to follow. It's stick and carrot. We give them the choice.'[14]

Moussa having responded insufficiently to the carrot, and Attici never having been offered it, Laperrine hit them both with the stick. In June 1908, he received permission to establish a military post, fifty kilometres east of Tamanrasset, from where he could belabour the Hoggar whenever he wished. He called it Fort Motylinski – he had wanted to call it Fort Foucauld, but Foucauld would not allow it – and, unlike most of the mud-brick constructions that France dotted throughout the Sahara, it was actually a fort worthy of the name. Perched on a rock in the centre of a wide valley, at an altitude of 1,800 metres, Fort Motylinski had presence. It was a sullen, crenellated edifice that struck a pose somewhere between the crusader castles of the Middle East and the fortified burgs alongside the Rhine. Looking at its gates, which threatened at any moment to disgorge a horde of cavalry, travellers passed swiftly on their way. So forbidding was Fort Motylinski's aspect that its commanding officer, Lieutenant Sigonney, had little to do. Sometimes he would lead routine patrols to Tamanrasset but mostly he presided over disputes between the *harratin* of the valley, and tended his garden. 'His ambitions are limited to growing chestnut trees,' wrote a visiting officer in 1911. 'He's got a dozen of them, and the highest is only thirty centimetres. He's prouder of them than Eiffel is of his tower.'[15] Foucauld would not have admitted it, but it was Fort Motylinski more than any degree of peculation by the marabouts that stifled Moussa's Islamic kingdom of the Hoggar.

Attici was more of a problem. Tripolitania being, however nominally, a part of the Ottoman Empire, Laperrine was barred from pursuing the Tuareg raiders across the border. Nor could he ask the Ottomans to deal with Attici themselves, for their influence had dwindled to the extent that, as with the Sultan of Morocco, they exerted little or no control beyond the major, coastal centres; the southern, desert region was one in which the inhabitants did much as they liked, overseen only by the consuls of Murzouk, Ghat and Ghadames who were at best indifferent to Attici's activities and on occasion actively assisted him. Laperrine's options were limited. Between April and August of 1908, he led his *méharistes* to the Adjer, where he rattled his stick along the Algerian–Tripolitanian frontier and deposited another redoubt, Fort Polignac, on the edge of the Tassili plateau to the north of the Hoggar, to guard against further raids. Attici might lurk menacingly in the dunes, but Laperrine's men would be waiting for him. So, too, would Foucauld.

Over the next years, Foucauld alerted Laperrine to every changing nuance of Hoggar society. A man named El Mahdi 'survives here by committing felonies';[16] Moussa's adviser, Ba Hamou, was, 'a pretty sinister character';[17] and Ba Hamou's cousin, Hadj Ali, was possessed of an evil spirit and was probably an enemy agent into the bargain. He gave Laperrine information about Moussa's intentions – opportunistic, but on the whole reliable – and warned him that the Tuareg were becoming increasingly aware of Islam's finer points, for which he blamed in part the burgeoning trade between the Tuat and the Hoggar that allowed marabouts to spread their gospel at will, and in part Attici's incursions from Tripolitania: 'We need to watch the marabouts more closely than usual, not those of this country but the ones from Tripolitania. The Turks send . . . emissaries of the lowest sort to spread false rumours and stir up the population.'[18] Nor did he restrict himself to providing information on the Tuareg. He had always stated that the occupying forces should be men of impeccable character and when they showed any sign of imperfection, he reported it. One officer, who was dallying with the local women, was dismissed on Foucauld's recommendation. When another, who had a reputation for cruelty, came to Tamanrasset, he refused to meet him. 'He is a dishonourable man, and I do not wish to shake his hand. And as I cannot refuse to shake hands with a French officer in front of the Tuareg, I'm off!'[19] He hovered on the outskirts for forty-eight hours until the man had left.

As well as reporting to Laperrine, Foucauld maintained a proprietary interest in the running of Fort Motylinski and pestered its young commander, Lieutenant Sigonney, with suggestions as to how he should conduct his affairs. He gave his advice 'with an admirable tact, with exquisite discretion and humility',[20] but also with an unwelcome degree of persistence. As one of his most admiring biographers was forced to admit, '[For an officer] to accept this non-official superior authority of the priest, his constant interposition in administrative and political affairs, even sometimes in military ones, required exceptional qualities.'[21] Nevertheless, Foucauld's interference seemed to have positive results. Increasingly, his letters to Laperrine read, 'Nothing new on the political front.'[22]

During this period Foucauld was, in the words of one observer, 'the true chief of the Ahaggar'.[23] It was his knowledge of the country and its people that allowed the French to construct Fort Motylinski. It was he who arranged tax relief and employment for individuals in need, and ordered condensed milk for sickly children, seed for the *harratin*, and tar products to cure mange in camels. He all but told Moussa what to do – 'His influence is very great,' Laperrine wrote. 'The *amenoukhal* Moussa makes no important decision without consulting him first.'[24] He also mediated between the inhabitants of the Hoggar and the occupying power. Sometimes he would even act as marriage broker for French soldiers smitten by native women, though, as all the 'engagements' came to nothing, it seems that Foucauld rather than the individual soldier had a lasting union in mind. Laperrine still mocked his enthusiasm: 'that fellow has always got Almighty God in his bedside table,'[25] he remarked. (The joke was taken up: when travelling with the monk, Gautier wrote that he wrapped God up in a large white tablecloth before putting Him in his saddle bag.) But his contribution to the colonial cause could not be ignored. His sworn goal was 'to give lands to France and souls to God',[26] and if he failed in the latter, he succeeded in the former. 'Always giving excellent advice,' Laperrine wrote, 'he was the principal agent in the pacification of the Tuareg in the Hoggar.'[27] Others agreed: 'He was the surest, the most confidential, the most discreet of all intelligence officers . . . His dominant characteristic was to be, first and above all, an officer of the Native Bureau . . . He will remain the model and the pattern for every officer of Native Affairs in any and every colonizing nation.'[28]

Despite these accolades, Foucauld remained uneasy about his position in Tamanrasset. He wanted to move about, to see more of the Tuat – he had recently purchased a house in In Salah – and to visit Beni Abbès, where caretakers were looking after his original hermitage and from where beckoned the rich spiritual pasture of Morocco. His unrest was exacerbated in August 1908 when he heard of horrible deeds in Casablanca, on Morocco's Atlantic coast. Since his accession in 1900, Sultan Abd el-Aziz had not endeared himself to his subjects. Thanks to international treaties over which he had no control – and large borrowing requirements, over which he did – he had become all but a puppet. France owned his debt; banks in Paris ran those in Morocco; customs officials in every major port were French, and so were the police. Attracted by a low cost of living and the prospect of quick profits, Europeans settled along the coast in large numbers. Popular resentment came to a head in July 1907, when a French mining company laid a railway alongside a Muslim cemetery in Casablanca. Outraged, the citizens of the town rose against the foreign interlopers. The scenes of rape, murder and destruction were so appalling that the French felt obliged to equal them. Lyautey sent a detachment of his hardest men to Casablanca where, on landing, they went about their business with practised brutality. By the time they had established a perimeter, hundreds of Moroccans were dead and the international port was firmly under French control. Foucauld should have reacted with dismay at the bloodshed. Instead he was irritated that he had not been involved. 'I told General Lyautey that, *wherever* there was a serious expedition, he had only to telegraph me, and I would arrive immediately,'[29] he complained to Guérin.

In fairness to Foucauld, this outburst was not a reflection of blood-thirstiness, nor even a desire to participate in some kind of crusade. He rejoiced in French successes but was losing interest in evangelism whether it be in Morocco or the Hoggar. He made this clear in a letter to Guérin: 'Preaching Jesus to the Tuareg, I do not believe Jesus wants that, not from me, nor from anyone. We must proceed very cautiously there, gently, get to know them, make friends with them. All that to lead them to Christianity in God's good time, maybe in centuries.'[30] As he would later state, '[Our mission is] to regard every human being as a beloved brother. To banish from our midst the spirit of militancy. Jesus has taught us to go like lambs amongst wolves, not to take up arms.'[31] No, his irritation stemmed probably from bore-dom – or maybe the *cafard*. He was by nature a man who wanted to be *doing*. He had to have a goal ahead of him. But at the scrap end of 1908 every goal seemed either futile or impossibly distant. The Tuareg showed no interest in Christianity and, as Foucauld acknowledged, it might be hundreds of years before they did. He had made no real con-verts in the seven years he had lived in the desert. Despite translating Tamacheq for up to ten hours a day, there was still so much to be done. And on top of his linguistic studies he had begun an amateur archaeological survey of the pre-Islamic artefacts and paintings that abounded in the Hoggar. Gloomily, he estimated it would take another ten years to finish the tasks he had set himself – and even then the job would be incomplete. The only progress on which he could congratulate himself was the daily march towards his own death. But while he welcomed the inevitable he could not, realisti-cally, claim it as something of his own doing. (He was now eating well and, despite his outward decrepitude, was surprisingly fit.) No wonder that he hankered after Morocco. At least Lyautey was producing results.

His ever-present smile concealed his depression from visitors. It even fooled Laperrine who, in a memoir of 1913, gave a jolly vignette of the hermit's existence: 'I have often been asked just what Foucauld could do to kill time. It is a godsend for him when he can get hold of a few elderly ladies of the Tuareg nobility, for it is they who are most well versed in the tribal traditions. On those occasions there is nothing more entertaining than to watch him holding court, pencil in hand, in the middle of an elite assembly of old dowagers sitting on the ground, chatting about everything while sipping their tea and smoking a pipe.'[32] Foucauld's letters, however, gave a far less cosy picture, revealing a man tormented by fears of age, loneliness and failure. The White Fathers had no more 'Gérards' to offer. Nobody from Constantine wished to pursue Motylinski's path. The archaeologists of Algiers did not want to leave their wives and were afraid to take them into the desert. 'The journey in winter is *ravishing*,' Foucauld tempted in vain. 'A woman will be charmed by the climate, the picturesque situation and the chance to help her husband in his work of civilization.'[33] And, he added, it was only fifty days by mule, horse or camel from the nearest railhead. Still, nobody wanted to accept his offer. 'Solitude is so sweet to me, but how many things could be done were I not alone,' he wote to Marie de Bondy on 20 September 1908. 'I am well, but I feel I am getting old. My work gets slower and slower and is that of a tired man. I have just reached my fiftieth year. I feel it, and would like to have around me others who could take my place when I am gone.'[34]

He had one last hope. There was a young orientalist by the name of Louis Massignon, who was currently studying in Cairo and with whom Foucauld had been corresponding since 1906. A non-believer, Massignon had at first been interested only in Foucauld's linguistic and anthropological studies, but of late his letters had displayed a surprising – and to Foucauld, delightful – religious urgency. The turning point had come in 1908 when Massignon was kidnapped by bandits while on an archaeological field trip near Baghdad. Threatened with torture and death, on suspicion of being a spy, Massignon contemplated killing himself. Then he had a vision. In his own words: 'Try at suicide out of incredible self-loathing; eyes closed and a sudden feeling of reverence before an inner fire judging me and consuming my heart, the certainty of a pure, ineffable, creative Presence suspending my sentence at the prayers of beings, invisible visitors to my prison, whose names suddenly burst upon me . . . *Foucauld!'*[35] Shortly afterwards, with no explanation, the bandits released him and, after treating him with great hospitality, sent him on his way. 'Besieged by grace,' Massignon described his adventures to Foucauld in a missive that ended with the words, 'How I suffered when God converted me! It is my entire life that he wished to make his!'[36] No better assistant could be imagined. Here was a man who had experience of Islam, who had lived in Arab countries and who had a desire to give his life for God – a man much like Foucauld himself. After a brief exchange of letters it was agreed that they should meet in Paris to discuss their positions.

Foucauld had for a long time been reluctant to return to France. It held memories, offered temptations and was a distraction from the task at hand. When his relations urged him to make the voyage, he responded sternly: 'Voyages for family radically contrary to monastic law; in leaving the Trappists I embraced a state more severe, not less severe, than theirs; moreover, such journeys are *a very bad example.*'[37] By 1909, however, his resolve had weakened. Perhaps, he admitted, he might allow himself a visit to his relations. Also, the trip would not be entirely self-indulgent: he needed to assess Massignon's suitability as a companion; and he wanted to drum up support for his latest brainchild, 'The Union of the Brothers and Sisters of the Sacred Heart'. The Union had its origins in the 'Third Order' he had previously suggested to Guérin, and was to comprise a group of lay men and women whose job was to spread Christian values in the desert not by teaching or preaching but by 'showing forth Christ in their lives'.[38] As he envisaged it, the Union would have 'the triple objective of bringing Christians back to living a life in conformity with the Gospel;

of developing among them the love of the Holy Eucharist and of rousing among them a movement for the conversion of infidels, and especially for the accomplishment of the strict duty that any Christian people have of giving a Christian education to the infidels in their colonies.'[39] And – although this was maybe too much to hope for – the Union might possibly act as an intermediary stage for those who wished to join Foucauld's harsher order of Little Brothers. On Christmas Day 1908, Foucauld left Tamanrasset, rode and walked through the oases of Ghardaia, Laghouat and El Goléa to Biskra, caught a train to Algiers, a ship to Marseilles and then another train to the capital. He stepped onto the platform on 18 February 1909.

Most French officers, on returning to civilization after a spell in the oases, experienced a sense of dislocation. Even Algiers seemed a roaring metropolis compared to life in the Sahara. Lean and sun-baked, obvious strangers to town, they were bewildered by the most basic aspects of Western existence: sleeping under sheets, walking on carpets, locking doors, buying shoes, wearing collars and ties, dressing for dinner and, strangest of all, going out for dinner. For the majority the period of transition was brief. Typically, a Saharian was given at least one month's leave per annum and it was rare for anyone to spend more than two years away from home, or to forget entirely the land and family to which he belonged. But Foucauld had not seen France in eight years, and until recently had not thought of ever returning there. For him, arriving in Paris was like arriving on an alien planet. So much had changed since he had last seen the city. The streets were busier, the air was smoggier, and the illuminations more garish. Cars, electric lighting and telephones, which had been relative novelties in 1901, were now commonplace. Street posters advertised products he had never heard of and newspapers carried meaningless columns on the latest political, commercial and sporting developments. Adding to the foreignness of it all was the weather. It had been a cold winter. The sky was grey, the trees were black, snow sagged on the rooftops and formed dirty ridges on the pavements. Still clad in his desert robes, but wearing a hat and overcoat against the chill, Foucauld walked into the sludgy, smoky world that was Paris in February.

He first visited Marie de Bondy at her home, 10 Avenue Percier. Then he went to see Huvelin, who was sick and in bed, but who had strength enough to give his blessing to the Union of Little Brothers and Sisters. After that, he saw Massignon and outlined his vision of their future. 'As long as we do not respect the human being in the non-Christian believers we are trying to "convert",' he said, 'we are betraying God. Conversion is not a shipping permit we attach to the conscience of others. It is a deepening of what is best in their religious loyalty.'[40] Massignon allowed Foucauld to lead him in an all-night vigil at the Basilica of the Sacred Heart in Montmartre. Here, he had his first doubts. It was 'a slow, dark, bare night, without consolation in that glacial, lofty tomb,'[41] Massignon recorded. The following morning he and Foucauld went to Mass at St Augustine's and, while waiting for Foucauld to robe himself, Massignon accepted another priest's invitation to serve at his own ceremony. At that moment, Foucauld emerged from the sacristy. As Massignon later wrote, it was the look on Foucauld's face that decided him: the monk was cross, jealous, annoyed that his pupil dared worship with anyone else. Massignon realized that Foucauld was too individual to share his burden – a burden of which only he knew the weight – with anyone else. Politely, Massignon said that he was uncertain if he wanted to become a Little Brother. He did, however, join the Union, and as one of its first members he accompanied its founder to the home of the Cardinal of Paris, where Foucauld hoped to receive approval for his demi-order. The two men were ushered into His Eminence's presence and for a while nobody spoke. At length the Cardinal said, 'It appears that you left the Trappists.' Foucauld agreed that he had. 'The best thing you could do would be to return to them,'[42] the Cardinal said. After a few minutes' silence the interview was terminated.

Foucauld did not give up. Bidding farewell to Massignon he booked a ticket to Viviers, the diocese in which he had first entered the priesthood and whose Bishop, Monsignor Bonnet, was a far more sympathetic character. 'I approve your plan, and I wish it complete success,' Bonnet said. 'I shall help you with my poor prayers. The work is worth devoting to it everything in one's power.'[43] Bonnet's power, on its own, was not very great. As he admitted, 'If God wants it to be realized, how many difficulties it is going to encounter and how much suffering will be required before it wins a place in the sun of the holy Church!'[44] Carrying this rueful blessing, Foucauld travelled from Viviers to Grasse to see his sister Marie. A mother of six children, Marie was barely recognizable as the woman he had last seen in 1901. She had put on weight, had become depressed and fragile, and although applying herself courageously to her children's needs she spent more and more time either in church or in a book. As Jean-Jacques Antier, one of Foucauld's most recent biographers, has written, 'Like him, she was paying for the tragedies of their childhood.'[45] After a few sad days in her company he returned to Algiers on 8 March 1909. His tour had been unproductive and disheartening. But this was the stuff of Foucauld's career. He agreed with Bonnet's assessment: if the task was hard, 'that is no reason to back down. On the contrary, that should be an incentive to begin working valiantly.'[46]

His time in France had not been without its moments. Before leaving Paris he had visited Marie de Bondy's twenty-one-year-old son, François. She had advised him that he was a wastrel: he had lost his religion and was ruining himself just as Foucauld had done. She wanted him to see the boy and draw him back to the faith. Foucauld did as she asked, and on 25 February he knocked at the door of François de Bondy's luxurious bachelor apartment. (He had tried on the 24th but François was preoccupied with a member of the *Folies Bergère*.) François opened the door cautiously.

The wind was howling, [François wrote] it was cold and nasty. The snow was melting on the streets. I saw the black outline of a funny little priest. He entered the room and peace entered with him. The glow of his eyes and especially that very humble smile had taken over his whole person. Aside from that intelligent, searching look, tempered if not belied by the determined self-effacement so etched into his face, nothing remained of the Charles de Foucauld whom I remembered.

There stood before me a puny model of the secular priest,
owing to the pathetic black quilted overcoat, which hid almost
completely his missionary robes. It was only on his chest that I
could see something of the coarse white fabric, on which stood
out the cross and the cherry-red heart. In his hand he held a
pitiful clerical hat, which must have rolled in the mud, for it
was streaked with dirt. And I looked at that emaciated head,
the face of the anchorite through the ages, without any age
itself, lined and weathered, the scanty little salt-and-pepper
beard, the short-cropped hair and the gray skull.

Foucauld talked to François about his forthcoming novel – every
young man of François's ilk was writing a novel – and then departed
in a gust of sanctity that left the young man shaken.

After he was gone, I remained intrigued by this unusual visitor.
A blessing was on him in the room, and there still floated about
me something sweet and infinitely peaceful. He had said
nothing of a nature to upset me. There was an incredible joy
emanating from him . . . Having tasted 'the pleasures of life'
and able to entertain the hope of not having to leave the table
for a good while, I, upon seeing that my whole sum of
satisfactions did not weigh more than a tiny feather in
comparison with the complete happiness of the ascetic, found
rising in me a strange feeling not of envy but respect.

Why should he have over my mind this mysterious power?
He made no attempt to lecture me any more than he
endeavoured to convert Muslims. Perhaps he loved in me what
he himself knew of enthusiasm – even though mine was
directed toward everything counter to his ideals . . .

For the duration of that visit I had seen Charles surrounded
by a radiance, neither luminous nor visible, but perceivable to
some sense that we have not yet come to identify. So much
faith, hope and charity placed around him that nimbus which
painters, who can only appeal to the eye, depict as rays of gold.

Silent music, beneficial waves, bringing beatitude and dreams.
[Thus] the minute with Charles is engraved in me, eternal.[47]

The interview did nothing to steer François from his hedonistic
ways but it provided a snapshot of the unsettling force Foucauld now
possessed. Others, too, testified to the strange power of his presence,
describing it as something he did not exert but which simply
emanated from his very being. Today, cynics might call it the power of
fanaticism. In medieval times it would have been called a halo.

15

DJANET

Foucauld was invigorated by his stay in France. His ennui had disappeared and in its place had come a renewed determination. He spent a month at Beni Abbès and then transferred to Tamanrasset, stopping for a few days at In Salah where, on 11 May, he made a bravura appearance at the ceremony of the colours, 'dominating the horizon with the fine posture of a one-time cavalryman, reciting aloud the *Pater* as no one has ever recited it.'[1] He had expected to be tired by the journey but found himself pleasantly fit and by 11 June was brushing the dust out of his 'Frigate' (his shack in Tamanrasset) with gusto. For the rest of the year he applied himself to Jesus and, worship permitting, to his studies of the Hoggar. He wrote to Massignon, urging him to visit. 'The climate is like France, without the snow, rain or ice and is just as healthy,'[2] read one letter. (This was not strictly true: the Hoggar was now in its fourth year without rain and the *harratin* were dying.) 'If you want, you can live a monastic life before God, an apostolic life before God, while appearing to live no more than the studious life of a *Savant*.'[3] Having pleaded he then took a hectoring tone: 'You will follow me, and take my place when the time comes, all the while appearing as if a lay person.'[4] But Massignon prevaricated, and for the rest of the year Foucauld remained alone in his hermitage. By 31 August 1909, however, he was back on the trail, making yet another tour with Laperrine.

The last two years had been good for the Commander of the Oases. Apart from instituting Forts Motylinski and Polignac, Laperrine had also gained a small victory in the battle for precedence that grumbled between the Sahara and the Soudan. Although their joint border had been settled, and they existed (officially) in a state of perfect accord, and although individual officers did, indeed, get on perfectly well, there was still a lingering sense of antipathy between the two French commands. For Laperrine, the link-up on Soudanese territory in 1906 between his and Cortier's forces had not dispelled the memory of Timiaouine, where the Soudanese had so brusquely prevented him travelling to Timbuctoo. In 1908, however, his superior control of the desert was acknowledged when the Soudanese invited Lieutenant Sigonney for a meeting at Agadez. On the agenda was how the Motylinski garrison might protect the Soudan from incursions by Tripolitanian and Tuareg bandits; also how the two colonies might best work together in the future; and – this was what pleased Laperrine most – the Soudanese were having trouble with some of the northern tribes and would be grateful if, on his way south, Sigonney could lead his *méharistes* through their territory. The tribes were awed into quiescence, the week-long meeting, which was punctuated by blaring, musical festivals, ended in mutual congratulations and on the return journey Sigonney compounded his triumph when he encountered a group of Hoggar Tuareg who had decamped to the border: it was where they always went when the Hoggar was drought-ridden, as it now was; but their absence had weakened Moussa's position and so Sigonney drove them home. Laperrine's adjutant, a young officer named Léon Lehuraux who later produced a stream of jingoistic but well-informed books on the Sahara, could not hide his glee: 'One more time [the Tuareg] realized that we could reach them wherever they went, and that a lasting *entente cordiale* reigned between the Saharians and the Soudanese.'[5] The *entente* became even more *cordiale* in 1909, when the Soudanese asked Laperrine to settle a few outstanding queries. How should they regulate trans-Saharan cara-vans? How should they create a regular postal service between the two colonies? What should they do about the cross-border movement of nomads and their flocks? Another meeting was required, this time with the Colonel in person. It was to be held at Gao on the River Niger.

In choosing Gao, the Soudanese were saving as much face as they could. The officer in charge of the Haut-Sénégal and Niger district, Colonel Venel, wanted to settle the differences between the two colonies. He knew also that Laperrine's great ambition was to travel from In Salah to Timbuctoo. But to allow him within the gates would have been too humiliating a climb-down. So Venel chose Gao, an out-post to the east of Timbuctoo, whose position on the Niger Loop, or 'Boucle', he hoped would compensate for its lack of fame. Gao was also far enough north to fall within the sphere of the Soudan's own brand of semi-nomadic Tuareg who, like the tribes Sigonney had subdued the year before, needed a demonstration of power. Laperrine accepted, and left In Salah on 8 April with fifteen *méharistes*. Moussa in person acted as his guide. After skirting the western edge of the Ténéré, they reached Gao on 12 June.

Lehuraux was cock-a-hoop. 'The Chaamba's arrival on the banks of the Niger was a sensational event. Never had the Tuareg of the *Boucle* imagined that the Algerians, with whom their comrades in the Hoggar and the Adjer had so often met in bloody combat, would one day water their camels in the *Bahr*, as the Saharan nomads call the river.'[6] What Lehuraux did not mention was the difference in climate. Laperrine had led his men from the dry, and relatively disease-free desert to the humid, pestilential fringe of the tropics. Where they stood, they were safe. But river blindness, bilharzia, dengue fever, yellow fever and malaria waited just a few days' journey downriver. Venel wanted Laperrine to make that journey. He had changed his mind, and would prefer it if they met at Niamey, his regional command post, further to the south. Unfazed, Laperrine left his men at Gao and caught a canoe to Niamey where, for a week, he and Venel discussed their positions. When they left the negotiating table they had not only agreed their administrative and strategic requirements but had also redrawn their joint border (to Laperrine's advantage). The Niamey Convention, to give it the name under which it was later ratified by the French government, was possibly a better way of carving up the continent than the standard one of drawing lines on a map in a distant European capital. Nevertheless, there is something strange, albeit appropriately Conradian, in the image of two white men, dressed in colonial uniform, huddled over a table in a steamy office on the banks of the Niger and deciding singlehandedly just where a nation should start or stop. If such considerations impinged upon Laperrine or Venel, they made no impression on Lehuraux: it was all being done, he wrote, 'for the greater good of France's prestige in Africa'.[7]

Laperrine left Niamey on 21 June and, gathering up his *méharistes*, travelled north to the Hoggar where he met Foucauld for a tour of Tamanrasset and its environs. So far, the Tuareg had impressed him with their loyalty: Moussa had been a perfect guide; a number of his Hoggar chieftains had travelled 800 kilometres to escort him over the last stage; their wives and children had lined up outside his tent to greet him; in all, he could find no fault in them whatsoever. They showed every sign of being as faithful as his own Chaamba. His policy had been 'to show force in order to avoid using it'[8] – to borrow Lyautey's words – and he had succeeded so well that when his puny troop of *méharistes* rode into Tamanrasset the Tuareg interpreted their weakness as a token of friendship. If the French dared enter the Hoggar in such small numbers it was a sign that they respected their allies and were willing to put themselves under their protection. In addition, Laperrine's reputation as the 'children's general' was beginning to pay dividends. 'They respected the fact that I knew all of their relatives: wives, children, young girls, young men. An uninterrupted procession wound its way to my camp.'[9] Overjoyed by the success of his policies, Laperrine roamed the Hoggar like an indulgent god of war, distributing largesse and goodwill as he went. Foucauld, meanwhile, hovered attentively at his side, interpreting, advising and occasionally directing.

Laperrine returned to In Salah on 30 September 1909, having spent six months away from the oases. The tour had been successful in every way, and he had nothing but praise for his *méharistes*. 'During the whole journey I could not have been more satisfied with everyone,' he wrote in his official report. 'French, Arabs and Touareg alike rivalled each other in zeal, showed the greatest spirit, and endured without complaint the very serious privations that I imposed upon them.'[10] But then he expected nothing less, for this was the only attitude that could conquer the desert. He tried hard to impress this fact on the Algerian and Parisian authorities. 'Unless one has led one of these trips, or taken part in a similar policing operation, one cannot imagine the excellent character of our Saharians,' he reiterated. 'Their resilience in the face of fatigue, hunger and thirst is a matter of amour-propre. There is never a complaint, even when circumstances are such that the chef is obliged to repeat the miracle of the loaves and fishes. When reading them their evening orders I have often had to include instructions of the following kind: for such-and-such a reason we cannot get fresh supplies until this time instead of that time; I've given you provisions to last from 15 to 30 April; you'll have to make them last until 8 May. I've given you three days' water; but from the latest information, it seems that we will not reach another well until noon on the fifth day; you will have to be sparing with your water, etc. . . . I wonder how these orders would be received by any other company in the Sahara?'[11] He emphasized, too, the way his men made light of diseases that in a normal unit would be seized upon as an excuse for hospitalization. '[Even when ill] they continue for as long as they can remain upright, and if they do admit that they are unwell, it really means they are on the point of death. Frequently, they die on arrival at the infirmary, or even before they reach it. Some show signs of scurvy; others, in their last days, are hit by sudden attacks of consumption; but the doctors' diagnosis is always the same: these men have driven themselves to the point of exhaustion, they have given more than their constitutions could bear. *I can think of no finer eulogy*.'[12]

Anticipating bureaucratic queries as to why the *méharistes* should have to suffer so severely, Laperrine pointed out that they had little choice. 'Our job as Saharians requires this superhuman effort . . .

There is no question of being gentle with the men: the mission we have been given requires us to ask of them the impossible. The authorities should recognize their services and reward them accordingly.'[13] He drew the authorities' attention to the fact that the forty-four Frenchmen and 356 Chaamba based at In Salah were expected to patrol a radius of 800 kilometres and that on his recent trip to Gao he had traversed an area the size of France, Spain and Portugal combined. The only response was a message to the effect that the Minister of War had no need of geography lessons, hadn't asked him to visit Gao in the first place, and would be pleased if Laperrine could explain reports that had been transmitted from the Ottoman Embassy concerning events on the Tripolitanian border.

This was Laperrine's downfall. The border with Tripolitania was like that between Algeria and Morocco: in the more densely populated coastal regions there was a clearly demarcated frontier, but in the deeper desert, where Tripolitania abutted Algeria, no boundary had been confirmed. By 1909, in anticipation of a final accord to which diplomats were moving sluggishly, France and the Ottoman Empire had agreed a neutral zone over which neither side had sovereignty. France, however, was a wealthy, industrial nation, the Ottoman Empire an inchoate anachronism on the point of bankruptcy, and the neutral zone reflected this fact. It encompassed no French territory and stretched so far into Tripolitania as to almost reach Ghat, one of the country's southernmost trade centres. The agreement, which looked so fine on paper, was a sham on the ground. The Ottomans continued to patrol the neutral zone as if it were their own and even installed a garrison right in the middle of it. They also supported Attici's displaced Tuareg warriors in their raids into French territory, and they gave refuge and arms to the Senoussi, an Algerian-born body of Muslim fundamentalists whose political and religious motivations made them a potentially far more dangerous foe than the Tuareg. As for the French, they too acted as if the disputed area were their own. From Fort Polignac patrol after patrol went into the Tripolitanian desert. Occasionally the two sides met, sometimes with ridiculous consequences: once, when a French column routed a caravan led by

Ottoman officers, they had to collect the fallen luggage and return it to its owners. To Laperrine the situation was insupportable. Before leaving for Gao he told Nieger to take a detachment of *méharistes* to Fort Polignac from where he was to exert himself to the fullest. Nieger had *carte blanche* but Laperrine drew his attention to Djanet, a strategically important oasis not far from Ghat, from where Fort Polignac could reprovision without the long trudge to and from In Salah. Nieger did exert himself, and he did so in a journey whose mix of geographical and military ambitions epitomized Laperrine's reign over the Sahara.

Nieger left In Salah at the beginning of April. The accepted route to Fort Polignac led north-east from In Salah to Temassinin and then south-east, following a series of established wells. Nieger decided to complete the triangle by crossing the barren and hitherto unexplored Tassili plateau. This sheet of black stone, littered with boulders of every size, seemed to confirm the Tuareg legend that the Sahara was a playground of the gods. European wisdom stated that rocks were moved by glaciers, but the rocks of the Tassili fitted no such orderly explanation. Some the size of cathedrals, others smaller than dominoes, they looked as if they were the product of an erratic, centuries-old tournament of *pétanque*, hurled down on the landscape and, at irregular intervals, swept into ravines by some distant, divine hand. Wells were few and far between, having been deliberately collapsed to deter invaders, and those that remained were mostly foul. The guides were unreliable, for nobody had travelled this way in decades, and Nieger was forced to navigate by compass alone. Dr Robert Hérisson, whom Laperrine had ordered to accompany the expedition, was horrified.

Recently posted to In Salah, Hérisson was keenly aware of his status as a newcomer – his baggage having been lost en route, he had arrived with only a cello and, having no uniform, for twenty days had to wear a set of borrowed Arab robes – but even so, he was unprepared for his first desert journey. His legs and back ached from spending ten to twelve hours at a time perched on a camel. He wearied of a meat-only diet – meat, he noticed, that as it dried assumed a peculiar green and

purple tinge – and the water sickened him. 'When I lift my canteen to
my mouth, my stomach rises in disgust at the first taste,' he recorded.
'I have a horror of everything made from this liquid – soup, coffee, tea.
I drink only what is necessary to stay alive. I cannot prevent myself
groaning under my breath, everytime I have to swallow this revolting
brew. It gets worse as we go on. After the first days, the best is gone.
It becomes concentrated by evaporation and seepage, becomes
blacker and thicker. The taste of leather, of tar and of rancid butter is
overwhelming.'[14] The lack of hygiene disturbed him: there was no
water for shaving or washing; and despite veiling themselves in the
Tuareg style, their faces became covered in sand, which collected in
their eyes, ears and nostrils, and formed a glutinous silt at the corners
of their mouths. Above them circled large black crows who, every
time the column halted, swirled down in malevolent flurries to peck
at the camels' humps. Hérisson slept in the open, and beneath the
folded burnous that was his pillow he kept a loaded revolver against
the Tuareg raid he expected every night. Once, when the party went
six days without finding fresh water, he seriously thought they were
doomed. Still, he comforted himself half-heartedly, if he'd stayed in
France he might have died of pneumonia or typhoid.

In compensation, their existence had a certain barbaric splendour,
as when they cooked a couple of antelopes brought in by the
Chaamba. 'It was an impressive spectacle. To and fro in the darkness,
lit by the flickering red light of a blazing wood fire, moved men who
were ragged, thin, black and desiccated, unwashed for ages, wrapped
in bandoliers of cartridges, knives hanging from their belts. The two
gutted carcases, the fire, the shadows that rose and fell, and above it
all the vast, azure heaven . . . dotted with silver stars – it was like
living in the stone age.'[15] Sometimes there were storms of a dramatic
quality that Hérisson had never before witnessed – abruptly, at
midday, the sky turned black, lightning crackled to and fro amidst the
rocks, and huge, hot raindrops splashed down, within seconds transforming the parched party into so many lumps of damp cloth. Then,
just as suddenly, the sun was beating down on them again. (In the
aftermath of one of these downpours, Hérisson ordered his batman to

launder his clothes in a pool of water that had collected in the rocks. The man pounded a shirt for a few moments then draped it over his bare back while he pounded the next. In temperatures of up to 50 °C the first shirt dried in the time it took to wash the second. He had barely finished before the pool evaporated.) After that came the evenings, when the thermometer fell below zero and unfamiliar constellations glittered in a still-blue sky – in the Sahara, Hérisson noted, the sky never went completely black, even at night.

Natural wonder was matched by intellectual stimulation. Before Hérisson left In Salah, Laperrine had instructed him that his duties were those of a scientist as much as a doctor. He was to make a record of everything that might be of interest to the professors in Algiers – botany, anthropology, geology and, above all, any scrap of knowledge that might assist in a better understanding of the Tuareg and their past. Hérisson met few Adjer Tuareg and those he did refused to accept money, food or shelter and swore eternal enmity to France. As for their past, when he offered them a slice of roast lizard that the Chaamba had thrown on the fire, they refused haughtily. They did not eat lizards, they said: lizards were the reincarnation of their ancestors. But Hérisson had a thick skin and ignored these put-downs, concentrating instead on the evidence before him. On every side, signs of prehistoric life abounded. In caves and beneath overhanging rocks he found ancient paintings of antelopes, humped cattle, camels and ostriches, whose beauty he tried vainly to reproduce in his journal. Stone arrowheads, axes and other implements littered the ground in such profusion that he stopped collecting them. The plateau was covered with piles of boulders that he at first mistook for route-marking cairns but which, when he dismantled them, revealed human bones that fell to dust as he lifted them up. He did not know where these relics came from, but he suspected they belonged to a time far older than that of the Tuareg. The scale of the landscape and the quantity of remains made him feel as if he was walking through the cinders of a dead city. The sense of trespass was overpowering.

On 19 April 1909, a small, grey swallow, flying north to Europe, landed on the metal trunk containing his medical gear. It was so exhausted that Hérisson was able to take it in his hands, give it water, and then place it on a branch of a nearby tree. The next day it was gone. 'It was very strange,' he wrote. 'If I was superstitious, I might think it was a spirit come to make sure of my good health, to know whether to lead us from that place or leave us to carry on.'[16] He did not have long to wait for an answer. In the early days of May, having spent a month on the Tassili plateau, their camels slouched into Fort Polignac.

For Nieger the trek had been nothing special. For Hérisson it was a triumph. 'We had not discovered America,' he wrote, 'but with only a compass we had opened new stretches of desert that nobody had dared cross in such a manner.'[17] Fort Polignac was hardly civilization. It had not yet been completed, and Tuareg captives from the Adjer were still hauling the last mud bricks into place. But it was big, and it was safe. Within its walls lay stores of food, ammunition, water – Laperrine had sited it around a well – and, most importantly as far as Hérisson was concerned, it offered company. The commanding officer was one Lieutenant Nivelle, a cheery youngster, in his twenties like Hérisson, who gave the new boy every encouragement. He shouldn't be embarrassed in the slightest at having lost his baggage, he said. The very same thing had happened to him, and he had not even been left with anything as useful as a cello: on reaching In Salah his worldly possessions had consisted of a parasol and a soda siphon. The two youngsters became friends and in the evenings they scampered up the ropes and planks left behind by the builders to watch from Fort Polignac's unfinished battlements the sun blaze down over the Tassili.

Nieger gave Hérisson only a few days' recuperation before marching south to Djanet. He took Nivelle and his fifty *méharistes* with him, as well as a troop of infantry and an eighty-millimetre cannon that he had ordered from Ouargla. Now Hérisson had new cause for fright. They marched through wooded defiles that were perfect grounds for ambush. Trigger-happy, they fired at everything, nearly decimating a flock of goats who rustled through the bushes. But when they neared

Djanet, Nieger ordered complete silence. They moved in noiselessly, rejecting advances from surrounding tribes, until they emerged on a hill overlooking their target. The oasis looked peaceful enough, but from its small fort there flew an Ottoman flag. While one of Nieger's sergeants reconnoitred the palm groves, leaping thorn fences over a metre high with his rifle in his hand, Hérisson prepared for his first taste of combat. On his right shoulder he slung his bag of medical equipment, and on the left a Lebel carbine and a hundred cartridges. 'The inhabitants of Djanet had not heard of the Red Cross,' he wrote nervously. 'It was too late, and perhaps not the best time, to explain to them what it was.'[18]

When Nieger's sergeant returned, it appeared that Hérisson's services might not be needed. Unconventionally, and with remarkable candour, the people of Djanet sent word that they couldn't decide whether to fight or not. Half of them were very keen but the other half, they apologized, were tepid. By return, Nieger said they had half an hour to make up their minds, and while they were doing so, he invited them to study a small, white rock, about four metres by three, which lay to the north of the fort and was about the same distance from his position as the fort. Ranging his cannon, he sent three shells in quick succession into the rock. 'To a man, the inhabitants declared themselves friends of France,' Hérisson wrote. 'They raised the white flag and sent a new delegation to confirm their best intentions.'[19] Nivelle led his *méharistes* into the fort and personally hoisted the *tricouleur*. Then, after his men had prayed in the mosque and kissed a sacred Koran that was reputed to have belonged to a saint, he led them out again. After that, the French went back to Fort Polignac.

It had been a small operation, more a snook-cocking than a conquest. But if its military impact was insignificant, its diplomatic repercussions were far-reaching. Paris had not instructed Laperrine to advance on Djanet and, communications in Tripolitania being swifter than in Algeria, the government was affronted to hear of his action first from the Ottomans. Not that they particularly minded, but there was an etiquette to these matters and Laperrine had transgressed it.

When he reached In Salah after the Gao expedition, Laperrine read his correspondence and realized, like many Saharan officers before him, that his time was up. To forestall his dismissal he applied for a posting to France. His application was accepted and on 8 November he was given the colonelcy of the 18th Chasseurs in Lunéville. The transfer did not take effect until the following summer, however, and during that time Laperrine continued to prowl the Sahara. He told nobody of his forthcoming departure.

One of his first troubles that winter was Foucauld. On leaving Laperrine's tour in 1909, the monk had loped into the Hoggar in search of a retreat where he could complete his translations. The place that seemed best was Assekrem, a rocky peak 2,700 metres above sea level. It was solitary but not hopelessly so, for when it rained the Tuareg took their flocks to graze the scrub on the hillside below. Returning to Tamanrasset, he asked Laperrine's assistance in building a small stone shack there. Laperrine refused. He did not want Foucauld to go to Assekrem and he did not even want him to stay in Tamanrasset. His scouts had warned him that an Adjer war party was on its way and it would be best if Foucauld left the region for a while. *Méharistes* gathered up those locals who wanted French protection but Foucauld would not budge. Hérisson, now the medical officer at Fort Motylinski, wrote, 'He will remain alone in his quarters, unarmed, unguarded, under the sole protection of God. I realize that he is determined to die murdered. That is the end he foresees and longs for.'[20]

The expected attack from Adjer did not materialize and in the spring of 1910 Laperrine gave in to Foucauld's demands. He sent a team of masons from Fort Motylinski to construct a rough, stone shelter for his friend and as they were building it he went on his last tour of the Hoggar. He wanted to know how many men he could rely upon to defend the Hoggar against attacks from Tripolitania and ordered a *fantasia*, or ceremonial review of Moussa's troops. The *fantasia* was to be held in *oued* Tmeriri, a river bed situated in one of the Hoggar's higher valleys and covered with thickets of ethel trees. Laperrine took up position on a hummock overlooking the *oued*, and with Foucauld, Sigonney and a few other officers awaited the display. From a neighbouring valley, Moussa's men moved slowly into the *oued*, their white shields glimmering through the branches. Then, at Laperrine's command, the war-drum was beaten. Five hundred warriors burst from the trees and charged towards the Frenchmen, drawing up at the last moment in a cloud of dust. Laperrine remained immobile but was secretly delighted by the display. The last time a *fantasia* had been performed was in the Soudan. It had resulted in the death of a French colonel, all his orderlies and several onlookers.

Hérisson accompanied Laperrine and Foucauld as they made their tour, and described their daily routine.

For lunch or dinner, a big rug is spread on the ground in the shade of some tree if there is one, or in the Colonel's tent, which is quite large. Each gives his table-gear, can, and cup to the cook, who places them anyhow. There is no precedence. When all is ready, they sit down to table, squatting like tailors on the edge of the rug. The cook brings the dish. Each man has his little wheaten cake cooked under the ashes. The Colonel calls upon anyone he likes to help himself the first. Then they talk away and there is no restraint. The Colonel always invites all the French in the neighbourhood to his table – quartermasters, corporals, gunsmiths and joiners. They will pay nothing to the mess. Sometimes he has them served first. They take any place whatever at table, just by chance. Father de Foucauld always comes at noon, with a bottle of white muscat, his sacramental wine . . . At table we do not talk about serious things; we tell stories, jokes, and chaff the Colonel's cook. Father de Foucauld laughs. The Colonel has a very varied and amusing stock of stories, which he says are true. He is a very charming raconteur. Father de Foucauld smiles when everybody else laughs. But if the story goes a little beyond the limits of propriety, he hears nothing, he is deaf, and seems to be thinking of other things. Then someone remarks that the conversation has taken 'a silly turn' and that the Father must be scandalized; but if excuses are made, he protests that he was not listening and did not hear; no one was embarrassed.

During the 'rounds' he used to come with a black servant and a hired camel, without tent or camp bed. He slept on the ground in his blankets. The greater part of the time he took a pack-camel without a saddle. Not to lose time he wanted us to go on, and to come and join us at the place agreed upon, doubling his stages and doing eighty kilometres a day at five kilometres an hour, and, as far as possible, using a route still unexplored by the French. He then arrived with little bits of paper full of notes and sketches, quite small, but very clear, like those of his Morocco exploration, and put them all into the Colonel's hands.[21]

In the evenings, Foucauld would take Hérisson for a stroll and advise him on the practicalities of life in the Hoggar. Hérisson fell under his spell. 'Father de Foucauld, unlike what is said of celebrated men, became immeasurably greater when one saw him every day and close by.'[22]

Perhaps it was as well that Laperrine was returning to France for, behind his informality and joviality, he was on the point of disintegration. The man who had survived the awful journey through the Erg Chech, who had criss-crossed the Sahara and who had led his *méharistes* from In Salah to the Soudan, had finally reached his limits. On this last tour of the Hoggar, he became slower and slower, dismounting from his camel every two hours to rest. Perhaps he was suffering from a mild form of tuberculosis – he had been to an Alpine spa a few years before – or maybe he was just exhausted. It was probably the latter. Hérisson recorded how, after a daily journey of eighty kilometres, Laperrine began work as soon as his tent had been erected. 'He sits down, drafts his orders, reads his reports, writes to the Minister, to the Governor of Algiers, to the papers. He is an indefatigable worker. I admire the unity of his life. He lives for his work beyond and above everything else.'[23] He also recorded that through long habit Laperrine had become an insomniac. Once an officer entered Laperrine's quarters and, seeing him slumped over his desk, retreated on tip-toe. As he left, a voice came from behind, 'I do not sleep.'[24] Even Foucauld acknowledged that the Colonel had overreached himself. 'Laperrine spends himself beyond measure,' he wrote, 'he has impressed all who are under his orders with a wonderful energy and activity. The last six years, the amount of work the officers under his orders have done, and what has been effected from the military, administrative, geographical, and commercial points of view, are unheard of.'[25]

The respect that Laperrine commanded was awesome. Shortly after Djanet, Hérisson asked his Arab batman what he would do if there was holy war between the West and Islam. 'Cut your throat,'[26] the man replied. Hérisson then asked him why he served France at all. His answer was that he did not serve France; he served men like Laperrine and Nieger, men who were warriors and who understood the Sahara. When Laperrine left the desert in June 1910, to be followed a few years later by Nieger, who shared the blame for Djanet, their supporters felt they had been betrayed. 'Our officers have given France colonies that they have accepted grudgingly, at the risk of sacrificing their careers and knowing that for all their efforts they will be disavowed and blamed by officialdom,' wrote Hérisson. 'These men [in government] are acting contrary to a tradition of which they are sincerely and violently unworthy.'[27] Foucauld was just as indignant. 'Since the age of twenty-one [Laperrine] has not spent three years in France . . . It is he who gave the Sahara to France, *in spite of her*, and at the risk of his career, and he it is who united our Algerian possessions with our colony in the Soudan.'[28]

Laperrine and Foucauld never saw each other again in the Sahara. They continued to write, and Laperrine did his best to ensure that Foucauld's advice was passed to the appropriate authorities. On one or two occasions, when organizing his Union of lay missionaries, Foucauld dropped into Lunéville. But from 1910, Laperrine belonged to France's war machine as it moved towards the long-awaited conflict with Germany. His last act as Commander of the Oases was to arrange Moussa's promised trip to France. Escorted by

Nieger and accompanied by a small group of Tuareg nobles, the *ame-noukhal* of the Hoggar was treated to a full display of France's might. The itinerary, as one contemporary remarked disparagingly, was 'meant to astound rather than appeal to the heart, a visit such as governors who have no paternal feeling of responsibility can order'.[29] Moussa watched bayonet charges and artillery experiments – 'People with such means of destruction are crazy if they go to war against each other,'[30] he said, uncomprehendingly – then was led on a dizzying parade of munitions factories, stud farms, palaces and Montmartre night-clubs. He was shown waterfalls, lush fields, herds of fat, docile cattle, and the Moulin Rouge. Foucauld's in-laws put him up at their estate, and at a military parade in Longchamps a general pinned the Légion d'Honneur to his chest.

Moussa felt uncomfortable. 'France is nothing but a vast garden,' he later told Hérisson. 'Peace reigns among the multitudes: the bustling, agitated people you pass in the streets don't attack you or rob you. You can come and go amidst countless strangers without having to carry a sword or a dagger for your security. God must love the French to have given them such prosperity. But we could not wait to get back home, to our country, our families, to be amongst our own people with our servants, our goats and our camels.'[31] When the time came to board the ship at Marseilles, he did so with an appreciation of France's might and an honest bewilderment as to why it was wasting it in the Sahara. 'I saw your sister and spent two days at her home,' he wrote to Foucauld. 'I saw your brother-in-law. I visited their grounds and their chateau. And you, you live in Tamanrasset as if you were poor.'[32]

16

HERMIT OF ASSEKREM

The year 1910 was a bad one for Foucauld. To the loss of Laperrine was added the deaths of Guérin and Lacroix in May, followed by that of Huvelin in August. He tried to see the positive side. Of Guérin, for example, he wrote, 'What luck, to be so young, only thirty-seven, and already called home.'[1] But as he told Marie de Bondy, 'All these voids leave me to face a future that may offer obstacles of many kinds.'[2] In another letter, 'I feel more and more that I am not up to my task: I get tireder and tireder, I have more work on hand than I can manage, there is so much that is wrong around me.'[3] To distract himself, he packed eighteen months' supplies and retreated to Assekrem to complete his Tamacheq dictionary with Moussa's secretary and interpreter, Ba Hamou (the same Ba Hamou whom he had told Laperrine was a bad influence). The chapel at Assekrem was not comfortable, being little more than a stone corridor with a couple of open windows and an altar at one end. It took an hour to reach the nearest well, which was 490 metres downhill and so paltry that if an antelope had been there first Foucauld would have had to wait another hour for it to refill. Yet it overlooked vistas that would have made an alpinist weep. All around lay the ragged, unclimbed peaks of the Hoggar, as beautiful in their starkness as the purest, snow-capped Swiss mountain. In the hours before dawn, when the Saharan breezes blew at their strongest, Foucauld stood on his mountain top and gazed towards infinity. 'The view is more beautiful than can be expressed or imagined,' he wrote. 'The very sight of it makes one think of God, and I can scarcely take my eyes from a sight whose beauty and impression of infinitude are so reminiscent of the Creator of all; and at the same time its loneliness and wildness remind me that I am alone with Him . . . From my window I can look out over the mountains and watch the sun rise behind them. I am above them all. I have a wonderful view toward the south and west and need to go only 500 metres to see the sun set. At least every other day there is a big wind that makes you think you are at the seaside.'[4]

He told his friends not to worry about his well-being: 'As for food, I am like Noah in the Ark, or like somebody who is going for a sixteen-month sea voyage without touching at a port.'[5] But after six months' work, in which he made great progress in his translations, he was forced to leave Assekrem. One reason was that Ba Hamou, the evil interpreter – who seems in reality to have been a pragmatic and long-suffering man – said that he couldn't stand it any longer. Another was that they were both seriously ill. Foucauld had indeed packed eighteen months' supplies, but they consisted only of flour, couscous, sugar, salt, pepper, dates and coffee. In the absence of any fresh meat or vegetables, both men were now suffering from scurvy. In comparing himself to a man on a long sea-voyage Foucauld had been less fanciful than he supposed.

Foucauld's return to Tamanrasset gave him the food he needed for physical recovery and the company that was essential to his psychological health. Despite having chosen a life of solitude, he complained throughout his Saharan career about loneliness. He referred outwardly to his lack of spiritual companionship, and inwardly to the loss of his parents. But there was a part of him that still yearned for European company, although he went out of his way to deny it. Nieger recorded that 'One evening, as he strolled outside his pathetic hovel, he observed, "I have a horror of the world and its hypocrisy." He was speaking of our world. I cannot believe he attributed to the Touareg, whose faults and vices he knew so well, a moral level superior to ours.'[6] This, however, was hypocrisy in itself, for when not railing against his loneliness Foucauld liked to bemoan the moral turpitude of the Tuareg – as, for example, in a letter to Sigonney, dated 3 June 1910: 'Your astonishment at Touareg morals does not cause me any surprise. They are too alien from our experience for us to believe. Fundamentally it is a society of Apaches: the men live by robbery, while the women applaud them and live as they please.'[7] In truth, Foucauld was happy to have fellow Europeans about him, and their increased presence during the winter of 1910–11 helped to restore his flagging vigour.

Hérisson was a frequent visitor to Tamanrasset, sometimes bringing his cello which, battered, broken and warped though it was, could still carry a tune. Foucauld disapproved of such frivolities but couldn't hide his interest. Marching out of his shack, he demanded to know what Hérisson had been up to in Fort Motylinski. Hérisson replied that he had learned a bit of Arabic, a bit of Tamacheq, had cured one man of bronchitis, another of rheumatism and a third of syphilis. He had also been playing his cello. 'It's a waste of time playing the cello,'[8] Foucauld grumbled, poking at the twisted instrument. He was taken aback when Hérisson said that Tuareg women considered his cello a musical giant compared to their one-stringed violins, and on listening to a few slow waltzes ten of them had agreed to be vaccinated against smallpox.

Nieger, working out his notice like Laperrine, was another *habitué* of the 'Frigate'. Unlike Hérisson, who was full of cheery anecdotes, Nieger observed Foucauld with a sharp, military eye. 'He had a will of iron, and it kept his impatience under control. He barely raised his voice when expressing an opinion. It was only in moments of crisis that his cavalry officer reflexes surfaced. Then, energy and decisiveness in his gestures, his voice and his plans formed a surprising contrast with his usual gentleness. He sought contact with us only when it was useful to the cause. His kindness could not hide his impatience at putting up with purposeless visits. His indulgence and patience came in different doses: unbelievably large for children and ordinary folk, then smaller and smaller according to the intellectual level of his interlocutor.'[9]

When he first came to Tamanrasset, Foucauld had written: 'As long as France is not involved in a European war, it would seem that this place will remain in security; were there to be a war, however, there would probably be insurrections throughout the south, and here as much as anywhere else.'[10] France was not yet at war but the diplomatic knots on which European peace depended were already beginning to unravel and, as Foucauld had predicted, Africa became involved. The Great Powers who decided Europe's fate were Britain, France, Germany, Austria-Hungary, Russia and the Ottoman Empire. Mutually antagonistic, and in some cases on the brink of collapse, these six imperial powers controlled the fate of a majority of the world's population. Should one of them fall it would start a chain reaction of land-grabbing by the other five, the consequences of which were potentially disastrous. In 1909, the Ottoman Empire began to crumble.

The Young Turks who seized power in Constantinople that year had as their agenda the democratization of a corrupt state and the transformation of an autocratic Sultan into a constitutional monarch. They succeeded in the latter and, to some extent, in the former. But they did so at the expense of a centuries-old tradition that for many peripheral nations was all that bound them to Constantinople. Over the next few years, the Ottoman fringes became fair game for anyone who wanted them. Russia supported Bulgaria in its successful bid for independence; Austria-Hungary moved slyly into Bosnia; and Italy, which until now had been an outsider in the game, made its bid for Great Power status by occupying Tripolitania. On 4 October 1911 the Italian navy bombarded Tripoli. It then did the same to Benghazi before sending a 100,000-strong force to mop up a Turkish army less than a third its size. On 18 October 1912, Rome and Constantinople signed the Peace of Ouchy and Italy, like every other European nation, at last found its place in the sun.

For France, the rearrangement of North African politics brought mixed benefits. It allowed them surreptitiously to extend their frontier so that Djanet became part of Algeria. But it also provided encouragement for the Senoussi, who had not liked Turkish rule in the first place and resented even more strongly the arrival of the Italians. Inflamed by the speeches of wandering marabouts, Tripolitania's Islamic population sided with the Senoussi. Attacking now the Italians and now the French, they overturned Laperrine's careful preparations. Their fury, manifesting itself first in Tripoli, boiled down into the desert. Border incidents became common-place. In the winter of 1911–12 two French patrols were massacred by Senoussi warriors.

The situation brought out Foucauld's least Christian element. 'Such misdemeanours should be severely punished,' he instructed one officer. 'The inspirer, if not the author, is that cursed marabout Abidine, whom you must have known at Timbuctoo. If I were you, this is what I would do. I would collect all the available *méharistes*. I would take them down to South Morocco, where he is supposed to be [hiding]. I would catch the villain, stand him up immediately against a wall – and plug twelve bullets into his skin.'[11] Against the Senoussi, Attici and his men seemed like mere opportunists, and when they were trounced by *méharistes* from In Salah, Foucauld sent the garrison commander a congratulatory letter. 'The flight of Attici bothers no one but himself. It's the best thing for us, on one condition, that he never be allowed, neither he nor [his fellow chief] Sidi ag Khatkhat, to return to French territory, with orders to shoot them without any form of legal process if ever they set foot on it again. The banishment is the best thing that could have happened, and that they have done it to themselves is the best thing for us . . . To have killed them would have had something odious about it, but perpetual banishment under pain of death settles everything.'[12]

He was relatively complacent about the effect the upheavals would have on the Hoggar. 'It leaves the Touaregs completely cold,' he reassured his cousin. 'They do not know the Italians exist and don't care tuppence about the Turks.'[13] This was not entirely true, for Senoussi marabouts had already begun to move down the Saharan trade routes, sometimes even attaching themselves to military columns. But in general his assessment was correct. The Tuareg had far more important things on their minds that winter, one being that it had not rained in Tamanrasset for twenty months and the other being that the two harvests of 1911 (wheat in the spring, millet in the autumn) had both been devastated by locusts. 'Results: 1) there is not a bit of food in the land – I have not been able to buy *one litre* of any sort of grain, wheat, barley or millet; 2) nobody has any clothes for they get these by selling butter, beasts, etc.' Infant mortality stood at 25 to 30 per cent and the people were, as Foucauld wrote, 'in a shocking state of distress'.[14]

Paris was not bothered. Why should it worry about a few raids across a border that it barely knew existed and in which it had little interest? Italy was a modern, industrial power; it should have no trouble subduing a few raggle-taggle rebels. If the uprising spilled into the Algerian Sahara, Laperrine's *méharistes* of In Salah, Fort Polignac and Fort Motylinski were more than capable of dealing with it. In fact, the French were feeling very happy about North Africa because in March 1912 Lyautey had at last given them Morocco – not on a platter as a colony, but more conveniently on the sideboard as a Protectorate, a succulent dish from which they could pick at will, leaving any bones or gristle to the newly installed puppet government. 'Algeria, Tunisia, Morocco, the Soudan, the Sahara, what a beautiful empire!' Foucauld exulted. 'Providing that we civilize it, Frenchify it . . . in fifty years this empire will be an admirable extension of France.'[15] As far as Paris was concerned, its possessions were secure.

The desert, previously a controlled zone through which non-military personnel could travel only with permission from Algiers or Paris, was declared open to all Europeans. Many came, in many different ways. The German Imperial Aero Club was interested in a traverse of the Sahara by plane, dirigible and car. In February 1912, Foucauld received notice that a Polish philosopher was walking from Algiers to Timbuctoo, eating nothing but dates on the way. In December, *The Times* reported that a six-wheeled, propeller-driven sledge had carried one General Bailloud 200 kilometres between

Biskra and Touggourt. (Of this wondrous device no more seems to have been heard.) And, of course, a party of surveyors set out once again to chart a route for the trans-Saharan railway.

The group, which included the omnipresent Chudeau, was accompanied by *méharistes* under the command of Nieger and by a hard-faced young lieutenant named Paul Duclos, recently posted to In Salah. Unlike Hérisson, he had come fully-equipped and was impatient to get ahead. He thought the operation a waste of time. Remembering the efforts of Ferdinand de Lesseps who, between 1881 and 1891, had spent 20,000 lives and millions of francs attempting to build the Panama Canal, he wondered how France's conscience could allow even the concept of a Transsaharian. It would be expensive, dangerous and pointless. 'The whole Sahara won't fill a single train a year,'[16] he complained to his father. Duclos was not impressed by the surveyors, whom he described as 'insatiable infants', who spent more time 'suckling' than working. When they reached the Hoggar in April he was ready to murder one individual. 'He lies back on the saddle as if he was a piece of luggage. He covers his eyes with goggles, muslin and a hood. From time to time he instructs the natives to collect stones and only moves when he needs to drink. This, apparently, is the way one builds railways.'[17] He wasn't very impressed by Foucauld either. When Nieger ordered him to collect Foucauld from Tamanrasset, Duclos wrote, 'I brought the hermit away with me . . . We are likely to make him commit the sin of gluttony, for ordinarily he lives on cooked barley ground up with some dates. He offered some to me, saying it was not very attractive but "it is so nourishing; and the water here is so good, and the sunsets wonderful!" The water tasted stale to me, and the sun seemed to go down in a bonnet of cotton-wool instead of a crown of glory. The hermit pushes evangelical charity a long way when he exalts the elements by anticipation.'[18]

Impervious to the officer's cynicism, Foucauld darted up to Assekrem to collect the barometers he had left there the previous year, and spent a fortnight taking readings and giving the surveyors topographical advice. He thought the Transsaharian an excellent project and he did so both as a priest – 'The railroad is a powerful means for spreading civilization, and civilization aids Christianization. Savages cannot be Christians'[19] – and as an imperialist: 'It is a necessity for preserving our African empire and for enabling us to transport to the Rhine, if need be, as many troops as possible.'[20] After his stay in Nieger's camp Foucauld returned to Tamanrasset, leaving Duclos to grumble his way south.

The traverse of the Sahara had become a fixation for the French. Ever since the days of Foureau and Lamy it had presented a challenge that was political, practical and personal. Politically, a crossing demonstrated French might. Practically, there was always something that had to be imposed on the desert – roads, telegraph lines, railways – and personally, it was a goal sought by every man who had ever had a taste of desert life. There was an element of marvel in its achievement. He who crossed the Sahara saw sights forbidden to all but a few mortals and battled an environment so extreme as to rate comparison with the Poles. Let Peary, Shackleton, Scott and others boast about their Farthest Norths or their Farthest Souths. France had the Sahara.

Duclos couldn't give a fig. He hated almost everything about the trip. He thought the Tuareg, with their shields and lances, were like actors from a comic opera and swore that their only good quality was being able to act naturally in front of a camera. The country, like them, was 'more ugly than picturesque, more dismal than savage'.[21] And when he reached Agadez, the expedition's destination, he described it as 'a verminous town, just as miserable as In Salah but without the sand'.[22] On the way back, 'I promise that some of the wells cannot be said to contain anything that chemically fits the description H_2O.'[23] He described the water in one word – '*pouah!*' (In his journal, he wrote '*eau natronée*', a phrase that added a further taint of putrescence with its recollection of the natron baths in which Egyptian Pharaohs were mummified.) He hated the prolonged journeys, during which he wrapped his head in a muslin veil that had once been white but was now stained grey from sweat. After a swig of salty water he tried to 'become a man for whom the outer world does not exist – or at least I repeat to myself with a growing obstination that I have become such. But there is always some movement of the camel, or a stray shaft of sunlight that penetrates my veil and my driver's goggles, to tell me otherwise.'[24] When they halted he tried to blank it all out by wrapping himself in his burnous – 'Honestly: these dry, hot winds burn your skin; some kind of screen is essential.'[25] Then, after a short rest, the ordeal started again, leading him to Djanet, which he denounced as completely indefensible from a military standpoint, and in its lack of creature comforts even more appalling than either Agadez or In Salah.

Duclos may have been overly acerbic, and he may have dramatized the discomfort of his journey for effect, but his complaints were not unjustified. For most Frenchmen desert travel was an alien and unpleasant experience. The meals were dreary, consisting usually of tinned sardines, the water was almost always foul and the routine was monotonous. In Duclos's opinion, 'If it is true that the daily repetition of the same acts in the same manner differentiate the bourgeois from the artist, then there is no one more bourgeois than a Saharian on the march.'[26] There was, however, an undeniable wonder in crossing this waterless ocean and Duclos, despite his antipathy, described it very well in his description of the journey to In Salah.

> The officer gets up a bit before daybreak. As soon as he is up he is ready (for he sleeps fully clothed). On leaving his tent he sniffs the air, finds it chilly, and warms his hands in front of a fire of roots or dried camel dung. The coffee has boiled. He drinks it, trying to ignore the fact that it tastes more of tar from the goatskin than Arabian mocha. Fully awake, he stirs the men. The drivers load the camels, with a concert that would put Wagner to shame: swearwords in every language and, for the brass section, a groaning that is enough to make one shudder – these 'placid' camels make the most terrible noise. A luminous dawn rises. The desert reveals itself, always the same: a circle of land, round and calm as the sea. Sometimes on the horizon a rosy outline indicates the presence of dunes; sometimes there are *garas*, rocky tables that look as if they

have been set for giants. Now there is sand underfoot and now sharp rocks, slabs of stone that seem to have fallen from the sky and smashed in the wake of some planetary cataclysm.

En route I go ahead with the guides, who lead their camels by the bridle – until the sun comes up it is best to keep warm by walking. We travel directly . . . in the direction of In Salah, which resembles a magnetic pole on which the guides converge like human compasses. I have had some experience of these strange beings, more like homing pigeons than civilized men. They have led me from well to well without straying off course and I have yet to fathom how they navigate in this featureless nothingness. For four or five days they go, '*hak, hak,*' meaning, 'There, there in front of you,' and then, at the allotted hour, the little, black rectangle of a well appears at your feet – no walls, no beams, just a tiny blot in the plain that you only notice when you are about to fall into it.

The sun rises, red, round and enormous, as if it had been plucked from a Japanese flag. Within a few minutes it is brutally triumphant. You throw off your burnous, wrap your head in a 'Cheich' and perch yourself on your camel. Thereafter, for hours on end, the animal carries you at a slow, undulating pace . . . towards a Bethlehem that has no star above it, nor a God in its stable.[27]

There were just two things that Duclos admired about the Sahara. The first was the glorious omnipotence that colonial service conferred. 'Isn't it strange being a military commander in the Oases?' he wrote to his father. 'There you are, a man who would be an unimportant cavalry officer in France, acting as unconstitutional sovereign of a country larger than your own. Yesterday you took orders from your Colonel and worried if you'd set your alarm in time for manoeuvres. Today you control a whole people – peoples, even . . . When you leave for a tour of your realm . . . tribes make months-long pilgrimages to meet you. As king of the Sahara you are not answerable to any Chamber of Government and although you are under the Governor

General of Algiers it takes at least a month for messages to get through. In the meantime, you have *carte blanche*.'[28]

The second thing that Duclos appreciated, even more than power, was the scenery. On returning to In Salah he scrambled up a dune to watch the sun go down. 'The sky was clear, and on its rim the sun was a huge, red balloon . . . dropping swiftly from view. But even as it fell it continued to dazzle, almost as if inviting me to turn my back and marvel at the dying landcape . . . I did so, and there the Tidikelt lay at my feet. To the north, the angular rocks of the Tadmait formed a shadowy girdle. To the south and east, a gentle slope rose towards a sky so blue as to be almost transparent. And against this tawny backdrop the desert undulated like a comet's tail, in which everything was tinted gold; here, on the crest of a dune, a gold that was almost white; there, in the dip between two wrinkles, a dull gold, almost brown; and elsewhere, thanks to a celestial hand that seemed to have waved a comb across the sand, gold of such variety as to defy the imagination of any landscape painter.'[29] Through it all stretched the Tuat, a river of green terminating in the bronze citadel of In Salah. When his reverie was over Duclos slid down, knee-deep in sand, with a speed that astonished him – 'It wasn't like the escalators you find in modern cities, but a positive railway'[30] – and returned to barracks life. In Salah, which had seemed a city of bronze when viewed from above, became a village of mud brick, the Tidikelt a mass of formless sand, the Tuat a straggly line of palms outlined against the night sky. 'Imagination,' he wrote sadly, 'gives way to reality.'[31]

Back at Tamanrasset Foucauld was feeling positive. '[Our] North African colonial empire, with sixty million inhabitants, will be in an advanced state of material progress, criss-crossed with rail lines, populated by inhabitants accustomed to handling our weapons, and whose elite will have been educated in our schools.'[32] He warned, however, that it was pointless winning territory if France did not also win the hearts of its inhabitants. 'If we have not learned by then how to hold these people to us, they will drive us out. Not only will we lose our entire African empire, but it will become, only a few hours away by sea, on the other shore of the Mediterranean, a hostile neighbour, fearsome and barbaric.'[33] His answer was to make them 'brothers equal to us, brothers like us'.[34] But this was exactly what the North Africans did not want. To be equal to the French – maybe. To be like them – never. Over the past decades Paris had made numerous attempts to assimilate its Algerian subjects, passing various decrees that, true to the doctrine of Liberty, Fraternity and Equality, permitted Algerians to apply for French citizenship. Yet they were worded reluctantly and did not confer full equality – 'French Muslim of Algeria' was the best an Algerian could aspire to – and were never accepted by the *colons*, or white settlers (or more pejoratively the *pieds noirs*) who, like all ruling minorities, feared the undermining effect of liberalism on their own position. The decrees were never accepted by the Algerians either, for they stipulated that anyone receiving the benefits of French citizenship would have to remove themselves from the jurisdiction of Islamic law and, as was obvious, this was not equality but surrender.

Well-meaning in theory, France's programme of naturalization was merely a redefinition of status that allowed a human to shift from being 'one of them' to 'one of us'. Algeria's downtrodden Jewish community embraced the opportunity, but the Muslims refused: between 1866 and 1934 only 2,500 accepted the offer. Even the Tuareg, who were in Foucauld's words 'very lukewarm Muslims',[35] preferred their own ways to those of Europe. They recognized France's might, accepted French rifles, French artesian wells, French supplies and fought under French officers, but they did so under duress and would have been much happier if only they had been left alone. In Tunisia, where the concept of 'Frenchification' was applied less forcefully – if one disregarded the large statue of Cardinal Lavigerie placed at the gates to the *medina*, or old town, of Tunis – the feeling was the same. And in Morocco, where Resident-General Lyautey not only understood and respected Islam but ordained that his administration did so too, the populace would still have liked it if the French had stayed in France. What only a very few French understood was that the people of North Africa honestly did not want to become French.

In 1913 Foucauld did his best for the imperial cause by taking a twenty-two-year-old Tuareg on a tour of France. The man, named Ouksem, had grown up under French rule and, as Foucauld told his friend, was 'intelligent, upright, serious. I treat him like my child, and he shows me a most affectionate devotion'.[36] He was also the heir-apparent to a Tuareg chief and therefore worth cultivating. Ouksem's trip followed the same pattern as Moussa's. He travelled first-class on a steamer to Marseilles, was taken around a dreadnought, invited to numerous churches, introduced to Foucauld's family, displayed in Paris and then – 'Your Touareg should see the Alps'[37] – hauled off by Laperrine to Switzerland before returning three and a half months later to Algeria. Foucauld considered it a triumph. In Paris he and Ouksem were hailed by crowds and on one occasion, when the young Tuareg was invited to join family prayers, he refused to enter the chapel but apparently shed tears at the sight of such devotion. 'Ouksem was not sad or sick for a moment the whole time of our journey,' Foucauld rejoiced, 'and he never ceased being as nice as possible.'[38]

The hard-bitten Saharan officers to whom Foucauld related these stories were sceptical. Of the Paris reception one Colonel Augieras wrote, 'They had been invited to an officers' mess on the Place de l'Opéra. There de Foucauld said he showed himself on the balcony beside the young Touareg who was in his Ahaggar costume. This spectacle soon drew a crowd and, above all, soon attracted the attention of a number of milliners from a big shop nearby. Father de Foucauld emphasized over and over again the success of his Touareg ... The Touareg was, it seemed to me, the *mouchard* (spy) of Laperrine. I've heard him also called *caoued* by the Arabs, a word meaning "informer".'[39] Lehuraux, normally a supporter of Foucauld, scoffed at Ouksem's tears of modesty. 'I think it more likely,' he wrote, 'that if Ouksem was really shedding tears, they were for his beloved Ranbechicha, to whom he had been married only a few days before his departure for France. I saw Ouksem on his return from this memorable trip ... he did not give the impression of having kept a very clear memory of anything he had seen. He seemed above all pleased to be returning soon to his own tents and to his nomad life again, and pleased also to be bringing to his young wife the many presents that he had brought back for her from France.'[40]

In 1913 Foucauld made another trip to France, this time to persuade Massignon to join him in the desert. But Massignon refused: he had an offer from the Sultan of Turkey to study in Cairo and was also about to get married. It was Foucauld's last visit to France and when he returned to Tamanrasset he did so with a sense of finality – possibly futility, too. Even if people were willing to join his Union nobody was willing to join his Brotherhood, and there seemed no likelihood of any religious community being established in the Hoggar during his lifetime. In 1912, on his way to Algiers, he had made an impassioned speech to a gathering of White Sisters, ending with the words, 'Who among you, my sisters, would like to sacrifice herself for the Touareg?'[41] Proving that the crusading spirit was not limited to their male counterparts, every woman in the congregation rose silently to her feet. The religious and military authorities, however, would not countenance it. Although anti-clericalism had abated in Paris, the White Fathers were still nervous of attention; and although Laperrine had left for France, the military still shared his suspicion of interfering do-gooders. Both parties agreed that it was best if the missionaries stayed where they were.

Foucauld had reached a point in his life when he was no longer able to rejuvenate himself. The journey of 1913 was his last stab at christianizing the Hoggar, and from that year he resigned himself to the solitude of Assekrem and the 'Frigate'. He did not reject civilization and applauded the few trappings that came his way. When General Bailloud arrived at Tamanrasset (not this time by propeller but by camel) with an apparatus to test the reception of radio waves, Foucauld placed his ear against it and was excited to hear a transmission from the Eiffel Tower. 'Fascinating!' he wrote to Laperrine. 'What a pity Nieger didn't have the TSF [*Telegraphe Sans Fil*] on his last transsaharan mission.'[42] But he was getting older and wearier. Hérisson recalled a Christmas when Foucauld sat down and told him his life story, recounting the death of his parents and the walks he used to take with his grandfather through the woods of

Sauverne and Alsace, where the only sounds were those of the birds and the insects. 'I liked the solitude,' he said wistfully. Then he dropped into a reverie. 'Le Père Foucauld saw himself once again as a child,' Hérisson wrote. 'His face fell and he dreamed aloud, forgetting that I was there. Suddenly he came to himself, saw me, and apologized with a sad smile, "You must understand, I have always been a savage." '[43]

At the end of 1913 Foucauld added a codicil to his will. 'I wish to be buried at the place where I die, a very simple interment, without a coffin, the grave quite plain and without a monument, surmounted only by a wooden cross.'[44]

17

'IT IS THE HOUR
OF MY DEATH'

Freshly washed but already oozing sweat, Lieutenant Paul Duclos sat naked on the chair of his shower apparatus. His feet were immersed in the water that had collected in the tin tub. Now and then, a drop of water fell onto his head from the dying rose. The thermometer stood at 48 °C. Bent over a block of paper, he tried to describe to his father the discomfort of life in In Salah during the months of July and August. 'By day one retreats to a dark, well-sprinkled room, ventilated by electric fans set at their fastest or by large "punkas" operated from outside by a native. All sunlight is blocked out, and in this artificial night, the sufferer lies like an ancient warrior, naked from head to foot, on a low bed that allows him to enjoy the chill of the damp flagstones. He drinks iced lemonade through a long straw, without moving, without even shifting his head, and thereby gains a modicum of interior coolness. If he sleeps he struggles not to think of anything, for even thinking is too much of an effort. When he gets up it is only to plunge himself in a nearby bath: but the water from the pipes is too warm and he has to throw in a block of ice to reduce it to an acceptable temperature. This is the moment, if he is still capable of reading, when he might open a curtain – but he does

it artfully, so that only a single ray falls on his book or journal.'[1] Duclos
had read that Anglo-Saxons thought their climate made them hardier
than the Latin races. 'Let them come here to see how stupid that
theory is,' he scoffed, 'The struggle against centigrade, when the
mercury is pushing 40, that's what hardens a man's character and stirs
the dullest brain.'[2]

In July and August of 1914, the weather was memorably hot. It was
hot in France and it was hot in Britain, Germany and Austria-Hungary.
From London's Hyde Park to Berlin's Unter den Linden, parasols
blossomed as fashionable society paraded to the last strains of a vanishing epoch. It was very hot in the Sahara too. Throughout that
summer, the officers of In Salah, Fort Motylinski and Fort Polignac
cloistered themselves in their rooms, waiting for September's respite.
What September 1914 delivered, however, was the news that for the
past month France and Germany had been at war. Abruptly, the
desert emptied. The notions of freedom and individualism that
had inspired so many Saharians vanished in a gush of patriotism. Who
wanted to be in Africa when there was a chance to avenge the
humiliation of 1870? The languid routine of garrison life was replaced
by bustle and commotion, as hastily arranged caravans siphoned every
non-essential man northwards. Foucauld was not immune. When a
courier from Fort Motylinski alerted him to the crisis at 5 a.m on 3
September, he wrote immediately to Laperrine. 'Could I not be
useful at the front as a chaplain or stretcher bearer? If you don't write
to me to come, I'll stay here until the peace. If you tell me to come,
I'll leave at once and at a good pace.'[3] It took two months for
Laperrine's reply to get back to Tamanrasset. When Foucauld opened
the telegram it contained one word – 'STAY'. Laperrine was writing
under the assumption that the war would be over by Christmas. From
the gloom of his shower tub, Duclos gave a more realistic assessment:
'Don't pray for me,' he wrote to his parents, 'Don't pray for us. Pray
for France. After forty-four years of waiting, the reign of justice will
be terrible.'[4]

Despite the withdrawal of many of their troops, the French
remained confident that they would not lose their North African

territories. Lyautey, against orders, had concentrated his men in the heart of Morocco, instead of along the coast, in the certainty that any uprising would come from within rather than without – a policy that ensured that despite bloodshed the country remained under French control throughout the war. In Algeria, the military could always call upon armed settlers to help quash any rebellion. In the Hoggar, the Tuareg were indifferent to whatever went on in Europe. And France could rely on Italy to patrol the Tripolitanian border. Italy had yet to take sides in the combat but relations were cordial between commanders on the ground. 'War has been declared between France and Germany,' the Italian commander of Ghat warned his counterpart at Fort Polignac. 'If Italy comes out [for the Germans] I will attack you tomorrow with all my strength. Meanwhile, here's a bottle of Asti.' The French officer replied, 'The wine is excellent. Thank you. I have left half the bottle so that I can give you the last glass when you bring me your surrender. I have 100 *méharistes* and if we come to blows you will be cut off from your supplies and will starve in a horrible and unpleasant manner.'[5]

In the spring of 1915, however, Italy joined the battle against Germany and Austria-Hungary, and its North African troops, like those of France, were withdrawn to Europe. In the few years it had been in Tripolitania, Italy had never truly penetrated the heart of the country. Along the coast, thousands of settlers had made a living for themselves, as the French had done during their early conquest of Algeria, but inland their garrisons were little stronger than those of their Ottoman predecessors and when the demands of war weakened them further still, the Senoussi moved in. No longer a band of rebels, the Senoussi had become a large, well-organized force, who had the support of Germany and Turkey. In January 1915 they drove the Italians out of Ghat, seizing a quantity of supplies – rifles, artillery and ammunition, plus food to last a column six months in the field – that made them equal to any other force in the vicinity. (The retreat over the Tassili to Fort Polignac of the 250-odd Italians stationed in Ghat is one of the First World War's many forgotten horror stories.) Hitherto, France had always relied on its superior weaponry: the *méharistes* were excellent at their job but there were times, such as at Djanet, when it was necessary to bring out the big guns. Now the Senoussi had big guns too, and thanks to the Turks they knew how to use them. For the first time in its Saharan history, France was facing the enemy on equal terms.

In Tamanrasset, Foucauld did his best for the war effort. He set the Tuareg women to knitting, as wives and daughters in Europe were already beginning to do; he took stock of his stores – 'one best-quality wax candle, 0.75 long and 0.22 thick, burns for five hours,'[6] – and he cut down on his food. Rationing was something that Foucauld excelled in, and he took it, of course, to its limits. Hérisson's replacement at Motylinski, one Dr Vermale, was disgusted at being summoned to treat him for scurvy. 'He leads the most unhygienic life imaginable. Incessant work, without ever going out or taking exercise – unbelievably foolish! I only got here just in time.'[7] (Luckily for Foucauld, Hérisson had planted fig, apple, pear and apricot trees at Motylinski; their first fruits may have assisted in his recovery.) There was an involuntary form of rationing, however, that Foucauld did not enjoy. Previously, he had been able to count on an annual dribble of visitors – from Motylinski, from In Salah, officers, soldiers, civilians. 'It is very convenient,' one man wrote of the 'Frigate'. 'One might find there one officer with his folding table, writing his report in the chapel, the Colonel in the main part of the establishment, a third officer poring over maps on the table in the doorway, and Father de Foucauld writing on a stool at the foot of his bed.'[8] Now, fewer and fewer Europeans came to his shack and Foucauld, no longer the firebrand of his youth, missed their company. The Tuareg had formed an affection for him – he had been invited to pray for Moussa's dying aunt – but they did not fill the gap. 'Tomorrow it will be ten years since I first said Mass in Tamanrasset,' he wrote to Marie de Bondy, 'and not a single conversion.'[9] But he had his Tamacheq translations to occupy him, and if he could not speak to his friends he could at least write to them.

Throughout 1915 and the early months of 1916, Foucauld kept his friends and relatives up to date with every development in the Sahara.

Couriers were harder to come by than the early days when he had plotted with Guérin in code, and he said what he felt, at leisure, without trying to conceal his feelings. To Marie de Bondy, of a battle between Moussa and the Senoussi, he wrote: 'It was far from here. Don't worry. What a contrast between nature, so silent, so beautiful, so peaceful, so quiet in our deserted mountains, and human beings who everywhere, always, and for motives habitually so low and shameful disturb the peace of creation.'[10] Turning to Flanders: 'The present war makes me think of the Crusades. Never had I understood them properly . . . Now, I understand. It was Christian civilization, the independence of nations, the liberty of the Church that were at stake, as now.'[11] To Laperrine, on hearing that a priest had been called up, Foucauld wrote: 'How do I go about getting to the front (because I would rather stay here than be at G.H.Q or behind the lines)? Between the tiny unit I am and zero there's little difference, but there are moments when everyone should enlist.'[12] By the spring of 1916 he did not have to enlist. The war was upon him.

Over the previous six months, border skirmishes had grown in number and in violence. On 2 October 1915, 3,000 Senoussi killed one Captain Bermond and half his 400-strong force at the outpost of Oum-Souig. The oasis of Dehibat was attacked on eleven separate occasions. In November the Senoussi began to infiltrate the Adjer, and in February 1916 they advanced on Djanet. The first Paul Duclos heard of it – he was now Captain Duclos of In Salah, officer-in-charge of the Tidikelt – was when two *méharistes* emerged from the Tassili on 14 March to hand him a note. It was written by the sergeant in charge of the Djanet garrison, and informed him that since 6 March Djanet had been besieged by a force of more than 1,000 Senoussi, armed with artillery and machine-guns. Trapped in what Duclos had already described as an indefensible position, the sergeant and his fifty men asked his assistance. Duclos set out immediately, but when he arrived on 26 March he was two days too late. On the 24th, their fort in ruins and most of their number dead, the garrison had blown up their magazine and made a desperate bid for freedom. None of them had survived. Unable to dislodge the enemy, Duclos called for reinforcements and on 16 May, after a three-day battle, he eventually retook Djanet. But the fort was in such a mess, and so difficult to supply, that he was forced to withdraw. Soon afterwards Forts Polignac and Flatters were also abandoned.

Fort Motylinski was now even more isolated than ever before. Moreover, it was drastically undermanned, its commander, Captain de la Roche, having taken his *méharistes* 500 kilometres south to fight raiders on the Soudanese border. The officers he left in charge, Lieutenant Charlet and Sub-Lieutenant Constant, were inexperienced and had only twenty-five soldiers to face the Tripolitanian hordes. 'The Senoussis have the road open before them,'[13] Foucauld wrote unhappily to Laperrine.

From this point, according to one of Foucauld's biographers, '[he] did not merely advise: he himself gave orders and they were instantly executed'.[14] He set up five observation posts in the Hoggar and ordered that 'at the first call for help, or the first alarm, general mobilization will be effective for all men able to bear arms'.[15] He pointed out to Lieutenant Charlet that his plans for Fort Motylinski's defence were 'unworkable and absurd':[16] the fort was strong but it had no well of its own and could not withstand a serious siege; a much better idea was to build a new fort at Tamanrasset. It was done. Working under Foucauld's supervision, and to his own plans, in 1915 a group of soldiers from Fort Motylinski erected a new bastion on a 275-metre rise to the east of Tamanrasset. Fifteen metres square, with turrets at each corner, and walls that were five metres high and two metres thick, it was surrounded by a dry moat, two metres wide and one metre deep. Within were a chapel, a storeroom, a magazine and a good, deep well. Stairs led to terraces from which defenders could fire at the enemy through chamfered notches in the walls. It had one door, accessible only by a narrow bridge across the moat, which led to a brick corridor at the other end of which was another door. The outer door was equipped with heavy locks and metal bars; it was so small that one almost had to crawl through it and was protected by a firewall set just over a metre from the entrance. If one ignored the render of mud that smoothed its corners and turned its stairs into gentle ripples, it could have been built by any one of

France's medieval architects. Even Foucauld was slightly surprised at what he had done. 'I have transformed my hermitage into a fort,' he told Laperrine. 'When I look up at my battlements, I cannot help thinking of the fortified convents and churches of the Middle Ages. How the ancient things return, and how that which one thought gone forever reappears!'[17]

In his letters to Duclos he took a harder and ever more militaristic line. 'As to the big chiefs of Africa, I think it is necessary to suppress them and to substitute for them a well-chosen French administration. Moussa can be left until his death but should have no successor. To perpetuate the rule of the amenokals is to confirm the existing evils and drape them with the Tricolour.'[18] When Duclos wished to apply tighter discipline, Foucauld supported him enthusiastically. 'I agree with you entirely on all points: on the absolute necessity of the severe repression of the crimes committed, of the desertions, the goings over to the enemy, on the necessity of expelling the undesirable, the spies, and sowers of trouble . . . Not to repress severely encourages the criminals and encourages others to follow them. It means losing the esteem of all, subdued or unsubdued, who see only weakness, timidity, fear – and it discourages the loyal, who see the same, or almost the same, treatment meted out to faithful and deserters, those who submit and those who rebel.'[19]

Foucauld's bluster could not compensate for France's weakness in the field. The army had consolidated its position but still did not have enough troops to control the area effectively and the Tuareg, who might have filled the gap, were either going over to the enemy in dribs and drabs or were simply not there, having fled to the Soudanese border. Their flight was not a matter of cowardice but of survival, for the Hoggar was gripped by appalling drought. On 20 February 1915, Foucauld had written, 'In the nine and a half years I have been here it has rained twice; once, nine years ago, for 36 or 48 hours, and once five years ago, for 3 or 4 hours. The flocks are hardly more than a memory.'[20] The Tuareg's herds of goat and sheep were one-fifth of the number that they had been; the goats no longer gave milk; half the camels had perished, those that remained were too weak to carry any appreciable load; grain supplies were low, five successive waves of locusts having devoured the previous year's harvest. There was no rain for the rest of 1915 and the summer brought a new plague of locusts. Moussa remained loyally by Foucauld's side, but in January 1916 he was ordered south to relieve Captain de la Roche, leaving behind a representative who, although a capable man, did not command the same respect as an *amenoukhal*. Throughout the Hoggar there were increasing signs of unrest and almost every week brought alarms – some real, most false – of small raids from Tripolitania, the Soudan or Morocco.

Alone in Tamanrasset, Foucauld made a tempting target. When Captain de la Roche returned to Fort Motylinski it was just in time. As he later recalled, 'already in June and again in September a plot had been made against [Foucauld] by six men whose names were told me. I had four of them seized and shot. The two others escaped me.'[21] One of them, Abdennebi, hid in the Hoggar, and the other, El Madani ag Soba, fled to Djanet. Apart from an entry in his diary that he had treated El Madani a few weeks earlier for eye problems, Foucauld made no mention of these conspiracies. But he was troubled enough by the overall situation to write a lengthy letter to Laperrine at the end of September 1916.

> The dark spots are the Senoussi and above all the attitude Algiers is taking towards them. If Algiers insists on retreating, its trouble is the whole Sahara; if Algiers orders an energetic resistance and the retaking of our lost frontier, all will be well. In order to repress the Senoussi in an exemplary fashion, it is evident that we would need reinforcements. The enemy must have at least 500 modern rifles, three cannon and a machine-gun.
>
> Here we have had a big alarm, which seems only to have been a false one, [on 20 September a deserting corporal from the Tidikelt had attacked a French caravan with 300 Senoussi and had inflicted many casualties before being driven back] but it had the very good effect of obliging Fort Motylinski to make serious preparation for its defence and showed us which

were the natives upon whom we should count. It is agreed that my hermitage, with its good well, its provision of victuals that I have, and its solid walls shall be the place of refuge for the garrison of Motylinski, if the lack of water or a too heavy bombardment should force them to evacuate the fort. Tamanrasset would then be, until further happenings, the link with In Salah.

I have been given fourteen rifles and two cases of cartridges with which, if the natives around me are loyal, I can defend myself against light weapons if they are unsupported by artillery. So we are working here to make the fort as strong as possible. Women, children, the aged, and the flocks have fled from here and taken refuge in the mountains. The alarm has gone out through the countryside, and people and beasts are hiding themselves and being hidden, and the provisions, too, are being hidden or buried.

The days pass, and the patrols come and go without bringing any fresh information.[22]

Foucauld was not entirely alone in Tamanrasset. On 23 September, when a courier announced that Fort Motylinski had fallen, ten *harratin* offered to help him defend his fortress. It was a false alarm, but Foucauld was gratified by their support. And when Moussa heard the news and trotted into town with fifty warriors, the hermit was elated. The *amenoukhal* had arrived too late to do anything but he had made the effort and this was an encouraging sign. '[He] has behaved admirably,' he told Laperrine, 'and has come back immediately to Tamanrasset . . . to defend the white marabout.'[23] On 15 October Foucauld informed Laperrine that rain had at last fallen. Far from doing any good, the deluge collapsed the irrigation system and swamped the plateau. 'The flooding has not created as much pasture as we had expected. Insects and aphids devoured the grain as soon as it sprouted. I fear a harsh famine this winter.'[24] Lacking the provisions to stay long in the Hoggar, and being needed in the south, Moussa left in early November.

Since the war had begun, Foucauld's letters had become longer and more frequent, his journal entries briefer and more intermittent. His journal for 24 November read, 'Met with Captain de la Roche.' On 26 November he wrote, ' Convoy with ammunition passes through.' On 28 November, with relief, 'Finished work on Tuareg poetry collection.' The short, bland sentences contained warnings whose importance would only become obvious at a later date. On 20 October, for example, he had written eight innocuous words: 'Saw six men from Amsel seeking El Madani.'[25] As he completed his last entry on 28 November, El Madani was already seeking him.

In September 1916, De la Roche had reported that El Madani's group numbered 'twenty-eight Harratin assassins led by seven or eight white Touaregs'.[26] During the following months it had been augmented by a further twenty-eight disaffected *harratin*. They moved through the night, careful to avoid Fort Motylinski and any patrolling *méharistes*, and reached Tamanrasset on the evening of 1 December. They herded their camels behind a wall and then, after a short discussion, deputed El Madani to make the first move.

Foucauld had eaten his habitual dinner of dates and couscous at 5 p.m. on 1 December 1916, and was catching up with his correspondence. There were four letters that evening, to Marie de Bondy, to his sister, to Louis Massignon and to Laperrine. The last was in response to a request for information about activity in the Adjer. 'I will put it in a postscript tomorrow,' Foucauld wrote, 'when the post will return from Motylinski.'[27] He was pleased to say that 'It does not seem to me that at present there is any danger from Tripolitania and the Senoussi: our troops are strongly reinforced and I hope they will be able to force the enemy back beyond our frontier. There have been no alarms since September and the country is very quiet.'[28] The bi-monthly courier had already passed by that morning but his bag was sealed and the letters it contained could not be read until Captain de la Roche had opened the package. Normally, it was twelve hours before the courier returned to deliver Foucauld's post and collect the outgoing mail. Today, he seemed to be in a hurry as, at 7 p.m., there came the familiar three knocks on the outer door of Foucauld's fort and the cry

'Your post is here.' Foucauld pushed the door ajar and put his hand through the gap. El Madani and two of his men yanked him out and tied his elbows behind his back.

Of what happened next there exists only the word of Paul, Foucauld's faithful yet despised slave, who had settled in Tamanrasset after quitting his religious employment, and a deposition given by one of El Madani's band, who was captured and interrogated by the Saharians. El Madani apparently wanted no more than to kidnap Foucauld and ransack his fort for the weapons, and above all the gold, that he was certain were hoarded within. He found the rifles but not the gold, so sent his men to find Foucauld's slave. Paul was trussed up alongside his master. (They would have liked to have shot him, but felt it beneath their dignity to kill a slave.) Then they began to question the two captives. Where was their money? Where were the soldiers? What were the men at Fort Motylinski planning? Paul could not, and Foucauld would not, tell them anything. When they threatened to kill Foucauld if he did not speak, and ordered him to accept the Islamic faith, he simply replied, '*Baghi n'mout*' ('It is the hour of my death').[29]

Turning to easier business, the raiders left them sitting against the wall while they continued their pillage. Later that night, however, the sentinels gave a shout: two *méharistes* were approaching. El Madani and his men moved out to ambush them, leaving a fifteen-year-old boy named Sermi ag Thora in charge of the two prisoners. The *méharistes*, who were making a courtesy visit on their way to Motylinski, swayed slowly towards the fort, unaware of any danger, the villagers too scared to warn them. At El Madani's command, his men fired a volley. The lead *méhariste* was killed instantly. The second one turned to escape but had not gone fifty metres before his camel was brought down and then he too was despatched. Amidst the firing it was unlikely that anyone heard the single shot from inside the fort.

Fearing that the two troopers were going to be murdered, Foucauld moved instinctively to warn them. Sermi ag Thora placed the muzzle of his rifle against Foucauld's head. Simultaneously, there came the first, sharp burst of rifle fire. Jittered, the boy pulled the trigger. The bullet entered Foucauld's head below the right ear and exited through his left eye, embedding itself in the wall near the hinges of the door. 'The marabout supported himself with his right hand,' Paul remembered, 'He neither moved nor cried out. I did not think he was wounded. It was only a few minutes later that I saw the blood flowing. His body slid down slowly and he fell on his side. He was dead.'[30]

Foucauld had once written, 'The light! In the clear light of faith, I can make out a thousand new objects of which I formerly knew nothing. Without faith I would still be in the dark, I would be walking in the night, my foot striking a thousand obstacles. Now, faith illuminates those shadows like a blazing sun. With faith the road appears bathed in light and the goal of our journey shines at night in the distance like a great city whose dazzling outer wall sits atop a high mountain.'[31] Whether it was the right road, and whether he travelled along it in the proper manner, are questions that can be debated interminably. The only certainty is that on 1 December 1916, in a shabby mud village in the middle of the desert, he reached its end. Perhaps the glittering city of his anticipation awaited him. It would be nice to think it did.

The raiders were disconcerted to find their hostage dead. They had a short argument over whether they should bury the body or take it with them and claim a ransom. In the end they stripped it and left it outside the door to the fort. Then there was the question of Paul. Some were for killing him but here, at last, the *harratin* of Tamanrasset intervened. Approaching El Madani nervously, they informed him that although Paul had served Foucauld for many years he had refused to be baptized and was therefore still a true Muslim. El Madani agreed, and ordered him to be released. After this, he and his men built a fire from Foucauld's furniture and cooked one of the *méharistes'* camels. The following morning a third *méhariste* plodded unsuspectingly into Tamanrasset. It was the courier from Fort Motylinski, carrying the mail to which Foucauld had hoped to add a postscript. He very nearly escaped. The raiders' first shots were wide of their mark, and the courier turned to flee. He had almost reached shelter when a bullet hit his camel. As the animal fell to its knees, the *méhariste* tried to load his rifle but was overwhelmed by El Madani's men. He begged them, in Allah's name, to spare him. They held his arms and legs and shot him through the back of the head.

El Madani ordered the villagers to be brought together. According to Paul's testimony, 'They assembled us on the other side of the fig grove and said, "The soldier who came this morning, bury him in the Muslim cemetery, since he recited the formula. The others, don't bury them . . . Go back to work in your fields. We shall soon return." The Harratins were in a joyful state. They said to each other, "The French are finished. Imam El Mahdi has come." '[32] When the raiders left that day, the villagers bricked up the door to the fort and, ignoring El Madani's orders, buried all four corpses. The three *méharistes* were placed in the fort's moat and shovelled over. Foucauld was interred alongside them, but with greater formality: planks from a packing crate were put around him in lieu of a coffin; scraps of his manuscripts were placed in the grave; then he, too, was covered by the sands of Tamanrasset.

Paul brought the news to Fort Motylinski at noon on Sunday, 3 December. De la Roche reacted swiftly. He led a group of *méharistes* in pursuit of the raiders and on 17 December attacked their camp. He managed to kill a number but most of them escaped, including El Madani and Sermi ag Thora. In their tents he discovered a pair of Foucauld's sandals. Abandoning the chase, he turned south for Tamanrasset, which he reached on 21 December. When he entered the fort, he found it strewn with debris. El Madani had taken everything of value: rifles, ammunition, food, even the communion wine. Scattered on the floor of the chapel were Foucauld's journal, the four letters he had written on the evening of 1 December, and hundreds upon hundreds of pages covered in his small, tidy script, that had once been his collection of Tuareg mythology and his Tuareg dictionary. Digging through the sand, De la Roche uncovered Foucauld's religious paraphernalia: his rosary, his tabernacle containing the Host (donning white gloves, De la Roche later served it to one of his sergeants), and the hand-drawn stations of the cross that he had brought with him from Beni Abbès. He collected all these items and took them back to Motylinski from where he sent them to France via In Salah and Algiers. When the dictionary was reassembled the final entry read, '*Ta mella, (tas)*' ['to die a violent death'].[33]

De la Roche forwarded Foucauld's four letters, which arrived at the same time as the news of his death. Each recipient reacted in a different way. Foucauld's sister fell into a depression from which she never recovered and which hastened her death in 1919. Marie de Bondy was horrified, but resilient; in 1918, however, her house burned down and she died a few months later. Louis Massignon, serving on the Western Front, leaped onto the parapet and shouted, 'Foucauld killed in the Sahara! He has found the passage; he has arrived!' Miraculously, no Germans shot at him and he collapsed back into his trench. 'Through a bizarre exchange, he is killed and I am protected,'[34] he muttered. He remembered the occasion until his death in 1962. Laperrine, also at the front, showed no emotion. He requested instead an immediate transfer to the Sahara. The authorities approved the move and in 1917 he boarded a steamer for Algiers. In his baggage he packed a mauve notebook.

18

DUNE FLIGHTS

Moussa wrote to Foucauld's sister, Marie de Blic, on 13 December 1916:

May the one God be praised,

To Her Ladyship, our friend Marie, sister of Charles our marabout . . . As soon as I learned of the death of our friend, your brother Charles, my eyes were shut. All is darkness for me. I have wept and I have shed many tears and I am in deep mourning. His death has brought me much sorrow. I myself am far from the place where the treacherous thieves and deceivers killed him . . . But if God so wishes we shall kill them, the people who have killed the marabout, until our vengeance is done.

To your daughters, your husband and your friends, say, 'Charles the marabout has not died for you alone, he has also died for us all'. May God grant him mercy and may we meet with him in paradise.

The 20 Safar 1335, Moussa ag Amastane, *amenouhkal*.[1]

How this message was received by the pious de Blic household is not recorded. But it is safe to say that if they liked Moussa's promise of vengeance they would have liked much better to have had a peek into Laperrine's mauve notebook. Laperrine was proud of his notebook and he showed it once to a fellow officer. 'See this?' he said, 'It contains the names of Foucauld's assassins. They're all here, and I have memorized them. There are 103, arranged in alphabetical order. When I kill one I cross his name off the list.'[2] How Laperrine came to the figure of 103 is a mystery, every source stating that El Madani's troops numbered fifty at best. But maybe the newly returned General had called in some favours, and added a few more names to the list. Fifty or a hundred, Laperrine was determined to hunt the assassins down. He was determined, too, to bring order to a desert that he had left secure in 1910 but which was now in disarray.

Before he addressed the contents of his mauve notebook, there were formalities to attend to, one of which was the official inquiry into Foucauld's death. Held at Motylinski between June and September 1917, and involving the interrogation of many Tuareg and *harratin*, it laid the blame not on any specific plot but on an overall disaffection. 'From the general point of view, it may be said that at the time of Father de Foucauld's assassination all hearts in the Hoggar had been won over to the cause of our enemies, and that their dearest wish was for our speedy and final disappearance from the region.'[3] There was no evidence that any of the Hoggar Tuareg had been involved, the ringleaders having come from the Adjer. 'Nothing, up to the present, makes us think that a single *imrad* or Touareg noble . . . favoured the plan. Nevertheless, the event is still quite recent and a wise prudence bids us leave time to do its work of making things plain before being affirmative on this point.'[4] When time did do its work, several writers accused both Moussa and Ouksem of complicity: they had heard of the intended attack and knew that France was losing control of the region; at the same time they were unwilling to desert the colonial masters on whom they depended. Their answer, therefore, was to absent themselves and await the outcome. The idea is plausible but unprovable. While it is true that neither Moussa nor Ouksem was at Tamanrasset, it is also true that the drought obliged them to move out and that, as the inquiry found, Foucauld himself had ordered the few remaining Tuareg to flee to the hills. Laperrine did not believe that the Tuareg were the culprits. He favoured a grander conspiracy. At Ouargla, on 20 October 1917, he dictated a note that was appended to the inquiry's findings. 'In my opinion the assassination of the Reverend Père de Foucauld is to be connected with the letter found at Agadez in the papers of [a captured rebel] in which a European (German or Turk) advised him as a first measure, before stirring up the populations, to kill or take as hostages Europeans known to have influence over the natives and native chiefs devoted to the French.'[5]*

Having completed his report, Laperrine moved south to deal with the remains of his friend. He could not leave him in the ditch, which would fill with water at the next rains, so, on 9 December, he exhumed the body and re-interred it on higher ground. At his feet he buried the three *méharistes* who had also died in the attack. He was struck by the differences between the three cadavers. The *méharistes* had decomposed but Foucauld was still intact. 'Your brother was as if mummified,' he wrote to Marie de Blic, 'and he could still be recognized. The transfer of his remains has been a most emotional experience.'[6] Foucauld had been buried in the position in which he had been shot – on his knees, elbows tied behind his back – and had stiffened in that posture. Laperrine had difficulty moving him. 'We were obliged to inter him in that position, so as not to break his limbs; we simply wrapped him in a shroud.'[7] He was placed in a simple grave, marked only by a black wooden cross without any inscription, but Laperrine had plans for a more permanent monument in the shape of a large cross of Hoggar granite (placed five metres

---

*This was not wholly vindictive. Germany had long machinated against France in North Africa and had actively encouraged a rumour that had gained currency following the Kaiser's 1899 visit to Constantinople, in which Wilhelm II was believed to be the Caliph's cousin. During the last years of the war an important Senoussi leader was evacuated from Tripoli by U-Boat.

away, so as not to further contravene the hermit's wishes), which he assured Foucauld's sister would be visible from a great distance.

Laperrine's visit to Tamanrasset was part of a comprehensive shake-up of the Saharians and of the entire region. He was horrified by how incompetent his elite force had become. In place of the '*gens de poudre*',[8] whom he had so carefully recruited, the *méharistes* of 1917 were mostly shepherds and out of work labourers who had bought a camel and enlisted in the hope of making a few francs. And the camels were not the fabled *méharis* of yore but decrepit specimens, purchased in the certainty that they would die on a journey of any length and that when they did so the army would reimburse their owners for the cost of a pedigree animal. The French officers and NCOs were 'demoralized and querulous'.[9] In the Saharians' defence, it was fair to say that the pick of them, French and Algerian alike, had been called to fight in Flanders. But that was no excuse in Laperrine's eyes for slovenliness. He also disagreed – like Foucauld – with Algiers' policy of abandoning its outer stations in the desert. In his opinion it could only have 'a most deplorable moral effect'.[10] There should be no backsliding: 'We must shout aloud; let it be known to friends and enemies that we are determined to give no ground.'[11]

Having left In Salah in November 1917, he did not return until April 1918. During these five months he led his camel troops to Timbuctoo and, returning to the Hoggar, caught up with Moussa with whom he spoke frankly. It had been seven years since they had last met and the *amenoukhal* all but prostrated himself before his old commander. Laperrine accepted his homage and informed him, curtly, what he expected of an ally of France. In October 1918 Laperrine retook Djanet. Later he also reoccupied Polignac. Between December 1918 and June 1919, he made another grand tour, travelling 4,500 kilometres from In Salah to Agadez and then back through the Hoggar and the Adjer, accepting the submission of every tribal leader he met. On his return, he wrote, 'I have identified the main vices that afflict the Saharian organization and have ordered, as a priority, certain measures to be put in place.'[12]

In October 1919, Laperrine was recalled to Algiers. While he had been in the Sahara he had performed miracles. He had stabilized the

Hoggar and reasserted France's presence on the Tripolitanian border. He had, however, crossed off very few of the names in his mauve notebook. In 1918 a party of *méharistes* accounted for seven men, finding in their camp a number of Foucauld's possessions. But the seven were not enough, even when augmented by those whom De la Roche had killed in 1916, to satisfy Laperrine. When he departed for Algiers he did so with regrets. The list in his mauve notebook was almost untouched.*

The Sahara that Laperrine left in 1919 was a very different desert from the one he had first encountered twenty-odd years before. At almost every major oasis French engineers had dug artesian wells that spouted at a prodigious and apparently uncontrollable rate. In some places the output was so far in excess of the population's needs that it formed huge lakes of a kind that had not been seen for 10,000 years – and on whose stagnant surfaces malaria-carrying mosquitoes bred happily. Surveyors, prospectors and scientists had added their own form of erosion to rocks that had hitherto been scoured only by the wind. People who had never seen a white face found themselves surrounded by little forts containing men in blue uniforms who, when not shooting at them, dug gardens and nurtured plants of an alien dispensation. Here and there, on hilltops, radio antennae made a mockery of the desert's solitude. The Hoggar Tuareg, once the acknowledged masters of the Sahara, were now servants to a greater power. And, above all, the combustion engine had arrived.

The first unmetalled road had been built between Algiers and In Salah as early as 1916, and a few weeks before his death Foucauld had recorded the completion of the In Salah–Tamanrasset link. A car had arrived at In Salah that year, but its driver had not dared continue to Tamanrasset. During his post-1916 pacification of the Sahara Laperrine had made reluctant use of lorries to transport his *méharistes* when they ran out of camels. In February 1918 a 16-horsepower Renault, fitted with caterpillar tracks, coughed fitfully through the

*(In 1946 El Madani was brought to trial. He was acquitted under the Statute of Limitations.)

dunes. By 1920 the road had been extended from Tamanrasset to the Soudanese border and the Sahara boasted a network – most of it traversible, some of it covered by sand, some of it still under construction – totalling almost 4,500 kilometres. Planes, too, had made an appearance. In January 1917 a small squadron had nested at Biskra from where it distributed bombs and propaganda leaflets across the Adjer and in February 1919 a fleet of cars raced five 80-horsepower Farman bi-planes from Colomb-Béchar to Ouargla. The Farmans got there first, but only two survived the journey, and they beat the cars by just a day which was not much of a showing. Nevertheless, the Minister of War was so impressed that he ordered the creation of a joint Algerian–Tunisian air force.

Laperrine was unsure about these new developments. He didn't like cars, which he thought were far less practical than camels, but he accepted their advent and, eventually, showed an interest in their workings. When, for example, one officer completed the journey to In Salah, he was greeted by a shabby chap, obviously a mechanic, who wanted to know how the trip had gone. The officer replied that it had been as good as could be expected and, since he was standing there with nothing to do, could he help him with his car? The man obliged and when the job was finished, he was thanked for his work. The officer then asked where he could find General Laperrine. The mechanic stuck out his hand. 'Pleased to meet you.'[13]

Having come to terms with the automobile, Laperrine was soon seduced by the aeroplane. Since he first saw these sputtering machines on his return to France in 1910 he had been intrigued by their potential. On the Western Front he had seen what they could do. In the Sahara, what could they not do? They were the ideal instrument of desert conquest. With their ability to cover hundreds of kilometres per day, landing and taking off at will; with their machine-guns and bombs, who could stand against them? (Not the Morrocans, who were deluged with Spanish clusters of mustard-gas during the early 1920s.) In 1920, therefore, on his return to Algiers, Laperrine was overjoyed to be part of a major aerial adventure.

General Robert Nivelle, the artillery commander whose creeping barrages had wreaked havoc on the German army at Verdun and who was now in command of the North African military, had already decided that it would be instructive for the Hoggar Tuareg to see the power of his air force. His plan was that five planes under Commandant Rolland and Lieutenant Poivre would fly to Tamanrasset and back, an event that would be something of an aviatic coup as well as a demonstration of France's might. In 1919, however, the French government hit upon an even grander scheme: two specially adapted planes, piloted by Commandant Vuillemin and Lieutenant Dagnaux, would fly from Paris to the Soudan, a journey fraught with danger but one that would demonstrate conclusively France's control over its colonies. Nivelle was almost beside himself with excitement. 'One should not look upon this first attempt to cross the Sahara by plane as a mere sporting achievement,' he told a reporter from the *Echo de Paris*. 'It is a matter of national importance.'[14] He explained the benefits that would accrue. During the war, he said, Soudanese products had not reached France because there were no ships to carry them; as a result (and as usual) foreigners had stolen the nation's trade. If a regular air service existed then France would never again be dependent on the mercantile marine of other nations. Also, a proper survey of France's African colonies was essential and planes, equipped with cameras and the keen eyes of their navigators, were the best means of making such a survey. Moreover, he concluded triumphantly, these surveys were essential to the construction of a trans-Saharan railway.

Nivelle's explanations were visionary, but they were also nonsense. No plane in existence could carry any appreciable quantity of goods over so great a distance. In the 'Turnip Winter' of 1916–17 no planes had made even the trip to Algiers where, as Duclos recorded, the citizens lived in over-stuffed splendour while European nations blockaded themselves into starvation. Navigators' memory could not be relied upon for maps, and cameras were little better because, with the exception of one or two landmarks such as the Hoggar, most stretches of the Sahara looked the same. As for the Transsaharian, it had been made redundant by the arrival of cars and even Gautier, one of the railway's more enthusiastic supporters, had to admit that the automobile offered at present a more practical means of crossing the desert. Whatever Nivelle might say, the flight was an unnecessary act of showmanship. Then, those were the grounds on which France had occupied most of North Africa, so why stop now? Besides, Nivelle had a personal interest in the flight. He had secured permission to accompany Vuillemin and Dagnaux as the first high-ranking officer to overfly the Sahara. And that, in part, was the reason why Laperrine had been recalled to Algiers. While General Nivelle was flying over the desert in which Laperrine had spent his life, Laperrine was to sit at Nivelle's desk and do whatever paperwork might accrue in his absence.

The proposed flight would have been a relatively straightforward affair if all it had involved had been the planes taking off from Algiers and landing in the Soudan. But this was not the case. The only directional pointers in the Sahara were the newly built roads, and these were what the planes had to follow. With the exception of Vuillemin and Dagnaux, whose planes were fitted with extra fuel tanks, the squadron had to refuel every five hours. They could have flown by compass alone but in such extremes of temperature and altitude – not to mention the buffeting they received at every landing – the accuracy of their compasses could not be depended on. The exercise therefore became rather pointless as the planes had to be preceded through most of their journey by lorries carrying drums of fuel that were deposited at prearranged depots along the roadside – preferably at oases – and which had to be guarded by Laperrine's *méharistes*. If Nivelle had wanted to cross the Sahara he could have done so more efficiently by car or by camel, but he chose the plane. And he chose Laperrine to organize the ground support. Laperrine did not complain. In combination with Sigonney, he set up the fuel depots and he arranged for Tuareg and Chaamba sentries to protect them. He had the road marked by white or black stones, depending on whether it ran over sand or rock; he had it emblazoned with white crosses that would be easily visible from the air. He contacted the Haut-Sénégal and Niger authorities and had them clear landing strips and prepare fuel dumps. On 1 February 1920 he met all the aviators at Algiers and told them what to do. 'It's very simple,' he said, 'Don't leave the roads.'[15]

M. Louis Breguet, who had constructed the 300-horsepower bi-planes in which the aviators were to fly, gave a nervous interview to *Le Temps*. 'This flight is one of the most arduous enterprises to date. Personally, I would like to have seen it put off until the manufacturers' new designs were ready (principally those involving engines), until the infrastructure of the route had been better organized and, above all, until a more favourable season. I know from long experience in aerial research how this time of the year can present difficulties.'[16] The approach of spring was in the Sahara, as in Europe, a time of unpredictable weather. It might rain, it might be warm, it might be windy. The desert might blossom; it might not. Whatever the weather did, however, its one constant was its inconstancy. And unlike Europe, which threatened fliers with no more than the occasional shower, the Sahara held terrors unimaginable to the average pilot. Vuillemin did not consider himself an average pilot. A gung-ho cavalier of the skies, he laughed at the weather. He also seems to have laughed at his colonial companions, thinking their sortie a pitiful enterprise compared to his own. Whenever possible he intended to fly at his own speed, in his own time and in the direction he saw fit. He would follow the roads as far as they went but his joy was in completing the journey using his own aeronautical skills.

On Tuesday, 3 February, the seven bi-planes sputtered out of Algiers' Hussein-Dey aerodrome. Five of them, led by Commandant Rolland and Lieutenant Poivre, had Tamanrasset as their goal, the other two under Vuillemin were destined for the Soudan. Laperrine saluted them as they took off and watched enviously as they clambered into the sky. They were hardly in the air when the one carrying Nivelle coughed, sank below the others and turned back. Its motor, as Breguet had feared, had failed. When the plane landed, things moved fast. In between Nivelle's taking off and landing, a telegram had arrived recalling him immediately to Paris. He ordered Laperrine to take his place and follow the flight to its next stop, where he should alert the others not to leave without his plane, which would be with them as soon as it had been mended. Laperrine commandeered a taxi, gave the driver his directions – 'Biskra, please'[17] – offered him a bottle of rum if he put his foot down, and reached his destination at 6 a.m the following day, having stopped only once to refuel.

Laperrine's plane having caught up, the squadron took off from Biskra at 7.30 a.m. on 7 February into a sky dotted with clouds and by the same evening were at Ouargla. Here they lost their first plane, which flipped onto its back as it came in to land – fortunately without injuring the pilot. Sigonney was waiting to greet them. He repeated the instructions given by Laperrine. 'I said to them simply this: always follow the track that I have marked for you. It will lead you safely to the arranged landing spots and if you have a break-down the *méharistes* patrolling the road will find you and help you.'[18] By the afternoon of 8 February they were at In Salah, but at the cost of a second plane, which had returned to Ouargla with engine trouble and crashed on its subsequent take-off. On 9 February they nearly lost a third plane: despite all warnings, Vuillemin insisted on flying into a sandstorm; he was forced down before he even cleared the oasis, miraculously suffering no damage beyond a broken propeller. On the 14th, however, the weather cleared and they were once more on their way – except for Dagnaux, whose engine had failed.

'Everything that was not black rock was yellow sand,' Rolland wrote. 'It was like a yellow sea dotted with islands and in the distance lay the steep coast of the Hoggar, riven with fjords.'[19] The first three planes landed at Tamanrasset at 4.30 p.m. where Moussa gave them an elaborate welcome. 'It was feast after feast,'[20] Lieutenant Poivre recalled. There were sword fights, dances and camel races. In return Laperrine distributed presents to the Tuareg and held a parade in which he decorated every European in sight: soldiers, fliers, mechanics and truck drivers. According to Rolland, Laperrine remained sombre amidst the revelry. At one dinner he confided that before leaving Algiers he had learned that his father had drowned in a shipping accident. 'All Laperrines seem to die violent deaths,'[21] he remarked.

Tamanrasset was the point at which the squadron separated, Rolland's remaining planes returning to Algiers on the 17th, while the Soudanese team continued its journey. Laperrine remained downcast. 'He was more worried for us than for himself,' Rolland wrote. 'He feared that on our journey north we would meet with the bad weather so common at this time of year.'[22] That same day, in confirmation of Laperrine's fears, Rolland was forced down in the desert and had to be rescued from his blazing aircraft by two *méharistes*. Yet Laperrine had good reason to worry for his own future. Of the two long-distance planes only Vuillemin's remained. Laperrine was therefore to travel in one of the standard Algerian models piloted by one Lieutenant Bernard. In addition, the two pilots had decided it was essential that Bernard be accompanied by a mechanic, a young man named Marcel Vasselin who had come to Tamanrasset in a lorry as part of the support team. The planes being only two-seaters, the General would have to sit on Vasselin's knees. When the Breguets took off on 18 February, Laperrine found himself perched uncomfortably, his head projecting above the windscreen, in the rear cockpit of an overloaded craft that had fuel for only five hours' flight. Nevertheless, he reckoned all would be well. Their course was for Tin Zaouaten, the other side of the Iforas mountains, with a brief stop to refuel at the oasis of Tin Rharo. Even with its extra burden, the Algerian Breguet expected to be able to complete the distance, so long as the weather stayed clear.

The weather did not stay clear. Before take-off, clouds of sand were visible on the horizon, driven by a south-easterly wind, but Vuillemin was confident they could fly over them. The accounts of what happened next are confused. The plan was that Vuillemin would take the lead, on the understanding that if he lost his way Bernard would overtake him and correct his path. Vuillemin later stated that 'We put all our confidence in General Laperrine's navigational abilities, for he had crossed the Sahara eleven times on foot or by camel; we considered him sufficiently experienced in a plane because he had just travelled 1,800 kilometres and had kept his bearings perfectly.'[23] Contradictorily, Vuillemin also said that they had arranged to steer by compass (his compass) for the first part of the route, using photographs supplied by Laperrine to identify Tin Zaouaten – but not Tin Rharo, which was a tiny, water-filled hole in the desert. 'What I have never been able to understand,' said one man (identified by Laperrine's biographer only as Commandant X), 'was how the General agreed to rely on Vuillemin's compass. He should have insisted that he did not leave the track.'[24] But Laperrine seems to have believed that they *were* following the track. As the sandstorm thickened below them, it became harder to follow the markings. 'I can't see it any more,' he wrote on a scrap of paper that he passed to Bernard. A little later: 'With the wind and the sun I can't see anything.'[25] What they could see was Vuillemin's aircraft so they followed that. 'The commandant looked as if he knew where he was going,'[26] Laperrine wrote in his diary.

Unbeknownst to any of them, Vuillemin's compass had broken and was steering them twenty degrees to the east. At 10.30 a.m. they had not yet sighted Tin Rharo, and Bernard warned Laperrine that they had only an hour's fuel left. At 11.30 he took the plane down. Descending from a height of 3,500 metres he had time to make repeated SOS calls on his radio, but there was no reply to show that he had been heard. Meanwhile, 1,000 metres ahead of them, Vuillemin puttered determinedly onwards. Then they entered the storm. For a short while they flew blind, buffeted by violent winds and, all at once, they were fifteen metres from the ground. Realizing that they were going to crash, Bernard cut the engine to prevent a fire and coasted in. The right wing touched the ground, then both wheels buried themselves in the sand and the plane somersaulted onto its back.

Strapped into his harness, and protected by the Breguet's upper wing, Bernard survived the impact unscathed. The other two were less fortunate. Vasselin was caught between the plane and the ground, his head in the sand, while Laperrine, who had not been wearing a harness, was crushed between Vasselin and the windscreen. When Bernard dragged them free, Vasselin was able to move but had contusions down his back and his right leg. Laperrine, who could at first do little more than slump speechless against the plane, had broken his left collarbone and several ribs and had a badly bruised knee. They were dismayed but not disheartened for they had prepared for such an eventuality. Before setting off Vuillemin had lectured them on what to do if a plane came down: if it landed on firm ground the second plane would rescue them (he did not explain how five men were to fit into a two-seater); if the surface was bad, the other plane would 'fly over, fix the spot exactly, and make a report of the situation in order to give every possible assistance to the search and rescue parties'.[27] But if Vuillemin's plane was somewhere above them they could not see it through the storm, and when the wind died, the sky was empty. They were surrounded by kilometre upon kilometre of empty dunes.

Vuillemin later wrote that he had seen Bernard's plane enter the cloud of sand and had spent half an hour trying to locate it before continuing to Tin Rharo which, by his compass, should have been nearby and from where he could summon help. It was at this point, according to his report, that he realized his compass was faulty. Unable to find Tin Rharo he flew on. At 5 p.m. he reached the edge of the desert and, spotting what appeared to be a camp, touched down for the night. The camp was deserted, devoid of food and fuel. 'We ate a cold meal,' he recorded, 'and slept in the plane, rifles to hand, woken at every instant by the cries of wild beasts.'[28] The following morning, with 150 litres of fuel remaining, Vuillemin headed south and at 8 a.m. on 19 February, landed at the Soudanese outpost of Ménaka. Looking at his map – a splendid one that had been personally prepared by Laperrine – he saw that Ménaka was 200 kilometres east of Gao and that if he followed a clearly marked river bed the Niger was only 150 kilometres to the south-west. 'The officer in charge of the post, Lieutenant Salies of the colonial infantry, received us very well,' Vuillemin wrote. 'The natives were stupefied . . . when the plane landed and two French officers stepped out of it. Tuareg who had seen it flying overhead made journeys of four or five days to ask an explanation from the Lieutenant. The moral effect was impressive. [Lieutenant Salies] had gathered the tribal chiefs of every sector: some of them walked 150–200 kilometres to see the plane.'[29] In the afternoon they tried to inflate a balloon carrying an aerial via which

they could radio news of their arrival to Gao along with a request for
fuel. But the balloon leaked so they sent a courier instead, whose
message alerted the world to Vuillemin's achievement, adding inci-
dentally the news that Laperrine's plane was missing. It would take
several days for the courier to reach Gao and another five for a fuel
convoy to reach Ménaka. Vuillemin, who assumed that Bernard and
Laperrine were at Tin Zaouaten, tinkered happily with his plane
and waited for the fuel to arrive. On 1 March a return courier pelted
into Ménaka accompanied by a group of *méharistes*; he carried orders
that every available man should look for Laperrine's plane. Even at
this juncture Vuillemin did not seem concerned. He seized upon the
méharistes avidly. 'I drew them up and explained to them what a plane
was, what its uses were in peace and war. They seemed enormously
interested, far more so than the blacks who thought it was just something else that Frenchmen did.'[30] While Vuillemin held his audience
in thrall, Bernard, Laperrine and Vasselin were dying.

At noon on the day of their crash, when it became obvious that
Vuillemin was not going to rescue them, Bernard forced Laperrine
to drink a few mouthfuls of 'emergency alcohol'. He revived and
began to issue orders. '*Mes enfants*,' he said, 'we must try to eat, then
we will rest until the morning and see what tomorrow brings.'[31]
Trusting to his knowledge of the desert, *les enfants* looked through
their supplies and found a *gigot* of gazelle. Laperrine managed only
a few mouthfuls before falling asleep. Afterwards, Bernard and
Vasselin made an inventory of their provisions. It comprised ten
300-gramme tins of preserved meat, twenty biscuits, 250 grammes
of chocolate, a carton of condensed milk, another of sugar and
ten two-litre bottles of water. Bernard also had half a litre of alcohol
and a rifle. These rations, designed for a landing on the road
where *méharistes* patrolled constantly, looked frighteningly small in
the open desert.

On the morning of 20 February Bernard unfastened the Breguet's
compass and gave it to the General. If, by Laperrine's reckoning, they
had gone too far to the east they should reach the Iforas mountains by
following a north-westerly course. A high dune rose in the distance

and it was there that Laperrine said they should go: once on a height he would recognize the terrain. They departed that evening, carrying their food and their water. The water was rationed to a litre per man per day. The food needed no rationing: their mouths were so dry they could hardly swallow it. Laperrine told them to be of good heart; the road was only fifty kilometres away. But when they tramped to the top of the dune there was no road. All they could see was sand, hundreds of thousands of hectares of the stuff, rolling into the distance. Laperrine ordered them to rest for a while before resuming the march. By 3 p.m., still surrounded by dunes and with no sign of the road, Laperrine admitted defeat. At 7 a.m. on 21 February, they arose – 'the usual hour,'[32] wrote Vasselin wearily – they retraced their steps. If rescuers were looking for them, the plane was an obvious target. It was also the only home they had: better, perhaps, to die amidst familiar surroundings.

The way back seemed far longer than the way out. When they rested between 11 a.m and 4 p.m. Laperrine scribbled a message in the sand: 'We are walking back to our plane which is fifteen kilometres from here.'[33] He signed it in French, Arabic and Tamacheq. But he gave no bearing. He had long ago given up on his compass and had no sense of direction beyond the line of their own, recent footprints. On the morning of 22 February, Laperrine was so weak that Bernard and Vasselin had to support him either side. Four hundred metres from the plane, Laperrine collapsed. 'Leave me, *mes enfants*,' he said, 'Go to the machine and put down your things. You can come back for me later.'[34] They took him by the arms and dragged him on. Back at the plane, they reviewed their situation: they still had eleven litres of water which, if they restricted themselves to half a litre per day, would last them perhaps a week; and if that ran out there was fourteen litres of coolant in the plane's radiator. If they did not exert themselves and rationed themselves carefully, they might live another three weeks. They sought shade under the Breguet's wings where at midday the temperature was 45 °C.

At Ménaka, Vuillemin was fiddling contentedly with his plane. In the Hoggar, however, people had begun to worry. Lieutenant Pruvost, who was in charge of the stations south of Tamanrasset, and who had little faith in Vuillemin or any other aviator, had arranged his own fail-safe system: each station would light a beacon when the planes passed over them and then proceed by camel and lorry to the next; if a beacon was not lit then they would know that the planes were in trouble. At midday on 18 February, a beacon had failed to light. By the 22nd, having heard no news, Pruvost commandeered a lorry and left for Tin Rharo which he reached at midday on the 24th. Nobody had seen Laperrine's plane. But a *méhariste* stationed fifty kilometres south-west of Tamanrasset claimed to have heard the sound of an engine to the east. Immediately, Pruvost despatched one courier to alert In Salah and another to ask for a detachment of *méharistes* from Tin Zaouaten. On 28 February, In Salah sent a telegram to Moussa: 'I count on you and your people to carry out the rescue of General Laperrine. You will remember in your heart he who has been your benefactor and whom you call your father. Only men who know the region can operate swiftly and well; they will be paid.'[35] But by some telegraphic quirk the message did not reach Tamanrasset until 5 March. The Tin Zaouaten *méharistes* arrived at Tin Rharo on 29 February and two days later were scouring the desert.

On 1 March Pruvost heard from Colonel Delestre, commander of the Timbuctoo region, who announced that he was on his way to Tamanrasset, that Vuillemin had landed at Ménaka, and that Laperrine was safe. This latter, probably a garbled version of Vuillemin's original message, filled Pruvost with relief. But he ordered his men to keep searching, just in case.

On 3 March in Ménaka, while waiting for his fuel to arrive, Vuillemin wrote, 'Nobody has found General Laperrine . . . I am beginning to be seriously worried.'[36] On the same day Bernard and Vasselin decided to abandon Laperrine and walk south out of the desert. 'I give you my blessing,' he said. 'Go south, *mes enfants*, but if you do, you will never come back alive.'[37] They made him as comfortable as they could, buried a three-litre flask of water by his side and gave him a length of rubber tubing as a makeshift straw. Then they said their farewells and walked south. After climbing three

ranges Bernard collapsed on a dune and told Vasselin to leave him
there. Vasselin picked him up and dragged him back to the plane.
The journey took three and a half hours. On reaching the Breguet
they saw that Laperrine had drunk nothing. When they poured him
some water he was too weak even to hold the cup. Vasselin wrote on
4 March, 'The General complains more and more and we expect him
to die at any moment. He has difficulty swallowing his chocolate.
This is a dismal day. We see birds of prey fly over us, croaking. They
have scented death among us.'[38]

On 5 March, Bertrand and Vasselin awoke to find that Laperrine
was trying to crawl into the dunes. They pulled him back and offered
him water. But his mouth was full of blood. He motioned with his
head that he had something to say. 'People think they know the
desert,' he whispered. 'People think I know it. Nobody really knows
it. I have crossed the Sahara ten times and this time I will stay here. I
am sorry. I have failed you.'[39] At midday he asked for water. Three
hours later, as the three men lay in the shade of the plane, Bernard
remarked to Vasselin that Laperrine had not spoken for a while. They
gave him a shake. He was dead. They dragged his body into one of
the furrows left by the plane's wheels, covered it with sand and placed
on top of it a spare tyre and his hat. Then they returned to the boiling
shade of the Breguet.

The following day, another of Colonel Delestre's messages reached
Pruvost at Tin Rharo. 'I have every reason to hope that the General
and his companions are safe and sound . . . I expect that before long
you will have heard good news from Tamanrasset. I will be with you
soon to share it.'[40] When Delestre reached Tin Rharo on 7 March, he
learned that the good news had yet to arrive and that Pruvost's search
parties had found nothing. It wasn't for want of trying: one group had
travelled 425 kilometres in eight days; a single *méhariste* had sped
down the road to Tin Zaouaten, covering the 160 kilometres in a
remarkable forty-eight hours; another man had gone through 600 kilometres of desert in five days; one solitary Tuareg was still out there
and would not return until a month had passed. On the afternoon of
his arrival, Delestre took Pruvost's lorry and left for Tamanrasset.

On 10 March, with supplies running low, Pruvost was forced to abandon the search. At 6 a.m. he left Tin Rharo and led his *méharistes* back to their home camp, just north of Agadez. To save time, he decided not to follow the usual line of wells but to take a short-cut through a hitherto unexplored stretch of desert. Normally, he would have travelled by night, but his guides advised against it: they did not know these dunes and would rather cross them in daylight. It was completely by chance, therefore, that Pruvost spotted an odd shape in the sand. 'Suddenly,' he wrote, 'at about a kilometre's distance we saw an object that we could not make out. Then two men appeared and fired three rifle shots. [The Saharians' standard SOS.] We realized that this strange thing was Laperrine's overturned plane.'[41] The *méharistes* collected Bernard and Vasselin and fed them soup and cups of sugary tea. When they recovered they told Pruvost what they had been through. They had eaten toothpaste. They had drunk glycerine and tincture of iodine from the medical chest. They had broken the compass and drunk the water inside it. They had drunk eau de Cologne. They had tried to drink their own urine.

On 15 March Pruvost disinterred Laperrine. 'He was wearing his flying clothes,' Pruvost recorded, 'and had no shoes on his feet.'[42] He wrapped him in a strip of canvas torn from the fuselage, which bore the *tricouleur* and the Breguet's insignia – a 'G' – then loaded him onto a bier made of aluminium tubes that he tore from the aeroplane, and dragged him back to Tamanrasset. He was buried alongside his old friend, Foucauld. His *méharistes* dug the grave, then knocked together a couple of planks of wood and stuck them on the mound.[*]

---

[*]Laperrine's death was the low-point of a hugely expensive enterprise. Of the fifty-four support vehicles that set out, only nine arrived in Tamanrasset and only three made it back to Ouargla on 17 July. In total, they had gone through 1,000 tyres and 2,000 inner tubes. Additionally, 700 camels had died. It was estimated that the journey would have been a quarter the price if undertaken in traditional fashion.

19

THE DYING DAYS

Foucauld's wish had been that he should lie undisturbed where he died: 'I *forbid* that my body be transported or removed from the place where God has decreed that my pilgrimage shall come to an end.'[1] The only people who obeyed his wishes were the inhabitants of Tamanrasset. Laperrine had moved his body in 1917, and twelve years later it was decided that his pilgrimage should begin afresh. On 18 April 1929, accompanied by several high-ranking officers and members of Algeria's civil administration, Monsignor Nouet, Apostolic Prefect of the Sahara, oversaw the exhumation of Foucauld's corpse for removal to El Goléa. Ostensibly the reinterment was for religious purposes: Foucauld, who had been ignored by the papal machine for so long (and had ignored it in return), was now a candidate for canonization on the grounds that he had died a martyr's death; it was necessary therefore that his remains be shifted from Tamanrasset lest they become the focus of a cult. How this reasoning worked is a mystery: it was far easier for would-be cultists to visit El Goléa than it was for them to make the long journey to Tamanrasset. Culpability probably lay with the military, who may not have wanted a horde of worshippers travelling through a desert that was still not very safe.

And the politicians may have had a hand in it too. The year 1930 was the centenary of France's invasion of Algeria, a year in which every device was employed to celebrate the permanence and stability of the colony. Festivals were organized, authors were commissioned to write congratulatory histories (on rich, glossy pages with fold-out panoramas of Algiers), parades were held and foreign dignitaries were invited to view them. Given that Foucauld was now an important figure, why not draw him closer to the centre of things?*

The corpse had deteriorated since Laperrine had last remarked on its extraordinary mummification. Rain had fallen in the intervening years and despite the General's best efforts, Foucauld's grave had become waterlogged. Parts of his torso had decomposed and his legs and arms had separated from the trunk. On behalf of the White Fathers, Monsignor Nouet ordered Foucauld's heart to be picked from the mess and reinterred beneath the granite cross Laperrine had erected in his honour. Stern-faced men in blue kepis saluted the tiny casket as it went back into the sand. The other remains were crated, loaded onto a camel and taken to El Goléa where similar obsequies were observed. The Catholic Association of Nancy had donated money for a lasting memorial to a man they considered a saint, and so it was not beneath a simple wooden cross that Foucauld found his last rest, but an immense granite slab on which was chiselled:

Awaiting the judgement of the Holy Church
Here lies the remains of God's servant
Charles de Jésu – Vicomte de Foucauld
1856–1916
Died in the odour of sanctity

*Indeed, come the centenary, one of the few events reported by the British press was a visit by the Governor-General to El Golea, ostensibly to show visiting botanists what an oasis looked like. His motor cavalcade was escorted through the palms by several hundred Touareg, firing rifles in the air. Whether or not the party saw Foucauld's tomb is not recorded – but they undoubtedly did – just as they saw the large *tricouleur* flying above the mosque.

December 1, 1916
at Tamanrasset
Assassinated by dissident Senoussi
A victim of his charity and his apostolic zeal[2]

Some found it strange that this most spiritual of characters should be commemorated in such heavy-handed style – "a triumph of banality," spluttered one biographer, "[a] monstrous piece of masonry,"[3] – yet the memorial was fitting enough, for as well as living and dying in imitation of Jesus, he had also lived and died in the service of colonialism. His spiritual contract had been fulfilled; it seemed that the temporal one was open-ended.

A more lasting legacy was the creation of the order for which Foucauld had always yearned. In 1933 Massignon and others helped found the first community of Little Brothers of the Sacred Heart in southern Oran, and soon there was a branch at Tamanrasset. In the same year a community of Little Sisters sprang up in Montpellier. The Little Brothers and Sisters spread across the world, their communities augmented by those of other orders, all of whom were inspired in some way or other by Foucauld's example. Today they can be found in France, Italy, Spain, Belgium, Venezuela, Haiti, Canada and the Congo, in numbers that would have delighted their founding father. In 1936, for example, one Sister Magdalene created the non-cloistered Petites Soeurs de Jésus. When she died in 1991 her sub-sect had 1,400 members from sixty nationalities. None of Foucauld's followers could match his capacity for self-denial – there would be a lot fewer of them if they did – but they revere his memory. 'We are almost astonished,' wrote one follower in 1958, 'at having been led so far by a man who taught us no spiritual doctrine nor bequeathed us any special tasks to carry out other than to adore the Holy Eucharist and to take the gospel seriously in our daily life. It is precisely this silence in speech and this severity that fulfil our expectations. For each of us, Brother Charles is a witness who does not let us rest and who unceasingly urges us to take seriously the demands of the gospel.'[4]

Laperrine suffered much the same fate as Foucauld. A huge stone pyramid was erected above his grave, bearing the rather bland inscription, 'Strong in battle, resigned in the face of suffering, he never forgot to think of others.'[5] On suitable occasions the obelisk was draped with flags. The fort at Tamanrasset was strengthened, garrisoned and named after him. For future generations he became one of the heroes of Saharan conquest. He was never, however, seen as the *great* hero. That honour fell to Lyautey, who became a near divinity following his death in 1934. (Photographs of his marble catafalque, guarded by soldiers of the African army, and emblazoned with the single, golden word LYAUTEY, are nothing short of awesome.) But then Laperrine had never wanted to be a great hero. He was too sardonic, too idiosyncratic to fit the ideal: even when he was at the top of his profession a subordinate observed that in a roomful of generals he was the one who stood out from all the rest. It was meant as a compliment but it underlined Laperrine's essential difference from other career soldiers. What he had wanted, like Foucauld, was to be left alone to do his job and, if possible, to be left alone to do it in the desert. His wish had been granted.

As for the empire which both men served, by the time of their deaths it had become an object of admiration to other nations. The British, who had long sneered at France's imperial programme, were impressed by the North Africa they now saw. It seemed stable and prosperous, a shining example of how the white man could bend the barbarous continent to his will. 'Twenty years ago,' wrote one traveller in 1924, 'with a few Arabs and as many camels, I wandered in these vast silent sands where the murmur of stream and the rustle of trees are always absent. To-day those sands behold trains, zeppelins, hear aeroplanes and motor caterpillar cars humming like bees . . . The Romans . . . made great strides in the North of Africa, and have left some wonderful monuments behind. But there is no evidence that they ever conquered the Sahara. The French have conquered it . . .'[6] It is impossible to come away from Algeria without an increased respect for the French as colonists.'[7]

Europeans revelled in the marriage of western civilization and oriental romance. One tourist who visited the oasis of Touggourt was enthralled by an Arab café. 'I stood in the door some while, sipping coffee and looking. Outside the night was white as milk. The open space and the houses round looked as if they had been snowed on. There was a faint odour in the air of dust and spice, decay and sweetness mixed, the familiar smell of the East, always the same. A few ghost-like figures in their winding-sheets crossed the place and vanished into unseen openings. Then I turned my head, and beside me was this darkly-glowing interior and swarthy pomp of colour. It is not enough to say of colouring like this that it is deeper, richer, stronger than ours. It is all this of course, but it is more than all this. It is different in kind. In the East colour is a substantive, in the West it is an adjective. We have coloured things; the East has colour.'[8] Those words were written in 1905, but the description still held true twenty years later – even truer perhaps, once the oases were accessible to more and more travellers. The same writer also wandered through the Algiers suburb of Mustapha in late spring, when it was deserted, the hotels closed for the season and the gardens empty: 'The roses were full-blown and . . . every moment a tuft of petals broke and fell as I walked under the trellissed pergolas.' Blossom seemed to be tumbling from the very sky, turning air and earth yellow with flower. 'Never,' he wrote, 'have I seen decay so lovely.'[9]

Algeria's visitors eulogized the country's exoticness but never participated in it. They appreciated the decay of roses but not that of a people; they liked to stand in the doorways of cafés rather than enter them; and while rejoicing in the flowers of Mustapha they ignored the reality of Algiers – a blanched, alien sprawl that, for all its noise and energy, remained a leprous growth on North African soil. What they really saw, and admired, was the superficial flourish of might that permitted them to be there in the first place and which lent the native population an appearance of willing servility. 'The French are excellent colonists,' concluded one Briton in 1926, 'and now all is peace, happiness and brotherhood.'[10]

Of course, it was not all peace and brotherhood. For most of the 1920s French soldiers struggled to subdue Morocco's discontented Berber population and no sooner had they gained control of the southern Atlas than fresh disturbances broke out in Algeria, where a newly politicized population was beginning to raise its voice. Pan-Islamic factions demanded independence while a pro-French elite – those

educated in government *medrasas* by people like Motylinski – insisted
that Algeria become fully integrated with France but with its own
separate Islamic identity. Meanwhile, the *colons*, or French settlers,
who found both ideas equally unthinkable, took every step to block
reforms. The 1930s became, for Algeria as for Europe, a decade of
racism, repression and violence. In 1934, when a drunken Jewish soldier
urinated against a Constantine mosque, twenty-seven people died and
forty-eight were injured in the ensuing riots. France tried to calm its
colony: in 1940, Pétain's Vichy government appointed four Muslims to
serve in the Council of Government of Algiers (the Council never met,
to the delight of the *colons*); and as the Second World War progressed,
further minor concessions were made. But the changes satisfied neither
party and the *colons* became so intransigent that even the most accom-
modating reformers lost hope. 'What does this mean if not that the
Algerian problem . . . is essentially a *racial and religious one*?' wrote one
Algerian, on reviewing the *colons*' hostility. 'The hour has passed when
an Algerian Moslem will ask to be anything but a Moslem Algerian.'[11]

On 8 May 1945, at the close of a war in which North African soldiers had played a prominent part – as they had done during the First
World War and, indeed, the Franco-Prussian War – Algiers decked
itself in triumphant *tricouleurs*. It was too much for the nationalists.
Flags not seen since the days of Abd el-Kadir were waved in the
streets, and riots flamed throughout the country. Over the next four
days, one hundred Europeans were killed. The French military, still
burning from the humiliation of their defeat by Germany, reacted
viciously. Planes, ships, infantry and armoured columns were
employed to quell the 'rebels'. By the time they had restored order,
10,000 Algerians were dead, thousands of them killed by summary
execution. In 1946, Paris made a final attempt to bring Algeria within
the metropolitan fold, but the *colons* once again refused to cooperate.
By then the Algerians had already chosen their path. 'The revolt of
May, 1945, dug a ditch we could no longer cross between the two
communities,' said one leader. 'It made us decide to take up arms.'[12]

By the 1950s, Algeria was no longer as beautiful as it had been
thirty years before. While other European nations divested them-

selves of their colonies – reluctantly, and not without 'emergencies', to use a British euphemism – France lagged obstinately. Its Far Eastern territories went in 1954, after a long and bloody war; Morocco was handed back to its inhabitants in 1956, as Tunisia had been in 1955. (One of the Tunis government's first acts was to remove the statue of Cardinal Lavigerie that stood outside the *medina*.) But Algeria was a different matter. There were now two million white settlers living there and although many people complained about the expense of the colony, the government could not afford to let it go. When, in 1956, Algerians used terrorism to topple the regime, the military used brute force to suppress them. The unrest started in the old quarter of Algiers, a warren of dilapidated buildings and narrow streets untouched since Ottoman times, whose geography was impenetrable to all but its inhabitants. French troops regained control of the capital after a long and bloody battle, only to find that the focus of rebellion had now shifted to the countryside. Over the space of a few years Algeria became the same ungovernable colony it had been in the 1830s and 1840s, with white villagers huddling together for security while the army scoured the country for an elusive enemy, the slight difference being that in 1830 the French had horses and rifles, whereas now they had helicopters and machine-guns. What truly differentiated the situation in the 1830s and the 1950s, however, was France's attitude to the Sahara.

While the massacres continued in the countryside, and as the bombs exploded in Algiers' cafés, the desert became the placid backdrop to Ionesco-like absurdities. Here, it was suggested, in an empty space the size of the United States, France – nay, Europe – could prove its status as a world power. The Sahara had oil, it had natural gas (a product whose value was only being realized in the 1950s), it had minerals and incalculable reserves of underground water. It also had the world's largest inland missile testing range, an attraction that was touted as if it were a hotel's heated swimming pool or private golf course – the interested parties being not sales reps but members of NATO. Enthusiasts spoke of 'Eurafrica', a nebulous partnership between Europe and Africa, wherein the capital of the former would be used to develop the resources of the latter to the benefit of both. The notion had already been suggested in the 1920s by Erik Labonne, a former Resident-General of Morocco who saw the way the world was going: 'A disintegrated and impoverished Europe,' he wrote, 'is measuring its tiny strength against the vast development of the United States and Soviet Russia. Africa is its only hope: the Continent which, if Europe can decide on a joint plan for its development, will allow Europeans to break away from their small, peninsular existence and find their unity in a common effort.'[13] His words carried even more weight in the 1950s. 'Eurafrica' was nothing more than a redefinition of imperialism, but it appealed to a continent coming to terms with its downfall and whose plans for a new future relied, occasionally, on templates from the past. France was the driving force behind 'Eurafrica' (which in unguarded moments was sometimes mentioned in the same breath as the 'French Union', a commonwealth of ex-colonies) but other members of Europe's new-formed Common Market also showed an interest. West Germany, in particular, was keen to invest. And so, during the late 1950s, money was thrown at the Sahara.

Lunatics of every persuasion hastened to the honey-pot. In an age when the split atom seemed the answer to everything, horrendous applications were suggested. According to one author – whose testimony seems incredible – there were proposals to create underground reservoirs by dropping a nuclear device down the drill shaft ('[It] would only be visible on the surface in the form of a huge pimple . . . radioactive pollution of the water would not be a serious threat . . . The Sahara is the Promised Land for the peaceful use of atomic explosions.').[14] The odd megaton here and there might rejuvenate failing oil wells. And there were serious plans to blast atomically a new port on the Atlantic coast; all being well, a 'clean bomb' would be detonated in 1965. Once again the Transsaharian rose phoenix-like, and once again it flamed down in ashes, leaving only a proposed extension of the existing narrow-gauge line from Colomb-Béchar to Adrar, the dunes over which it ran to be stabilized by spraying them with oil. In its place came even wilder schemes. In 1953 one man wanted to divert the River Niger at Timbuctoo to create a navigable waterway leading to Taoudeni where it would then separate, one half running to the Atlantic, the other extending to In Salah from where it would be diverted by pipeline to Fort Flatters and then flow northwards down an ancient *oued* towards the Mediterranean. A yet more ambitious concept was the creation of an inland Saharan sea by cutting a canal from the Mediterranean to the chain of *chotts*, or salt marshes, surrounding Biskra, some of which lay thirty metres below sea level. This was an old idea, first suggested in the 1870s by Captain François Roudaire and supported by Ferdinand de Lesseps. Studies had shown it to be perfectly feasible – on a par with building the Suez Canal – and only the lack of return had deterred investors. But now that the Sahara was potentially profitable, the canal received new attention. In 1957 Roudaire's great-grandson formed a group called ARTEMIS, 'Association de Recherche Technique pour l'Étude de la Mer Intérieure Saharienne.' What ARTEMIS proposed was very simple: a twenty-megaton hydrogen bomb buried at a depth of 750 metres would create a crater three kilometres in diameter; fifty such bombs, detonated simultaneously, would within seconds blast the world's largest man-made waterway and flood almost 5,000 square kilometres of desert. Thankfully, ARTEMIS went into liquidation two years later.

What was worrying about these crackpot schemes was not their idiocy – the desert had always attracted more than its fair share of foolishness. At the beginning of the century one Jacques Labaudy had declared himself Emperor of the Sahara before being committed to a Long Island asylum in 1915; in 1941 the Nazis had toyed with the idea of a trans-Saharan pipeline for ground-nut oil; and in the 1920s a German named Herman Sorgel had considered transplanting the Mediterranean to the Sahara. Reasoning that the Mediterranean lost more water by evaporation than was replaced by the rivers flowing into it, he wanted to dam the Dardanelles and the Straits of Gibraltar. As the Mediterranean fell at a rate of one metre per year, the dams would produce hydro-electricity that could be used to desalinate the water and pump it into the Sahara. At the end of the process the desert would be green, the sea would be dry and Europe would no longer be separated (by water, at any rate) from the continent in which it was to fulfil its destiny.

No, the disturbing aspect was that the thinking that spawned such lunacies – the same thinking that gave rise to 'Eurafrica' – still informed governmental policy. Throughout the 1950s, France made a determined effort to save the Sahara for the benefit of itself and its European collaborators. Steps were taken to 'decolonialize' the desert, to separate it from coastal Algeria – that heartland which, as every politician knew in his soul, must sooner or later go – and to preserve it for the West when everything else was lost. Decolonialization had already been applied to the French Soudan, where Mali, Chad, Niger and other nations had been granted autonomous membership of the French Union as a step towards independence. But an independent Sahara was not an option because, if divorced from its neighbours, there was nothing around which to build a state. It was a flawed argument but one that had a kernel of logic: even if the Sahara was attached to Algeria it would still remain a zone where accepted notions of nationhood did not apply; administration was the best anyone could hope for. And that being the case, why should Algeria instead of France be the administrator? The desert's last ruler, if it could be said to have a ruler, had been Moussa. When Moussa died in 1920, shortly after Laperrine, it had been in the certainty that France offered the best future for his people. On his death the military had taken control, following Foucauld's advice, and forty years on they showed no intention of relinquishing it. Accordingly, the Sahara was 'decolonialized' upwards. From being a colony it was promoted in 1957 to the status of *département* – two *départements* to be precise, one with its capital at Colomb-Béchar, the other centred on Laghouat – and was given its own Ministry in Paris, its own bureaucracy, its own budget, its own revenue-raising powers and its own quasi-autonomous governing body, the OCRS, 'Organisation Commune des Régions Sahariennes', whose influence extended wherever possible into the French Union territories of the Soudan.

It fooled nobody. France was merely using political reorganization to cloak its desire to control a commercially valuable asset. And a pretty thin cloak it was too. The ploy had already failed once, in the Suez Crisis of 1956, when France and Britain – a nation whose own policy towards imperial dismemberment was never entirely straight-forward, particularly in the Middle East – had intervened as peace-makers between Egypt and Israel, and had then sent armed forces to seize the Suez Canal. Their subsequent, US-forced with-drawal broke the governments of both London and Paris. Still, however, France pursued a semi-imperial agenda. Outsiders were disquietened by this blindness to reality. In 1958 the author Herbert Luthy wrote, 'Words like "Eurafrica" and "French Union" have an unreal, ghostly sound against the background of the Algerian tragedy; yet precisely because this appalling conflict between a legal fiction and a reality can only end with the destruction of a myth, the myth of the "mother country of the peoples", so it will become the threshold across which France finally steps out of the magic circle of historical self-adulation into the open: as a nation amongst nations. The question is not whether this will happen but at what cost and how late?'[15]

For certain elements in France, no cost was too great and 'late' had no meaning at all. Paris was determined to keep the Sahara – and not only to keep it but to invest in its future. Bodies private and public applied themselves to a wasteland from which they hoped to reap huge rewards. The Tuareg, erstwhile masters of the sands, were smothered by sheer weight of acronym. There was S.N.REPAL (Société Nationale de Recherche et d'Exploitation des Pétroles en Algérie) and its associated company CREPS (Compagnie de Recherche et Exploration de Pétrole au Sahara). There was BRP (Bureau de Recherches de Pétrole) and CFP (Compagnie Française des Pétroles) and ZOIA (Zones d'Organisation Industrielle et Stratégique en Afrique). Scientists from SODETEP (Société de Developpement de Techniques de la Pluie Provoquée) sought to produce artificial rain and established little hutments in the Hoggar from which its employees recorded the passage of clouds. Technicians from ENERSOL (Société d'Études et d'Applications Industrielles de l'Énergie Solaire), aided by ARESA (Association pour la Recherche sur l'Utilisation de l'Énergie Solaire en Algérie) developed solar furnaces – elaborate, James Bondian dishes that swivelled with the sun and could smelt ore at temperatures of more than 3,000 °C – while associated companies experimented with novel forms of wind turbine. The increased rainfall and free energy for which these bodies strove was to the benefit of bodies such as BUMIFOM (Bureau Minier de la France d'Outre-Mer), which controlled mineral-prospecting (Outre-Mer was a deliberate reference to the kingdoms French crusaders had created in Palestine). Meanwhile, PROHUZA (Centre d'Études et d'Informations des Problèmes Humains dans les Zones Arides) studied the effects of extreme heat on the employees of all the above: after one survey in which it found that an oil worker lost eight kilograms per day through perspiration, it advised that three years in the Sahara was enough to destroy the average man.

The military resented the multi-initialled intruders. For the preceding thirty years the French army had run the desert on its own. With ever-decreasing amounts of money and less thanks it had maintained the peace and nurtured what it hoped was a pro-French environment. Now it was acting as nursemaid to an alliance of bureaucrats and capitalists that had no feeling for the Sahara. Professional Saharians laughed at the oil men who dined in air-conditioned canteens decorated with scenes of the French Alps. They scoffed, too, at PROHUZA's declaration that a man was finished after three years' desert service: anyone with a smattering of colonial history knew that Foucauld, Laperrine and other dedicated officers had spent decades in the Sahara. According to one lieutenant, the newcomers were 'barbarians who have no sense for the beauty of a sunset'.[16] To corporate eyes these sentiments were as anachronistic as the Tuareg themselves: the march towards modernity could not wait for a few sentimentalists. In Napoleonic fashion, the OCRS assuaged its warriors with a new medal, the *Ordre du Mérite Saharien*. It also reminded them that they were not there to fight the oil companies but the 'terrorists' of FLN. The *Front de Libération Nationale* could not muster as many capital letters as its opponents but it was a potent, nationalistic force that held coastal Algeria in its thrall and had already begun to bomb French installations in the desert.

In 1958 France's unstable Fourth Republic – which had gone through twenty-four governments since its creation in 1946 – was replaced by the Fifth Republic, whose leader, General de Gaulle, finally admitted defeat. In 1959 he granted Algeria a degree of self-determination. Pointedly he did not include the two Saharan *départements*, which were still considered as belonging to France. But the FLN did not agree: they wanted full independence and full control of the Sahara as well. For the next four years, a tripartite war raged between the FLN, the French military and colonial paramilitaries, during the course of which hundreds of thousands died, many of them innocent civilians. The unrest spread to France, where it very nearly brought about a civil war until, in 1962, De Gaulle at last signed a peace treaty with the FLN. In the following year Algeria adopted its first constitution as a democratic and independent republic. Slowly at first, and then in increasing numbers, the white settlers abandoned their property and fled to France. By the end of the decade, in what was one of the largest displacements of humanity since the Second World War, there remained barely a few thousand from a community that had once been numbered in millions. Fittingly, Algerians now took their pick of abandoned farms and businesses just as the French had done during the nineteenth century. They turned the cathedral of Algiers back into the mosque it had originally been, and they demolished the statues and memorials that the French had erected to celebrate their conquest. Then they addressed the reconstruction of their national identity – a problem that would prove more complicated than anyone envisaged.

After 133 years, France's grand African venture was at an end. Everything it had built it had lost, everything to which it had aspired was redundant. The Transsaharian, and the empire it was supposed to connect, survived only in memory and in archives – as did the men who had been part of the colonial dream. The Sahara was now part of Algeria and apart from its southern boundary, which had been agreed so long ago at the Convention of Niamey, little remained of

Laperrine's presence and even less of Foucauld's. The *méharistes* were gradually superseded by planes, helicopters and cars; the few converts that the White Fathers had made left soon after independence; and the community of Little Brothers that maintained the station at Tamanrasset were driven out in the 1980s.

Had Foucauld and Laperrine wasted their lives? Not really. They lived within the circumstances of their age and subscribed to prevailing ideals. Foucauld could even be congratulated for manufacturing a creed of self-denial that continued long after his death. The tragedy of their existences lay not so much in time as in landscape. They had entered a region that defied Western notions of permanence, and they had died there still believing that they had made an impact. But the Sahara was the same after their deaths as before – a vast expanse of sand and rock in which nothing would really change and upon which nothing could leave a lasting impression. Professor Gautier, who had travelled up and down the desert, and had seen both Foucauld and Laperrine in action, gave them an apt, if depressing, epitaph: 'The only endemic disease of the Sahara,' he wrote, 'is madness.'[17]

SOURCES AND REFERENCES

The following abbreviations have been used:

CBA – Carnet de Beni Abbès
CS – Correspondances Sahariennes
CT – Carnets de Tamanrasset
FH – Foucauld & Huvelin, Lettres Inédites
HSND – Archives of the State Historical Society of North Dakota

1 Absinthe and Barracks

1 M. Preminger, *The Sands of Tamanrasset*, Peter Davies, London, 1961, p. 44.
2 D. Porch, *The Conquest of Morocco*, Jonathan Cape, London, 1986, p. 5.
3 L. Phillipps, *In the Desert*, Edward Arnold, London, 1905.
4 J. Cooley, *Baal, Christ, and Mohammed*, John Murray, London, 1967, p. 165.
5 Phillipps, op. cit., p. 49.
6 Ibid.
7 Ibid., p. 50.
8 B. Vandervoort, *Wars of Imperial Conquest in Africa, 1830–1914*, UCL Press, London, 1998, p. 60.
9 Phillipps, op. cit.
10 A. Knox, *The New Playground, or Wanderings in Algeria*, C. Kegan Paul & Co., London, 1881, p. 69.
11 Ibid., p. 58.
12 G. Cooke, *Conquest and Colonisation of North Africa*, Blackwood, Edinburgh, 1860, p. 2.

13 Ibid., p. 10.
14 Ibid., pp. 10–11.
15 Ibid., p. 237.
16 Ibid., p. xiii.
17 Knox, op. cit., p. 461.
18 *Cambridge History of Africa*, Vol. V, CUP, Cambridge, 1976, p. 488.
19 C. Agerre (trans. M. Brett), *Modern Algeria*, Hurst & Co., London, 1991, p. 21.
20 Alphonse Daudet, quoted in *Cambridge History of Africa*, op. cit., p. 472.

2   A Painful Void

1 A. Fremantle, *Desert Calling*, Hollis & Carter, London, 1950, p. 19.
2 Ibid., p. 19.
3 Ibid., p. 23.
4 Ibid.
5 Ibid., p. 28.
6 Ibid., p. 27.
7 C. Foucauld, *Lettres à un ami de Lycée*, Nouvelle Cité, Paris, 1982, p. 88.
8 Fremantle, op. cit., p. 31.
9 R. Bazin (trans. P. Keelan), *Charles de Foucauld*, Burns Oates & Washbourne, London, 1923, p. 9.
10 Ibid.
11 Fremantle, op. cit., p. 42.
12 Ibid., p. 36.
13 Ibid., p. 37.
14 Ibid., pp. 41–2.
15 Foucauld, op. cit., p. 124.
16 Fremantle, op. cit., p. 45.
17 Foucauld, op. cit., p. 116.
18 Fremantle, op. cit., p. 46.
19 Ibid.
20 Foucauld, op. cit., p. 116.
21 Bazin, op. cit., p. 10.

3   Into the Desert

1 R. Bazin (trans. P. Keelan), *Charles de Foucauld*, Burns Oates & Washbourne, London, 1923, p. 64.
2 H. Duveyrier, *Journal de Route*, Challamel, Paris, 1905, p. xiv.
3 Ibid., p. xxii.
4 H. Duveyrier, *Exploration du Sahara: Les Touaregs du Nord*, Challamel Ainé, Paris, 1864, p. 371.
5 A. Duponchel, *Le Chemin de Fer Trans-Saharien*, Hachette, Paris, 1879, p. 355.
6 Ibid., p. 341.
7 Ibid., p. 342.
8 Ibid.
9 A. Knox, *The New Playground*, C. Kegan Paul, London, 1881, p. 168.
10 P. Gaffarel, *Les Colonies Françaises*, Germer Baillière, Paris, 1880, p. 3.

11 Ibid., p. 4.
12 Ibid., p. 5.
13 P. Gaffarel, *Les Explorations Françaises Depuis 1870*, Degorce-Cadot, Paris, 1882, p. 176.
14 D. Porch, *The Conquest of the Sahara*, Jonathan Cape, London, 1985, p. 114.
15 Ibid., p. 117.
16 Ibid., p. 124.

4 Reconnaisance au Maroc

1 C. Foucauld, *Lettres à un ami de Lycée*, Nouvelle Cité, Paris, 1982, p. 116.
2 Ibid.
3 E. Gautier, *Un Siècle de Colonisation*, Félix Alcan, Paris, 1930, p. 173.
4 Ibid., p. 172.
5 A. Fremantle, *Desert Calling*, Hollis & Carter, London, 1950, p. 57.
6 Ibid., p. 115.
7 R. Bazin (trans. P. Keelan), *Charles de Foucauld*, Burns Oates & Washbourne, London, 1923, p. 11.
8 Foucauld, op. cit., p. 118.
9 C. Foucauld, *Reconnaissance au Maroc*, Société d'Éditions Géographiques, Maritimes et Coloniales, Paris, 1939, p. 12.
10 Fremantle, op. cit., p. 64.
11 Ibid., p. 59.
12 Foucauld, *Lettres* . . . op. cit., p. 125.
13 Fremantle, op. cit., p. 69.
14 Ibid., p. 67.
15 Foucauld, *Reconnaissance* . . . op. cit., p. 30.
16 Ibid.
17 Ibid., p. 31.
18 Ibid., p. 30.
19 Ibid., p. 32.
20 Bazin, op. cit., p. 18.
21 Fremantle, op. cit., p. 76.
22 Ibid.
23 Bazin, op. cit., p. 36.
24 Fremantle, op. cit., p. 77.
25 Ibid., p. 76.
26 Foucauld, *Reconnaissance* . . . op. cit., p. 61.
27 Ibid., pp. 92–3.
28 Ibid., p. 136.
29 Bazin, op. cit., p. 39.
30 Ibid., p. 35.
31 Foucauld, *Reconnaissance* . . . op. cit., p. 133.
32 Ibid., p. 223.
33 Ibid., p. 222.
34 Ibid., p. 219.
35 Bazin, op.cit., p. 41.
36 Bazin, op. cit., p. 53.

37 Ibid.
38 Ibid., p. 54.
39 Ibid.
40 Ibid., p. 55.
41 Ibid., p. 56.
42 Ibid.
43 Foucauld, *Reconnaissance* . . . op. cit., p. 409.
44 Ibid., p. 410.
45 Ibid., p. 411.
46 Ibid., p. 429.
47 Fremantle, op. cit., p. 93.
48 Ibid., p. 94.
49 Ibid.
50 Foucauld, *Reconnaissance* . . . op. cit., p. 21.
51 Ibid., p. 14.
52 Bazin, op. cit., p. 60.
53 Foucauld, *Lettres* . . . op. cit., p. 134.
54 Ibid., p. 135.
55 Bazin, op. cit., p. 65.
56 Fremantle, op. cit., p. 123.
57 Bazin, op. cit., p. 71.
58 Ibid.
59 Ibid., pp. 67–8.
60 Fremantle, op. cit., p. 144.
61 Bazin, op. cit., p. 75.

5 Senegalese Hooligans

1 L. Lehuraux, *Laperrine Le Saharien*, Éditions de l'Encyclopédie de l'Empire Français, Paris, 1947, p. 17.
2 S. Howe, *Les Héros du Sahara*, Armand Colin, Paris, 1931, pp. 79–80.
3 D. Porch, *The Conquest of the Sahara*, Jonathan Cape, London, 1985, p. 130.
4 Ibid. p. 127.
5 Howe, op. cit., p. 51.
6 Porch, op. cit., p. 128.
7 Ibid., p. 129.
8 Ibid.
9 Ibid., p. 131.
10 Ibid., p. 129.
11 Howe, op. cit., p. 86.
12 *Bulletin de la Société de Géographie*, Tome XVI, 1895, 388.
13 P. Vuillot, *L'Exploration du Sahara*, Challamel, Paris, 1895, pp. 334–5.
14 Lehuraux, op. cit., p. 26.
15 Ibid., p. 28.
16 Ibid., p. 29.
17 *Bulletin de la Société de Géographie*, op. cit., 388.
18 Porch, op. cit., p. 142.

6 The Monk's Friend

1 A. Fremantle, *Desert Calling*, Hollis & Carter, London, 1950, p. 133.
2 Ibid.
3 Ibid., p. 140.
4 Ibid., p. 145.
5 Ibid., p. 143.
6 Ibid., p. 147.
7 Ibid., p. 148.
8 R. Bazin (trans. P. Keelan), *Charles de Foucauld*, Burns Oates & Washbourne, London, 1923, p. 94.
9 Fremantle, op. cit., p. 148.
10 Ibid., p. 145.
11 HSND.
12 HSND.
13 D. Porch, *The Conquest of the Sahara*, Jonathan Cape, London, 1985, p. 154.
14 Ibid.
15 Ibid.
16 Ibid.
17 D. Dresden, *The Marquis de Morès: Emperor of the Bad Lands*, University of Oklahoma Press, Norman, 1970, p. 242.
18 Ibid., p. 243.
19 Ibid., p. 236.
20 Ibid., p. 245.
21 Ibid., p. 247.
22 Ibid., p. 248.
23 Ibid., p. 251.
24 Ibid.
25 Porch, op. cit., p. 157.
26 Ibid.
27 Dresden, op. cit., p. 251.
28 Porch, op. cit., p. 157.
29 Dresden, op. cit., p. 254.
30 Ibid., p. 255.
31 Ibid.
32 Porch, op. cit., p. 159.
33 Dresden, op. cit., p. 256.
34 Porch, op. cit., p. 160.
35 Ibid., p. 153.
36 É. Hourst (trans. N. d'Anvers), *French Enterprise in Africa*, Chapman & Hall, London, 1898, p. 505, 512.
37 Porch, op. cit., p. 163.
38 L. Phillipps, *In the Desert*, Edward Arnold, London, 1905, p. 74.

7 From Algiers to the Congo

1 F. Foureau, *Documents Scientifiques de la Mission Saharienne*, Vol. I, Masson, Paris, 1903, p. ii.

2 F. Foureau, *D'Alger au Congo par le Tchad*, Éditions L'Harmattan, Paris, 1990, p. 1.
3 *Bulletin de la Société de Géographie*, Tome XVI, 1895, 41.
4 Ibid., 42.
5 Ibid.
6 S. Howe, *Les Héros du Sahara*, Armand Colin, Paris, 1931, p. 56.
7 Foureau, *Documents* . . . op. cit., p. 2.
8 Ibid., p. 3.
9 D. Porch, *The Conquest of the Sahara*, Jonathan Cape, London, 1985, p. 167.
10 Ibid., p. 166.
11 Ibid.
12 *La Géographie*, Tome IV, 1901, 476.
13 Porch, op. cit., p. 167.
14 Foureau, *D'Alger* . . . op. cit., p. 110.
15 Ibid., p. 139.
16 Porch, op. cit., p. 167.
17 Foureau, *D'Alger* . . . op. cit., p. 130.
18 Ibid., p. 136.
19 Ibid., p. 190.
20 Ibid., pp. 190–1.
21 Ibid., p. 191.
22 Ibid., p. 199.
23 Ibid., p. 309.
24 Ibid., p. 204.
25 Porch, op. cit., p. 174.
26 Foureau, *D'Alger* . . . op. cit., p. 407.
27 *Journal of the Royal Geographical Society*, Vol. XVII, Jan–June 1901, 140.
28 Porch, op. cit., p. 177.
29 Ibid., p. 178.
30 *Journal of the Royal Geographical Society*, op. cit., 142.
31 Ibid.
32 Foureau, *D'Alger* . . . op. cit., p. 441.
33 Porch, op. cit., p. 183.
34 Ibid., p. 187.
35 Ibid., p. 189.
36 Ibid.
37 Ibid., p. 191.
38 Ibid., p. 192.
39 Ibid.
40 Ibid.
41 Ibid., p. 193.
42 Ibid.
43 Ibid., p. 194.
44 *Journal of the Royal Geographical Society*, op. cit., 142.
45 Ibid., 143.
46 Ibid.
47 Ibid.
48 Ibid., 144.

49 Ibid.
50 Foureau, *D'Alger* . . . op. cit., p. 617.
51 *Journal of the Royal Geographical Society*, op. cit., 144.
52 Foureau, *D'Alger* . . . op. cit., p. 667.
53 *Journal of the Royal Geographical Society*, op. cit., 146.
54 Porch, op. cit., p. 203.
55 Ibid., pp. 204–5.
56 Ibid., p. 205.
57 Ibid., p. 207.
58 *Journal of the Royal Geographical Society*, op. cit., 150.
59 Foureau, *D'Alger* . . . op. cit., p. 792.
60 Ibid., p. 517.
61 Porch, op. cit., p. 208.
62 Foureau, *D'Alger* . . . op. cit., pp. 797–8.
63 *Bulletin de la Société de Géographie Commerciale*, Tome XXII, 1900, 353.
64 Ibid., 357.
65 Foureau, *D'Alger* . . . op. cit., p. 798.

8 'Think that you are going to die a martyr'

1 *Journal of the Royal Geographical Society*, Vol. XV, Jan–June 1800, 177.
2 S. Howe, *Les Héros du Sahara*, Armand Colin, Paris, 1931, p. 80.
3 G. Gerster (trans. S. Thomson), *Sahara*, Barrie and Rockliff, London, 1960, p. 6.
4 D. Porch, *The Conquest of the Sahara*, Jonathan Cape, London, 1985, p. 222.
5 Ibid., p. 235.
6 A. Fremantle, *Desert Calling*, Hollis & Carter, London, 1950, p. 150.
7 R. Bazin (trans. P. Keelan), *Charles de Foucauld*, Burns Oates & Washbourne, London, 1923, p. 97.
8 Fremantle, op. cit., p. 155.
9 FH, Huvelin to Foucauld, 2 August 1896.
10 C. Foucauld, *Selected Writings*, Orbis Books, New York, 1999, p. 38.
11 Fremantle, op. cit., p. 163.
12 Ibid., p. 166.
13 Ibid.
14 Ibid., p. 168.
15 Foucauld, op. cit., p. 38.
16 Fremantle, op. cit., p. 174.
17 FH, p. 51.
18 Fremantle, op. cit., p. 188.
19 Ibid.
20 FH, Huvelin to Foucauld, 20 March 1900.
21 Fremantle, op. cit., p. 190.
22 Ibid.
23 Ibid., p. 194.
24 Ibid., p. 196.
25 Ibid., p. 198.
26 Ibid.

9 Beni Abbès

1 *The Times*, 3 July 1901.
2 *The Times*, 2 May 1901.
3 *The Times*, 29 April 1901.
4 *The Times*, 25 May 1901.
5 *The Times*, 2 May 1901.
6 *The Times*, 27 November 1900.
7 *The Times*, 29 April 1901.
8 A. Fremantle, *Desert Calling*, Hollis & Carter, London, 1950, p. 209.
9 C. Foucauld (trans. B. Lucas), *Letters from the Desert*, Burns & Oates, London, 1977, p. 84.
10 Ibid.
11 Ibid., p. 83.
12 CS, Foucauld to Guérin, 22 August 1901.
13 J-J. Antier (trans. J. Smith), *Charles de Foucauld*, Ignatius Press, San Francisco, 1999, p. 178.
14 H-P. Egdoux, *L'Exploration du Sahara*, Gallimard, Paris, 1938, p. 158.
15 Ibid.
16 Ibid., p. 159.
17 Ibid.
18 Antier, op. cit., p. 179.
19 Ibid.
20 Ibid., p. 185.
21 S. Home, *Lyautey of Morocco*, Hodder & Stoughton, London, 1931, pp. 182–3.
22 D. Porch, *The Conquest of the Sahara*, Jonathan Cape, London, 1985, p. 274.
23 Antier, op. cit., p. 186.
24 Fremantle, op. cit., p. 216.
25 Antier, op. cit., p. 188.
26 Fremantle, op. cit., p. 225.
27 FH, Foucauld to Huvelin, 15 December 1902.
28 Fremantle, op. cit., p. 225.
29 CS, Foucauld to Guérin, 4 February 1902.
30 Fremantle, op. cit., p. 235.
31 Antier, op. cit., p. 191.
32 Ibid.
33 CS, Foucauld to Guérin, 4 February 1902.
34 Fremantle, op. cit., p. 222.
35 CS, Foucauld to Guérin, 28 June 1902.
36 CS, Guérin to Foucauld, 17 September 1902.
37 CS, Guérin to Foucauld, 27 March 1902.
38 CS, Guérin to Foucauld, 13 March 1902.
39 CS, Guérin to Foucauld, 17 September 1902.
40 Antier, op. cit., p. 193.
41 FH, Foucauld to Huvelin, 22 November 1907.
42 Fremantle, op. cit., p. 209.
43 Antier, op. cit., p. 194.
44 Fremantle, op. cit., p. 224.

45 G. Gorrée (trans. D. Attwater), *Memories of Charles de Foucauld*, Burns Oates & Washbourne, London, 1938, p. 69.
46 FH, Foucauld to Huvelin, 26 October 1905.
47 CS, Guérin to Foucauld, 17 September 1902.
48 Ibid.
49 Fremantle, op. cit., pp. 226–7.
50 Foucauld, op. cit., p. 109.
51 CBA, 20 April 1903.
52 Fremantle, op. cit., p. 224.
53 FH, Huvelin to Foucauld, 18 May 1902.
54 FH, Foucauld to Huvelin, 15 December 1902.
55 CS, Foucauld to Guérin, 30 September 1902.
56 Fremantle, op. cit., p. 229.
57 Antier, op. cit., p. 189.
58 Ibid., pp. 195–6.
59 Fremantle, op. cit., p. 226.
60 Ibid., p. 225.
61 Ibid., p. 230.
62 CS, Foucauld to Guérin, 11 December 1902.
63 CS, Foucauld to Guérin, 9 March 1903.
64 CS, Guérin to Foucauld, 26 January 1903.
65 CS, Foucauld to Guérin, 31 December 1902.

10   Laperrine's Command

1 E. Gautier, *La Conquête du Sahara*, Armand Colin, Paris, 1925, p. 99.
2 D. Porch, *The Conquest of the Sahara*, Jonathan Cape, London, 1985, p. 239.
3 Ibid., p. 251.
4 J. Germain and S. Faye, *Le Général Laperrine*, Plon, Paris, 1922, p. 9.
5 L. Lehuraux, *Laperrine*, Éditions de L'Encyclopédie de L'Empire Français, Paris, 1947, p. 55.
6 Ibid., p. 56.
7 Ibid.
8 Ibid.
9 Ibid., pp. 56–7.
10 Ibid., p. 57.
11 Ibid.
12 Ibid.
13 Ibid.
14 Porch, op. cit., p. 262.
15 Ibid.
16 Lehuraux, op. cit., pp. 57–8.
17 Porch, op. cit., p. 260.
18 Ibid., p. 247.
19 Ibid., p. 269.
20 Ibid.
21 Ibid.
22 Ibid.

23 Ibid., p. 263.
24 H-P. Egdoux, *L'Exploration du Sahara*, Gallimard, Paris, 1938, p. 181.
25 Ibid.
26 Ibid., p. 182.
27 Ibid., p. 183.
28 Ibid.
29 Porch, op. cit., p. 260.

11   A Tour of the Interior

 1 A. Fremantle, *Desert Calling*, Hollis & Carter, London, 1950, p. 234.
 2 M. Serpette, *Foucauld au Désert*, Desclée de Brouwer, Paris, 1997, p. 26.
 3 Fremantle, op. cit., p. 231.
 4 CBA, 7 February 1905.
 5 CBA, 21 June 1903.
 6 Ibid.
 7 CS, Foucauld to Guérin, 29 April 1903.
 8 J. Germain and S. Faye, *Le Général Laperrine*, Plon, Paris, 1922, pp. 96–7.
 9 CBA, 26 August 1903.
10 Germain, op. cit., p. 98.
11 CBA, 13 December 1903.
12 Ibid.
13 Ibid.
14 L. Lehuraux, *Laperrine Le Saharien*, Éditions de l''Encyclopédie de l'Empire Français, Paris, 1947, p. 75.
15 Fremantle, op. cit., pp. 236–7.
16 Lehuraux, op. cit., p. 66.
17 Ibid., p. 78.
18 CS, Laperrine to Regnault, 19 February 1904.
19 Fremantle, op. cit., p. 244.
20 Ibid.
21 Ibid., p. 247.
22 Ibid., p. 249.
23 Ibid., pp. 244–5.
24 CS, Laperrine to Regnault, 19 February 1904.
25 CBA, 8 April 1904.
26 Fremantle, op. cit., p. 251.
27 CBA, 16 April 1904.
28 Ibid.
29 CBA, 22 April 1904.
30 CBA, 17 May 1904.
31 J-J. Antier (trans. J. Smith), *Charles de Foucauld*, Ignatius Press, San Francisco, 1999, p. 219.
32 CBA, 26 May 1904.
33 CBA, 7 June 1904.
34 Fremantle, op. cit., p. 252.
35 CBA, 14 June 1904.
36 Antier, op. cit., p. 219.

37 CBA, 7 October 1904.
38 Antier, op. cit., p. 220.
39 Fremantle, op. cit., p. 255.

12 Towards the Hoggar

1 CS, Foucauld to Guérin, 20 February 1905.
2 A. Fremantle, *Desert Calling*, Hollis & Carter, London, 1950, p. 257.
3 Ibid.
4 Ibid.
5 J-J. Antier (trans. J. Smith), *Charles de Foucauld*, Ignatius Press, San Francisco, 1999, p. 226.
6 Ibid., p. 227.
7 Ibid.
8 CBA, 15 April 1905.
9 L. Lehuraux, *Laperrine Le Saharien*, Éditions de l'Encyclopédie de l'Empire Français, Paris, 1947, p. 116.
10 R. Hérisson, *Avec le Père Foucauld et le Général Laperrine*, Plon, Paris, 1937, p. 30.
11 D. Porch, *The Conquest of the Sahara*, Jonathan Cape, London, 1985, pp. 275–6.
12 Ibid., p. 276.
13 Ibid., p. 277.
14 Fremantle, op. cit., p. 263.
15 Porch, op. cit., p. 278.
16 Ibid., p. 286.
17 Ibid., p. 287.
18 Antier, op. cit., p. 229.
19 Fremantle, op. cit., pp. 265–6.
20 E. Gautier, *Un Siècle de Colonisation*, Félix Alcan, Paris, 1930, p. 142.
21 Ibid., p. 157.
22 Fremantle, op. cit., p. 267.
23 Porch, op. cit., p. 291.
24 Ibid.
25 CBA, 4 July 1905.
26 Fremantle, op. cit., p. 268.
27 Porch, op. cit., p. 59.
28 Antier, op. cit., p. 234.

13 'I choose Tamanrasset'

1 CT, 11 August 1905.
2 A. Fremantle, *Desert Calling*, Hollis & Carter, London, 1950, p. 271.
3 J-J. Antier (trans. J. Smith), *Charles de Foucauld*, Ignatius Press, San Francisco, 1999, p. 237.
4 Fremantle, op. cit., p. 273.
5 CT, 23 October 1905.
6 Ibid.
7 FH, Foucauld to Huvelin, 26 October 1905.
8 Fremantle, op. cit., p. 276.

 9 FH, Foucauld to Huvelin, 15 July 1906.
10 Fremantle, op. cit., p. 277.
11 E. Gautier, *Un Siècle de Colonisation*, Félix Alcan, Paris, 1930, p. 149.
12 Ibid.
13 Ibid.
14 CT, 17 May 1906.
15 R. Bazin (trans. P. Keelan), *Charles de Foucauld*, Burns Oates & Washbourne, London, 1923, p. 247.
16 Fremantle, op. cit., p. 278.
17 Ibid., p. 280.
18 Ibid.
19 Antier, op. cit., p. 250.
20 S. Howe, *Les Héros du Sahara*, Armand Colin, Paris, 1931, p. 216.
21 Bazin, op. cit., p. 249.
22 Ibid.
23 Ibid., pp. 249–50.
24 Ibid., p. 250.
25 Ibid., p. 251.
26 Ibid., p. 252.
27 Ibid.
28 Ibid., p. 253.
29 Ibid., pp. 254–5.
30 Ibid., p. 253.
31 Ibid.
32 Ibid.
33 CS, Foucauld to Guérin, 6 March 1907.
34 Fremantle, op. cit., p. 285.
35 Ibid.
36 Bazin, op. cit., p. 253.
37 Ibid.
38 CS, Foucauld to Guérin, 22 July 1907.
39 Ibid.
40 Ibid.
41 CT, 31 January 1908.
42 CS, Foucauld to Guérin, 24 January 1908.
43 Ibid.
44 CS, Laperrine to Guérin, 3 February 1908.
45 CS, Laperrine to Guérin, 11 February 1908.
46 CS, Foucauld to Guérin, 6 March 1908.
47 Bazin, op. cit., p. 257.
48 CS, Foucauld to Guérin, 1 June 1908.
49 Ibid.
50 Ibid.
51 Ibid.
52 CS, Laperrine to Guérin, 22 July 1908.
53 Howe, op. cit., p. 120.

14 White Marabout

1 *La Géographie*, Tome XII, 334.
2 Ibid., 335.
3 Ibid.
4 Ibid.
5 L. Lehuraux, *Laperrine*, Éditions de l'Encyclopédie de l'Empire Français, Paris, 1947, p. 93.
6 Ibid., p. 94.
7 Ibid., p. 95.
8 Ibid.
9 Ibid.
10 Ibid., p. 96.
11 Ibid.
12 Ibid., p. 98.
13 *La Géographie*, Tome XIV, 241.
14 J. Germain and S. Faye, *Le Général Laperrine*, Plon, Paris, 1922, p. 82.
15 P. Duclos, *Lettres d'un Saharien*, Soubiron, Alger, 1933, p. 137.
16 A. Fremantle, *Desert Calling*, Hollis & Carter, London, 1950, p. 289.
17 Ibid.
18 Germain, op. cit., p. 128.
19 Fremantle, op. cit., p. 295.
20 Ibid.
21 Ibid.
22 Germain, op. cit., p. 128.
23 Fremantle, op. cit., p. 294.
24 J-J. Antier (trans. J. Smith), *Charles de Foucauld*, Ignatius Press, San Francisco, 1999, p. 267.
25 Fremantle, op. cit., p. 266.
26 Ibid., p. 245.
27 R. Bodley, *The Soundless Sahara*, Robert Hale, London, 1968, p. 132.
28 Fremantle, op. cit., p. 242.
29 CS, Foucauld to Guérin, 6 March 1908.
30 Antier, op. cit., p. 268.
31 Ibid.
32 Ibid.
33 M. Serpette, *Foucauld au Désert*, Desclée de Brouwer, Paris, 1997, p. 60.
34 Antier, op. cit., p. 267.
35 Ibid., p. 270.
36 Ibid.
37 Fremantle, op. cit., p. 299.
38 Ibid., p. 300.
39 Ibid., p. 301.
40 Antier, op. cit., p. 270.
41 Ibid., p. 271.
42 Fremantle, op. cit., p. 301.
43 Antier, op. cit., pp. 272–3.
44 Ibid., p. 273.

45 Ibid.
46 Ibid.
47 Ibid., pp. 271–2.

15 Djanet

1 J-J. Antier (trans. J. Smith), *Charles de Foucauld*, Ignatius Press, San Francisco, 1999, p. 273.
2 J-F. Six, *L'Aventure de l'Amour de Dieu*, Éditions du Seuil, Paris, 1993, p. 62.
3 Ibid., p. 63.
4 Ibid.
5 J. Germain and S. Faye, *Le Général Laperrine*, Plon, Paris, 1922, pp. 40–41.
6 L. Lehuraux, *Laperrine*, Éditions de l'Encyclopédie de l'Empire Français, Paris, 1947, p. 106.
7 Ibid., p. 107.
8 Ibid., p. 104.
9 Ibid., p. 108.
10 Ibid.
11 Ibid., pp. 108–9.
12 Ibid., p. 109.
13 Ibid.
14 R. Hérisson, *Avec le Père Foucauld et le Général Laperrine*, Plon, Paris, 1937, p. 51.
15 Ibid., p. 50.
16 Ibid., p. 58.
17 Ibid., p. 68.
18 Ibid., p. 146.
19 Ibid., p. 147.
20 Ibid., p. 185.
21 R. Bazin (trans. P. Keelan), *Charles de Foucauld*, Burns Oates & Washbourne, London, 1923, pp. 289–90.
22 Ibid., p. 291.
23 Hérisson, op. cit., p. 246.
24 Ibid., p. 250.
25 Bazin, op. cit., p. 293.
26 Hérisson, op. cit., p. 148.
27 Ibid., p. 151.
28 Bazin, op. cit., p. 293.
29 Ibid., p. 294.
30 Antier, op. cit., p. 278.
31 Hérisson, op. cit., pp. 306–7.
32 Antier, op. cit., p. 279.

16 Hermit of Assekrem

1 A. Fremantle, *Desert Calling*, Hollis & Carter, London, 1950, p. 304.
2 J-J. Antier (trans. J. Smith), *Charles de Foucauld*, Ignatius Press, San Francisco, 1999, p. 279.
3 G. Gorrée (trans. D. Attwater), *Memories of Charles de Foucauld*, Burns Oates & Washbourne, London, 1938, p. 122.

4 Fremantle, op. cit., p. 308.
5 Ibid.
6 Antier, op. cit., p. 277.
7 Gorrée, op. cit., p. 120.
8 R. Hérisson, *Avec le Père Foucauld et le Général Laperrine*, Plon, Paris, 1937, p. 188.
9 Antier, op. cit., p. 277.
10 Fremantle, op. cit., p. 271.
11 Ibid., p. 310.
12 Ibid.
13 Gorrée, op. cit., p. 129.
14 Ibid., p. 130.
15 Antier, op. cit., p. 291.
16 P. Duclos, *Lettres d'un Saharien*, Soubiron, Alger, 1933, p. 151.
17 Ibid., p. 155.
18 Ibid., p. 153.
19 Antier, op. cit., p. 290.
20 Ibid.
21 Duclos, op. cit., p. 156.
22 Ibid., p. 158.
23 Ibid.
24 Ibid., p. 159.
25 Ibid.
26 Ibid., p. 113.
27 Ibid., pp. 113–14.
28 Ibid., p. 138.
29 Ibid., pp. 146–7.
30 Ibid., p. 146.
31 Ibid., p. 147.
32 Antier, op. cit., p. 291.
33 Ibid.
34 Ibid., p. 292.
35 R. Bazin (trans. P. Keelan), *Charles de Foucauld*, Burns Oates & Washbourne, London, 1923, p. 298.
36 Antier, op. cit., p. 292.
37 Fremantle, op. cit., p. 314.
38 Ibid., p. 315.
39 Ibid.
40 Ibid., p. 314.
41 Antier, op. cit., p. 293.
42 M. Serpette, *Foucauld au Désert*, Desclée de Brouwer, Paris, 1997, p. 171.
43 Hérisson, op. cit., p. 191.
44 Fremantle, op. cit., p. 315.

17 'It is the hour of my death'

1 P. Duclos, *Lettres d'un Saharien*, Soubiron, Alger, 1933, p. 72.
2 Ibid., p. 71.
3 A. Fremantle, *Desert Calling*, Hollis & Carter, London, 1950, p. 316.

4 Duclos, op. cit., p. 185.
5 Ibid., p. 199.
6 Fremantle, op. cit., p. 317.
7 Ibid.
8 Ibid., p. 318.
9 Ibid.
10 Ibid., p. 319.
11 Ibid.
12 Ibid.
13 Ibid., p. 320.
14 Ibid.
15 Ibid.
16 Ibid.
17 Ibid., p. 321.
18 Ibid., pp. 321–2.
19 Ibid., p. 322.
20 G. Gorrée (trans. D. Attwater), *Memories of Charles de Foucauld*, Burns Oates & Washbourne, London, 1938, p. 144.
21 Fremantle, op. cit., p. 322.
22 Ibid., pp. 322–3.
23 Ibid., p. 323.
24 J-J. Antier (trans. J. Smith), *Charles de Foucauld*, Ignatius Press, San Francisco, 1999, p. 311.
25 CT, 20 October 1916.
26 Fremantle, op. cit., p. 322.
27 Ibid., p. 324.
28 Gorrée, op. cit., p. 155.
29 Antier, op. cit., p. 317.
30 Ibid., p. 319.
31 Ibid.
32 Ibid., p. 321.
33 Fremantle, op. cit., p. 327.
34 Antier, op. cit., p. 322.

18   Dune Flights

1 J-J. Antier (trans. J. Smith), *Charles de Foucauld*, Ignatius Press, San Francisco, 1999, p. 323.
2 E. Gautier, *Un Siècle de Colonisation*, Félix Alcan, Paris, 1930, p. 179.
3 R. Bazin (trans. P. Keelan), *Charles de Foucauld*, Burns Oates & Washbourne, London, 1923, p. 345.
4 Ibid.
5 Ibid.
6 Antier, op. cit., p. 323.
7 Bazin, op. cit., p. 352.
8 J. Germain and S. Faye, *Le Général Laperrine*, Plon, Paris, 1922, p. 161.
9 Ibid.
10 Ibid., p. 159.

11 Ibid.
12 Ibid., p. 164.
13 Ibid., p. 60.
14 Ibid., p. 209.
15 Ibid., p. 213.
16 Ibid., p. 211.
17 Ibid., p. 215.
18 Ibid., p. 218.
19 Ibid., p. 222.
20 Ibid., p. 223.
21 Ibid. p. 224.
22 Ibid.
23 Ibid., p. 264.
24 Ibid., p. 223.
25 L. Lehuraux, *Laperrine*, Éditions de l'Encyclopédie de l'Empire Français, Paris, 1947, p. 137.
26 Ibid.
27 Germain, op. cit., p. 229.
28 Ibid., p. 265.
29 Ibid., p. 266.
30 Ibid., p. 267.
31 Ibid., p. 231.
32 Ibid., p. 234.
33 Ibid., p. 235.
34 Ibid., p. 236.
35 Ibid., p. 240.
36 Ibid., p. 267.
37 Ibid., pp. 243–4.
38 Lehuraux, op. cit., p. 139.
39 Ibid., p. 245.
40 Ibid., p. 246.
41 Ibid., p. 247.
42 Ibid., p. 250.

19 The Dying Days

1 R. Bodley, *The Warrior Saint*, Robert Hale, London, 1954, p. 286.
2 Ibid., p. 288.
3 Ibid., p. 287.
4 J-J. Antier (trans. J. Smith), *Charles de Foucauld*, Ignatius Press, San Francisco, 1999, p. 332.
5 S. Howe, *Les Héros du Sahara*, Armand Colin, Paris, 1931, p. 348.
6 C. Kearton, *The Shifting Sands of Algeria*, Arrowsmith, London, 1924, p. 27.
7 Ibid., p. 25.
8 L. Phillipps, *In the Desert*, Edward Arnold, London, 1905, p. 151.
9 Ibid., p. 43.
10 A. Wilson, *Rambles in North Africa*, Jonathan Cape, London, 1926, p. 32.
11 J. Cooley, *Baal, Christ, and Mohammed*, John Murray, London, 1967, p. 278.

12 Ibid., p. 279.
13 G. Gerster (trans. S. Thomson), *Sahara*, Barrie and Rockliff, London, 1960, p. 255.
14 Ibid., pp. 274–6.
15 Ibid., p. 246.
16 Ibid., p. 248.
17 Ibid., p. 263.

BIBLIOGRAPHY

Agerre, C. (trans. M. Brett), *Modern Algeria*, Hurst & Company, London, 1991

Antier, J-J. (trans. J. Smith), *Charles de Foucauld*, Ignatius Press, San Francisco, 1999

Arnaud, E. and Cortier, M., *Nos Confins Sahariens*, Émile Larose, Paris, 1908

Bazin, R. (trans. P. Keelan), *Charles de Foucauld: Hermit and Explorer*, Burns Oates & Washbourne, London, 1923

Benhazera, M., *Six Mois chez les Touaregs du Ahaggar*, Adolphe Jourdan, Algiers, 1908

Bernard, A. and Lacroix, N., *La Pénétration Saharienne (1830–1906)*, Imprimerie Algerienne, Algiers, 1906

Bernard, F., *Quatre Mois dans Le Sahara: Journal d'un voyage chez les Touareg, suivi d'un aperçu sur la deuxième mission du Colonel Flatters*, Delagrave, Paris, 1881

Blanc, Captain, *Récit d'un officier D'Afrique*, Alfred Mame et Fils, Tours, 1842

Bodley, R., *The Warrior Saint*, Robert Hale, London, 1954

—— *The Soundless Sahara*, Robert Hale, London, 1968

Brosselard, H., *Voyage de la Mission Flatters*, Jouvet, Paris, 1883

Cannon, W., *Algerian Sahara*, Carnegie Institution, Washington, 1913

Cooke, G., *Conquest and Colonisation of North Africa*, Blackwood, Edinburgh, 1860

Cooley, J., *Baal, Christ, and Mohammed*, John Murray, London, 1967

Dresden, D., *The Marquis de Morès: Emperor of the Bad Lands*, University of Oklahoma Press, Norman, 1970

Duclos, P., *Lettres d'un Saharien*, Soubiron, Alger, 1933

Duponchel, A., *Le Chemin de Fer Trans-Saharien*, Hachette, Paris, 1879

Duveyrier, H., *Exploration du Sahara: Les Touaregs du Nord*, Challamel Ainé, Paris, 1864

—— *Journal de Route*, Challamel, Paris, 1905

Egdoux, H-P., *L'Exploration du Sahara*, Gallimard, Paris, 1938

Fage, J. and Oliver, R. (eds.), *The Cambridge History of Africa*, Vol. 5. Cambridge University Press, Cambridge, 1976

Foucauld, C., *Reconnaissance au Maroc*, Société d'Éditions Géographiques, Maritimes et Coloniales, Paris, 1939

—— *Père de Foucauld & Abbé Huvelin: correspondance inédites*. Desclée, Paris, 1957

—— *Lettres et Carnets*, Éditions du Seuil, Paris, 1966

—— *Lettres à un ami de Lycée*, Nouvelle Cité, Paris, 1982

—— *Carnets de Tamanrasset*, Nouvelle Cité, Paris, 1986

—— *Carnet de Beni Abbès*, Nouvelle Cité, Paris, 1993

—— *Correspondances Sahariennes*, Éditions du Cerf, Paris, 1998

—— *Selected Writings*, Orbis Books, New York, 1999

Foucauld, C. (trans. B. Lucas), *Letters from the Desert*, Burns & Oates, London, 1977

Foucauld, C. and Calassanti-Motylinski, A., *Textes Touaregs en prose*, ÉDISUD, Aix-en-Provence, 1984

Foureau, F., *Au Sahara: mes deux missions de 1892 et 1893*, Paris, 1897

—— *Documents Scientifiques de la Mission Saharienne* (2 vols), Masson, Paris, 1903

—— *D'Alger au Congo par le Tchad*, Éditions L'Harmattan, Paris, 1990

Fremantle, A., *Desert Calling: The Life of Charles de Foucauld*, Hollis & Carter, London, 1950

Gaffarel, P., *Les Colonies Françaises*, Germer Baillière, Paris, 1880

—— *Les Explorations Françaises Depuis 1870*, Degorce-Cadot, Paris, 1882

Gautier, E., *La Conquête du Sahara*, Armand Colin, Paris, 1925

—— *Un Siècle de Colonisation*, Félix Alcan, Paris, 1930

Gautier, E. (trans. D. Mayhew), *Sahara: the Great Desert*, Frank Cass & Co., London, 1970

Germain, J. and Faye, S., *Le Général Laperrine*, Plon, Paris, 1922

Gerster, G. (trans. S. Thomson), *Sahara*, Barrie and Rockliff, London, 1960

Gorrée, G. (trans. D. Attwater), *Memories of Charles de Foucauld*, Burns Oates & Washbourne, London, 1938

Hérisson, R., *Avec le Père Foucauld et le Général Laperrine: Carnet D'Un Saharien 1909–1911*, Plon, Paris, 1937

Home, S., *Lyautey of Morocco*, Hodder & Stoughton, London, 1931

Hourst, É. (trans. N. d'Anvers), *French Enterprise in Africa. The Personal Narrative of Lieut. Hourst of his Exploration of the Niger*, Chapman & Hall, London, 1898

Howe, S., *Les Héros du Sahara*, Armand Colin, Paris, 1931

Kearton, C., *The Shifting Sands of Algéria*, Arrowsmith, London, 1924

Knox, A., *The New Playground, or Wanderings in Algeria*, C. Kegan Paul & Co., London, 1881

Largeau, V., *Le Sahara Algérien*, Hachette, Paris, 1881

Lehuraux, L., *Laperrine Le Saharien*, Éditions de l'Encyclopédie de L'Empire Français, Paris, 1947

Leroy-Beaulieu, P., *Le Sahara, Le Soudan, et les Chemins de Fer Transsahariens*, Paris, 1904

Phillipps, L., *In the Desert*, Edward Arnold, London, 1905

Piquet, V., *La Colonisation Française Dans L'Afrique du Nord*, Armand Colin, Paris, 1912

Porch, D., *The Conquest of the Sahara*, Jonathan Cape, London, 1985
—— *The French Foreign Legion*, Macmillan, London, 1991
—— *The Conquest of Morocco*, Jonathan Cape, London, 1986
Preminger, M., *The Sands of Tamanrasset*, Peter Davies, London, 1961
Serpette, M., *Foucauld au Désert*, Desclée de Brouwer, Paris, 1997
Six, J-F., *L'Aventure de l'Amour de Dieu*, Éditions du Seuil, Paris, 1993
Vandervoort, B., *Wars of Imperial Conquest in Africa, 1830–1914*, UCL Press, London, 1998
Vignon, L., *La France dans L'Afrique du Nord*, Guillaumin, Paris, 1887
Vircondelet, A., *Charles de Foucauld*, Éditions de Rocher, Monaco, 1997
Vuillot, P., *L'Exploration du Sahara*, Challamel, Paris, 1895
Wilson, A., *Rambles in North Africa*, Jonathan Cape, London, 1926
Wingfield, L., *Under the Palms of Algeria and Tunis* (2 vols), Hurst and Blackett, London, 1868

INDEX